A Companion to Marx's *Grundrisse*

A Companion to Marx's *Grundrisse*

David Harvey

VERSO

London • New York

First published by Verso 2023
© David Harvey 2023

1 3 5 7 9 10 8 6 4 2

Verso
UK: 6 Meard Street, London W1F 0EG
US: 388 Atlantic Avenue, Brooklyn, NY 11217
versobooks.com

Verso is the imprint of New Left Books

ISBN-13: 978-1-80429-098-9
ISBN-13: 978-1-80429-099-6 (UK EBK)
ISBN-13: 978-1-80429-100-9 (US EBK)

British Library Cataloguing in Publication Data
A catalogue record for this book is available from the British Library

Library of Congress Cataloging-in-Publication Data

Names: Harvey, David, 1935- author.
Title: A companion to Marx's Grundrisse / David Harvey.
Description: London ; Brooklyn, NY : Verso, 2023. | Includes
  bibliographical references and index.
Identifiers: LCCN 2022036533 (print) | LCCN 2022036534 (ebook) | ISBN
  9781804290989 (trade paperback) | ISBN 9781804291009 (ebook)
Subjects: LCSH: Marxian economics. | Capitalism.
Classification: LCC HB97.5 .H3538 2023 (print) | LCC HB97.5 (ebook) | DDC
  335.4—dc23/eng/20221011
LC record available at https://lccn.loc.gov/2022036533
LC ebook record available at https://lccn.loc.gov/2022036534

Typeset in Minion by Hewer Text UK Ltd, Edinburgh
Printed and bound by CPI Group (UK) Ltd, Croydon CR0 4YY

Contents

Author's Introduction

This *Companion to Marx's* Grundrisse is another contribution to what I call, in retrospect, "The Marx Project." I say "in retrospect" because it is only when I look back that I can see that I have been engaged on this project over many years. It did not begin with a conscious purpose or design: it just grew. The impulse behind the project, which began some two decades ago, has, however, remained both clear and constant. I felt a pressing need to communicate, as clearly and simply as possible, what it was that Marx had uncovered in his critique of classical political economy. I also wanted to explore how the insights gained thereby could usefully illuminate the sources of the economic, social, ecological and political troubles and dangers that were becoming more and more salient across the globe. Marx's writings, I felt, were incisively relevant to understanding why capital not only was failing to meet human needs, but was also totally unable to stave off the dangers of environmental degradation. His works helped explain why capital was bound in the long run to fail on both counts.

Most people, when confronted with Marx's voluminous works on the critique of political economy, find them difficult, intimidating and confusing. As a result, there have arisen a variety of interpretations of his work by scholars and activists alike, coalescing in some instances into what appear to be factions or even whole schools of thought as to what the correct line is for elaborating on Marx's theoretical contributions. Political parties of the left (particularly of a communist persuasion) have often shaped distinctive but somewhat rigid interpretations suited to their political situation and agendas. Marx, being the controversial figure that he is, has also attracted his share of personal vilification from opponents. Deliberate misrepresentations and false representations abound, along with more sophisticated and subtle attempts to undermine his views. All of this creates expectations and a climate of presumption and prejudgment that makes a simple and uncluttered reading of any of his texts virtually impossible.

My aim was and is to open a door into Marx's thinking and to encourage as many people as possible to pass through it and take a closer look at the texts and make of them what they will. I have no interest in trying to impose my own particular interpretations on anyone. That is why I call my books on Marx "companions" rather than guides. I cannot, of course, open a path to an understanding of Marx's thought without using my own experience and interests as crucial helpmates for interpretation. The fact that my main interest has been urbanization and uneven geographical development, at a variety of scales, clearly affects the way I evaluate Marx's texts. I imagine myself, however, accompanying the reader on a long hike in which I point out this and that particular feature here and there, drawing upon my long experience of working with the text, and highlight moments of epiphany for me, linking ideas together, when possible, while always wondering and asking what it is that you, the reader, might make of it all. In teaching Marx over the last fifty years, I have been incredibly fortunate to teach it to all sorts of different groups and audiences. I have learned immensely from the very divergent ways in which people can make sense of what Marx is saying. This is, of course, a tribute to the rich complexity of the texts; that they can speak so directly to so many different people living in such radically different situations and coming from such radically different cultural and intellectual traditions.

The *Grundrisse* is, by far, the most interesting and the most difficult book by Marx to work with. It is a set of notes that Marx was frantically writing to himself at a rather frantic time. Marx, throughout his lifetime, employed different modes of writing depending upon his audience. These can be categorized into four types. There was, first, the writing style adopted in his journalism, in his contemporary commentaries and in his correspondence. It is plainspoken and colloquial, even as it takes on difficult matters with some conceptual grace. Some of his serious writings on political economy were prepared for publication, such as Volume I of *Capital*. There, he is greatly concerned to use a language which he thinks his audience will understand. That audience was the literate fraction of a working class, the majority of whom were illiterate. The literate fraction was self-taught, quite sophisticated and, being autodidacts, unlikely to be subject to the disciplinary tropes of formal education. So, while *Capital* may appear to us as a difficult book, somewhat above the capacity of the average undergraduate in formal education to easily comprehend, this would not necessarily be true for the autodidact artisans that Marx was concerned to influence, primarily in Britain and France but also in the United States and beyond. My own hope in my Marx Project has been to recast Marx's language in a way more accessible to contemporary student audiences along with the autodidacts (yes, they still exist) in the labor unions and social movements. The third kind of writing is more experimental. It is constructed as a voyage of discovery, where Marx will unfold an argument, sometimes deploying novel and even arcane concepts for anyone willing to follow. This is characteristic of the manuscripts out of which Engels constructed both Volumes II and III of *Capital*. The fourth kind of writing is Marx writing purely for himself, using whatever tools and ideas that he has in his head, prepared to unleash a stream of his own consciousness, to set down possibilities and potential interrelations that may or may not turn out to be important in his more considered studies.

This last is the predominant style of the *Grundrisse*, and it is this that makes it such an exciting, frustrating, imaginative and sometimes boringly repetitive text to work with. Marx is, in short, just talking to himself. It is not sufficient to understand his language (which is distinctly his own). It is also important to understand his mode of thinking, which is, to put it mildly, somewhat elusive. But this is the form of writing that dominates in the *Grundrisse*.

One of the things that makes reading and interpretating the *Grundrisse* so difficult is determining whether Marx is advancing his own conceptual framework and interpretations or simply reporting upon that of others. For example, at the very outset of the introduction, he states: "Individuals producing in society—hence socially determined individual production—is, of course, the point of departure." We can read this as saying that this is where he, Marx, proposes to start; or as Marx saying that since this is where bourgeois political economy typically starts, then this is where he is obliged to start his own critical interrogation. The outcome is often a fusion of both. He may end up saying that socially determined individual production is a good and appropriate place to start provided we interpret the "individual" in a different way from that given in bourgeois political economy. I note, in passing, however, that Marx begins *Capital* with the commodity, which was definitely his own choice.

Marx does not think the bourgeois political economists were idiots, liars or mere apologists. Some of them may have been that, but certainly not Adam Smith and Ricardo and the host of other thinkers (like James Steuart, William Petty, Sismondi, Quesnay and even on occasion Thomas Malthus) who preceded or succeeded them. Marx regarded most of the bourgeois political economists as honest journeymen and scientists seeking desperately to understand the confusing and enormously complex political and economic changes occurring around them. They provided Marx with the raw materials for his own interpretations and, if only for that reason, commanded respect. But there is plenty of "unfinished business" in the *Grundrisse* (as well as in Marx's work in general) as to what is distinctive to Marx and what is derivative from the bourgeois political economy of the time. This is very much the case, for example, with respect to Marx's concept of value, which, to this day, has never been firmly defined to everyone's satisfaction. Marx, in the *Grundrisse*, is not always consistent with himself; he sometimes changes conceptual apparatuses in midstream. The meaning of key concepts evolves as the text unfolds. He is often unsure as to exactly where he is going. The result is a somewhat messy, complex but open and episodically incisive analysis. But, then, capital is a somewhat messy, complex economic system, and the *Grundrisse*, often by happenstance, mirrors this complexity in some pretty astonishing ways.

There are, however, different ways to read this text. A very close, deep and systematic reading would take a long time. It is easy to spend a week wrestling with the meaning of just a few pages. Other readings take a particular angle on Marx's thinking. For instance, philosophers might read it looking for how Marx is appropriating Hegel or Spinoza, while economists are typically drawn to how Marx is appropriating Adam Smith, David Ricardo and the socialist Ricardians. Marx frequently argues in opposition to Proudhon and the French socialists. I do not find that commentary particularly enlightening or interesting. For this reason, I tend to give the debate with Proudhon short shrift in this reading. I am, furthermore, not equipped, by intellect or temperament, to wrestle with the complexity of the Hegelian influence and the extensive philosophical explorations of Marx's language and method. I appreciate the work done by others on these topics but those interested in it must needs look elsewhere.

Marx was not only seeking in this text to come to terms with Ricardo and Hegel. He was also engaged, in my view, in a titanic struggle to emancipate himself from the limiting categories of Ricardian analysis and the prison house of Hegelian formulations. I here concentrate, therefore, on what Marx defines as his central mission in the *Grundrisse*. This he states as follows: "The exact development of the concept of capital is necessary since it is the fundamental concept of modern economics, just as capital . . . [is] the foundation of bourgeois society. The sharp formulation of the basic presuppositions of the [capital] relation must bring out all the contradictions of bourgeois production, as well as the boundary where it drives beyond itself" (331; see note on p. xxi). I anchor this reading of the *Grundrisse* around this problematic.

Marx was concerned not only to understand the concept of capital and its elaboration in the world of thought. He was also concerned to come to terms with capital as it was operating on the ground and how its abstract laws of motion, albeit riven with contradictions, were not only producing economic crises (such as that of 1857–58) but were also dictating conditions of life and labor for the mass of the population in the then capitalist world.

Capital is, of course, still with us, and the unfolding of its inner laws of motion, along with all its inner contradictions, is omnipresent, though perhaps dressed in new clothing and perhaps practiced at a much expanded scale. A dose of Marx's revelatory discoveries can therefore shed a great deal of light on our contemporary capitalist world, even as we recognize that this world is very much in flux and in some respects very different from the one which Marx inhabited. Yet there are also reasons to think that the chief elements of Marx's theoretical conception are more relevant now than they have ever been. When Marx was writing, industrial (as opposed to merchant) capital was dominant in only a small corner of the world—Britain, Western Europe and the Eastern seaboard of the United States. But the kind of factory conditions which Marx depicts in *Capital* in the chapter on 'the Working Day' can now be found in Bangladesh, China, Turkey, Brazil, India, Guatemala and South Africa (just to name a few places). Capital has, moreover, "scaled up" to the edge of the globe and, while this scaling up calls for theoretical adjustments, it deepens rather than lessens the contradictions to which capital as an economic system is prone. On the other hand, the complexity of class formations and class relations on the world stage makes the applications of some of Marx's theorizations, as we shall see, problematic.

There is, however, a structure to Marx's seemingly chaotic inquiry in the *Grundrisse*. It is important to be aware of this structure when studying the text. Marx aims to investigate the formation and functioning of capital as "a totality." This aspect of Marx's approach has largely been ignored in contemporary commentaries. I suspect the turn to Foucault and post-structuralism, which holds totalizing discourses and, ergo, any evocation of the concept of the totality, in anathema, is partly to blame. It may also be because earlier attempts to deploy the concept of totality (by, for example, Lukács) were found to be misleading and inadequate. But Hegel's concept of totality is of a closed, self-contained and self-sustaining entity, and it was this concept of totality that proved (correctly, in my view) to be so inadequate. Marx seeks to emancipate himself from this Hegelian conception. Marx's totality is open, evolving, self-replicating, to be sure, but in no sense self-sustaining, given its internal contradictions and its metabolic relation to both nature and to the cumulative historical achievements of human cultures. Marx depicts capital as an "organic" totality and treats it as a complex ecosystem in continuous historical formation. But Marx limits his inquiries, for the most part, to the totality of capital and not of everything. While capital may be the driving force, the foundational process within bourgeois society, it does not say everything that needs to be said about capitalism as a social formation. The theory of capital as a mode of production is one thing. The theory of capitalism as a social formation is quite another. In the *Grundrisse*, Marx mainly focuses on the former, even as some his asides clearly target the latter.

The ecosystemic analogy is important here. In the same way that researchers may conceptualize and isolate for study whole ecosystems such as the tropical rain forest, the tundra, wetlands or even urban ecosystems as totalities (each totality comprised of multiple species in relation or competition with each other, knitted together by energy flows including those emanating from outside), so Marx seeks to isolate for study capital's ecosystem (with its complex intersecting divisions of labor, competition, specializations of function, forms of distribution and money flows).

This totality of capital is, in some respects, like a human body (though this analogy will prove misleading if pushed too far). Marx, at one point, pursues exactly this analogy to elucidate the importance of differential turnover times. "In the human body, as with capital, the different elements are not exchanged at the same rate of reproduction, blood renews itself more rapidly than muscle, muscle than bone, which in this respect may be regarded as the fixed capital of the human body" (670). The human body circulates blood through the heart and oxygen through the lungs, ingests energy through the digestive system and the stomach, deals with waste through the liver and kidneys while coordination is exercised through the brain and the central nervous system. Each of these circulation processes is autonomous and independent (and subject to specialized knowledge in the form of cardiology, neurology, urology, etc.) but subsumed within the logic of the totality of a human body as a functioning system. It makes no sense to assign a hierarchical structure of importance or causality to the interactions and interrelations between all these different circulation processes. The failure of any one of them threatens the life and existence of the totality.

In the *Grundrisse*, Marx decomposes capital into different circulation processes. He begins with the study of monetary circulation. Not all money is capital. Capital is money circulating in a particular way. But monetary circulation has to be studied as autonomous and independent, performing all manner of social functions other than that required in the flow of money as capital. Money becomes money capital through its encounter with and purchase of the capacity to labor. This sparks an analysis of the circulation process of the capacity to labor (Figure 1). Capital (value) flows through the different moments of (1, p. xv) commodity purchase (labor power and means of production), (2) a labor process producing surplus-value, (3) realization through sale in the market, (4) distribution and (5) reinvestment. This forms a distinctive circulation process of capital in general (Figure 2, p. xviii). The flow of capital can be divided into two distinctive paths: those of circulating capital (with a turnover on an annual basis), and those of long-term fixed capital (e.g., machinery), together with flows into the consumption fund (e.g., housing) (Figure 3, p. 296). Fixed capital and long-term consumption fund formation take on a special character and significance. They both intersect with the circulation of interest-bearing capital, which supports and coordinates them. This connection is only occasionally mentioned in the *Grundrisse*, even though it is usually incorporated in the various plans that Marx lays out to guide his future work. The circulation of interest-bearing capital is taken up in detail, of course, in Volume III of *Capital*. There are other circulation processes that could be incorporated. But Marx leaves them to one side in the *Grundrisse*, except in the various plans. The circulation of state revenues through taxation and public investments is notably lacking, except for a brief commentary on road building.

Figure 1 The Circulation of the Capacity to Labor

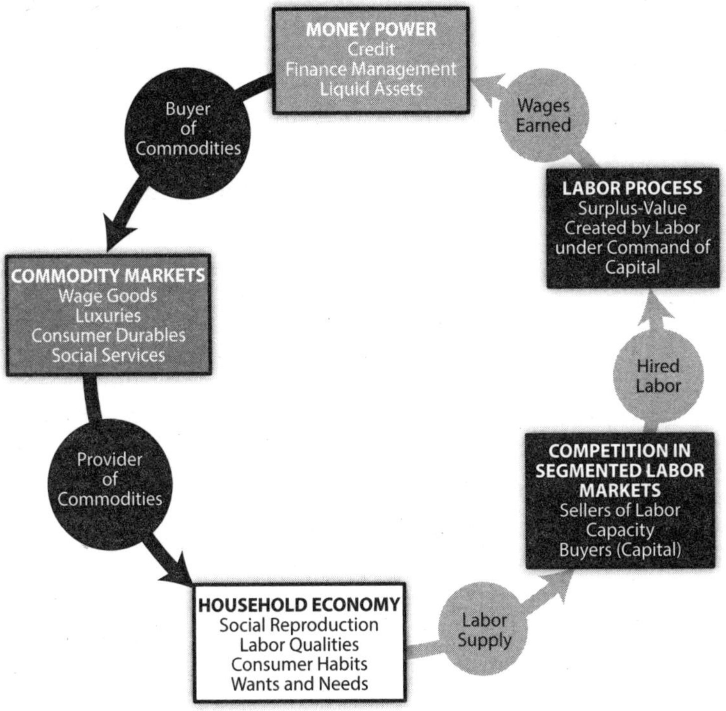

The totality of capital is not pregiven or predefined. It is not some ideal type waiting to be revealed or discovered, nor is it fixed and determinate with respect to its reach in space and time. While the idea of totality undoubtedly derives from Hegel, Marx reworks it and revolutionizes it (as he does with almost everything else taken from Hegel). For Marx, the totality is a network of historically specific social practices and relations built and evolving over time through human action. This network is constantly in the process of growth and transformation (perpetually "becoming," as he puts it) even as it exhibits certain tendencies toward permanence. The emphasis, however, is upon the fluidity of the processes that sustain and create it. But the crystallization of various features within the totality can guide, inhibit, imprison or exacerbate the processes that historically constitute it. This crystallization can, from time to time, become downright sclerotic. It then appears as if humanity has imprisoned itself in its own web of social (class) relations, institutional arrangements (e.g., the law) and social interactions. It constantly finds itself straining to break the bonds and barriers that it has itself created. This is the foundational contradiction within the capitalist mode of production.

The *Grundrisse* is structured as an inquiry into the different circulation processes that produce and support capital as a totality. We have:

1 The Circulation of Commodities through Exchange
2 The Circulation of Money as Money
3 The Circulation of the Capacity to Labor (Figure 1)
4 The Circulation of Money as Capital (Figure 2)
5 The Circulation of Fixed Capital (Figure 3)
6 The Circulation of Interest-Bearing Capital (not studied but mentioned in the *Grundrisse*)

Other circulation processes might be incorporated into this framework, such as the circulation of financial/banking capital and the circulation of state revenues. Volume II of *Capital*, it is worth noting, is dominated by the study of different circulatory systems beginning with the circulation of money, commodities and productive capital and the circulation of all three forms within capital as a whole. Later in that volume, Marx examines the circulation of fixed capital and studies working periods and turnover times, with subsequent chapters on the circulation of variable capital and surplus-value, culminating in the modeling of circulation relations between capital and labor in the so-called reproduction schemas. The *Grundrisse* is an illuminating precursor to much of that.

The boundedness of the totality (both structurally and geographically) is, to some degree, arbitrarily imposed by the investigator, even when there are strong concrete conditions that logically support a particular definition of boundedness. In the case of the human body, to follow on with this analogy, there are strong reasons to treat of it as a functioning totality in itself for purposes of medical investigation, diagnosis and analysis. But the general social conditions in which that body operates cannot be ignored in any approach to health conditions in society. While, for example, a cause of death might be very specific from the medical standpoint, the context of substance abuse and opioid addictions, of alienation and social anomie and of all the economic and social reasons that lie behind these phenomena are of great significance to understanding recent trends in morbidity. While Marx isolates capital—what he calls "the inner structure" of the social system—to concentrate attention on the production, consumption, realization and distribution of value, he clearly recognizes that there is a far broader totality within which this arbitrarily abstracted totality called "capital" has its being. Hence, in Figure 2, we see the metabolic relation to nature and the construction of a second nature through urbanization along with the production of space and place relations as contextually significant to the more narrowly defined and bounded model of capital circulation. The same can be said of capital's relation to human knowledge, social relations, culture and tradition in existing populations, to conditions of social reproduction and to

Figure 2 The Circulation of Capital in General

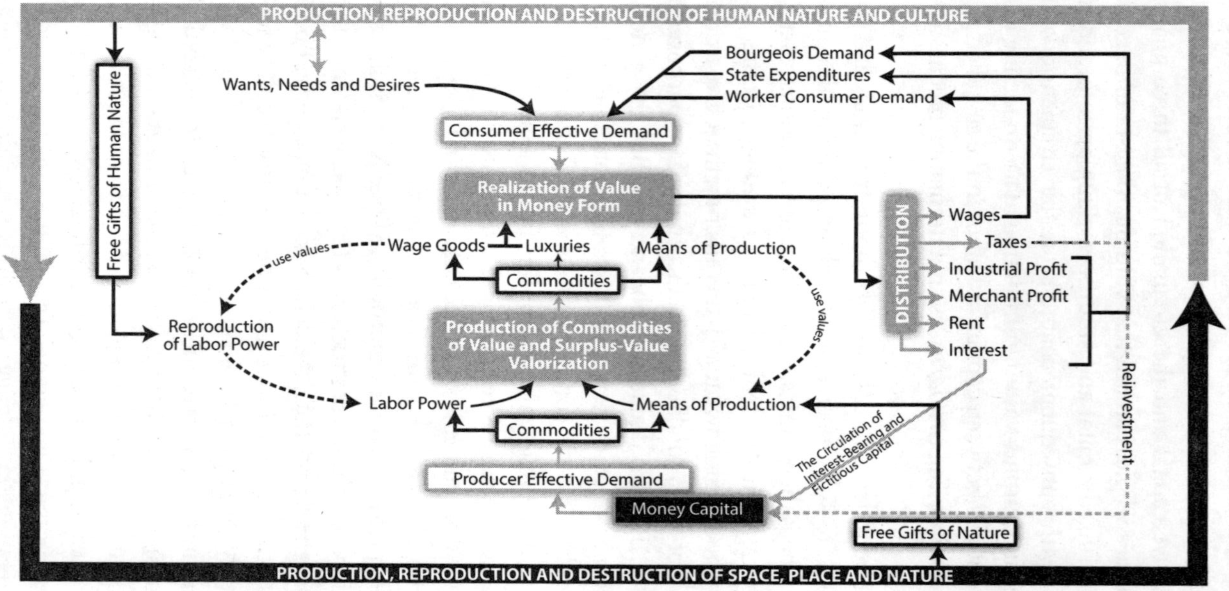

the constant shaping and reshaping of the wants, needs and desires that get expressed through the diverse expressions of human consumerism. What Marx subjects to analysis is the totality of capital within the much broader totality of capitalism. His reason for so doing is that he sees capital as the economic engine, the foundational power-house, the source of the abstract forces to which all of us are willy-nilly obligated and bound to some degree.

One word of warning on Marx's method of inquiry. He situates himself with respect to his subject matter in a very specific way. He typically interprets what he is looking at in a pure form free of contamination from so-called external influences (such as those just described) or particular complications. In the chapter dealing with money, for example, he proceeds as if the circulation of money capital has no role. Throughout the text, he frequently indicates issues that he will take up later or matters that we are not, at this point in the analysis, equipped to handle. This renders much of what he says contingent on context rather than definitive. Marx recognizes that many of his "fixed suppositions themselves become fluid in the further course of development. But only by holding them fast at the beginning is their development possible without confounding everything" (817). This is not an unfamiliar problem—how to capture process, movement and flow with categories that cannot be other than fixed? I frequently see citations from Marx presented as if they are final judgments when they should be presented as contingent statements. This does not mean the subject matter is useless. Quite the contrary. But care should be taken to recognize the assumptions and contextual conditions under which Marx is organizing his theorizing.

The theory he comes up with is, in general, contextualized by how capital was working in what Marx himself recognized to be his "little corner of the world." For most of his active intellectual life, he felt, rightly or wrongly, that the study of British industrial capitalism was showing to the rest of the world a picture of its own likely future. This is where he stands when thinking through the materials assembled in the *Grundrisse*. But, toward the end of his life, he began to question whether that presumption was warranted. Context matters. And, in the same way that he admitted that the theses of the *Communist Manifesto*, written in 1848, deserved to be reexamined and perhaps rewritten when republished (in what turned out to be their most influential version) in 1872, so he also had to acknowledge that the course of capital's "becoming" might look very different when viewed from the standpoint of the development of capitalism in Russia or elsewhere. A recent study by Marcello Musto on Marx's later life sheds helpful light on some of these questions.[1] Whether or not the image of our own future now lies in China is thus an interesting contemporary version of this question, and one open to debate of course. We all work from contexts even as we seek theoretical insights that might transcend those contexts. Marx is no exception.

But then there are passages in the *Grundrisse* where Marx throws all contextual caution and constraints to the winds and speculates, sometimes wildly, as to the true essence and qualities of capital as a transcendent power. His insights are brilliant, dramatic and often astonishing in their implications. These form, as a student once commented to me, the jewels that shine with such luster in the mud of all too often turgid analysis. Finding and toying with these jewels of incisive understanding is what makes the study of the *Grundrisse* so extraordinary and worthwhile as well as, dare I say it, fun.

Finally, I wish to dedicate this book to my thoroughly apolitical father. This probably seems strange coming from someone who is eighty-five years old. But I now see that I could not have done this work without his help and influence. He was employed in the Naval Dockyard in Chatham, in England, and during World War II found himself increasingly tasked with managing the emergency repair and refitting of damaged naval ships pretty much on his own initiative. He apparently fulfilled this task excellently well.

---

1   Marcello Musto, *The Last Years of Karl Marx: An Intellectual Biography*, trans. Patrick Camiller (Stanford, CA: Stanford University Press, 2020).

But, in 1950, when he was fifty-three, the Admiralty determined, in its infinite wisdom, that, in order to continue doing what he had been doing for the previous seven years, he must take a qualifying competitive examination in naval construction engineering. This was a person who had left school for an apprenticeship at age thirteen. For two years, after coming home from work and taking "high tea," he would retire to the front parlor and study his engineering texts for two or three hours every day (except weekends). He had to learn calculus, for example. He passed the national competitive exam with flying colors and was confirmed in his job position. My father and I did not get along (for reasons I need not go into). I felt he never approved of me. But I now realize how important it has been for me to earn his approval by emulating how and what he did in his studies, how he applied himself, at that time when I was fifteen years old. I have, consequently, never been fearful of undertaking long-term projects. Indeed, I value them and seek them out. Persistence and dedication pay off. Writing this companion to the *Grundrisse* has been like that. I have often had a picture of my father in my mind as I retired to some space for a couple of hours almost every day during Covid lockdown with my text and my laptop, to work on this project. While I have no idea what he would think of the content, he would, I hope, recognize and appreciate the manner of my effort. It has taken a long time for me to be able to say it, but: "Thanks, Dad!"

The edition of the *Grundrisse* to which I will refer is Karl Marx, *Grundrisse: Foundations of the Critique of Political Economy*, trans. Martin Nicolaus (London: Penguin Classics in Association with *New Left Review*, 1973 [reprinted 1993]). Note that phrases in italics reflect Marx's original text of the *Grundrisse* unless otherwise noted. I am also deeply indebted to Martin Nicolaus for his heroic efforts as translator of an extremely challenging text.

Marx's Introduction
Pages 83–111

What is here presented as the "Introduction" to the *Grundrisse* is, in fact, a separate and earlier text that only loosely connects to the main body of the manuscripts. As Martin Nicolaus, the editor and translator of the text, records (53–5), Marx apparently had some serious reservations about the manner of presentation of the "Introduction," and it is fairly clear that the materials have a somewhat tenuous relation to the main part of the work, even as they help frame and interpret the main text in important if not foundational ways. The "Introduction" helps us understand how Marx was positioning himself vis-à-vis the classical political economy that was the object of his critique. His discontents may also have derived from the fact that he had not yet freed himself enough from the propositions of classical political economy to construct his own independent perspectives. In the same way that he interrupts the flow of his argument in the main body of the *Grundrisse* with the observation that his formulations need revision because they are too idealist and, by implication, Hegelian (151), so he may have felt that this introduction was too Ricardian. The *Grundrisse* is, in many ways, Marx's coming to terms with the thought of both Hegel and Ricardo. The "Introduction," as I see it, reflects Marx's thinking at a certain stage of his "becoming" the fierce critic of capital that he ultimately became.

The "Introduction" has four parts. He begins with a brief critical commentary on the role of the individual in liberal theory. The second, and, by far, the most prominent and challenging part deals with "production in general" and the inner relations between production, distribution, consumption and exchange within what he terms the "totality" of capital. The third part entails a brief discussion on the method of political economy. The last two pages open up a laundry list of matters to be considered, culminating with some interesting observations on the relationship between ancient and modern modes of art and thought.

THE CRITIQUE OF LIBERAL INDIVIDUALISM

Marx announces his initial focus to be "material production." The starting point is "individuals producing in society—hence socially determined individual production" (83). This immediately poses the question of how individuals came to play such a crucial role in shaping what capital is about. Marx dismisses "the unimaginative conceits of the eighteenth-century Robinsonades" before going on to consider Rousseau's account in *The Social Contract*, "which brings naturally independent, autonomous subjects into relation and connection by contract."

This question of how to understand the role of the individual in relation to society in general and to private property and competitive entrepreneurialism in particular recurs throughout the *Grundrisse*. We will frequently return to it. Here Marx opens with a critique rendered much more explicit in Volume I of *Capital*.[1] There, Marx derides the way in which so many of the eighteenth-century political economists based their theorizing on the imaginary of rational economic man (*homo*

---

1   Karl Marx, *Capital: A Critique of Political Economy*, vol. 1, trans. Ben Fowkes (London: Penguin Classics, 1990), 170.

economicus) as depicted in Daniel Defoe's story of shipwreck and survival in the novel *Robinson Crusoe* (published in 1719). Defoe made it seem as if any rational individual when precipitated alone into a situation close to nature would "naturally" organize his productive life according to the principles of double-entry bookkeeping. Crusoe, having "learned from experience, and having saved a watch, ledger, ink and pen from the shipwreck, he soon begins, like a good Englishman, to keep a set of books," as he puts it in Volume I of *Capital*.[1] Not for the first time, we see capital and the individual as products of nature, when, for Marx, they are social and historical products.

The importance of *Robinson Crusoe* as a text was not only that it gave bourgeois political economists an imaginary basis for their theorizing but that it was a very popular story consumed by literate peoples everywhere (I read it as a child!). It gave popular support to the naturalness of economic calculation and entrepreneurial action at the same time as the introduction of Man Friday naturalized and endorsed colonial paternalism and the importance of racial distinctions. The way forward was to unite the brains of the white inhabitants of the temperate regions with the brawn of the black people of the tropics. I have long thought, however, that the bourgeois political economists chose the wrong Defoe story. Had they used *Moll Flanders*, they would there have found a character whose life reads like the wayward history of commodity capital in perpetual circulation. Flanders, who is a charming thief, seductress and liar, goes from riches to debtors' prison, from Britain to Virginia, all the time speculating with respect to her own desires as well as to those of others. One high point of the story comes when Flanders, on the point of penury, launches a last-gasp effort to rescue her financial fortunes by renting a horse and carriage, a mass of expensive jewellery and fashionable clothing to attend a country-house ball, where she so successfully seduces a young aristocrat that they get married that very night. On waking in the local inn the following morning, they

---

1 Ibid.

discover that neither of them has a penny to their names. When the shock wears off, they both see the humor of their situation and part on good terms. This is a wonderful exposé of the flippant emptiness of what commodity capital is all too often about, including the constant toying with wayward human desires. This contrasts with Crusoe's serious and stolid attempt to reconstruct the conditions of industrial capital in isolation on his island, protected from any market discipline apart from his ledger. (Incidentally, Defoe's novel *Captain Singleton* has a lot to say about piracy, globalization and primitive accumulation across Africa and the Indian Ocean, while his *Journal of the Plague Year* makes for interesting reading in the year of Covid-19!)

The political economy of the eighteenth century sought to naturalize the individual entrepreneur. Rousseau, in his *Contrat social*, endorsed this view. The "noble savage" or the social individual endowed with inalienable rights (sometimes construed as God-given) supported by private property, is seen as the "natural" basis upon which political economic institutions and theory should be constructed. The freedom of the sovereign individual lies at the basis of liberal theory. But for Rousseau, that dangerous and potentially unruly freedom is severely limited by the social contract. Marx turns this the other way around. "In this society of free competition, the individual appears detached from the natural bonds, etc. which in earlier historical periods make him the accessory of a definite and limited human conglomerate" (83). The original "natural" unit (if ever there was one) was not the individual but the kinship group, the band, the tribe or some other form of collective organization in which a tacit contract ruled (and he will later go into detail on such forms—see pages 471–514). In Marx's view, it took a certain kind of market exchange society to "dissolve" collective forms and create a situation in which the individual could act as an entrepreneur and claim the sovereign rights of private property for himself or herself. The individual and individualism, therefore, are by-products of the rise of a certain kind of society based on monetized market exchange, private property and capital accumulation. This is politically important. Current right-wing popular political thinking (in the USA in particular) is based on the sacrosanct qualities of individual freedom and liberty, as natural or God-given absolute rights that cannot be overridden by the state or any other form of collective power (there is nothing binding about any social contract). Marxism, or any socialist line of thought derivative of Marx, is therefore seen as the mortal enemy of individual liberty and freedom. Marx's response is to pose two questions. If capital did come into being as the "natural" consequence of such inalienable individual rights, then why do we live in a society characterized by wage slavery, the impoverishment of the mass of the people and the total and accepted violation of these supposed "inalienable" rights by capital on a daily basis (particularly in the labor process)? Second, if, as Marx puts it in Volume III of *Capital*, the realm of true freedom can only begin when the realm of necessity is left behind (or in President Roosevelt's formulation, "necessitous people are not free"), then why do those who so loudly proclaim their belief in individual liberty and freedom so fiercely resist all collective attempts to construct a world in which the necessity that curbs that freedom is eradicated? This second question enfolds the more particular paradox in which capital, through its remarkable pursuit of new technologies, develops the productive forces required to abolish the realm of necessity, while avidly denying the use of them to create a world of universal equality and well-being. This refusal to extend the realm of human liberty and freedom to all, even as the means to do so lie readily to hand, is a blot on human history. Marx wholeheartedly supports the quest to extend the realms of individual liberty and freedom to all. But he insists that the conditions in which these virtues can flourish have yet to be realized. It is pure fiction and fantasy (of the *Robinson Crusoe* sort) to say that the freedom of the sovereign individual existed at the creation.

Marx comments on only certain aspects of this whole argument in the "Introduction." He writes, for example, that "only in the eighteenth century, in 'civil society,' do the various forms of social connectedness confront the individual as a mere means towards his private purposes, as external necessity. But the epoch which produces this standpoint, that of the isolated individual, is also precisely that of the hitherto most developed social (from this standpoint, general) relations. The human being is in the most literal sense [a political animal], not merely a gregarious animal, but an animal which can individuate itself only in the midst of society" (84). Marx thus confirms the view that the individuation that makes entrepreneurialism possible is a social and historical product and not an attribute of some imagined natural order.

PRODUCTION IN GENERAL

When studying the *Grundrisse*, it is useful and important to collate all those passages where Marx comes back to the conditions required to extend human liberty and freedom. Here, however, Marx quickly switches his attention to production. He notes, contra the Crusoe story, that "production by an isolated individual outside society . . . is as much an absurdity as is the development of language without individuals living *together* and talking together" (84). But "whenever we speak of production . . . what is meant is always production at a definite stage of social development" (85). In the *Grundrisse*, it is "modern bourgeois production" that will be the main focus of attention. But it is also important to acknowledge that "all epochs have certain common traits, common characteristics." We need to assess what all of these different societies have in common (85). Marx therefore proposes to look at "production in general" as a "rational abstraction in so far as it really brings out and fixes the common element and thus saves us repetition."

This term "rational abstraction," alongside with that of "concrete abstraction," requires elucidation. For Marx, the concept of the commodity is a concrete abstraction. We see innumerable material exchanges involving the buying and selling of all manner of particular products. We cannot possibly consider the infinite number and variety of these material transactions, so we bring them all together and consider all of them as exemplary of the exchange of commodities. This is the concrete abstraction. We then build an economic theory on that basis. The basis is material (concrete), but the concept is abstract. Another level of abstraction—rational abstraction—arises out the interrogation of the theoretical content of commodity exchange. Value, for example, is a rational abstraction. It arises out of the study of commodity exchange as a concrete abstraction. The only rational answer to Marx's question as to what makes diverse commodities commensurable is that they all must have something in common, i.e., they are all products of human labor. The inference that value must be a manifestation of social human labor is a rational abstraction. This is how Marx puts his historical materialist technique into practice. This mode of approach is omnipresent in the *Grundrisse*. It also ultimately helps explain Marx's assertion that, within a capitalist mode of production, we are all of us concretely "ruled by abstractions," (e.g., movements in the interest or profit rate).

In the case of production in general, the "common element sifted out by comparison, is itself segmented many times over and splits into different determinations. Some determinations belong to all epochs, others only to a few . . ." (85). Again, it is useful to understand Marx's technique here. All forms of production relate, for example, to land, but the role and meaning of land varies (as we shall later see) from one situation or mode of production to another. The implication is that any macroeconomic transformation in the mode of production from, say, feudalism to capitalism, will entail a radical change in the role and meaning of, for example, land ownership and use. Furthermore, "if there is no production in general, then there is also no general production. Production is always a *particular* branch of production—e.g. agriculture, cattle raising, manufacturing, etc.—or it is a *totality*" (86). It is also produced through "a certain social body, a social subject" (such as the laborer) "which is active in a greater or sparser totality of branches of production." The topics that need to be elaborated are:

"Production in general. Particular branches of production. Totality of Production" (86).

It is here that Marx introduces us, for the first time, to the concept of a totality. This is a vital concept throughout the *Grundrisse*. Marx often frames his thinking in terms of the "totality" and its "moments." But bourgeois theorists (such as Adam Smith) typically introduce their subject matter (the study of the moments of production, consumption, distribution and market exchange) by hammering the "essential moments of all production" into "flat tautologies" (86). This is the heart of Marx's critique of classical political economy: it reduces the vibrant and fecund processes of even bourgeois economic life to the dead and lifeless qualities of the conjoining of static factors of production. This is then supplemented by the fact that "certain races, locations, climates, natural conditions such as harbours, soil fertility etc. are more advantageous to production than others." Such contingent conditions are then flattened into yet another "tautology that wealth is more easily created where its elements are subjectively and objectively present to a greater degree" (87).

Marx will later seek to free political economy from all such tautological formulations (which continue to dominate in economics to this day) through the gentle application of dialectics and a version of process-based philosophy. But here he is more concerned to show that the economists' real concern and aim is "to present production—see e.g. Mill—as distinct from distribution etc., as encased in eternal natural laws independent of history, at which opportunity *bourgeois* relations are then quietly smuggled in as inviolable natural laws on which society in the abstract is founded" (87). This is a far more pernicious way of naturalizing bourgeois production than the blatant manoeuvres of the Robinsonades. It is recognized, however, that society can "be considerably more arbitrary" with respect to distribution. Distributive socialism (of the Mill-ian or Ricardian socialist sort) is perfectly feasible under this formulation, but the socialization of production is impossible because it is part of the natural order governed by natural law. This "tearing apart" of "the real relation" between production and distribution is, for Marx, totally inadmissible. But this is what capital does.

"All production is appropriation of nature on the part of an individual within and through a specific form of society" (87). This brief mention of the "appropriation of nature" presages a long-running concern within the *Grundrisse* to understand what Marx later refers to as "the metabolic relation to nature." But here he races past this issue to expose the way "it is a tautology to say that property (appropriation) is a precondition of production," even as it is "ridiculous" to "leap from that to a specific form of property" such as "private property." Communal forms of property have been far more common throughout human history. "Every form of production creates its own legal relations, form of government, etc." (88). In short, "there are characteristics which all stages of production have in common, and which are established as general ones by the mind; but the so-called *general preconditions* of all production are nothing more than these abstract moments with which no real historical stage of production can be grasped." How, then, are we to grasp the nature of capital as a totality?

In the *Grundrisse*, Marx seeks to answer this question in incremental steps. His method is to start with basic concrete abstractions, build in the rational abstractions that arise within a given mode of production (such as value theory) and gradually pin together a picture of the totality in motion and formation. That picture begins to take shape toward the end of the analysis. Marx scrupulously refrains from going beyond where he is at in this process of defining the rules of operation within the theoretical totality in formation. Again and again, we find him saying of some topic (e.g., the credit system or the circulation of fixed capital) "this does not belong here yet" or "we will deal with this later," even as he is plainly seeking a framework for studying the totality of capital in all its fullness. On several occasions, however, he abandons all constraints and sets out a proposed plan for the study of the totality. Each plan is different. We have no way of knowing which one he might have followed had he had enough time to pursue any of them to their end point.

I propose, however, to reverse Marx's general approach here. I present a picture of the framework that Marx more or less completed in his political economic studies of capital (Figure 2). This picture of capital flows provides an initial map, and hence a way of locating where we are as we move through the text. There is always a "forest for the trees" problem in reading Marx. The map depicts the totality of capital (the forest) and it then provides a framework in which to understand how Marx is depicting the interrelations between the moments (the trees). Capital is defined as value in motion, and it is through this motion that all the moments are linked together. The diagram is a map of the primary flows of value within the totality.

At the base of the diagram, we see money capital, which is money being used as capital. The presumption is that the money form is well established and is already being used to circulate commodities, to measure value and so on. Not all money is capital, but capital cannot exist without at some point taking on the money form. In the next step, the capitalists use their money to buy commodities of an equivalent value in the marketplace. There are two kinds of commodities: means of production of all sorts (such as machinery and raw materials) and labor power (the capacity to labor). The implication is that commodity and labor markets are also already well-established. As owners of means of production and of labor power, capitalists bring these two factors of production together in the third step, a labor process under their command, in order to create a new commodity. This labor process is organized by capital to preserve the value of the labor power and the value of the means of production (thus creating a commodity equivalent to the original money value) while also adding a surplus-value. This is the moment of production. The surplus-value is derived from the laborer working beyond the time required to reproduce the value of their own labor power. The surplus-value is congealed initially within the value of the new commodity. In the next step, that commodity is taken to market, where its value is realized and monetized through sale. The capitalist, says Marx in Volume I of *Capital*, "stares in astonishment" because the money received is greater than the money initially laid out. The surplus-value is realized as money profit. This is the moment of realization. Once it is in the hands of the users, the commodity either disappears in the physical act of consumption or is recycled into the production process when purchased as means of production by other producers.

But there are many claimants to the monetary value reproduced and gained in production. Some of the money passes over to the workers as wages. Some is taken by the state in the form of taxes (though Marx surprisingly says very little about this). Some goes to the bankers who might have lent some of the money at the outset. Some goes to merchants who specialize in the selling of commodities. Some goes to landlords who charge a rent for the use of the land (or access to the raw materials embedded therein). And some remains for the capitalist producers, who set up the whole productive circulation in the first place. Taken all together, this is the moment of distribution.

But what do all these claimants do with the money they get? Quite a bit of it goes to support their consumption, which forms much of the demand to buy commodities in the market (final consumption). Some of it flows back into the money capital form for what Marx calls "productive consumption" (reinvestment). Before doing so, surplus moneys are typically brought together by the banks and financial institutions who direct much of it toward performing the role of money capital once more. This initiates the circulation of interest-bearing capital. And so the cycle begins again, though this time containing a division between money capital plain and simple and interest-bearing capital lent to entrepreneurs to get the cycle going or keeping it running smoothly (as in times of distress). But because surplus-value and profit are key features, the cycle becomes a spiral of never-ending growth (accumulation) through the circulation and production of capital. The spiral form takes over.

This spiral of capital, while abstractly presented, is grounded in the material world. At the base of Figure 2 we depict the grounding of capital accumulation in the physical material world of nature. The metabolic relation to nature is a critical feature in the evolution of the totality. It sets up certain conditions of possibility for different forms of human activity. We know the natural world is itself in constant flux and that it contributes directly to production through its fecundity and rich diversity. It is also constantly being modified by human action. In some presentations, therefore, an important distinction is made between first nature (original and unmodified) and second nature (the product of human action in the building of physical infrastructures, urbanization, the carving out of fields, the drainage of swamps, etc.). Problems in the metabolic relation to nature and in the construction of second nature frequently arise (e.g., pollution and climate change or virus pandemics) and are not easily resolved. Value flows within the totality are not, therefore, independent of the restraints of this material world. Nor do the flows of value occur without having major impacts upon that material world.

The same can be said of the human nature and culture that is systematically used, shaped, appropriated, and incorporated in the continuous flows of value. Capital accumulation is materially embedded in this world of immense human diversity. Capital appropriates and, in many instances, preys upon preexisting differentiations and divisions at the same time that it produces new differentiations in the divisions of labor according to its own technological requirements. Capital is always busily at work perpetually modifying the conditions of possibility for further capital accumulation. The growth of knowledge, science and human skills and the proliferation of human wants, needs and desires (many of which are directly produced by capital itself) often butt up against unintended consequences and runaway crises of confidence and fears, as humanity has to grapple with both the defects and the triumphs of its own products and its own often problematic evolution. As Marx will note, it is not only transformations in the metabolic relation with nature but transformations in human nature that are at stake. The history of capital is tightly bound up with the production of new wants, needs and desires, even as capital mercilessly caters to and manipulates them.

The totality of value flows that produce capital accumulation is embedded in a wider totality that encompasses all of humanity's activities as well as global ecological transformations. In the same way that Marx works through his theory of *capital* in terms of inner relations between production, consumption, realization, distribution, and reinvestment, so a theory of *capitalism* (a term that Marx rarely if ever uses) might usefully be deployed to describe the inter-relationalities of culture, nature, economy and politics in a far broader conception of how society works. The *Grundrisse* provides glimpses of what such a broader conception might look like. In particular, the several outlines that Marx provides for his projected further work lay a topical basis accompanied by some provocative glimpses as to what a theory of capitalism as a totality (as opposed to capital as a totality) might look like.

Finally, we need to integrate into the picture the previously neglected question of social reproduction. This, since the feminist interventions of the 1970s, has become a critical feature in how we understand the evolutionary dynamics of capitalism as well as of capital. Of all the contingent features that set boundaries to the conditions of possibility for endless capital accumulation, social reproduction exhibits the most intimate internal relation with the theory of capital as Marx defines it. Social reproduction not only covers the crucial features of the biological and social reproduction of the laborer and, hence, of labor power. It also encompasses the production of ways of daily life, the cultural dynamics of consumption, and social institutions such as the family, communal and political forms, gender relations, collective forms of consumption, institutions of governmentality and the organized articulation of spiritual and political values. Much of this is only touched upon in the *Grundrisse*, but Marx (and we) cannot avoid confronting such topics, even if only to lay them to one side (as

Marx for the most part specifically does) for purposes of the analysis of capital.

Figure 2 is a picture, a mental reconstruction of a totality in which capital (value) circulates through different moments before coming back to its moment of origin (as money capital). At that point, the circulation process begins again. Production, consumption, distribution, reinvestment and exchange are distinctive moments within that totality. But classical political economy lacked and continues to lack to this day an adequate conception of totality. It typically views each one of these moments as autonomous and independent (flattened tautologies), whereas Marx views them as autonomous and independent but subsumed within a network of inner relations between all the moments within the totality. The phrase "autonomous and independent but subsumed within" will frequently be appealed to in the subsequent analysis. I am often asked what it means. The best answer I have is that it is like raising a teenager: they perpetually insist, assert and practice their autonomy and independence, while being confined within the household economy for daily sustenance—and when things go wrong, as they invariably do, they race on home seeking parental protection. This is a good description of how the bankers behaved in 2007–8. They insisted on deregulation, on their infallible autonomy and independence, but when the crash came the paternalistic protection of the state was crucial to their survival. The whole world woke up to the threat of moral hazard.

None of the moments within the totality of capital can, in Marx's view, be understood independently of the relations prevailing between them. Production presumes consumption and realization. It likewise presumes (or, to use Marx's favorite word, "posits") distribution. The material base of the internal relations lies in the continuous flow of value through and across the different moments. This conception of the totality and its moments pervades the *Grundrisse*. But it often lies in the background as a tacit assumption rather than as an explicit formulation. It is left up to the reader, when reading this or that part of the text, to keep the framework of the totality in mind. It is for this reason that I present the structure of the totality at the outset.

On occasion, however, Marx does remind us of its importance. On page 278, for example, he writes,

> while in the completed bourgeois system, every economic rela-
> tion presupposes every other in its bourgeois economic form
> and everything posited is thus also a presupposition, this is the
> case with every organic system. This organic system itself, as a
> totality, has its presuppositions, and its development to its total-
> ity consists precisely in subordinating all elements of society to
> itself, or in creating out of it the organs which it still lacks. This
> is historically how it becomes a totality. The process of becom-
> ing this totality forms a moment of its process, of its
> development.

The totality is thus neither fixed nor static but in constant development and evolution. It is perpetually in "the process of becoming." How and why, we might now ask, did the world's central
banks and international financial institutions such as the
International Monetary Fund and the Bank of International
Settlements come to play the role they now have? Marx's method
opens up the possibility of asking such questions and locating the
answers in the framework of a much more sophisticated theory of
an evolving totality. The geographical field and terrain that capital
flow operates across and upon is also in perpetual flux. This,
however, is a matter that we will take up in more detail later.

PRODUCTION, CONSUMPTION AND DISTRIBUTION

In the "Introduction," Marx looks at the basic economic categories
through the lens of classical political economy. "It is necessary," he
writes, "to focus on the various categories which the economists
line up" next to production (88). "Production creates the objects

which correspond to the given needs; distribution divides them up according to social laws; exchange further parcels out the already divided shares in accord with individual needs; and finally, in consumption, the product steps outside this social movement and becomes a direct object and servant of individual need, and satisfies it in being consumed" (88). Commodities, economically speaking, disappear as use-values in the act of final consumption, though their monetized value marches on. In this system, "production appears as the point of departure, consumption as the conclusion, distribution and exchange as the middle, which is however itself twofold, since distribution is determined by society and exchange by individuals ... Thus production, distribution, exchange and consumption form a regular syllogism; production is the generality, distribution and exchange the particularity, and consumption the singularity in which the whole is joined together" (89).

In reflecting on the qualities of this syllogism, Marx admits there is "a coherence," but characterizes it as "a shallow one." He then repeats Mill's formulation: "Production is determined by general natural laws, distribution by social accident ... Exchange stands between the two as formal social movement; and the concluding act, consumption . . . actually belongs outside economics except insofar as it reacts in turn upon the point of departure and initiates the whole process anew" (89). Bourgeois critics of this formulation typically complain at the privileging of production over all else, but in so doing they view production and distribution as "autonomous and independent neighbours" with the result that "these moments were not grasped in their unity." This prompts Marx to comment on the way in which the rupture between production and distribution "made its way not from reality into the textbooks, but rather from the textbooks into reality" (90). It was, he says, "as if the task were the dialectic balancing of concepts, and not the grasping of real relations!" Given the heavy reliance on the dialectical balancing of concepts throughout much of the *Grundrisse*, we plainly ought to keep Marx's warning very much in mind. At the end of the day, it is the understanding of the real relations that matters.

Classical political economy depicts relationships between the different moments and recognizes there is some way in which "the whole is joined together." But Marx picks apart the "shallow" and "flattened" qualities of the syllogism that prevails within bourgeois economic reason and mourns the lack of an adequate ecological and organic framework to capture the internal relations within the totality. As we see from Figure 2, production is not production without flowing into consumption. Consumption does not work for long without adequate distribution. If distribution is blocked, then nothing else works. The question of whether production is more important in this flow than consumption or distribution is not, in Marx's view, a valid question. It would be like asking, are your liver or your lungs or your brain more important to your life than your heart?

The first step in Marx's inquiry is to examine bourgeois conceptions of the relations between consumption and production. There are two forms of consumption. There is final consumption, where the product is eaten, worn or otherwise used up. The other is the production of means of production, which flow back into the system as productive consumption (90). This distinction between final and productive consumption is important. For instance, in the crash of 2007–8 final consumption was severely curtailed in the United States. Chinese export industries lost much of their market and were in deep trouble. Millions of workers were thrown out of work and the Communist Party had to face up to the threat of massive unrest. The Chinese government launched a huge program of investment in infrastructures. They built railroads, they built highways. They invested in new plant and equipment. They built whole new cities and urbanized at an astonishing pace. They countered the lack of final consumption by a massive increase in productive consumption. By this strategy, the Chinese created perhaps as many as 30 million jobs in a couple of years. Their rising demand for raw materials coincidentally saved much of the global economy (Australia, Chile, some African countries) from prolonged and deep recession. When capital flows get blocked down one path, then they can move to another.

Behind this lies the contradictory unity between consumption and production. Consumption proper "is also immediately production" in the same way that production "is also immediately consumption. Each is immediately its opposite" (91). Stated this way, the relation between production and consumption appears as a tautology. But on closer inspection we see that "the product only obtains its last finish in consumption. A railway on which no trains run, hence which is not used up, not consumed, is a railway only [potentially], and not in reality. Without production, no consumption; but also, without consumption, no production; since production would then be purposeless" (91). Consumption often "creates the need for *new* production, that is it creates the ideal, internally impelling cause for production." But also "production produces consumption (1) by creating the material for it; (2) by determining the manner of consumption; and (3) by creating the products, initially posed by it as objects, in the form of a need felt by the consumer" (92). Capital actively produces the wants, needs and desires of consumers, but at the same time the independent and autonomous movements among consumers pressure production responses.

Marx converges on what he calls the three-fold identity between production and consumption (93).

(1) "*Immediate identity*: Production is consumption, consumption is production." The most obvious example is when I eat the omelette I have just produced or wear the dress I just made. In a peasant society, the collective consumes what it produces. (2) In the second case however, "one appears as a means for the other, is mediated by the other: this is expressed as their mutual dependence; a movement which relates them to one another, makes them appear indispensable to one another, but still leaves them external to each other. Production creates the material, as external object,

for consumption; consumption creates the need, as internal object, as aim, for production. Without production no consumption; without consumption no production." This is a convoluted way of describing a situation in which I produce an omelette or a dress for another to meet their need. Peasant communes may trade surpluses with one another, perhaps on a regular and repeated basis.

(3) The third point is more difficult: "Not only is production immediately consumption and consumption immediately production, not only is production a means for consumption and consumption the aim of production . . . but also, each of them, apart from being immediately the other, and apart from mediating the other, in addition to this creates the other in completing itself and creates itself as the other" (93). A common value circulates through the production and consumption of omelettes and dresses. The independence and autonomy of production and consumption are asserted and assured but the circulation of value and surplus-value requires that both the quantity and quality of consumption (e.g., the state of wants, needs and desires backed by ability to pay) accommodate or "be adequate to" the realization of the produced value in the market. But here "consumption accomplishes the act of production only in completing the product as product by dissolving it, by consuming its independently material form." The dissolution of the use-value of the product through consumption invites repetition and it is this repetition that defines what it means to be a producer (93). "On the other side, production produces consumption by creating the specific manner of consumption; and, further, by creating the stimulus of consumption, the ability to consume, as a need." Market exchange separates production from consumption but then brings them back together in a contradictory unity.

"This last identity," Marx goes on to note, is "frequently cited in economics in the relation of demand and supply, of objects and needs, of socially created and natural needs. Thereupon, nothing simpler for a Hegelian than to posit production and consumption as identical. And this has been done not only by socialist belletristes but by prosaic economists themselves, e.g. Say," who was an expert in reducing complex relations to "flat tautologies" (93–4). The chief tautology that haunted economic analysis for more than a century was in fact Say's law. This "law," which Ricardo endorsed, states that since every purchase is a sale and every sale is a purchase, there can never be a surplus of purchases or sales. They are always in equilibrium. If this is so, then there can never be a general economic crisis of overproduction or underconsumption, though there may be over- or under-consumption in particular sectors. Say's law dominated economic theory from Ricardo right the way through to the 1930s, when it was plainly nonsensical to say there cannot be a general crisis of underconsumption because everyone was obviously living in one. Keynes attacked Say's law frontally and it was abandoned in the 1930s. The simplest argument Marx advances against it is that when money (a potential store of value) mediates the exchange process, the sale of a commodity for money does not mandate that the money be used to buy a commodity. Situations arise in which economic agents have good reasons to hold money (a form of social power). In so doing, they may create a crisis condition which looks like an overproduction of commodities or an overaccumulation of capital. A version of Say's law was resurrected in recent times in the marketing of financial services. Since every credit is a debt and every debt is a credit, there cannot be an excess of either debts or credits. This version of the so-called "efficient-market hypothesis" caused a lot of trouble in 2008, when the credit markets did not in fact clear.

Most normal, rational, thinking persons would surely at this point feel frustrated and impatient with this endless elaboration of possible relations between foundational categories. To this, Marx might well reply that this is the kind of muddle that gets created in a classical political economy that insists on the categories of production, consumption, realization and distribution as autonomous and independent "thing-like" categories before trying to analyze and enumerate the relations that may exist between and within them. Marx takes the "flattened tautologies" of bourgeois economics and tries to instill them with active life and meaning through the circulation of value within the totality. The subsumption within the totality is what is missing from bourgeois political economy. What matters is the flow of value as it courses through the different moments of production, consumption, realization and distribution. These categories do not exist independently of each other. Production and consumption are conceptualized "as moments of one process" (94). So, while Marx concedes, in line with classical political economy, that "production is the real point of departure and hence also the predominant moment" it rests on "consumption as urgency, as need, [which] is itself an intrinsic moment of productive activity." Production "is the point of departure for realization and hence also its predominant moment; it is the act through which the whole process again runs its course. The individual produces an object and, by consuming it returns . . . as a productive and self-producing individual. Consumption thus appears as a moment of production" (94).

At this point, Marx does not know exactly what the totality looks like. This is what he wants to uncover. He then turns to look at distribution and production in the same way. "*Distribution* steps between the producer and the products, hence between production and consumption, to determine with social laws what the producer's share will be in the world of products." But this then poses the question: "Does distribution stand at the side of and outside of production as an autonomous sphere?" (94).

He prefaces his search for an answer with a commentary on how the economists typically posit everything doubly. "For example, ground rent, wages, interest and profit figure under distribution, while land, labour and capital figure under production as agents of production" (95). Capital is likewise posited doubly as an "agent of production" and "source of income." "Interest and profit thus also figure as such in production . . . They are modes of distribution whose presupposition is capital as agent of production. They are, likewise, modes of reproduction of capital." The result is that "the relations and modes of distribution thus appear merely as the obverse of the agents of production." It then appears (which does not mean that it is) as if "the structure of distribution is completely determined by the structure of production." It was this that led Ricardo to conceive of "the forms of distribution as the most specific expression into which the agents of production of a given society are cast" (96).

To the single individual, distribution is a social law determining their position in society. "As regards whole societies, distribution seems to precede production and to determine it in yet another respect." For example, "a conquering people divides the land" and "imposes a certain distribution and form of property." Or, to take another example, "a people rises in revolution and smashes the great landed estates into small parcels, and, hence, by this new distribution, gives production a new character." The distribution of the means of production and initial divisions of labor are precursors. "To examine production while disregarding this internal distribution within it is obviously an empty abstraction; while conversely, the distribution of products follows by itself from this distribution which forms an original moment of production" (96). This "again shows the ineptitude of those economists who portray production as an eternal truth while banishing history to the realm of distribution ... If it is said that, since production must begin with a certain distribution of the instruments of production, it follows that distribution at least in this sense precedes and forms the presupposition of production, then the reply must be that production does indeed have its determinants and preconditions which form its moments" (97).

These questions "all reduce themselves in the last instance to the role played by general-historical relations in production, and their relation to the movement of history generally. The question evidently belongs within the treatment and investigation of production itself," which means a return, of course, to the principles of historical materialism. This return is briefly foreshadowed by a paragraph or two on the history of conquest, colonialism (in Ireland and India), the Mongol invasions and the like, all of which radically transformed production and distribution relations.

Exchange, for its part, "is merely a moment mediating between production and its production-determined distribution on one side and consumption on the other, but, in so far as the latter appears as a moment of production, to that extent is exchange obviously included as a moment within the latter." But there is no exchange without the division of labor, and its intensity depends on the degree of development of production (99).

"The conclusion we reach," and here Marx summarizes as succinctly as he can, "is not that production, distribution, exchange and consumption are identical, but that they all form the members of a totality, distinctions within a unity. Production predominates not only over itself, in the antithetical definition of production, but over the other moments as well. The process always returns to production to begin anew" (99). If you look at Figure 2, you will see the eternal return to production. Production dominates over itself in the sense that the production of surplus-value predominates over the production of material commodities.

That exchange and consumption cannot be predominant is self-evident. Likewise distribution as distribution of products; while as distribution of the agents of production it is itself a moment of production. A definite production thus determines a definite consumption, distribution and exchange as well as *definite relations between these different moments.* Admittedly, however, *in its one-sided form,* production is itself determined by the other moments. For example, if the market, i.e. the sphere of exchange, expands, then production grows in quantity and the divisions between its different branches become deeper. A change in distribution changes production, e.g concentration of capital, different distribution of population between town or country, etc. Finally, the needs of consumption determine production. Mutual interaction takes place between the different moments. This is the case with every organic whole. (99–100)

When you approach the economy from the standpoint of this totality of moments, then you start to see things in a very particular light. If I impressionistically summarize what has happened here, then it would be Marx measuring the achievements of the bourgeois economists, which, he concedes, were substantial, against a theoretical stance which privileges processes, relationalities, flows and contradictory tensions, all operating within a framework of a historically constituted totality comprising the different moments of production, consumption, realization, distribution and exchange. The reduction of the rich and contradictory complexity of capital's economy to the flat tautologies of Adam Smith and Ricardo was, in Marx's view, a profound error, compounded by the characterization of production as natural and therefore immune to social control or amelioration. Echoes of the privileging of production in classical political economy can be found in Marx. That is where surplus-value and the production and reproduction of capital find their origin. But if the organic ecosystemic metaphor holds, the production of capital and surplus-value, along with the capitalist, is nothing outside of the totality of the circulation process that supports it.

I understand that the language and the conceptual moves performed here are somewhat unusual and hard to grasp on a first reading. But we live in a world driven by the circulation and accumulation of capital. To be sure, it is a messy, complex but incisive world, as we soon discover in our attempts to live a decent life within its purview. What Marx seems intent on inventing is a messy, complex but incisive mode of analysis that mirrors the real world unfolding around us. The clean analytics to which classical and neoclassical political economy aspire might be reassuring to those steeped in Cartesian or positivist ways of thought. But their notorious failures when confronted with crisis and other inconvenient conditions, such as those of 2007–8, to say nothing of 2020, suggest that some alternative conceptual model must be uncovered. And this is what animates Marx in his inquiries. His method may appear unduly complex, but then that method mirrors the qualities of the world we have to understand. It is the incisive vector within the totality of moments that we seek to uncover.

THE METHOD OF POLITICAL ECONOMY

The third part of Marx's "Introduction" concerns the method of political economy. It is rare for Marx to write about methods. Most of us learn Marx's method by following and observing his practices. So we need to pay close attention to what he has to say right here, even though it is the method of political economy rather than his own method that is the primary focus of attention. Fortunately for us, the critique of the former reveals much about the latter.

The political economists typically start with "the real and the concrete" conditions prevailing in a country, such as the population and its characteristics. While this appears adequate, Marx demurs on the grounds that "population is an abstraction if I leave out, for example, the classes of which it is composed. These classes in turn are an empty phrase if I am not familiar with the elements on which they rest. E.g. wage labour, capital, etc. These latter in turn presuppose exchange, division of labour," and so on. "If I were to begin with the population," Marx asserts, "this would be a chaotic conception of the whole" (100). Plainly, our intellectual and mental landscape is littered with "chaotic conceptions" from which we derive equally chaotic understandings and political strategies. Marx is at war with such chaotic conceptions. We should be as well. But if perchance we did commence at the starting point of a chaotic conception such as population, we would then "move analytically towards ever more simple concepts, from the imagined concrete towards ever thinner abstractions" until we arrive at "the simplest determinations. From there the journey would have to be retraced" until we "finally arrived at the population again, but this time not as the chaotic conception as a whole, but as a rich totality of many determinations and relations" (100). It is "this rich totality" with its "many determinations and relations" that Marx seeks to understand.

The earlier economists typically followed the first path of descent from the concrete to discover "through analysis of a small number of determinant, abstract, general relations such as division of labour, money, value, etc." (100). These findings formed the basis of their economic systems, "which ascended from the simple relations, such as labour, division of labour, need, exchange value, to the level of the state, exchange between nations and the world market." Marx concludes: "The latter [the ascent from the abstract to the concrete] is obviously the scientifically correct method. The concrete is concrete because it is the concentration of many determinations, hence unity of the diverse" (101). If the reader takes anything from reading the *Grundrisse*, let it be this general strategy. "Along the first path" (i.e., the descent from the concrete to the abstract), "the full conception was evaporated to yield an abstract determination; along the second, the abstract determination leads towards a reproduction of the concrete by way of thought" (101). Hegel wrongly concluded from this that the real was the product of thought, "whereas the method of rising from the abstract to the concrete . . . reproduces it as the concrete in the mind. But this is by no means the process by which the concrete comes into being." Marx illustrates this research strategy with the example of "the simplest economic category, say e.g. exchange value." This category presupposes the existence of "a population producing in specific relations; as well as a certain kind of family, or commune, or state, etc. It can never exist other than as an abstract, one-sided relation within an already given, concrete, living whole." But as a philosophical category it "leads an antediluvian existence." In the "philosophical consciousness" (and I assume he means Hegel here) for which the only reality is "conceptual thinking," the "movement of the categories appears as the real act of production" whose "product is the world" until such time as it receives "a jolt from the outside" (i.e., reality breaks out). The result is yet another tautology such that the "concrete totality is a totality of thoughts," which is not the product of the concepts themselves but of a process of the "working-up of observation and conception into concepts" (101):

> The totality as it appears in the head, as a totality of thoughts, is a product of a thinking head, which appropriates the world in the only way it can, a way different from the artistic, religious, practical and mental appropriation of this world. The real subject [concrete reality] retains its autonomous existence outside the head just as before; namely as long as the head's conduct is merely speculative, merely theoretical. Hence, in the theoretical method, too, the [active] subject, society, must always be kept in mind as the presupposition. (101–2)

We have to recognize, however, that the general and simpler categories often "have an independent historical and natural existence pre-dating the more concrete ones." For example, Hegel's *Philosophy of Right* opens with "possession" as the simplest juridical relation, but there are many different situations where "possession" takes on specific meanings. It is also the case that money existed historically before capital, banks and wage labor. "The path of abstract thought, rising from the simple to the combined, [could] correspond to the real historical process" (102). But that process has varied significantly over time and place, before arriving at the point of its distinctive bourgeois form. For example, money did not exist in precolonial Peru even though there was a sophisticated economy with divisions of labor, cooperation and exchange relations. "Further, although money everywhere plays a role from very early on, it is nevertheless a predominant element, in antiquity, only within the confines of certain one-sidedly developed nations, trading nations. And even in the most advanced parts of the ancient world, among the Greeks and the Romans, the full development of money, which is presupposed in modern bourgeois society, appears only in the period of their dissolution" (103). "This very simple category, then, makes a historic appearance in its full intensity only in the most developed conditions of society."

Labor, likewise, appears as a very simple if "immeasurably old" category that has a variety of meanings in relation to different social conditions. Only in the hands of Adam Smith did it begin to take on its modern bourgeois meaning:

> With the abstract universality of wealth-creating activity we now have the universality of the object defined as wealth, the product as such or again labour as such, but labour as past, objectified labour . . . Indifference towards any specific kind of labour presupposes a very developed totality of real kinds of labour, of which no single one is any longer predominant. As a rule, the most general abstractions arise only in the midst of the richest possible concrete development. (104)

This general principle is foundational for understanding those abstractions which will root his own political economy. It is, for example, only "in the midst of the richest possible concrete development" that "one thing" can appear "as common to many, to all. Then it ceases to be thinkable in a particular form alone." This will later become the foundation for Marx's conception of value (a concept waiting to be articulated). "This abstraction of labour as such is not merely the mental product of a concrete totality of labours. Indifference towards specific labours corresponds to a form of society in which individuals can with ease transfer from one labour to another, and where the specific kind is a matter of chance for them, hence of indifference" (104). Here we have "the point of departure of modern economics." It is here that "the simplest abstraction" which "expresses an immeasurably ancient relation valid in all forms of society, nevertheless achieves practical truth as an abstraction only as a category of the most modern society" such as that in the United States. "This example of labour shows strikingly how even the most abstract categories, despite their validity—precisely because of their abstractness—for all epochs, are nevertheless, in the specific character of this abstraction, themselves likewise a product of historic relations, and possess their full validity only for and within these relations" (105).

Marx's method here matches in certain ways the principles that pervade contemporary work on artificial intelligence. Artificial intelligence (AI) works best and indeed wholly rests on massive data sets. The more massive the data sets, the more accurate AI becomes. The competitive advantage that China possesses in this regard is self-evident. What AI is doing is abstracting relationalities from the "richest concrete determinations" with information technologies that were unthinkable in Marx's time. Yet Marx was dedicated to abstracting the laws of motion of capital from the richest concrete determinations deriving from individualized market exchange.

In the history of capital, Marx argues, the sort of totality represented in the three volumes of *Capital* may be a product of his thinking. But it is also a product of the historical process whereby the totality comes into being. For example, this system and the theory it engenders could not work unless there was free exchange. It is a system that will only work alongside the creation of private property rights, exchange relations, monetary forms and all the rest of it. The totality of capital comes into being. It does not pre-exist. Nor is it a product of thought. But what the thinking head tries to do is to come to terms with what the emergent totality encompasses and to uncover its laws of motion and development. This is the key point of Marxist political economy. Marx seeks to reconstruct in thought the totality that is being constructed through daily life and daily practices in the market, through commodity exchange, through production and consumption activities, and above all through surplus-value production.

A dialectical process attempts to capture the relation between how something is being represented as a totality and the social processes that are producing, sustaining or dissolving that totality. It is not as if the totality is something solid, fixed and determinate. It is perpetually in the process of modification and transformation.

As it is being transformed, so the conceptual apparatus that we use to represent it must also transform. Otherwise, we impose our concept of a totality on a situation where it is not working that way anymore. This is the kind of question which arises when it is said that "financialization changes everything." Interest-bearing capital does not circulate in the same way as industrial capital. It does not have to go through production in order to claim its part of the surplus. Banks can lend to landowners to buy land. Banks can lend to merchant capitalists. Banks can lend to workers so that they have credit cards and they can get mortgages to buy a house or a loan to buy a car. Banks do not have to go through production in order to earn interest. The circulation process Marx analyzes always goes back through production. What happens when a large portion of capital does not flow back through production?

The totality, even in Marx's time, is an incomplete theoretical representation, a simplified version. The task of economics and economic theory is to try to capture the totality and capture the nature of the relations (the laws of motion) between these different moments. In the historical succession of the economic categories, as in any other historical, social science, "it must not be forgotten that their subject—here, modern bourgeois society—is always what is given, in the head as well as in reality, and that these categories therefore express the forms of being, the characteristics of existence, . . . and that therefore this society by no means begins only at the point where one can speak of it *as such*" (106). It would seem, for example, that the most obvious starting point would be with landed property and ground rent because the earth is "the source of all production and all being." But "nothing would be more erroneous," Marx asserts. "In all forms of society there is one specific kind of production which predominates over the rest, whose relations thus assign rank and influence to the others" (106–7). The designations vary greatly (and Marx provides examples). But in bourgeois society, agriculture and the use of the earth "is entirely dominated by capital" and "capital is the all-dominating economic power" which forms both "the starting-point as well as the finishing-point, and must be dealt with before landed property." It would "be infeasible and wrong to let the economic categories follow one another in the same sequence as that in which they were historically decisive. Their sequence is determined, rather, by their relation to one another . . . which is precisely the opposite of that which seems to be their natural order or which corresponds to historical development." The same category can occupy divergent positions in different social stages (107).

This point then leads him to consider the ways in which, historically, many of these categories have been set up. The historical order in which these categories came into being is significant. Money, for example, precedes capitalism. Credit and debt precede capitalism. Land and property and extractions of surplus from land and property precede capitalism. Even wage-labor, as we shall see, precedes the rise of capital. But what happens, in the bourgeois form of capitalist society, is that all of those categories are given different and more flexible meanings as they are absorbed within a changing totality. And as the totality forms and evolves, so it reconfigures the moments and elements within it. We can reconstruct the "antediluvian" histories of the different categories which have long preexisted the advent of capital and which can carry over as feudal residuals within the hegemony of capital. But even those feudal residuals take on a different character. The credit and debt found in ancient Sumer or in the Roman Empire is completely different from the way in which debt, credit and the circulation of interest-bearing capital work in a bourgeois capitalist society. This is something that David Graeber fails to recognize in his otherwise fascinating *Debt: The First Five Thousand Years*. In ancient Sumer, there was no market in debt. Now we have hugely complicated debt markets and all sorts of financial products. Debt creation right now has a completely different configuration, and a different function, compared to debt creation in ancient Sumer. The same is true of land rent, which, within capitalism, becomes something radically different from that found in feudal times.

Marx's warning bears repeating. It would be "infeasible and wrong to let the economic categories follow one another in the same sequence as that in which they were historically decisive." The evolution of the meaning of categories is a matter of concern. While there is a giant leap from one mode of production to another, the meaning of the categories continues to evolve within the history of capital. For example, "the concept of national wealth creeps into the work of the economists of the seventeenth century— continuing partly with those of the eighteenth—in the form of the notion that wealth is created only to enrich the state, and that its power is proportionate to this wealth. This was the still unconsciously hypocritical form in which wealth and the production of wealth proclaimed themselves as the purpose of modern states, and regarded these states henceforth only as means for the production of wealth" (108). The relation between state and capital has also evolved, not necessarily in a linear fashion, and the dual and sometimes conflictual objectives of either enriching the state or enriching its dominant classes, or even, heaven forbid, its population as a whole, has been a fluctuating feature across the spectrum of capital's history.

THE FIRST PLAN

We then come to another major feature of the *Grundrisse*. On page 108, Marx sets out the first of several study plans to guide his future investigations into the nature of capital. It consists of a list of topics, concepts and categories that will need to be studied:

> The order obviously has to be (1) the general, abstract determinants which obtain in more or less all forms of society, but in the above-explained sense. (2) The categories which make up the inner structure of bourgeois society and on which the fundamental classes rest. Capital, wage labour, landed property. Their interrelation. Town and country. The three great social classes. Exchange

between them. Circulation. Credit system (private). (3) Concentration of bourgeois society in the form of the state. Viewed in relation to itself. The "unproductive" classes. Taxes. State debt. Public credit. The population. The colonies. Emigration. (4) The international relation of production. International division of labour. International exchange. Export and import. Rate of exchange. (5) The world market and crises. (108)

What is interesting about this wide-ranging list is how little of it is covered in the mass of Marx's political-economic writings (as opposed to his journalistic interventions, where his reading of parliamentary reports and the financial press, such as the *Economist*, featured large). While Marx asserts the existence of three great classes plus unspecified "unproductive classes," his emphasis upon credit, banking, taxes, state debt and international trade emphasize features of distribution (e.g., merchant and finance capital) that are spottily covered in Marx's works. Production, labor and money are not prominent topics except by implication in the first item. Above all, it is interesting to review this list of items in relation to a working concept of the totality. The theory of capital as a totality as represented in Figure 2 is, for example, far less expansive than would be required in this study plan.

This is, however, the first of several proposed plans. These were all reviewed in some detail by Roman Rosdolsky in *The Making of Marx's* Capital. This text has an interesting history. Rosdolsky was a Ukrainian immigrant to the United States (arriving in 1947 after surviving several years in Nazi concentration camps). When in the New York Public Library, he came across a rare German published version of the *Grundrisse* and immediately recognized its importance. He undertook a detailed study of it (as an independent scholar with no academic affiliation) with special emphasis upon the different study plans in relation to Marx's *Capital*. His book was published in German in 1968 (shortly after he died) and appeared in English 1977. The English version of the *Grundrisse*

(1973) and Rosdolsky's analysis of it (1977) had a huge impact upon me while writing *The Limits to Capital* (1982)—which was exactly the sort of impact of the *Grundrisse* that Rosdolsky had anticipated.

ART AND SOCIETY

The fourth section of Marx's "Introduction" begins with a wish list of potentially important topics that are mentioned without being analyzed in any depth. Marx begins with war and the role of the army and the relation of productive force in relations of exchange in the military. He notes the contrast between historical materialism, which is a social construct, and naturalistic materialism. He introduces the key dialectic of the concepts of productive force and relations of production without elaboration. The question of uneven development is likewise introduced both geographically (e.g., Europe, with its feudal residuals, versus the United States) and sectorally (e.g., as legal relations). The question of communications is posed.

The last part is a charming excursus into the question of how art relates to the distinctive eras in human cultural and material development (110–11). "It is well-known, of course, that certain periods of artistic development go way beyond what might be expected from the general development of society, the organization of material production and the like. Nevertheless certain forms of art, such as the epic forms, can no longer be produced."

> Is the view of nature and of social relations on which the Greek imagination and Greek [mythology] is based possible with self-acting mule spindles and railways and locomotives and electrical telegraphs? What chance has Vulcan with Roberts & Co., Jupiter against the lightening-rod and Hermes against the Crédit Mobilier? All mythology overcomes and dominates and shapes the forces of nature in the imagination and by the

imagination; it therefore vanishes with the advent of real mastery over them.

The difficulty lies, Marx asserts, "not in understanding that the Greek arts and epic are bound up with certain forms of social development . . . [but] that they still afford us artistic pleasure." To this Marx opines that "a man cannot become a child again, or he becomes childish. But does he not find joy in the child's naïveté, and must he himself not strive to reproduce its truth at a higher stage? Does not the true character of each epoch come alive in the nature of its children? Why should not the historic childhood of humanity, its most beautiful unfolding, as a stage never to return, exercise an eternal charm?" That is a question for the ages.

2

The Circulation of Money
Pages 115–238

I argued, in my own introduction, that the *Grundrisse* is shaped around the study of several different circulatory systems contained within the evolving totality of capital. In this opening section of the main text, the focus is on the circulation of money and the structures, forms and functions of monetary circulation in general. Capital, Marx will argue, arises out of circulation, since it rests on the principle of using money to make more money. The questions to be addressed here are not only "what is money?" but "how does it circulate?" "what functions does it perform?" and "what properties does it acquire that can be made use of and, if necessary, be augmented when the circulation of capital becomes more general?"

What separates capital from other modes of monetary aggrandizement (such as robbery, piracy, war, tribute, or buying cheap and selling dear) is the direct exploitation of living labor in production (the production of surplus-value). The money form and monetary circulation (along with the commodification of labor power) pre-exist the rise of capital. The question of how money circulates as money capital is taken up later. Here, we concentrate attention upon the circulation of money in general as a necessary precursor to understanding how capital uses money for its own purposes.

Unfortunately, Marx has several other issues in mind. The text begins with a detailed critique of the theories of money being propagated by Proudhon and his followers (most notably Darimon).[1] A great deal of attention is also paid to the material qualities required of those commodities (such as the precious metals) that function as money commodities. Historical materials are inserted in a nonsystematic way. Add to this the sheer difficulty and complexity of the topic (an issue that makes the well-worked-out money chapter in Volume I of *Capital* also difficult to navigate) and you have a recipe for a messy and somewhat tedious (to put it mildly) introduction to the general subject matter of the *Grundrisse*. Marx's later characterization of the *Grundrisse* as a "hopscotch" of ideas is here all too visible.

I propose, therefore, to skim the first hundred or so pages of the text rather lightly, to treat it as a somewhat erratic voyage of discovery that goes in different directions only to circle back on itself at various points. At one of these points, Marx accuses himself of being too idealist, and vows to "correct the idealist manner of the presentation" (151). This problem arises because Marx does not follow his normal historical materialist practice of beginning with concrete abstractions drawn from real life (with concepts like the use and exchange-value of the commodity). In his desire to take down Proudhon, he confronts him in the realm of ideas and theoretical and political argument mainly by way of a detailed refutation of the work of Darimon, a prominent Proudhonist of the time. This cannot be ignored because it reveals something substantive about the nature of money and the properties of monetary circulation as Marx understands them. And it turns out that what appears as a somewhat arcane debate from Marx's time has considerable contemporary relevance.

---

1   Alfred Darimon, *De la réforme des banques* (Paris, 1856).

MONEY AS THE ROOT OF CRISES

Money capital is an originary moment in the circulation of capital (see Figure 2). But not all money is capital. The aggregate circulation of money is the pool from which money capital is drawn and the pool to which it returns. Money plays a variety of social roles in capitalism and circulates according to the requirements of those roles. The centrality of money leads many, including Proudhon, to believe that monetary reforms could play a crucial role in the search to construct a more socially just economic system. In our own times, the fascination of some anticapitalists with alternative monetary forms, such as local moneys and cyber-currencies, is a continuation of this political tradition. Marx's qualified rejection of this tradition is therefore of interest.

The material basis for Proudhon's position lay in the monetary manifestations of crises in which lack of liquidity and the inaccessibility of credit played a crucial role in the impoverishment and bankruptcy of the artisan working classes and small businesses in general (particularly in Paris). The answer for Proudhon lay in monetary reforms and the provision of easy access to free credit. The major monetary reform was to free the monetary system from its restrictive basis in the money commodities of gold and silver. The latter placed limits upon monetary accommodation and, according to Proudhon, triggered and exacerbated the descent into crises. Marx disputes Proudhon's account. For Marx, the trigger for the 1848 crisis was harvest failure and the collapse of raw silk production. France had to import large quantities of these raw materials, and the only acceptable way to pay for them was to ship out gold. It was this that produced a "bullion drain" which supposedly fed back into the domestic economy as a diminution of the means of domestic circulation and a collapse of the domestic market along with rising unemployment. Proudhon therefore proposed to separate and insulate domestic monetary circulation from convertibility into gold and silver. In other words, the domestic economy should go off the gold standard. Marx did not believe this would ever be possible (and explicitly argued so in Volume III of *Capital*).

On this point, Marx ultimately turned out to be wrong. On August 15, 1971, President Nixon suspended convertibility of the US dollar, the world's reserve currency at that time, into gold at a fixed price. After World War II, foreign governments had been encouraged to hold their active reserves in dollars backed by their gold reserve stored in Fort Knox. But by the time that Goldfinger got round to robbing it in the great James Bond movie of 1964, not much gold was left there. President de Gaulle of France, among others, speculated that the dollar would not last at $35 per ounce. The United States was finding it hard to maintain the price, and US banks hated the resulting curbs on their international activities. So devaluation was on the cards. This created a one-sided bet. Keep reserves in dollars and risk devaluation, or convert to gold, which meant breaking even if no devaluation occurred or making a huge profit if it did. de Gaulle took the gold back to Paris. Nixon devalued. This was a critical marker in the history of capital. It was, in fact, the realization of Proudhon's dream (though nobody noticed or cared at the time). But the reasoning advanced by Marx against the Proudhonian position sheds light not only on why he thought the gold standard could not be abandoned but what the consequences of so doing might be. Since these consequences are turning out to be problematic in our own times, Marx's responses are of relevance. The price of gold and floating currency exchange rates reflect the aggregate relative productive capacities of each nation's currency, while central banks manipulate currency and interest rates to ensure stability.

But Proudhon's main objection to the monetary system was that the prices of commodities did not properly reflect labor effort and input. He looked to devise an alternative monetary system in which "time-chits" would be the mechanism of exchange, reflecting the actual hours of labor input. This idea is still with us. For example, in the 1990s there was a lot of interest in local economic trading systems and local moneys—for example, the Ithaca dollar and the Bristol pound. In New York City, a time exchange network has existed for many years. In Argentina, in the wake of the crisis of 2001–2, a vast barter network sprang up with coupons, to form an alternative monetary system to the peso. In the 1930s, similar alternative monetary systems arose throughout many European countries. Keynes found them interesting, particularly when they sought to incorporate an "oxidizable" element such that the money disappeared after a certain time if it was not used. The Argentinian system worked rather well for about two years. It helped to keep a sophisticated barter economy going at the popular level during a time when everything else had pretty much crashed. It later spawned oxidizable systems that incorporated some of the principles of cyber-currencies that became the focus of experimentation after 2000 or so. My point here is to contextualize the tradition of monetary utopianism that Marx was addressing in his dispute with Proudhon. Oddly, the situation of negative rates of interest of the sort seen in various places over recent years entails the possibility of introducing something akin to systematic oxidization of paper moneys!

Marx opens his critique by noting that Darimon fails to recognize that "the quantity of discounted bills and the fluctuations in this quantity express the requirements of credit, whereas the quantity of money in circulation is determined by quite different influences" (115). Marx complains at "the intentional muddling together of the requirements of credit with those of monetary circulation" (116). He then goes on to condemn Darimon's "hasty effort to present in the most lurid colours his preconceived opinion that the metal basis of the bank, represented by its metallic assets, stands in contradiction to the requirements of circulation" (119). It was, Darimon held, far too restrictive. Marx further complains of "Darimon's illusion that [the bank's] monopoly really allows it to regulate credit. In fact the power of the bank begins only where the power of the private 'discounters' stops, hence at a moment where its power is already extraordinarily limited" (124). The metallic basis for money is largely irrelevant except and insofar as foreign interests prefer payment in gold, rather than accepting the local banknotes which facilitate domestic exchange. The use and proliferation of local banknotes is not limited by the metallic base. The private discounting of bills by merchants is an entirely different operation and is not limited by the gold reserves. Whether or not I extend credit to accommodate the needs of my customers does not depend upon the gold reserves of the banks.

In a prescient analysis of our current situation, Marx fantasized what would happen when money was cut loose from its metallic base.

> Suppose that the Bank of France did not rest on a metallic base, and that other countries were willing to accept the French currency or its capital in any form, not only in the specific form of the precious metals. Would the bank not have been equally forced to raise the terms of its discounting precisely at the moment when its "public" clamoured most eagerly for its services? The notes with which it discounts the bills of exchange of this public are at present nothing more than drafts on gold and silver. In our hypothetical case, they would be drafts on the nation's stock of products and on its directly employable labour force: the former is limited, the latter can be increased only within very positive limits, and in certain amounts of time. The printing press, on the other hand, is inexhaustible and works like a stroke of magic. (121)

And this, of course, is exactly where we are now, since this hypothetical situation became a reality after August 17, 1971. The Federal Reserve (along with all the world's other central banks) has responded to every disturbance in the global economy with magical monetarist methods such as quantitative easing. The printing presses have worked overtime.

The consequence, as Marx saw it, would be that "the directly exchangeable wealth of the nation" would be "absolutely diminished" alongside of "an unlimited increase of bank drafts" (i.e., accelerating indebtedness) with the direct consequence of "increase in the price of products, raw materials and labour" (inflation) alongside a "decrease in price of bank drafts" (ever-falling rates of interest) (121–2). This is pretty much the situation we have now arrived at, without, so far at least, the rising prices of labor and means of production (low inflation except for assets such as stocks and shares, land and property and resources such as water rights). In Marx's view, magical monetarism would not enhance the wealth of the nation but only destroy the viability of financial institutions (as we saw in 2007–8) and trigger repeated crises in the financial system. The Proudhonist response was not to be content with "abolishing the metal basis and leaving everything the way it was" but "to create entirely new conditions of production and circulation" (122). After all, "did not the introduction of our present banks, in its day, revolutionize the conditions of production? Would large-scale modern industry have become possible," asks Proudhon, "without this new financial institution, without the concentration of credit which it created, without the state revenues which it created in antithesis to ground rent, without finance in antithesis to landed property, without the moneyed interest in antithesis to the landed interest" (122), and so on, down to the birth of stock companies? All of these transitions are presumed to be witness to the Proudhonian radical dream of revolution by financial means. "We have here reached the fundamental question," says Marx:

> Can the existing relations of production and the relations of distribution which correspond to them be revolutionized by a change in the instrument of circulation, in the organization of circulation? Further question: Can such a transformation of circulation be undertaken without touching the existing relations of production and the social relations which rest on them? If every such transformation of circulation presupposes changes in other conditions of production and social upheavals, there would naturally follow from this the collapse of the doctrine which proposes tricks of circulation as a way of, on the one hand, avoiding the violent character of these social changes, and, on the other, of making these changes appear to be not a presupposition, but a gradual result of the transformations in circulation. (122)

MONEY AND REVOLUTION

Can changes in the monetary system change everything? Could they lead to a peaceful and minimally disruptive transition to a more just social order? Marx's answer to both of these possibilities is a resounding "no" (122). He disputes Proudhon's account. To begin with, "modern credit institutions were as much an effect as a cause of the concentration of capital, since they only form a moment of the latter, and since concentration of wealth is accelerated by a scarcity of circulation . . . as much as by an increase in the facility of circulation." In his desire to refute Proudhon, Marx here appears to take the somewhat dogmatic position that monetary disruptions cannot in themselves lead to crises and that it is only in the case of production failures that the true generator of crises is revealed. Somewhat later in the text (129), Marx confirms that "a crisis caused by a failure in the grain crop is therefore not at all created by the drain of bullion, although it can be aggravated by obstacles that impede this drain." In Volume III of *Capital*, Marx abandons this position and accepts that the crises of 1848 and 1857 were primarily commercial and financial crises and that speculation and disruption in the financial system played an important formative role (as was the case in 2007–8 as well as in 1848).

Marx holds that the key production disruption in 1848 lay in harvest failure and disruption of domestic raw silk supplies, not in any of the internal contradictions (such as falling profit rates) that he later identifies as potential sources of crisis. To be sure, disruptions emanating from the metabolic relation to nature are common enough in the history of capital, and the Covid-19 pandemic in 2020 spectacularly illustrates the point. But this then leads to a conceptual if not theoretical problem concerning the material organic nature and boundedness of the totality as Marx specifies it for purposes of analysis.

From Figure 2, it would seem that there is an inner core of the totality occupied by the different moments of the conversion of money into money capital, the production of commodities and surplus-value, realization through a sale in the market, consumption, distribution of value across the different factions and reinvestment of money capital with the aid of financial institutions and the state. This leaves an outer band constituted by the metabolic relation to nature, social reproduction, cultural reproduction, institutional arrangements (the state and law) and the supply of the free gifts of human nature (wants, needs and desires as well as popular talents and skills), all of which contribute to capital creation and accumulation but exist in contingent contextual relations, to some degree shaped by capital itself (e.g., built environments, urbanization, cultural forms, the state and legal apparatuses, along with the changing cultural condition of human wants, needs and desires), to the activities occurring in the inner core. Whether the metabolic relation to nature is postulated as internal or external to the totality of capital, as Marx construes it, is an important question. When, in *Capital*, Marx asserts that capital, left to its own devices, will destroy the two sources of all wealth—"the labourer and the soil"—he is clearly taking a rather broader view of the totality than that described by capital's core internal relations. It is now widely accepted that human pressures on habitats through capital's expansion have made virus pandemics much more likely (as evidenced by the series of coronaviruses that have swept across the world over the last thirty years), while the evidence of capital's impact on climate change is now irrefutable. There is nothing weird about formulations of this sort. While we might look upon the human body as a totality in itself for purposes of medical intervention, just as important is the positionality of that body in relation to the larger questions of environmental conditions, economy, employment, sociality and culture in a much wider conception of the totality. While the proximate cause of death by opioid may be medically defined on a death certificate, the social and environmental conditions that led to opioid addiction are far broader. It is significant that the abandoned traditional working classes in the United States are mostly addicted to opioids, while the new and much overworked working classes in South and East Asia are mostly addicted to amphetamines. The concept of capital as a totality has to be fungible to encompass a broader terrain of determinant influences than those given by the inner core circulation of capital.

Marx does not, however, dismiss the importance of monetary innovations in facilitating capital circulation. We need to examine "whether the different civilized forms of money—metallic, paper, credit money, labor money (the last-named as the socialist form)— can accomplish what is demanded of them without suspending the very relation to production which is expressed in the category money" (123). Marx herewith inserts a caveat into his resounding "no." "Various forms of money may correspond better to social production in various stages; one form may remedy evils against which another is powerless; but none of them, as long as they remain forms of money, and as long as the money remains an essential relation to production, is capable of overcoming the contradictions inherent in the money relation, and can instead only hope to reproduce these contradictions in one or another form" (123). In the same way that "one form of wage labour may correct the abuses of another, but no form of wage labour can correct the abuse of wage labour itself," so the contradictions contained within the money form cannot be erased by monetary innovations, however important these may be.

Money plays a variety of roles in a capitalist society, and different forms of money play the different roles more or less effectively. Blockchain technology, to take a contemporary example, can reduce transaction costs. It is very effective at moving money around the world at high speed and in a costless way. Once upon a time, clearing banks were required to net out all the different countervailing claims of the different banks upon each other at the end of each day, so net balances could be paid. In the old days, the clearing banks actually were actual physical windows where the bank's representative took their checks and monetary claims on other banks for processing. The clearing process was laborious, time consuming and expensive. Then electronic clearing came, followed by cyber-currencies. Major consortia of banks have now developed their own collective cyber-currencies to facilitate instantaneous clearing between them. The need for clearing banks is much reduced and the term "window" is metaphorical rather than real.

Innovations within the financial system play an important role, therefore, in adjusting the speed and efficiency of monetary circulation. Marx plainly does not regard such innovations as irrelevant. Darimon, however, wanted to abolish the privileged position of gold and silver in the monetary system. This was, in his view, the greatest barrier to the fluidity and adaptability of monetary circulation to the needs of the direct producers. He wanted to degrade the money commodities to the rank of all other commodities (126). This would abolish all evil—but at the cost, Marx points out, of elevating all commodities to the monopoly position now held by gold and silver. All commodities would, in fact, be a form of money. "Let the pope remain," jokes Marx, "but make everybody pope. Abolish money by making every commodity money and by equipping it with specific attributes of money." From time to time, something like this happens. At the end of World War II in Germany, for example, cigarettes and chocolate became forms of money. When the ruble collapsed in Russia in the 1990s, bottles of vodka became the main currency.

At this point, Marx drops a one-liner into the conversation to great effect. "Frequently the only possible answer is a critique of the question and the only solution is to negate the question" (127). This is excellent advice, a very good principle but also a sharp tactic. Difficult situations can indeed be evaded by questioning and negating the questions being asked. But the principle also requires that one go deeper and deeper into the processes, the forces and the mental conceptions at work in particular situations. This is what Marx now attempts to do.

"The real question is: does not the bourgeois system of exchange itself necessitate a specific instrument of exchange? Does it not necessarily create a specific equivalent for all values? One form of this instrument of exchange or of this equivalent, may be handier, more fitting, may entail fewer inconveniences than another" (127). Marx here begins consideration of the role of the price system, exchange-values and value theory in relation to money. The question of value in the *Grundrisse* is tentative and uncertain, in a state of becoming rather than a secure anchor for the overall theory of capital.

This is the question that will dominate in the subsequent pages. But first we need to note another of Marx's cogent asides. "The impact of war," he writes, "is self-evident, since economically it is exactly the same as if the nation were to drop part of its capital into the ocean" (128). This is one of the few comments that Marx makes concerning the economics of militarization and war and the loss of capital such activities entail. It also anticipates Marx's later concern to build a theory of devaluation and capital loss into the general theory of capital accumulation. Any tendency toward overaccumu-lation, for example, might be resolved by channeling capital into wasteful and useless military investments and military ventures.

MONEY AND CRISES

After several pages going over the purported role of "bullion drains" in crisis formation, Marx concludes with the case of the Scottish banking system, which reflects the fact that "the Scots hate gold." The Scottish case is important "because it shows on the one hand how the monetary system can be completely regulated" so that "all the evils Darimon bewails can be abolished—without departing from the present social basis; while at the same time its contradictions, its antagonisms, the class contradiction etc. have reached an even higher degree than in any other country in the world" (133). In fact, "the Scottish banking and monetary system was indeed the most perilous reef for the illusions of the circula-tion artists." The Scots liberated themselves from the supposed chains of the metallic money commodities without accomplishing any of the revolutionary aims that Proudhon had in mind.

With this, Marx shifts to consider prices in relation to money commodities, such as gold, which can either appreciate or depreciate in value depending upon economic conditions (e.g., the California "gold rush" of 1848). Proudhon was concerned about the instability in market prices. The best response to this problem, Marx sarcastically comments, is to abolish prices and, hence, exchange (134). Unfortunately, exchange "corresponds to the bourgeois organization of society. Hence one last problem: to revolutionize bourgeois society economically. It would then have been self-evident from the outset that the evil of bourgeois society is not to be remedied by 'transforming' the banks or by founding a rational 'money system'" (134). While Marx may be quite correct to reject Proudhon's idea of the monetary system as the primary locus of revolutionary transformation, Marx fails here to consider the degree to which revolutionary transformations in labor practices might necessitate radical reorganizations in the monetary and financial system if they are to succeed. He does not take the question of socialist money seriously enough.

Convertibility—that is convertibility of any paper currency into gold, "legal or not—remains a requirement of every kind of money whose title makes it a value-symbol, i.e. which equates it as a quantity with a third commodity." Gold, for example, "is labour time accumulated in the past, labour time defined. Its title would make a given quantity of labour as such into its standard" (134). Gold is a proxy measure for labor time. Convertibility of paper moneys into gold ties the paper currencies to labor time. But what kind of labor time are we talking about here? "What determines value is not the amount of labour time incorporated in products, but rather the amount of labour time necessary at a given moment" (135). Marx is halfway to the definition of value in *Capital* as "socially necessary labour time." As living labor becomes constantly more productive, so "the labour time objectified in products constantly depreciates." Then, "if the hour of labour became more productive, then the chit of paper which represents it would rise in buying power, and vice versa" (135). In the eyes of many socialists, this would bring great benefits to the workers. But Marx refutes this claim. "The accumulation of this money, as well as contracts, obligations, fixed burdens etc., . . . would go to the benefit of non-workers" (136).

This points to a general problem. How frequently does it happen that proposals which purportedly will benefit the laborer, even those put forward by the socialists themselves, turn out to confer benefits primarily on the nonworkers (i.e., the capitalists)? This is the problem with "time-chits," and Marx is determined to expose the "delusions" of those who think time-chits can work to revolutionize social relations in a bourgeois world (though he perversely admits that a revolution in social relations might make time-chits viable). The most obvious problems derive from variations in the productivity of labor. If I spend ten hours on making something and somebody else spends five hours on making the same thing, and if the monetary reward is set by hours of actual labor, we have a situation where identical commodities will have two if not multiple money values. Furthermore, a time-chit received five years ago at a particular level of productivity means something radically different from that received for an identical commodity today.

Marx elsewhere expresses some sympathy with the idea of "time-chits" but states that this could only work in a situation of "direct social labour." What he meant by this is unknown. But here is my interpretation. If a group of associated laborers got together to organize not only production but social life, they might do so on the basis of time-chits that reflected hours of labor. In a time-share organization I might put in four hours of child-minding that I could exchange for four hours of yoga instruction that could be exchanged against four hours working on fixing the plumbing or building an extension to a dwelling. A centralized ledger of hours exchanged could be maintained (by a bank?) in which both offers and wants could be roughly coordinated in terms of work hours among the participants. There are all sorts of examples of communes and living arrangements where something of this sort (including the socialist kibbutzim in early Israel). This successfully works for a while. But everything depends on the social solidarity of the participants. As soon as social solidarity breaks down and trust evaporates among the participants, then the system collapses. Workable systems face enormous challenges when they attempt to scale up to the national, let alone the global level.

The big enemy of such alternative money systems is convertibility into conventional money. As soon as somebody decides that they would rather pay someone rather than put in their shift of hours cleaning the toilets, then the compact is broken. As soon as someone sells a property improvement made with time-shared labor on the market, that is the beginning of the end of viable time-sharing. Hence the significance of Marx's statement that "money destroys the community and becomes the community." Exchange and monetization (of everything, including, as Marx points out in *Capital*, conscience, honor, reputation and "immaterial worth") rests at the heart of the bourgeois economy of capital, and it is delusional to believe that all of this can be countered by time-chits. Proudhon has everything the wrong way round. While people may go out for a walk when the rain stops, Marx comments, in Proudhon's world they seem to go out for a walk to make sure the rain stops.

In the market, "the *value* (the real exchange value) of all commodities (labour included) is determined by the cost of production, in other words, by the labour time required to produce them. Their *price* is this exchange value of theirs, expressed in money. The replacement of metal money . . . by labour money denominated in labour time would therefore equate the *real value* (exchange value) of commodities with their *nominal value, price, money value.*" But in the market, "the value of commodities . . . is only their *average value. This average appears as an external abstraction*" (137). Market price in Marx's presentation is radically different from value. But Proudhon supposes no difference. Value, for Marx, is the social labor time, which is very different from the price realized in the market, which reflects conditions and vagaries of supply and demand, not social labor time input. The price can yo-yo up and down, whereas value should remain relatively constant:

Market value equates itself with real value by means of its constant oscillations . . . *Price* therefore is distinguished from *value* not only as the nominal from the real; not only by the denomination in gold and silver, but because the latter appears as the law of the motions which the former runs through. But the two are constantly different and never balance out, or balance only coincidentally and exceptionally. The price of a commodity constantly stands above or below the value of the commodity, and the value of the commodity itself exists only in this up-and-down movement of commodity prices. (137–8)

The difference between price and value, Marx notes, is the difference

between the commodity measured by the labour time whose product it is, and the product of the labour time against which it is exchanged, this difference calls for a third commodity to act as a measure in which the real exchange value of commodities is expressed . . . *Because price is not equal to value, the value-determining element—labour time—cannot be the element in which prices are expressed* . . . Because labour time as the measure of value exists only as an ideal, it cannot serve as the matter of price comparisons. (139–40)

Every commodity, Marx continues, "is = the objectification of a given amount of labour time." Consequently, "all commodities are qualitatively equal and differ only quantitatively, hence can be measured against each other and substituted for one another" (141). As a social relation, the quantity is not susceptible to direct measurement. It has to be represented. This is what money does. Value homogenizes all commodities and subsumes them under the value relation. "Value," he says, "is their social relation, their economic quality." The commodity's existence as value "is different from its existence as product . . . Its property of being a value not only can but must achieve an existence different from its natural one" (141). All of this is more clearly set out in Volume I of *Capital* as Marx explores the "double existence" of commodities as use-values and exchange-values, with value clearly separated out from exchange-value, which is not the case here.

After a few pages of convoluted argument in the *Grundrisse*, Marx attempts a tentative conclusion:

> The process then, is simply this: The product becomes a commodity, *i.e., a mere moment of exchange.* The commodity is transformed into exchange value. In order to equate it with itself as an exchange value, it is exchanged for a symbol which represents it as exchange value as such. As such a symbolized exchange value, it can then in turn be exchanged in definite relations for every other commodity. Because the product becomes a commodity, and the commodity becomes an exchange value, it obtains, at first only in the head, a double existence. This doubling in the idea proceeds ... to the point where the commodity appears double in real exchange: as a natural product on one side, as exchange value on the other. I.e. the commodity's exchange value obtains a material existence separate from the commodity ... The exchange value which is separated from commodities and which exists alongside them as itself a commodity, this is—*money.* (145)

It is this formulation that leads Marx to worry about his excessive reliance upon an "idealist method of presentation," upon what goes on "in the head" rather than emphasizing social practices.

It follows, Marx erroneously concludes, that "as value [the commodity] is money." In later works, he will make clear that money is a representation or an expression of value, which is very different from saying it *is* value. But

> just as it is impossible to suspend the complications and contradictions which arise from the existence of money alongside the particular commodities merely by altering the form of money

(although difficulties characteristic of a lower form of money may be avoided by moving to a higher form), so also is it impossible to abolish money itself as long as exchange-value remains the social form of products. It is necessary to see this clearly in order to avoid setting impossible tasks, and in order to know the limits within which monetary forms and transformations of circulation are able to give a new shape to the relations of production and to the social relations which rest on the latter. (145–6)

This is obviously meant to hammer home another nail in the coffin of Proudhon's project.

THE FUNCTIONS OF MONEY

Marx then lists some of the material properties of money as "(1) measure of commodity exchange; (2) medium of exchange; (3) representative of commodities . . .; (4) general commodity alongside the particular commodities" (146). This is a vague approach to the much firmer characterization of money in *Capital* as a measure of value; a means of circulation; a representation of value; a vehicle for saving; a foundation for relative prices; a form of social power; and an object of desire. The last of these properties is, however, here opened up for comment: "To the degree that production is shaped in such a way that every producer becomes dependent on the exchange value of his commodity, i.e. as the product increasingly becomes an exchange value in reality, and exchange value becomes the immediate object of production"—and producing commodities for exchange, not for my own use—"to the same degree, must *money relations* develop, together with the contradictions immanent in the *money relation*, in the relation of the product to itself as money. The need for exchange and for the transformation of the product into a pure exchange value progresses in step with the division of labour, i.e. with the increasing social character of production. But as the latter grows, so grows the power of money" (146).

But there are problems. "What originally appeared as a means to promote production becomes a relation alien to the producers. As the producers become more dependent on exchange, exchange appears to become more independent of them, and the gap between the product as product and the product as exchange value appears to widen. Money does not create these antitheses and contradictions; it is rather the development of these contradictions and antitheses which creates the seemingly transcendental power of money" (146).

Marx here draws our attention to the growing autonomy and independence of the money form, which endows it with a transcendental power. "The next question to confront us is this: are there not contradictions inherent in this relation itself, which are wrapped up in the existence of money alongside commodities?" (147). First, there is the "double, *differentiated* existence" of the commodity (use-value versus exchange-value), which undergirds "*antitheses* and *contradiction*" that "are not convertible into one another." Once the exchange-value is externalized; it "leads a double existence as a particular commodity, and as money." Exchange is "split into two mutually independent acts": exchange of commodities for money (C–M); and exchange of money for commodities (M–C). "Since these have now achieved a spatially and temporally separate and mutually indifferent form of existence, their immediate identity ceases" (148). This opens the way to the intervention of merchants, who step "between the producers" to form a "mercantile estate" which is not concerned with consumption but extracting money from their intermediations. Not far behind comes the "money business" which "separates from commerce proper" (149).

As you move away from barter, which is commodity-for-commodity exchange (C–C), to exchange mediated through money (C–M–C), then the splitting of exchange into the two acts C–M and M–C opens the possibility for the accumulation of money as well as for the interventions of merchant and money capitalists. Just because everybody has gone from C to M does not mean everyone must go from M to C. If everyone decides for some reason to hold money (and there are good reasons to do so, since money is a primary form of social power), then producers cannot sell their commodities for lack of a market. This leads into crises of the sort that Keynes identified: "The possibility of commercial crises is already contained in this separation" (149). Marx continues:

> Money can overcome the difficulties inherent in barter only by generalizing them, making them universal. It is absolutely necessary that forcibly separated elements which essentially belong together manifest themselves by way of forcible eruption, as a *separation* of things which belong together in essence. The unity is brought about *by force*. As soon as the antagonistic split leads to eruptions, the economists point to the *essential unity* and abstract from the alienation. Their apologetic wisdom consists in forgetting their own definitions at every decisive moment. (149–50)

Armed with a theory (Say's Law) that states that crises of overproduction are impossible, the economists viewed crises of overproduction as forcible restoration of the conditions presumed by their theory.

"Just as exchange value, in the form of money, takes its place as the *general commodity* alongside all particular commodities, so does exchange value as money therefore at the same time, take its place as a *particular commodity* . . . alongside all other commodities." Money "comes into contradiction with itself . . . by virtue of being itself a *particular* commodity" (150). The contradiction lies in the fact that the particularity of gold as a singular commodity is supposed to represent the universality of all social labor everywhere. This is plainly a fiction:

We see, then, how it is an inherent property of money to fulfil its purposes by simultaneously negating them; to achieve independence of commodities; to be a means which becomes an end; to realize the exchange value of commodities by separating them from it; to facilitate exchange by splitting it; to overcome the difficulties of the direct exchange of commodities by generalizing them; to make exchange independent of the producers in the same measure as the producers become dependent on exchange. (151)

The raw accumulation of money power by individual persons becomes not only possible but increasingly likely.

It is here that Marx notes the need to correct the idealist manner of his presentation! In order to do so, he goes back to time-chits. These could escape some of the contradictions, but only on such a limited basis as to be largely irrelevant. Banks could issue and record time-chits, but this would then be like "a meal ticket good for a dozen meals which I obtain from a restaurant, or a theatre pass good for a dozen evenings" (155). The bank would "be nothing more than a board which keeps the books and accounts for a society producing in common"; either that or "a despotic ruler of production and trustee of distribution," which would accord with the Saint-Simonian theory of associated production in which the bank would be elevated into "the papacy of production" (156). Depicting the Federal Reserve as the papacy of production by capital is an interesting image. Marx then transitions back (presumably in response to his excessive idealism) to a more historical materialist mode of inquiry:

The dissolution of all products and activities into exchange values presupposes the dissolution of all fixed personal (historic) relations of dependence in production, as well as the all-sided dependence of the producers on one another. Each individual's production is dependent on the production of all others; and the transformation of his product into the necessaries of his own life is [similarly] dependent on the consumption of all others ... This reciprocal dependence is expressed in the constant necessity for exchange ... Each pursues his private interest and only his private interest; and thereby serves the private interests of all, the general interest, without willing or knowing it ... The reciprocal and all-sided dependence of individuals who are indifferent to one another forms their social connection. (156)

Within this social scene, market individualism, which we encountered in the opening pages of the *Grundrisse*, is reconsidered. Individuals may appear free, but they are constrained by their reciprocal dependence on the work and exchange of others.

You do not have to care about the person you are exchanging with because you are simply interested in their money. "This social bond is expressed in *exchange value* ... the power which each individual exercises over the activity of others or over social wealth exists in him as the owner of *exchange values*, of *money*. The individual carries his social power, as well as his bond with society, in his pocket" (156–7).

The conclusion is that "exchange value is a generality, in which all individuality and peculiarity are negated and extinguished." The result is "something alien and objective," the "subordination" of individuals "to relations which subsist independently of them and which arise out of the collisions between mutually indifferent individuals. The general exchange of activities and products, which has become a vital condition for each individual—their mutual interconnection—here appears as something alien to them, autonomous, as a thing. In exchange value the social connection between persons is transformed into a social relation between things; personal capacity into objective wealth" (157).

FETISHISM AND ALIENATION

Alienation and fetishism are two key interrelated concepts in the Marxist lexicon. The next pages (157–68) include some of the most consequential theses that Marx explores in the *Grundrisse*. Here the nature and origin of both alienation and the fetishism implicit in bourgeois exchange relations are actively elucidated.

In *Capital*, Marx makes clear in the section on the fetishism of commodities how the market exchange of commodities creates a social world in which material relations exist between people (who perforce relate to each other in the marketplace not as persons but by way of their products), paralleled by social relations between things (because the comparative values of commodities reflect the application of social labor). Economic theory reflects and replicates this fetishism in the world of thought. This is what bourgeois economics is so adept at doing. But Marx wants to track the consequences for the worker—the living subject, the person who congeals their social labor in commodities—of living and working in a social world where such fetishisms prevail. The fetishisms of bourgeois economic theory conceal all of this. But Marx had the factory inspectors' reports on the working and living conditions of the British working class (along with Engels's *Condition of the Working Class in 1844*) to enlighten him. For Marx, the imperative was to engage with bourgeois theory and with historical reality to show how it was that those who produced the society's wealth through the application of their social labor received so little of it in return for their effort. While bourgeois theory deals with abstractions (such as the marginal contributions of land, labor and capital to the price of a product), Marx wants a theory to explain concretely the conditions of daily life and labor of the working classes. Getting beyond and behind the fetishisms of bourgeois political economy became central to Marx's project.

Alienation, which entails a certain fetishism, is a concept that has a troubled if not peculiar history in Marx's thought. While it is prominent in his early works, such as the *Economic and Philosophic*

Manuscripts of 1844, it disappears in the late 1840s as Marx explores principles of historical materialism (e.g., in *The German Ideology*) only to reappear big time as a central conception in the *Grundrisse*. It then fades as an explicit concept into the background of *Capital* and in his later works.

Most subsequent critical attempts to resurrect the concept have focused on Marx's early works. Little attention is paid to the radical reformulation of the concept in the *Grundrisse*. The "scientific" presentation of the concept in the *Grundrisse*, writes the Chinese scholar Zhang in his monumental work *Back to Marx* (2014), was

> fundamentally different from his past use of the humanist alienation conception . . . In fact, these were two completely different conceptions of alienation; the labor alienation in the *1844 Manuscript* was a humanist value postulate; the idealized essence that it formed was at odds with reality. This was a contradiction between imaginary and the real . . . The labor alienation in *Grundrisse*, on the other hand, was fundamentally Marx's reflection on real history. The objectified results of workers' past labor actually became the rulers and exploiters of today's workers. The "past" created by workers becomes the ruler of the "present" . . . Hired labor necessarily created a ruling power transformed out of itself: capital. This is the actual alienation of capital and labor relations that Marx describes.[1]

In the early Marx, universality is rooted in the supposed inherent qualities of our species being. The potentiality for realizing those qualities is frustrated by capital. The laborers who produce capital are denied the fruits of their labor (they stand in a relation of alienation to their product, to the value they produce and to the labor process in which they engage). The individual potential to achieve self-perfection (in social relations, in the relation to nature

---

1 Yibing Zhang, *Back to Marx: Changes in Philosophical Discourse in the Context of Economics* (Göttingen: Universitätsverlag, 2014), 481.

and in the experience of the labor process) is denied. The advantage of such a formulation is that it is forward-looking and aspirational. Our contemporary version of this idealist mode of thought is to react to the bigotry and violence of the right-wing movement in the United States with the claim that this is not who we Americans truly are. All we have to do is to regain our moral compass of practicing what it means to be a true American, and then all will be well. This is rank idealism at work.

But in the *Grundrisse*, alienation arises out of the historical tendency within capital to create the world market, to establish its social (class) and metabolic relations everywhere and to inscribe certain identifiable laws of motion into human history under the rule of the coercive laws of competition (159). The problem from the *Grundrisse* onward is to identify the laws of motion of capital and to understand how these laws govern the conditions of daily life and labor for the mass of the working population. The keystone of the theory of alienation in the *Grundrisse* occurs on page 164. We need to mark it well: "Individuals are now ruled by abstractions, whereas earlier they depended on one another. The abstraction, or idea, however, is nothing more than the theoretical expression of those material relations which are their lord and master."

While we may all passionately believe ourselves to be free individuals, we are, in practice, ruled by the abstractions of capital. While the behavior of bigoted right-wing white nationalists is incomprehensible when judged against the ideals of what it means to be a true American, it becomes much more comprehensible when placed against the background of the human and environmental destructions, depredations and degradations of life and labor wrought by Wall Street, corporate American greed, deindustrialization and the monopoly powers of Big Pharma and the high-tech companies, supported by ruling elites in the media and academia largely besotted by the superiority of the ruling neoliberal ideas of the current ruling class.

The political project for Marx is to liberate ourselves, in thought as well as in political and economic practices, from fetishism along with the constraints imposed by the abstract laws of capital, which redound so absolutely to the benefit of a ruling class. Alienation is not confined, as we shall later see, to the laborer. The capitalist, absent any state regulation, is compelled by the coercive laws of competition (a) to increase the length of the working day to its maximum; (b) to reinvest the surplus rather than to indulge in consumer pleasures; (c) to procure relative surplus-value through seeking out and adopting new technologies; (d) to produce increasing social inequality and an industrial reserve army; and much more. These are not free choices for the capitalists. But the subjective state of mind of the capitalist is largely set to justify or to create an apologetics for that which they must do given the coercive laws of competition.

Marx recognizes the contradictory character of the alienation that capital entails. Capital is not only a destructive but a constructive and creative force that transforms the world in positive as well as in negative ways. This will also be taken up in greater detail much later (409–10). How individuals and social movements confront such contradictions then becomes the big political question. The individual, psychologized (existential) alienation as articulated in Marx's early manuscripts here connects with a critique of the objective alienations of the *Grundrisse,* produced through the reproduction of capital on the world market. Workers may accept the objective alienations of wage labor in return for sufficient access to commodities to fulfil their personal wants, needs and desires. Alienated wage labor may in this way be offset by compensatory consumerism. Endless capital accumulation rests on the endless production and reproduction of wants, needs and desires backed by the ability to pay. In the *Economic and Philosophic Manuscripts,* Marx notes how "the extension of products and needs falls into contriving and ever-calculating *subservience* to inhuman, unnatural and imaginary appetites ... This estrangement ... produces sophistication of needs on the one hand and a bestial barbarization, a complete, unrefined, abstract simplicity of need, on the other."[1] It is not hard to see how such sentiments might be inserted into the *Grundrisse* account.

The foundation for Marx's historical materialist theory of alienation is laid out in detail in pages 157–68. I here attempt a summary of this argument, even as I would urge everyone to study the original text closely.

The argument begins with the initial recognition that in a market society "the reciprocal and all-sided dependence of individuals who are indifferent to one another forms their social connection. This social bond is expressed in *exchange value*" (156). Exchange, furthermore, "presupposes the all-round dependence of the producers on one another, together with the total isolation of their private interests from one another, as well as a division of social labor whose unity and mutual complementarity exist in the form of a natural relation, as it were, external to the individuals and independent of them." A whole social order is erected on the basis of this "free individuality." But there may well have been a historical progression that brings the bourgeois order to this point. "Relations of personal dependence (entirely spontaneous at the outset) are the first social forms, in which human productive capacity develops only to a slight extent and at isolated points. Personal independence founded on *objective* dependence is the second great form, in which a system of general social metabolism, of universal relations, of all-round needs and universal capacities is formed for the first time." This second stage, in which patriarchal and feudal relations get dissolved by commerce and money, paves the way for the modern order of "free individuality" (158).

The internal elaboration of the bourgeois order is riddled with contradictions. "Just as the division of labour creates agglomeration, combination, cooperation, the antithesis of private interests, class interests, competition, concentration of capital, monopoly, stock companies—so many antithetical forms of the unity which

---

1   Karl Marx, *Economic and Philosophic Manuscripts of 1844* (New York: International Publishers, 1964), 147–8.

itself brings the antithesis to the fore—so does private exchange create world trade, private independence creates complete dependence on the so-called world market, and the fragmented acts of exchange create a banking and credit system" (159). The tension between a supposedly free individuality and all these antithetical forms is palpable. "Within bourgeois society, the society that rests on *exchange value*, there arise relations of circulation as well as of production which are so many mines to explode it." Crises can break out all over the place. But not all is lost: "If we did not find concealed in society as it is the material conditions of production and the corresponding relations of exchange prerequisite for a classless society, then all attempts to explode it would be quixotic" (159). Individual initiative and entrepreneurial endeavor produce contradictory forces and possibilities as well as alien powers.

For example, a rolling contradiction between "commodities as exchange values and money" takes center stage. While "money owes its existence only to the tendency of exchange value to separate itself from the substance of commodities and to take on a pure form, nevertheless commodities cannot be directly transformed into money." They are physically commodities and that is that. This means that "the existence of money presupposes the objectification of the social bond," which in turn means "that people place in a thing (money) the faith they do not place in each other" (160). "Show me the money," says the trader, "follow the money," says the investigator, because that is the certifiable objective record for the transfer of social power from one individual to another. Money serves, says Marx, "only as the 'dead pledge' of society." It has this symbolic social property "because individuals have alienated their own social relationship from themselves so that it [the relationship] takes the form of a thing." We may even evaluate our self-worth in terms of how much money we have.

The creation of price lists and "the autonomization of the world market . . . [which] increases with the development of monetary relations (exchange value)" and "the independence and indifference of the consumers and producers to one another" underpins increasing alienation and crisis formation. But efforts are made to overcome alienation through the acquisition and collation of adequate information such as "lists of current prices, rates of exchange, interconnections between those active in commerce through the mails, telegraphs etc. (the means of communication)." Although "the total supply and demand are independent of the actions of each individual, everyone attempts to inform himself about them, and this knowledge then reacts back in practice on the total supply and demand. Although . . . alienation is not overcome by these means, nevertheless relations and connections are introduced thereby which include the possibility of suspending the old standpoint" (160–1). Marx here mentions, but without exploring further, the significance of developing general statistics on how the markets are working.

This again is an important point. The fiction that there is such a thing as a national economy (an artifact of the 1920s), the creation of national accounts (1930s), the World Bank accounting network (after World War II), the stock exchange record, the business press and media, all give the illusion of something happening (but always as a state of the world outside of us) that can be understood, analyzed and, most important of all, acted upon. The idea that this is all pure fetishism and fiction would be greeted by the economists with astonished disbelief. Yet this is the terrain upon which alienation and fetishism collide.

It is an insipid notion to conceive of this merely *objective bond* as a spontaneous, natural attribute, inherent in individuals and inseparable from their nature (in antithesis to their conscious knowing and willing). This bond is their product. It is a historic product. It belongs to a specific phase of their development. The alien and independent character in which it presently exists *vis-à-vis* individuals proves only that the latter are still engaged in the creation of the conditions of their social life, and that they have not yet begun, on the basis of these conditions, to live it. (162)

Again, we find Marx evoking the idea of a potentiality for something better that is not yet engaged. That potentiality is not predefined ideally as it was in the *Economic and Philosophic Manuscripts*, but it is open, even as it is circumscribed, as the harbinger of a possible future.

MONEY AND THE THEORY OF THE LIBERAL INDIVIDUAL

Universally developed individuals, whose social relations, as their own communal relations, are hence also subordinated to their own communal control, are no product of nature, but of history. The degree and universality of the development of wealth where *this* individuality becomes possible supposes production on the basis of exchange values as a prior condition, whose universality produces not only the alienation of the individual from himself and from others, but also the universality and comprehensiveness of his relations and capacities. In earlier stages of development, the single individual seems to be developed more fully, because he has not yet worked out his relationships in their fullness or erected them as independent social powers and relations opposite himself. It is as ridiculous to yearn for return to that original fullness, as it is to believe that with this complete emptiness history has come to a standstill. (162)

"The bourgeois viewpoint has never advanced beyond this antithesis between itself and this romantic [oppositional] viewpoint." That is the nostalgia for some supposed long-lost past, the whole romantic movement, which Marx himself had partially succumbed to in his earlier writings. Bourgeois culture produces its "other" in the form of anti-industrial romanticism. Keats, Shelley and Wordsworth, Byron and Blake, take anti-industrial, anticapitalist positions in a way that does not threaten capital or industrialism because it is rooted in a past that never was. The "antithesis between itself and this romantic viewpoint ... will accompany it as legitimate antithesis up to its blessed end" (162). Romanticism and what Terry Eagleton calls "the ideology of the aesthetic" have long structured the backward-looking critique of capitalist modernity.

This oppositional position requires definition.

> When we look at social relations which create an undeveloped system of exchange ... then it is clear from the outset that the individuals in such a society, although their relations appear to be more personal, enter into connection with one another only as individuals imprisoned within a certain definition as feudal lord and vassal, landlord and serf etc., or as members of a caste etc. or as members of an estate etc. In the money relation, in the developed system of exchange ... the ties of personal dependence, of distinctions of blood, education, etc. are in fact exploded, ripped up ... and individuals *seem* independent (this is an independence which is at bottom merely an illusion, and it is more correctly called indifference), free to collide with one another and to engage in exchange within this freedom; but they appear thus only for someone who abstracts from the *conditions*, the *conditions of existence* within which these individuals enter into contact (and these conditions, in turn, are independent of the individuals and, although created by society, appear as if they were *natural conditions*, not controllable by individuals). (164)

And so we come to the culminating formulation we earlier encountered: "These *objective* dependency relations also appear, in antithesis to those of *personal* dependence ... in such a way that individuals are now ruled by *abstractions*, whereas earlier they depended on one another. The abstraction, or idea, however, is nothing more than the theoretical expression of those material relations which are their lord and master" (164).

This is followed by an interesting coda:

Relations can be expressed, of course, only in ideas, and thus philosophers have determined the reign of ideas to be the peculiarity of the new age, and have identified the creation of free individuality with the ideological overthrow of this reign. This error was all the more easily committed, from the ideological stand-point, as this reign . . . appears within the consciousness of individuals as the reign of ideas, and because the belief in the permanence of these ideas, i.e. of these objective relations of dependency, is of course consolidated, nourished and inculcated by the ruling classes by all means available. (164–5)

And this, of course, is exactly what Margaret Thatcher so expertly accomplished as she promoted a neoliberal orthodoxy as the ruling ideas for which there was no alternative. This is not a minor point. Most presentations of the history of the neoliberal turn and its aftermath see it as emanating from the realm of ideas, in policies, in the displacement of state-managed demand-side thinking associated with Keynes by the entrepreneurial supply-side analysis of Hayek and Milton Friedman. In *A Brief History of Neoliberalism*, I insisted on an interpretation that rested on the configuration of class forces in the 1970s and the emergence of a class project to protect and enhance their centralized class power. In the course of pursuing this project, the ruling class embraced neoliberalism as their ruling idea. From Marx's standpoint the mission is always to reveal the "material relations which are the lord and master" of such ideas. The problem, of course, is that by the time the major institutions (such as the International Monetary Fund) adopted the ruling neoliberal ideas it then seemed as if these had originated in the minds of economists and policymakers. This fetish disguise has been largely successful, even among critics of the neoliberal program. The idealist interpretation dominates and the role of the ruling class is conveniently obscured. The fantasy takes root that all that is required to establish a more just social order is to change people's ideas, their mental conceptions of the world.

These are brilliant insights in lots of ways. We are ruled by abstractions arrived at through the free material practices of millions of participants. But the abstractions are not of any one person's making. Nor are they "controllable by individuals." We have created a world through the collective impact of our individual actions; a world of alienation and the play of the laws of motion of capital as abstract forces which become objectified and fetishized. We have clothed this material reality in a canopy of ruling ideas. But this interpretation of the economy of capital as a set of ruling abstractions is not unique to Marx. Adam Smith's theory of the hidden hand of the market (or Hayek's and Milton Friedman's articulation of supply-side orthodoxy) is in principle no different. Individuals, entrepreneurs acting out of their own self-interest, engage in all manner of practices and with all manner of motivations, but the market disciplines them in certain ways, supposedly, according to Smith, for the benefit of all. All economic theory is about the abstractions, the mental conceptions of the world, which rule in the name of the ruling class. What sets Marx apart is his insistence on identifying the class forces and the historical origins of these abstractions. This is what sets apart my interpretation in *A Brief History of Neoliberalism* from most other interpretations.

There is one important consequence of succumbing to the alienation and the fetishism inherent in bourgeois market exchange. If individuals do not freely choose but simply conform, even against their will, to the abstractions, then they have no moral or legal responsibility for their actions; they cannot be held accountable for the consequences. Abstractions cannot be held legally accountable, nor can abstractions be fined or sent to jail no matter how inhumane the consequences of their application and their rule. The fetishism of the market provides a convenient moral shield behind which capitalist entrepreneurs are enabled. Starting out, entrepreneurs, as good bourgeois citizens professing bourgeois virtues, proclaim their freedom and liberty to invest and accumulate. When things go wrong or bad things happen, they then portray themselves as helpless victims of a soulless market logic. The market is depicted, as Boisguillebert (cited by Marx) later does, as "the hangman of all things, the moloch to whom everything must be sacrificed" (199). In recent times, for example, the term "globalization" has been repeatedly used in this way to excuse and justify all sorts of invidious employment practices, environmental degradations and social inequalities, all wrought in the name of market logic and market freedoms: which outcome nobody claims as having animated their actions. No wonder the ruling class is so pleased with the manner in which it has articulated the ruling ideas of the neoliberal epoch.

Marx has been at great pains to show that "money does not arise by convention, any more than the state does. It arises out of exchange, and arises naturally out of exchange; it is a product of the same" (165). He now launches into a study of the physical properties of money commodities. I propose to skip this presentation (165–86) as of secondary interest although there are occasional insights. He notes for example that "the *precious* metals . . . split off from the remainder by virtue of being inoxidizable, of standard quality" (166). This quality of being inoxidizable is important, particularly if the need exists for a physically stable vehicle for long-term saving. Marx returns several times to the origins of money via the history of exchange and the connection between the money form and labor time. "The objectification of the general, social character of labour (and hence of the labour time contained in exchange value) is precisely what makes the product of labour time into exchange value; this is what gives the commodity the attributes of money, which however, in turn imply the existence of an independent and external money-subject" (168). Note here that labor time is connected to exchange-value rather than to value (as it is in *Capital*). "The truth is that the exchange-value relation—of commodities as mutually equal and equivalent objectifications of labour time—comprises contradictions which find their objective expression in a money *which is distinct from* labour time" (169). If this was true in Marx's time, then it would be triply so in today's global capitalism.

There then follows a brief excursus into how all of this might look under conditions of communal production and distribution:

> On the basis of communal production, the determination of time . . . remains essential. The less time the society requires to produce wheat, cattle etc., the more time it wins for other production, material or mental. Just as in the case of an individual, the multiplicity of its development, its enjoyment and its activity depends on economization of time. Economy of time, to this all economy ultimately reduces itself. Society likewise has to distribute its time in a purposeful way, in order to achieve a production adequate to its overall needs . . . Thus, economy of time, along with the planned distribution of labour time among the various branches of production, remains the first economic law on the basis of communal production. (173)

Marx does not say what kind of communal organization he has in mind. Some have taken this comment as a justification for Soviet-style five-year plans, whereas others see it as advice to local communes to organize themselves efficiently to maximize the free time of their members. Did not Marx, after all, praise free time for all as the true measure of how far we had progressed toward socialism?

Marx finally returns to the question of how to understand monetary circulation (which is what we have been waiting for all along). "The circulation of money, like that of commodities, begins at an infinity of points, and to an infinity of different points it returns." This is "the spontaneous and natural circulation process" prior to the mediation of the banking system. Marx's aim is "to find out to what extent this circulation is determined by particular laws." He immediately sees that "if money is a vehicle of circulation for the commodity, then the commodity is likewise a vehicle for the circulation of money . . . The circulation of commodities and the circulation of money thus determine each other" (186). But there are also moments of total independence. For example, the total money in circulation and its velocity depends not on commodities but on "the overall character of the mode of production," which will also "determine the circulation of commodities more directly." There then follows a brief evocation of what this world looks like:

> The mass of persons engaged in exchange (population): their distribution between town and country; the absolute quantity of commodities, of products and agencies of production; the relative mass of commodities which enter into circulation; the development of the means of communication and transport, in the double sense of determining not only the sphere of exchange, in contact, but also the speed with which the raw material reaches the producer and the product the consumer; finally the development of industry, which concentrates different branches of production, e.g. spinning, weaving, dyeing, etc., and hence makes superfluous a series of intermediate exchanges. (187)

Marx here constructs the imaginary of a typical industrial capitalist city-region, such as Manchester in his time, as a context to "establish the general concept of circulation or of turnover."

But this first requires a concept of price, since there can be no exchange without prices (both ideal and realized). "Money only circulates commodities which have already been *ideally* transformed into money." When they are taken to market, they have a notional price tag on them. Circulation therefore requires first that commodities are priced, and second that a circle of exchange spreads over the whole surface of society as a totality "in constant flux." Note here the insertion of the concept of totality into his presentation. "Money then exists as the exchange value of all commodities alongside and outside them. It is the universal material into which they must be dipped, in which they become gilded and silver-plated, in order to win their independent existence as exchange values." Consequently, "money is in the first instance that which expresses the relation of equality between all exchange values: in money, they all have the same name" (188–9).

What does all this betoken for our understanding of monetary circulation? "The real circulation of commodities through time and space is not accomplished by money. Money only realizes their *price* and thereby transfers the title to the commodity into the hands of the buyer, to him who has proffered means of exchange. What money circulates is not commodities but their titles to ownership; and what is realized in the opposite direction . . . is again not the commodities but their prices" (194). It then follows that "the quantity of money required for circulation depends not only on the sum total of prices to be realized, but on the rapidity with which money circulates." Marx here introduces us to the key concept of velocity of monetary circulation (the number of times a dollar bill can change hands in a day), which can "substitute for the quantity of circulating medium," though "only up to a certain point" (195). A possible contradiction is then identified between money as a measure of value and money acting as a medium of exchange (196).

What follows is a sketch of the overall qualities required for monetary circulation to perform the tasks required of it:

> What is essential is that exchange appear as a process, a fluid whole of purchases and sales . . . Circulation as the realization of exchange values implies: (1) that my product is a product only in so far as it is for others; (2) that it is a product for me only in so far as it has been alienated . . .; (3) that it is for the other only in so far as he himself alienates his product; which already implies (4) that production is not an end in itself for me, but a means. (196)

Now it must appear passing strange to think of all this as wrapped up in a seemingly simple and unproblematic act of market exchange. But it is precisely Marx's technique to break down such seemingly simple acts and identify all the potentially problematic moments within them. This is what he is doing here:

Circulation is the movement in which the general alienation appears as a general appropriation and general appropriation as general alienation. As much, then, as the whole of this social movement appears as a social process, and as much as the individual moments of this movement arise from the conscious will and particular purposes of individuals, so much does the totality of the process appear as an objective interrelation, which arises spontaneously from nature; arising, it is true, from the mutual influence of conscious individuals on one another, but neither located in their consciousness, nor subsumed under them as a whole. Their own collisions with one another produce an *alien* social power standing above them, produce their mutual interaction as a process and a power independent of them. Circulation, because a totality of the social process, is also the first form in which the social relation appears as something independent of the individuals . . . Circulation as the first totality among the economic categories is well suited to bring this to light. [see Figure 2] (196–7)

This is the point at which the first form of circulation within the totality of capital is clearly established, both theoretically and practically: so mark it well! The comment that this is the first totality implies there are more to come.

But Marx is here also picking apart what is involved when Adam Smith cheerfully advances his theory of the hidden hand of the market as a power above any one person's control and which operates for the benefit of all. The preconditions for this first totality were earlier established as an adequate pricing system for all commodities and "not isolated acts of exchange, but a circle of exchange, a totality of the same, in constant flux, proceeding more or less over the whole surface of society; a system of acts of exchange" (188).

Marx follows up this conclusion with a critique of Say's law, which we considered earlier. He points out here that the law would be formally correct in a system of barter and expresses his amusement at the contortions of the economists who lusted after money to liberate them from the constraints of barter only to theorize the circulation of money as if it were founded on barter (198). It is, he concludes "in the nature of money to solve the contradictions of direct barter as well as of exchange value only by positing them as general contradictions" (200). If the commodity "cannot be realized in money, it ceases to be capable of circulating, and its price becomes merely imaginary . . . The commodity requires not simply demand, but demand which can pay in money. Thus, if its price cannot be realized, if it cannot be transformed into money, the commodity appears as *devalued, depriced*" (198). This is the first comment on the importance of devaluation in Marx's theory of capital. It follows on from his critique of Say's law. If everyone hoards money, then sales languish and commodities will be devalued and depriced and a general crisis will ensue.

Rather than elaborate upon this, Marx prefers instead to comment on the different forms and ways in which money gets used. He notes with some amusement, for example, that, if a commodity worth £1 sterling is exchanged for a fake pound note, which is then used to buy something of equivalent value, then the fakeness of the pound note does not matter (210). When money simply functions as a medium of circulation for commodities, any circulating medium will do. It is only when you want money to represent saved value that the fakeness matters.

There is a fascinating prose poem by Baudelaire, made much of by Jacques Derrida in *Given Time*. The poet is surprised when his companion gives a franc to a beggar they encounter on the street. The poet compliments his companion on his generosity. His companion says not to worry, the coin is fake. The poet is appalled and remonstrates with his companion, who simply replies that the beggar is ecstatic because he thinks he has got a real coin. So, what is wrong, says his companion, with giving a fake coin when it confers such intense pleasure, at least for a time, given the beggar's otherwise miserable existence. The capitalist totality is riddled with fakery of this sort.

"A specific distinction does enter between a commodity in circulation and money in circulation. The commodity is thrown out of circulation at a certain point," to be consumed. "The function of money, by contrast, is to remain in circulation as its vehicle, to resume its circular course always anew like a *perpetuum mobile*" (201–2). When we go back to the circle of C–M and M–C, then, while the exchange of commodities as use-values makes sense, "by contrast, exchanging money for money makes no sense, unless, that is, a quantitative difference arises" (202). Hence the importance of profit!

Here comes a major transition point in Marx's argument. "The specific form M–C–C–M therefore just as correct as the other, which appears as the more original, C–M–M–C. The difficulty is that the other commodity is qualitatively different; not so the other money. It can differ only quantitatively" (203). This obviously opens the way to examine the circulation of money as capital and the category of profit with which, as yet, "we have nothing to do." Marx thus chooses to reroot this alternative form of circulation in the practices of barter. But it takes a few pages to get to the point where "money becomes a subject as instrument of circulation, as medium of exchange." Money then becomes "the general representative" of "exchange value; and, as such, as the *representative* of every other commodity of equal exchange value, it is the general representative" (211). "It *represents* the price of the one commodity as against all other commodities, or the price of all commodities as against the one commodity. In this relation it is not only the *representative* of commodity prices, but the *symbol* of itself."

Money as gold and silver . . . can be replaced by any other *symbol* . . . In this way symbolic money can replace the real, because material money as mere medium of exchange is itself symbolic. It is these contradictory functions of money, as measure, as realization of prices and mere medium of exchange, which explain the otherwise inexplicable phenomenon that the *debasement* of metallic money, of gold, silver, through admixture of inferior metals, causes a depreciation of money and a rise in prices.' (212)

In the seventeenth and eighteenth centuries, the problem of debasement of the currency was a chronic problem that had to be addressed by the state. One predatory technique was coin clipping—shaving off some silver from silver coins. It became a capital offence, and Isaac Newton seems to have taken some sadistic pleasure, in his role as Master of the King's Mint, in having coin clippers publicly hung on Tyburn gallows for their sins. A century or so earlier, one could be burned at the stake for religious heresy but, by the time of John Locke (the primary advocate of religious liberty) and Newton, it was sin against the currency that was a capital offence!

Plainly, money is absolutely necessary for a world in which market exchange is widespread. "Strike out money, and one would thereby either be thrown back to a lower stage of production . . . or one would proceed to a higher stage, in which exchange value would no longer be the principal aspect of the commodity because social labour, whose representative it is, would no longer appear as socially mediated private labour" (214). Marx tantalizing links the vision of socialism with the abolition of exchange-value. Some way would have to be found to organize production, distribution and consumption to escape the power of the ruling abstractions. This is a tall order, and Marx provides no hints as to what this might look like. He also links money with the representation of social labor (as opposed to exchange-value directly) and is envisaging a radical if vaguely specified reorganization of the production and distribution matrix along wholly different, nonmarket, perhaps democratic socialist, lines.

Marx then takes up "the third attribute of money, in its complete development," which "presupposes the first two and constitutes their unity" (216). The "second quality of money," recall, is "money as medium of exchange and realizer of prices" (208). The first quality is measure of exchange-value (189). The third attribute arises as money acquires "an independent existence outside circulation."

Gold can step outside circulation "as a *particular* commodity" embodied in "luxury articles, gold and silver jewelry" or simply hoarded as "treasure."

This aspect "latently contains its quality as capital." Marx is here signaling the imminent transition from the study of the circulation of money to the circulation of money capital in which "money itself is posited (1) as precondition of circulation as well as its result; (2) as having independence only in the form of a negative relation, but always a relation to circulation; (3) as itself an *instrument of production*" and thereby stamped as "a particular moment of this process of production" (217). The mediating link is the function of money as an independent form of social power appropriable by private persons. This social power is not absolute. It is contingent upon the continuing uses of money as measure of exchange-value, vehicle for price formation and medium of circulation. The power arises out of the simple fact that money can satisfy "every need, in so far as it can be exchanged for the desired object of every need, regardless of any particularity . . . With money, general wealth is not only a form, but at the same time the content itself. The concept of wealth, so to speak, is realized, individualized in a particular object" (218).

THE IDEOLOGY OF MONEY AND THE MONETIZATION OF EVERYTHING

The opening of a new notebook in the *Grundrisse* often provokes Marx to refocus. This is certainly what happens here. The focus suddenly switches to wealth, an ideal concept, which is materially realized in money, whose "substance is wealth itself considered in its totality in abstraction from its particular modes of existence." Marx elsewhere makes a clear distinction between wealth and value, but here that distinction is hidden from view (in part, I suspect, because the theory of value has yet to be fully developed). "Exchange value forms the substance of money and exchange value is wealth." Money, in contrast to all the wealth bound up in the particularity of commodities, "is the general form of wealth" even as particular commodities form its substance. Thus, in the first role, money is wealth itself; in the other (that of commodities), it is the general material representative of wealth. "Money is therefore the god among commodities" (221). When *Forbes* comes up with its list of the wealthiest and therefore most powerful capitalists in the world, it measures their wealth not only by the amount of money they control but also by the monetary value of all their properties and assets (stocks and shares, real estate and property, commodities, intellectual property rights and a whole set of intangibles such as reputation). This is what Marx is getting at here when he combines direct wealth (the money) with the monetary representation of wealth in the form of commodities to get at total wealth.

The language here is completely different. It is really about the anthropology, the psychology that is attached to the money fetish and what that means. The language is also somewhat convoluted, so I shall try to isolate the essential points. Money represents, Marx says, "the divine existence of commodities, while they [the commodities] represent its earthly form. Before it is replaced by exchange value, every form of natural wealth presupposes an essential relation between the individual and the objects, in which the individual, and one of his aspects, objectifies himself in the thing" (221). Money, on the other hand, has an independent existence outside circulation. As "an individuated, tangible object," money may be "found, stolen, discovered" and thereby "tangibly brought into the possession of a particular individual." From performing its "servile" roles as measure and medium of circulation, it "suddenly changes into the lord and god of the world of commodities" (221). While its initial relation to the individual appears as purely accidental, it nevertheless confers by virtue of its character "a general power over society, over the whole world of gratifications, labours, etc." (222).

Money becomes the fetish object of desire. This goes back to the *Economic and Philosophic Manuscripts*, where Marx provides a graphic description of the power of money in bourgeois society. Money is the extent of my power. I am ugly, but I can, if I have money, buy beautiful women. I thus do not appear ugly anymore. I am bad, dishonest, unscrupulous, stupid, but money is honored, and hence also its possessor. I lack talent but I can buy intelligent people to serve me—so I appear very smart. He goes on in this vein at length.

"Money is therefore not only *an* object, but also *the* object of greed ... Greed as such, as a particular form of the drive, i.e. as distinct from the craving for a particular kind of wealth, e.g. for clothes, weapons, jewels, women, wine, etc., is possible only when general wealth ... has become individualized in a particular thing, i.e. as soon as money is posited in its third quality." This greed is, however, "the product of a definite social development, not *natural*, as opposed to historical." Marx is fiercely opposed to the widespread commonsense view that human greed is natural and therefore inevitable, inscribed in our DNA and impossible to eliminate. To back up his position, he notes how the ancients despised money as inherently evil. We, too, often refer to it as the root of all evil. Marx notes the historical differentiation of the manifestation of greed as either hedonism or miserliness (222). He also notes how monetary greed "necessarily brings with it the decline and fall of the ancient communities." This sentiment plays a prominent role in Marx's sense of history. Money "is itself the community and can tolerate none other standing above it" (223). The undermining of the ancient world through monetization is noted. The more money develops in its third role, as a means of production, "the more the decay of their community advances." Or, as he puts it on the next page "where money is not itself the community, it must dissolve the community" (224).

The monetization of everything appears to be an unstated evolutionary law of capital as a totality. The era of neoliberalism has witnessed this law at work with awesome results. Rights, like health care and education, have been converted into commodities to be traded on the market. They have been monetized. "Monetary greed, or mania for wealth, necessarily brings with it the decline and fall of the ancient communities." At a certain stage of their economic development, "money necessarily appears in its third role, and the further it develops in that role, the more the decay of their community advances . . . It is inherent in the simple character of money itself that it can exist as a developed moment of production only where and when *wage labour* exists." In this case, it becomes "a driving wheel for the development of all forces of production, material and mental . . . The owner of money, in the ancient sense, is dissolved by the industrial process" (223).

"As *material representation of general wealth*, as *individualized exchange value*, money must be the *direct* object, aim and product of general labour, the labour of all individuals. Labour must directly produce exchange value, i.e. money." Note here that Marx is relating wage labor directly to exchange-value (money) rather than value. "Greed, as the urge of all, in so far as everyone wants to make money, is only created by general wealth. Only in this way can the general mania for money become the wellspring of general, self-reproducing wealth" (224). Monetary profit is clearly the prime animator for this drive toward wealth creation. But the agent is wage labor, so the progress of monetization connects to the historical formation of wage labor. This leads Marx to construct the following tentative formulation.

"It is the elementary precondition of bourgeois society that labour should directly produce exchange value, i.e. money; and, similarly, that money should directly purchase labour, and therefore the labourer, but only in so far as he alienates his activity in the exchange. *Wage labour* on one side, *capital* on the other . . ." (225). So here, finally, Marx begins to bring the class relation between capital and labor into view. But he steadfastly adheres to his earlier assertion (202) that he wants "nothing to do" with this relation at this point in his investigation. He remains totally focused on the contradictions of the monetary form:

> It is inherent in the attribute in which it here becomes devel-
> oped that the illusion about its nature, i.e. the fixed

insistence on one of its aspects, in the abstract, and the blind-ness towards the contradictions within it, gives it really magical significance behind the backs of individuals. In fact, it is because of this self-contradictory and hence illusory aspect, because of this abstraction, that it becomes such an enormous instrument in the real development of the forces of social production. (225)

By way of conclusion, Marx writes:

> Money thereby directly and simultaneously becomes the *real community*, since it is the general substance of survival for all, and at the same time, the social product of all. But as we have seen, in money the community is at the same time a mere abstraction, a mere external, accidental thing for the individual and at the same time, merely a means for his satisfaction as an isolated individual. The community of antiquity presupposes a quite different relation to, and on the part of, the individual. The development of money in its third role therefore smashes this community. (226)

The transition from one mode of production to another (for that is what we are looking at here) entails far-reaching creative destruction.

Rather than take up the class relation, Marx returns to his preoc-cupation with the exact form in which money can be the obvious manifestation of wealth. Coins work well as a means of circulation but perforce assume a national and local character. The universal form of money lies with the money commodities of gold and silver. "Only in this way is it the material representative of *general* wealth. In the Mercantilist System, therefore, gold and silver count as the measure of the power of the different communities" (226). Although mercantilism has been largely abandoned as an adequate economic theory of capital, it is still true to this day that "no matter how much the modern economists imagine themselves beyond Mercantilism, in periods of general crisis, gold and silver still appear in precisely this role, in 1857 as much as 1600" (227).

It is at this point that Marx breaks off to give brief consideration as to how all that he has written so far might integrate with the plan he has in mind to write a magnum opus on the critique of classical economy and the study of the laws of motion of capital. Plainly, he views the materials he has assembled so far as a basis, as the first part, of the book or books he has in mind.

> The internal structure of production ... forms the second section; the concentration of the whole in the state the third; the international relation the fourth; the world market the conclusion, in which production is posited as a totality together with all its moments, but within which, at the same time, all contradictions come into play. The world market then, again, forms the presupposition of the whole as well as its substratum. Crises are then the general intimation which points beyond the presupposition, and the urge which drives towards the adoption of a new historic form. (227–8)

This is the second of several outlines in the *Grundrisse*. Clearly, books on the state and international relations are missing and the state of the world market lies in the background of *Capital* as opposed to the foregrounding of industrial capital in Britain. But, interestingly, the concern with the totality, its moments and its contradictions firmly frames the inquiry.

The remaining few pages of the chapter on money are taken up with minor questions regarding the relations between coinage and the money commodities, how money can be stabilized as a measure of value, how money functions on the world stage, all the while noting the way in which money depends upon its functions as measure and medium of exchange even as it negates these functions when it steps outside those roles (and in a way negates them) to perform its third function as capital. The relation between hoarding (as a form of false accumulation) and putting money into circulation is also discussed.

Marx has lain the basis for analysing the complexity of money and the fetishisms that surrounds its usages. The contemporary push toward monetization of everything announces the acceleration of capital's evolution, the elements of which were there for all to see even in Marx's time.

Some years ago, I sat down with some undergraduates and asked them what they wanted to do after they got their degrees. The answer was that they all wanted to earn enough money to have a good life. No one professed any interest or ambition to do anything in particular. Money proscribed the limit of their ambition. The psychology of all this was some time ago commented upon by Keynes. He looked forward to the day "when the accumulation of wealth is no longer of high social importance," for then "there will be great changes in the code of morals. We shall be able to rid ourselves of many of the pseudo-moral principles which have hag-ridden us for two hundred years, by which we have exalted some of the most distasteful of human qualities into the position of the highest virtues. We shall be able to afford to dare to assess the money-motive at its true value. The love of money as a possession—as distinguished from the love of money as a means to the enjoyments and realities of life—will be recognized for what it is, a somewhat disgusting morbidity, one of those semi-criminal, semi-pathological propensities which one hands over with a shudder to the specialists in mental disease. All kinds of social customs and economic practices effecting the distribution of wealth and of economic rewards and penalties, which we now maintain at all costs, however distasteful and unjust they may be in themselves because they are tremendously useful in promoting accumulation of capital, we shall then be free at last to discard."[1]

---

1   See John Maynard Keynes, *Essays in Persuasion* (New York: Classic House Books), 199.

3

Alien Capital Meets Alien Labor
Pages 239–304

If the circulation of money is "the first totality among the economic categories of capital" then the second is the circulation of money as capital. This arises from that function of money "in which money appears not only as medium, nor as measure, but as end in itself" (215). That end, of course, is profit.

In Figure 2, money capital is located at the base of the flow diagram, and from there a flow of value is injected into the general circulation process of capital which passes through the different moments of production, consumption, realization and distribution, before returning to the circulation process in the form of money capital once more. This is the macroeconomic structure of capital flows. There is a parallel narrative structure within the *Grundrisse* that runs from the infinite variety of concrete commodity exchanges to the different forms of money that facilitate not only commodity exchange along with other social functions (such as storing value) but also provide the medium through which the abstract laws of motion of the circulation and accumulation of capital can proceed. This narrative from the concrete to the abstract rests upon multiple microinvestigations into every nook and cranny of the process of money circulation intertwined with

capital creation and circulation. These microinvestigations sometimes go on for pages and, even worse, often lead Marx into all
sorts of picayune arithmetic calculations of rates of return (in later
sections specified in a currency called thalers), on mass deploy-
ments, on production structures and the impact of technological
adjustments, and so on. There is, as a result, a serious "forest for
the trees" problem in reading Marx. I will focus here on the macroeconomic forest rather than the trees. At the same time, as was the
case in the money section, there are astonishing moments of brilliant insight that need to be dwelt upon at length. And then, lurk-
ing always in the background, is the evasive and constantly evolving plan for the *magnum opus* Marx has in mind.

There is, however, one general theoretical problem that pervades
the analysis. I have been reluctant to introduce materials from
Capital into this account. But in this instance, I feel obliged to do
so. In *Capital,* Marx operates with the three basic categories of use-
value, exchange-value, and value. These categories are interrelated
but autonomous, and the initial (Ricardian) treatment of value as
socially necessary labor time separates value theory (based on
labor input) from exchange-values (based on prices realized in the
market). While Marx recognizes, as we saw earlier, the distinction
between values that arise out of market exchange and values
derived from labor input, in the *Grundrisse* he does not separate
these categories. Value, for the most part, is equated with exchange-
value as it emerges out of some sort of fusion of labor inputs realized as market prices. In other words, value internalizes both labor
inputs and market prices. When Marx does take up the difference,
it is to contrast the ephemerality and instability of the market price
component relative to the relative stability of the labor input
component (a distinction recognized in classical political economy between so-called "natural" or equilibrium prices, supposedly reflecting labor input, and the instability of realized market
prices [determined by fluctuations in demand and supply]. When
Marx uses the term "value" in the following text, it has to be understood as exchange-value in the *Grundrisse* sense and not "value" as

it is defined in *Capital*. The failure to clearly separate market exchange prices and labor values hobbles the analysis in certain respects. As I think is generally accepted, Marx's lack of clarity on value theory is one of the outstanding problems of the *Grundrisse*. Marx consequently struggles on occasion with how to theorize capital. For example, my own preferred definition of capital as value in motion does not fit easily into Marx's thinking here.

MONEY AND CIRCULATION

Since capital originates in circulation, it makes sense to return to the circulation of money to identify those features that are critical for understanding the nature of capital. "The special difficulty in grasping money in its fully developed character as money—a difficulty which political economy attempts to evade by forgetting now one, now another aspect, and by appealing to one aspect when confronted by another—is that a social relation, a definite relation between individuals, here appears as a metal, a stone, as a purely physical, external thing which can be found, as such, in nature, and which is indistinguishable in form from its natural existence. Gold and silver, in and of themselves, are not money. Nature does not produce money, any more than it produces a rate of exchange or a banker" (239). The "fundamental contradiction contained in exchange value" (between physical use-values and the social practices of exchange) "here emerges in all its purity."

As opposition to "the ruling relations of production grows," so "artful tinkering with money is then supposed to overcome the contradictions of which money is merely the perceptible appearance." Indeed "some revolutionary operations can be performed with money" but they effectively "leave everything as it was." Marx deploys an instructive metaphor. "One strikes a blow at the sack, intending the donkey. However as long as the donkey does not feel the blows on the sack, one hits in fact only the sack and not the donkey. As soon as he feels it, one strikes the donkey and not the sack." Marx is determined to hit the donkey of capital hard, in spite of the deep protections of the monetary sack. In this case, he condemns the operations "directed against money as . . . merely an attack on consequences whose causes remain unaffected" (240). As we earlier established, tinkering with the money form, as Proudhon advocates, cannot overcome the contradictions. Yet it is also true that "all inherent contradictions of bourgeois society appear extinguished in money relations as conceived in simple form; and bourgeois democracy even more than the bourgeois economists take refuge in this aspect . . . in order to construct apologetics for the existing economic relations" (240–1). Such apologetics constitute the sack, a web of ideological protections that must be dismantled.

Marx delves deeper into what happens at the moment of exchange in well-developed markets. "The individuals, the subjects between whom this process goes on, are simply and only conceived of as exchangers . . . Each has the same social relation towards the other that the other has towards him. As subjects of exchange, their relation is therefore that of equality." This is a vital and foundational point. "Furthermore, the commodities which they exchange are, as exchange values, equivalent." Equality and equivalence are key features of this market process. There are "only three" formally distinct moments within this exchange process: "the subjects of the relation, *the exchangers* . . . ; the objects of their exchange, exchange values, *equivalents* . . . ; and finally the act of exchange itself" (241). Exchange rests on "the differences between their needs and between their production." This "gives rise to exchange and their social equation in exchange . . . Regarded from the standpoint of the natural difference between them, individual A exists as the owner of a use value for B, and B as the owner of a use value for A. In this respect, their natural difference again puts them reciprocally into the relation of equality" (242). The reciprocity of needs means the exchangers have to recognize each other as needy human beings. They cannot be indifferent to one another: "each of them reaches beyond his own particular need etc., as a human being, and . . . they relate to one another as human beings; . . . their common species-being"—a rarely mentioned concept in the *Grundrisse*, drawn from the idealism of the *Economic and Philosophic Manuscripts*—"is acknowledged by all" (243). In addition to the quality of equality, there also enters in the quality of freedom. "Although individual A feels a need for the commodity of individual B, he does not appropriate it by force, nor vice versa, but rather they recognize one another reciprocally as proprietors, as persons whose will penetrates their commodities. Accordingly, the juridical moment of the Person enters here, as well as that of freedom" (243).

In exchange, "each serves the other in order to serve himself; each makes use of the other, reciprocally, as his means." Equality, freedom, reciprocity, the compatibility of mutual interests in the midst of differentiation and the bonding of otherness under the banner of our common species-being, all emerge as crucial features of market exchange.

> Out of the act of exchange itself, the individual, each one of them, is reflected in himself as its exclusive and dominant (determinant) subject. With that, then, the complete freedom of the individual is posited . . . the common interest exists only in the duality, many-sidedness, and autonomous development of the exchanges between self-seeking interests . . . Equality and freedom are thus not only respected in exchange based on exchange values, but, also, the exchange of exchange values is the productive, real basis of all *equality* and *freedom*. As pure ideas they are merely the idealized expression of this basis; as developed in juridical, political, social relations, they are merely this basis to a higher power. And so it has been in history. (244–5)

Marx then goes on to contrast the politics of liberal political theory, which so clearly rests on exchange, with Roman law and medieval practices. In bourgeois market exchange "the money system can indeed only be the realization of this system of freedom and equality" (246). Furthermore,

> in so far as money here appears as the material, as the general commodity of contracts, all distinction between the contracting parties is, rather, extinguished . . . In so far as money, the general form of wealth, becomes the object of accumulation, the subject here appears to withdraw it from circulation only to the extent that he does not withdraw commodities of an equal price from circulation . . . If one grows impoverished and the other grows wealthier, then this is of their own free will and does not in any way arise from the economic relation. (246–7)

Plainly, there is something missing from this account and the liberal political theory that it supports. "In present bourgeois society as a whole, this positing of prices and their circulation etc. appears as the surface process, beneath which, however, in the depths, entirely different processes go on, in which this apparent individual equality and liberty disappear" (247). We forget, for example, that "the objective basis of the whole of the system of production, already in itself implies compulsion over the individual" (248). The individual is already bound by relations (abstractions) other than that of exchange and is "already *determined* by society . . . What all this wisdom comes down to is the attempt to stick fast at the simplest economic relations, which, considered by themselves, are pure abstractions," ignoring entirely "the opposition between labour and capital" (248). The failure to acknowledge the class relations is fatal. This prompts a brief critique of the French socialist position, which lauded the freedom and liberty given by bourgeois exchange relations and concentrated their political program on countering the perversions attributable to the money form and the centralization of money capital and power. "Liberté, Egalité, Fraternité" was, for example, the primary slogan in the French Revolution. "The proper reply to them is: that exchange value or, more precisely, the money system is the system of equality and freedom, and that the disturbances they encounter ... are merely the realization of *equality* and *freedom*, which prove to be inequality and unfreedom" (248–9). The slogan of the French Revolution was drawn from the bourgeois market. Political pursuit of its ideals was destined to hit the dead end of bourgeois utopianism.

How the bourgeois vision of equality, freedom and reciprocity is inverted to appear as inequality and unfreedom then needs to be explored. But why does Marx spend so much time on this question? First, I think Marx wanted to recognize that the powerful political ideals of equality, freedom and reciprocity had a real material basis in the process of commodity exchange in the market. They were not fanciful constructs conjured out of the human brain or natural God-given rights. Even if they are, they are meaningless until, as the Bible puts it, they are made flesh. Second, he wanted to expose the way in which these ruling ideas, encapsulated into bourgeois liberal political theories and free trade doctrines, benefited the ruling classes (and continue to do so today as the neoliberal political assault on collective action in favor of a persuasive ideology of individual liberties and freedoms along with free trade demonstrates). And, third, he wanted to wean socialists (particularly in France) away from falsely believing that the world of true liberty, equality and fraternity could be achieved by reforms in circulation in general and money in particular.

While Marx is obsessed with the "errors" of the French and European socialists—Proudhon and, later, Bakunin in particular—his critique is beautifully positioned in our own times to take on the libertarian tradition, as articulated by Ayn Rand, Nozick and others, along with the anti-statism of much of the radical right in the United States. The power of this tradition cannot be overemphasized. For example, Alan Greenspan, the Delphic Oracle of the Federal Reserve from 1987 to 2006, responsible for the interest-rate politics that led into the financial crash of 2007–8, was a devoted follower of Ayn Rand, as are many others in the Republican Party together with their major corporate donors. But when the suggestion that one should wear a mask to guard against a virus is greeted as an offense against a God-given right to individual liberty and freedom, then the bourgeois libertarian tradition, though materially grounded in acts of exchange, achieves the height of its absurdity. It becomes the subject of important ideological battles. The slogan of the French Revolution is bourgeois to its core, as is the neoliberal embrace of market freedoms and individual liberty in our own time. The beneficiaries of this ideological politics are, of course, the bourgeoisie in general and the top 1 percent in particular.

Marx begins his counterattack on all of this with the simple observation that "*money as capital* is an aspect of money which goes beyond its simple character of money" (250). Or, "*money as capital* is distinct from *money as money*" (251). But he immediately encounters a problem. Some uses of money as a form of capital clearly preceded the full development of the monetary system, while it is also clear that later elaborations of the money form led to the creation of the global money market as a future totality. The creation and accumulation of capital lies in between these two positionings. The rise of a money market as a future totality will obviously become an important feature in the history of capital (251). What is interesting is that Marx appears to accept that this will indeed be the case, but at this point he has no interest in exploring the growth of money markets in even the sketchiest of detail. This is left for future generations to work out. Marx instead seeks to grapple with and define the concept of capital, and thereby explain in what sense money "goes beyond" its simple character of money when it becomes capital. The materials that follow are convoluted and indecisive, as Marx struggles to come up with a clear definition of what capital actually is (as opposed to what it appears to be in everyday life situations) in the absence of a clear definition of value. The argument is sometimes hard to follow, but there are some key moments that inform the subsequent narrative.

(1) "Capital is not a simple relation, but a *process*, in whose various moments it is always capital" (258). In other words, capital is a process and not a thing. This is a crucial finding.

(2) "That money is the first form in which exchange value proceeds to the character of capital, and that, hence, the first *form* in which capital *appears* is confused with capital itself" (259). Just because money is the launching pad for capital, this does not mean that money *is* capital, as many suppose.

(3) "Exchange value deriving from circulation . . . preserves itself within it and by means of it." Circulation is therefore "not the movement of [capital's] disappearance" but rather "its self-realization as exchange value" (260). Capital as a process is self-replicating and ultimately continuous.

(4) Circulation "is no longer a simple positing of equivalents . . . but rather *multiplication* of itself." Exchange-value "posits itself as exchange value only by realizing itself; i.e. increasing its value" (263). Expansion through profit-making is inevitable.

(5) "Exchange value posited as the unity of commodity and money is *capital*, and this positing itself appears as the circulation of capital. (Which is, however, a spiral, an expanding curve, not a simple circle)" (266). Capital in its process takes on different material forms (as commodities and as money). The circular flow in Figure 2 needs to be replaced by a spiral representation.

(6) "The first presupposition is that capital stands on one side and labour on the other, both as independent forms relative to each other" (266). The class relation is crucial.

(7) "The labour which stands opposite capital is *alien* labour, and the capital that stands opposite labour is *alien* capital" (266). Mutual alienation exists at the core of the labor–capital relation.

(8) "Fixed as wealth . . . as value which counts as value, [a sum of money] is therefore the constant drive to go beyond its

quantitative limit: an endless process. Its own animation consists exclusively in that; it *preserves* itself as a self-validated exchange value distinct from a use value only by *constantly multiplying itself*" (270). Capital entails endless, cumulative and exponential accumulation. It has to grow or die.

(9) "Labour not as an object, but as activity; not as itself *value*, but as the *living source* of value" (296). The exchange relation between capital and labor in the market is qualitatively different from all other forms of market exchange.

Readers might want to skip the sometimes excoriating and puzzling details and pass to the next section, but I need to go over the details.

Marx begins his exploration with a brief examination of the "retail trade, in the daily traffic of bourgeois life as it proceeds directly between producers and consumers, in petty commerce." Here and here alone "does the motion of exchange values, their circulation, proceed in their pure form" (251). The social relation that dominates here is between buyers and sellers and "all other aspects are here extinguished." How to integrate this world of petty-bourgeois commerce into the general theory of capital is a bit of a problem that Marx tends to put to one side. While Marx may be formally correct to say that we cannot theorize capital by examination of this sector, the size and political influence of this sector in today's world economy cannot easily be dismissed. The street vendors of New York are not irrelevant to the economy as a totality, and the petty bourgeoisie has long been the home for a politics based on market exchange rather than proletarianized labor. When the Emperor Napoleon scathingly dismissed the English as a "nation of shopkeepers" he made an important political point. In what follows, however, Marx will ignore this question.

Marx proceeds instead to open up the question of value. He immediately asserts that "the concept of value precedes that of capital, but requires for its pure development a mode of production founded on capital" (251). He helpfully observes that the economists "sometimes consider capital as the creator of values ... while at other times they presuppose values for the formation of capital." Marx looks at this historically. Value arises as a meaningful category through the historical elaboration of certain social practices which increasingly express the power of value as an abstraction that rules over social action. Behind this there appears to be a process of "becoming" in which both the practice and the theoretical category coevolve. "This determination of value, then, presupposes a given historic stage of the mode of social production and is itself something given with that mode, hence a historic relation. At the same time, individual moments of value-determination develop in earlier stages of the historic process of social production and appear as its result" (252).

Marx then speculates as to where those "individual moments" might be found and quickly homes in on the idea that "it is not capital but the relation of landed property which appears as its real basis." The trouble is that "modern landed property ... cannot be understood at all, because it cannot exist, without capital as its presupposition ... It is, therefore, precisely in the development of landed property that the gradual victory and formation of capital can be studied, which is why Ricardo ... examined the relations of capital, wage-labour and ground rent within the sphere of landed property, so as to establish their specific form." This leads into a somewhat inconclusive conclusion. "The history of landed property, which would demonstrate the gradual transformation of the feudal landlord into the landowner, of the hereditary, semi-tributary and often unfree tenant for life into the modern farmer, and of the resident serfs, bondsmen and villeins who belonged to the property into agricultural day-labourers, would indeed be the history of the formation of modern capital" (252–3). This lies at the center of Robert Brenner's controversial interventions as to the true origins of capital through transformations on the land (particularly in England), rather than through international trade and the operations of merchant capital. While this doubtless forms an important perspective on capital's history, and Marx will return to it later in the *Grundrisse* as well as in *Capital* (Volume I, Part Eight and the chapter on the history of landed property in Volume III), he seems to be content to put such matters behind him with the observation that "we are dealing here with developed bourgeois society, which is already moving on its own foundation" (253).

Marx then switches to consider capital in relation to circulation. "Capital comes initially from circulation, and, moreover, its point of departure is money" (253). This is "the first form in which capital as such appears, M–C–C–M; that money is exchanged for commodity and the commodity for money; *this movement of buying in order to sell, which makes up the formal aspect of commerce, of capital as merchant capital*, is found in the earliest conditions of economic development." Marx offers some observations on the historical role of merchant capital, along the same lines as he considered landed property. He concedes the historical importance of commodity exchange, even that exchange mediated by money, in preparing the way for the historic rise of capital. But the problem is that circulation "*does not carry within itself the principle of self-renewal. The moments of the latter are presupposed to it*, not posited by it" (254). The term "posited," which Marx uses frequently, designates something that must be created in order for a process to be completed, in contrast to "presupposed," which designates something that already exists and can therefore be used. "Commodities constantly have to be thrown into [circulation] anew from the outside, like fuel into a fire. Otherwise it flickers out in indifference . . . Circulation, therefore, which appears as that which is immediately present on the surface of bourgeois society, exists only in so far as it is constantly mediated" (255). There is no mandate implicit in an act of exchange that says it must be repeated. That mandate, if it exists, must come from somewhere else. When we add to this (as we shall later see) that the equality and equivalence presumed in bourgeois exchange relations contradicts entirely the principle of expansion contained in the profit principle, then we get to the standard conclusion that capital cannot originate within or be perpetuated through acts of exchange.

What mediates this, what goes on "behind the backs" of the exchangers is, of course, the act of commodity production. This brings us back to "the point of departure; *production* which posits, creates exchange values; but this time, *production which presupposes circulation as a developed moment* and which appears as a constant process, which posits circulation and constantly returns from it into itself in order to posit it anew" (255). This movement leads toward "value-producing labour" and "production for exchange value" (256).

The example Marx uses is that of the wool trade in England, which arose in response to the import of Netherlands commodities in the sixteenth century (257). "In order then to produce more wool, cultivated land was transformed into sheep-walks, the system of small tenant-farmers was broken up etc., clearing of estates took place etc. Agriculture thus lost the character of labour for use value, and the exchange of overflow," while the occasional wool surpluses that earlier flowed from England to Europe from the fifteenth century on

> lost the character of relative indifference in respect to the inner construction of production. At certain points, agriculture itself became purely determined by circulation, transformed into production for exchange value. Not only was the mode of production altered thereby, but also the old relations of population and production, the economic relations that corresponded to it, were dissolved. Thus, here was a circulation which presupposed a production in which only the overflow was created as exchange value; but it turned into a production which took place only in connection with circulation, a production which posited exchange values as its exclusive content. (257)

I cite this example at some length to illustrate that Marx's views on the roles of landed and merchant capital in the transition to capitalism were solidly grounded in his historical geographical knowledge. This story of the transformation of the wool trade and its impact on British society has since been well-documented broadly along the lines that Marx described. The irony that British industrialism was preceded by agrarian extractivism has been duly noted. Commodity production creates exchange-values on the presupposition of exchange which then requires (posits) the creation of more channels of exchange in order to complete its process. The assertion that capital originates in production and not in circulation or exchange is a standard trope in Marxian theory, but it is here backed up by the scrutiny of micropossibilities and a study of how transformations in circulation contributed to changes in the mode of production, in this case in agriculture.

In the subsequent pages, this theoretical breakthrough is elaborated upon at length and in detail. "This movement appears in different forms, not only historically, as leading towards value-producing labour, but also within the system of bourgeois production itself, i.e. production for exchange value" (256). Notice here that value-producing labor is directly associated with exchange-value. But Marx's reluctance to explore some version of the labor theory of value is here explained by the fact that labor is a trans-historical category, which means that "*nothing is easier than to demonstrate that capital is a necessary condition for all human production*" (258). The danger is that capital will simply be explained in terms of objectified labor, which means that "*capital is conceived as a thing, not as a relation.*" "If it is said that capital is exchange value which produces profit, or at least has the intention of producing a profit, then capital is already presupposed in its explanation, for profit is a specific relation of capital to itself. Capital is not a simple relation, but a *process*" (258).

This is a profound and vital finding. Capital is defined as a process, not as a thing (even though it is objectified as different things at different moments in its process) and not even as a relation (though it internalizes a crucial social class relation, as we shall see).

This "process" has to be investigated. "To develop the concept of capital, it is necessary to begin, not with labour, but with value, and, precisely, with exchange value in an already developed movement of circulation." Once again, value and exchange-value are here merged. "As soon as money is posited as an exchange value which not only becomes independent of circulation, but which also maintains itself through it, then it is no longer money. For this as such does not go beyond the negative aspect, but is *capital*" (259).

Now we see much more clearly that money is not capital. But capital is money at a certain moment of its process. That is different from saying that money is capital. The relationship between money and capital becomes problematic:

> That money is the first form in which exchange value precedes the character of capital, and that, hence, the first *form* in which capital *appears* is confused with capital itself . . . This is a historic fact which, far from contradicting our development, rather confirms it. The first quality of capital is, then, this: that exchange value deriving from circulation and presupposing circulation preserves itself within it and by means of it; does not lose itself by entering into it; that circulation is not the movement of its disappearance, but rather the movement of its real self-positing as exchange value, its self-realization as exchange value. (259–60)

As a result, all other forms of exchange are extinguished in this act of exchange. If I barter with you and you give me some bananas and I eat the bananas, the bananas disappear. They have left the system. The commodities leave the system along with their value. Consumption takes commodities out of the system. Petty commodity production entails the creation of commodities, mediation through the market, and then their disappearance through consumption. There is no necessity of any kind of self-expansion, self-realization or even self-renewal in that. But Marx recognizes that capital as a process of circulation does not disappear. The money value does not disappear; it remains within the system. Much of the production of means of production stays within the system. The value which is created stays within the system even though the material commodity that is consumed does not. The process of capital is self-replicating. Quite simply, the process is value in motion that presupposes circulation and preserves itself within it and by means of it. It does not lose by entering it. In other words, value (exchange-value) is being reproduced.

"The immortality which money strove to achieve by setting itself negatively against circulation," through for example the hoarding of gold, "is achieved by capital, which preserves itself precisely by abandoning itself to circulation" (261). In that circulation, "capital becomes commodity and money alternately; but (1) it is itself the alternation of both these roles; (2) it becomes commodity; but not this or that other commodity, rather a totality of commodities. ... The identity ... which it obtains is that of being exchange value and, as such, money." In effect, although Marx does not say so here, money as the representative of the totality of exchange-values itself becomes a commodity. "If we speak here of capital, this is still merely a word. The only aspect in which capital is here posited as distinct from direct exchange value and from that of money is that of exchange value which preserves and perpetuates itself in and through circulation." (262) It is going to be the process definition which counts.

After navigating some of the complex possibilities in the sphere of circulation, Marx recognizes that "exchange value, as regards its content, was originally an objectified amount of labour or labour time," which after being launched into circulation becomes "tangible money." This then becomes "objectified exchange value ... which yields itself to labour ... so as to renew itself and to begin circulating again by itself. And with that it is no longer a simple positing of equivalents" but "rather *multiplication* of itself." Money "*as capital has lost its rigidity, and from a tangible thing has become a process*" (263). As a result, "the labour objectified in the exchange value posits living labour as a means of reproducing it, whereas, originally, exchange value appeared merely as a product of labour." From here onward, the role and relation of living labor to the process of capital circulation gradually moves to center stage. At this point, Marx inserts another outline of the proposed structure of the magnum opus he has in mind:

> I. (1) General concept of capital. – (2) Particularity of capital: circulating capital, fixed capital. (Capital as the necessaries of life, as raw material, as instrument of labour.) (3) Capital as money. II. (1) *Quantity of capital. Accumulation.* (2) *Capital measured by itself. Profit. Interest. Value of capital*: i.e. capital as distinct from itself as interest and profit. (3) *The circulation of capitals*. (α) Exchange of capital and capital. Exchange of capital with revenue. Capital and prices. (β) *Competition of capitals.* (γ) *Concentration of capitals.* III. Capital as credit. IV. Capital as share capital. V. *Capital as money market.* VI. Capital as source of wealth. The capitalist. After capital, landed property would be dealt with. After that, wage labour. All three presupposed, the *movement of prices*, as circulation now defined in its inner total- ity. On the other side, the three classes, as production posited in its three basic forms and presuppositions of circulation. Then the *state*. (State and bourgeois society. – Taxes, or the existence of the unproductive classes. – The state debt. – Population. – The state externally: colonies. External trade. Rate of exchange. Money as international coin. – Finally the world market. Encroachment of bourgeois society over the state. Crises. Dissolution of the mode of production and form of society based on exchange value. Real positing of individual labour as social and vice versa.) (264)

This astonishing prospectus was nowhere ever close to being realized, but it acts as some sort of guide to thinking about the totality of capital as Marx speculatively envisaged it in all of its complexity and fullness. It also constitutes some sort of invitation to later students, thinkers, theorists and class-struggle warriors to open up in whole or in part some aspect of this totality for closer inspection. This is what Marx does as he returns to his main theme, after a couple of pages debating some arcane points with Proudhon.

THE SPIRAL FORM: THE ALIENATION OF CAPITAL AND LABOR

"The wholeness of circulation, regarded in itself, lies in the fact that the same exchange value, exchange value as subject, posits itself once as commodity, another time as money . . . It is just this movement of positing itself in this dual character and preserving itself in each of them as its opposite, in the commodity as money and in money as commodity." This yields a fuller definition of capital. "Exchange value posited as the unity of commodity and money is *capital*. And this positing itself appears as a circulation of capital, which is however, a spiral, an expanding curve, not a simple circle" (266). The shift from cyclical analysis to a spiral form is significant. Whereas, up until now we have been talking about a cyclical activity (and portrayed it as such in Figure 2), Marx now introduces us to the idea that, if there is a multiplication going on, we are no longer dealing with a cyclical process but with a spiral form. And what is this spiral about? Where does the growth come from?

This prompts Marx to change perspective. "Let us analyse first the simple aspects contained in the relation of capital and labour." So, finally, we take up the class relation that is going to play such a crucial role in the definition of capital. "The first presupposition is that capital stands on one side and labour on the other, both as independent forms relative to each other; both hence also alien to one another. The labour which stands opposite to capital is *alien* labour and the capital which stands opposite labour is *alien* capital" (266). This powerful formulation is self-explanatory. But the thought that alienation lies at the heart of the class relation which grounds capital as process comes like a bolt from the blue. It shatters entirely the friendly, positive ideology that attaches to the equality, freedom and reciprocity earlier derived from the study of bourgeois exchange relations.

We are then made aware of what it is that bourgeois exchange relations and market processes conceal. It is not only the relation between capital and labor that is hidden from view but the alienation of both capital and labor in their relation. The founding constitutions in the bourgeois world—such as the constitution of the United States—have nothing to say about the capital–labor relation, let alone about their mutual alienation. None of this is ever directly mentioned. The US Constitution is a perfect document for regulating exchange relations and enforcing private property law. The language is redolent with ideals of equality, freedom and reciprocity, but it is hopeless when it comes to the collective rights of labor—let alone in confronting the mutual alienations of both capital and labor in the production of both capital and the capitalist. The one constitution that tried to incorporate the perspective of labor was the Portuguese constitution of 1975, when the socialists and communists took power. They tried to write a constitution which guaranteed the rights of labor against capital. It did not last very long in the face of competition in the world market. The "abstractions" of capital ruled.

It is the mutual alienation that is so striking in this initial formulation. Both labor and capital lose something important. But what? Why "alien capital"? Why can it not be just capitalist? "Alien labour" is easiest to understand because the capitalist appropriates the capacity to labor from the laborer (Figure 1). Labor becomes alienated in the production process. But Marx insists it is alienated as soon as it takes on the commodity form. When labor power becomes a commodity, then the laborer who is the bearer of that commodity is obliged to alienate their capacity to labor for the benefit of capital. The experience has nothing to do with the individuality of the laborer. What the laborer feels or thinks does not matter: capital is interested only in appropriating the capacity to labor, in labor power as a commodity. The humanity that is implied in bourgeois market exchange disappears and gives way to indifference on the part of capital vis-à-vis the laborer.

The alienation of capital is different but just as devastating. Capital enters into its process, not as a free individual (of the sort described in market exchange) doing whatever they like. Capitalists are tightly bound and ruled by abstractions. They are forced to do whatever has to be done, and this means, as we shall see, producing surplus-value or going out of business. The pride capitalists may take from their product counts for naught in the competitive realm of the market, and market forces oblige them to appropriate alienated labor at the lowest cost. In other words, once they are enmeshed in the system, both the capitalist and the laborer are alienated unfree beings from the very beginning; not as a result of the system but as a presupposition. Both capitalists and laborers have to offer themselves into this system as alienated beings. At a certain point, we may even feel sorry for the capitalist. In *Capital*, for example, Marx makes much of the Faustian dilemma between the capitalist satisfying the lust for enjoyment while living under the impulsion to reinvest.

In the case of labor, the options are different. In simple exchange, "labour was structured in such a way that the product was not of direct use value for the labourer, not a direct means of subsistence. This was a general condition for the creation of exchange value, and of exchange value in general. Otherwise the worker would have produced only a product—a direct use value for himself—but not an exchange value" (266–7). Marx continues,

> As soon as it has obtained motion from capital, this use value exists as the worker's specific, productive activity; it is his vitality itself, directed toward a specific purpose and hence expressing itself in a specific form. In the relation of capital and labour, exchange value and use value are brought into relation; the one side (capital) initially stands opposite the other side as *exchange value*, and the other (labour), stands opposite capital as use value. (267–8)

The bringing together of the use-value and the exchange-value of capital converts money into "money as capital" (269).

"The only utility whatsoever which an object can have for capital can be to preserve or increase [capital]" (270). With money, value

> is capable of no other motion than a quantitative one; to increase itself . . . For that reason, [exchange] value which insists on itself as value preserves itself through increase; and it preserves itself precisely only by constantly driving beyond its quantitative barrier, which contradicts its character as form, its inner generality. Thus, growing wealthy is an end in itself. The goal-determining activity of capital can only be that of growing wealthier, i.e. of magnification, of increasing itself. (270)

The contradiction is that this goal defies the rules of equality and equivalence as established in bourgeois market exchange.

Money, as a representative of general wealth, does not have "the capacity of buying all pleasures, all commodities, the totality of the material substances of wealth . . . Fixed as wealth . . . it is therefore the constant drive to go beyond its quantitative limit: an endless process. Its own animation consists exclusively in that; it *preserves* itself as self-validated exchange value distinct from use value only by *constantly multiplying* itself" and "it is damned difficult for Messrs the economists to make the theoretical transition from the self-preservation of value in capital to its multiplication" (270–1). If capital is necessarily about the endless growth of exchange-value (wealth), how does that square with the rules of bourgeois exchange, which promote equality and equivalence?

"The only use value . . . which can stand opposite capital as such is that which increases, multiplies and hence preserves it as capital" (271). The only use-value that can do this is living labor, "labour which is still objectifying itself, *labour* as subjectivity," which brings us to the conclusion that the only use-value "which can form the opposite pole to capital is *labour* (*to be exact, value creating, productive labour*)" (272).

This is a stunning, although, in certain respects, rather circumscribed, conclusion. Marx immediately points out that "labour as mere performance of services for the satisfaction of needs has nothing whatever to do with capital, since that is not capital's concern. If a capitalist hires a woodcutter to chop wood to roast his mutton over" then the woodcutter "gives him his service, a use value, which does not increase capital." But the woodcutter receives money and as with all other services this is categorized as "consumption of revenue" and "not consumption of capital." If I hire somebody to clean out my gutters or get the snow off my driveway, this is not a capitalist transaction. This is me just using my revenues and the recipient performing a useful service for me in return for a monetary payment. The performance of such services "cannot fall under the category of productive labour. From whore to pope, there is a mass of such rabble. But the honest and 'working' lumpenproletariat belongs here as well; e.g. the great mob of porters, etc." in seaport cities (272). In the next page or two, Marx briefly considers the distinction, made much of by Adam Smith, between productive and unproductive labor. The first volume of Marx's *Theories of Surplus Value* is devoted almost entirely to Adam Smith, whose theories of productive and unproductive labor are judged here to be "correct from the standpoint of bourgeois political economy" (271). Marx himself is more circumspect, although he seems to accept that the mere performance of services for the satisfaction of the bourgeoisie has nothing to do with endless accumulation, the multiplication of capital and the production of surplus-value.

This has some awkward implications. A large segment of contemporary wage labor is given over to supplying labor power in return for wages drawn not from the circulation of capital but from the circulation of revenues (as in state employment or security guards for the affluent bourgeois families and baby-minders for waged workers). It is all very well to dismiss this as "not capital's concern," but the mass of wage laborers so employed have an important political role to play, and it is invidious to exclude them from the active working class of supposedly "productive" laborers. Marx's ultimate solution in *Capital* will be to switch from a physical and material definition of productivity to a social definition in terms of surplus-value production and appropriation, so that teachers and entertainers can be productive if they are employed by a capitalist who appropriates surplus-value from their work. This is particularly important today, when many services are organized as capitalist enterprises and when some of the more politically militant movements are among teachers, health-care providers and delivery workers (Marx's porters), while the traditional definition of productive laborers in auto, steel, etc., has become far less important numerically and politically. In the *Grundrisse*, Marx simply announces that he will later return to consider this topic "in more detail" (273).

Marx continues his provocations by announcing that "capital exchanges itself . . . only in connection with *not-capital*, the negation of capital, without which it is not capital; the real *not-capital* is labour" (274). It is tempting to read this as Marx lapsing into some version of Hegelianism. Even if that is so, the comment deserves elaboration. Let us see where Marx goes with it. The exchange between capital and labor, Marx explains, splits into two qualitatively different and even contradictory processes. First, the worker sells his commodity, capacity to labor, which has a use-value, and since it is a commodity, also a price. Second, the capitalist obtains labor as "value-positing activity" that "maintains and multiplies capital, and which thereby becomes the productive force, the reproductive force of capital." This double process does not occur in simple exchange as with all other commodities. So there is something special going on here. The exchange between capital and labor is no ordinary commodity exchange.

The original statement concerning negation takes the form of an abstract proposition to be investigated. It focuses on the way in which labor produces capital, the instrument of its own oppression, alienation and negation, while capital produces a working class whose political mission is to negate the power of capital. This is what the abstract proposition proposes. This is what has to be investigated. At this point, however, Marx chooses to insert another plan for the *magnum opus*:

> *Capital*. I. Generality: (1) (a) Emergence of capital out of money. (b) Capital and labour (mediating itself through *alien* labour). (c) The elements of capital, dissected according to their relation to labour (Product. Raw material. Instrument of labour.) (2) *Particularization of capital*: (a) Capital circulant, capital fixe. Turnover of capital. (3) *The singularity of capital*: Capital and profit. Capital and interest. Capital as value, distinct from itself as interest and profit. II. *Particularity*: (1) Accumulation of capitals. (2) Competition of capitals. (3) Concentration of capitals (quantitative distinction of capital as at same time qualitative, as *measure* of its size and influence). III. *Singularity*: (1) Capital as credit. (2) Capital as stock-capital. (3) Capital as money market. In the money market, capital is posited in its totality; there it *determines prices, gives work, regulates production*, in a word, is the *source of production*; but capital, not only as something which produces itself (positing prices materially in industry etc., developing forces of production), but at the same time as a creator of values, has to posit a value or form of wealth specifically distinct from capital. This is *ground rent*. This is the only value created by capital which is distinct from itself, from its own production. (275)

Note here Marx's return to the framework of universality, particularity and singularity considered in his general introduction. Also in this case, the outline morphs seamlessly back into the text. But he here makes some assertions that seem somewhat at odds with where he is at in the rest of the *Grundrisse*. First is the idea that "in the money market capital is posited in its totality, there it *determines prices, gives work, regulates production*, in a word is the *source of production*." This is, perhaps, an advance reference to the position he takes at one point in Volume III of *Capital*, where the money market is viewed as a kind of central nervous system for the regulation and control of capital flows both geographically and sectorally. The money market, for all the importance assigned to it here, is almost totally ignored in the rest of the *Grundrisse*, while credit and interest-bearing capital are only lightly touched upon. The second seeming oddity is that "capital as a creator of values, has to posit a value or a form of wealth specifically distinct from capital. This is *ground rent*. This is the only value created by capital which is distinct from itself, from its own production. By its nature as well as historically, capital is the *creator* of modern landed property, of ground rent" (275–6). It entails "the dissolution of the old form of property in land." The "new arises through the action of capital upon the old" and it is in this sense that capital can be regarded as the "creator of modern agriculture." Marx here binds himself to the Ricardian distinctions between ground rent, capital and wage labor as the core relations in capital's economy and, somewhat surprisingly, justifies them. He even goes on to conclude that "the inner construction of modern society, or, capital in the totality of its relations, is therefore posited in the economic relations of modern landed property, which appears as a process." This poses the question of "how does the transition from landed property to wage labour come about?" (276).

The justification is that capital has to create modern landed property and ground rent out of feudal land relations because land is a primary means of production, the fertility and location of which is a free gift of nature. This free gift of nature must be commodified and owned lest laborers appropriate it (free) for themselves. The purpose of ground rent is to erect a barrier between the laborers and this free gift to ensure the supply of alienated labor to capitalist production. This explains why the creator of values, capital, has "to posit a value or a form of wealth specifically distinct from capital" in the form of ground rent. The laborers are, consequently, as alienated from the land (and nature) as they are from their own capacity to labor. Ground rent rests on the commodification of the land, the formation of the proletariat and the creation of modern agriculture.

"Historically, this transition is beyond dispute . . . landed property is the product of capital . . . and agriculture, driven by capital, transforms itself into industrial agronomy . . . Only in this way is the application of science possible for the first time, and the development of the full force of production" (276). This is a prescient account of the inevitable industrialization of agriculture that only became widespread after 1945 and global after 1970 or so. But Marx also emphasizes the importance of the transformation of labor relations. He wants to show how the "cottiers, serfs, bondsmen, tenants for life, cottagers, etc. became day labourers, wage labourers, i.e, that wage labour in its totality is initially created by the action of capital on landed property" then supplemented by the proprietor of the land who clears the land "of its excess mouths, tears the children of the earth from the breast on which they were raised and thus transforms labour on the soil itself" into a mere social relation in which wage workers "produce for profit instead of for revenue." Today we would mourn the loss of family farming in the face of industrialized corporate agriculture. The rule here is that "although capital can develop itself completely as commercial capital . . . without this transformation of landed capital, it cannot do so as industrial capital. Even the development of manufactures presupposes the dissolution of the old economic relations of landed property. On the other hand, only with the development of modern industry to a high degree does this dissolution at individual points acquire its totality and extent" (277). Once more, we encounter the idea of capital as an emerging totality in transformation. In this case, England is "the model country" for observing the "*total restructuring of the mode of production* (agriculture) itself."

This culminates in a general commentary on capital as an organic totality (which was cited earlier).

It must be kept in mind that the new forces of production do not develop out of nothing, nor drop from the sky, nor from the

womb of the self-positing idea, but from within and in antithesis to the existing development of production and the inherited,
traditional relations of property. While in the completed bourgeois system every economic relation presupposes every other
in its bourgeois economic form, and everything posited is thus
also a presupposition, this is the case with every organic system.
This organic system itself, as a totality, has its presuppositions,
and its development to its totality consists precisely in subordinating all elements of society to itself, or in creating out of it the
organs which it still lacks. This is historically how it becomes a
totality. The process of becoming this totality forms a moment
of its process, of its development. (278)

The totality is perpetually in "the process of becoming." It is
therefore ongoing and as relevant today as it was in Marx's time.
How and why, we might now ask, did the world's central banks and
the international financial institutions, such as the International
Monetary Fund and the Bank for International Settlements come
to play the role they now have? Where does the progressive industrialization and corporatization of agriculture come from? Marx's
method opens up the possibility of asking such questions and
locating the answers in the framework of a much more sophisticated theory of an evolving totality of capital today. The geographical field and terrain that capital flow operates across and upon is
also in perpetual flux as it inevitably expands. Marx continues:

If within one society, the modern relations of production, i.e.
capital, are developed to its totality, and this society then seizes
hold of a new territory, as e.g. the colonies, then it finds, or
rather its representative, the capitalist finds, that his capital
ceases to be capital without wage labour, and that one of the
presuppositions of the latter is not only landed property in
general, but modern landed property; landed property which,
as capitalized rent, is expensive, and which, as such, excludes
the direct use of the soil by individuals. Hence Wakefield's

theory of colonies followed in practice by the English government in Australia. Landed property is here artificially made
more expensive in order to transform the workers into wage
workers, to make capital act as capital, and thus to make the
new colony productive. (278)

Productive of surplus-value, it goes without saying. All of this has
to precede the development of industrial capital.

The final chapter of Volume I of *Capital* deals with Wakefield's
theory of colonization and its implications for labor control.
This passage also inspired much of my own thinking about the
role of what I call a "spatial fix" to the problem of overaccumulation of capital. Surplus capital accumulating in Britain needed
new outlets, so it flowed abroad (in Marx's time to the United
States, Australia, Argentina, etc.), only to find it could not function as capital without a captive labor force. The UK government
therefore sought to impose a land policy on Australia, as
Wakefield suggested, one that mobilized landed capital to
prevent free movement onto the land by the migrant population, who were then forced to market their labor capacity in
order to live. In this brief paragraph, Marx acknowledges the
role that geographical expansion (through colonization or impe-
rialist interventions) might play in the evolution of capital as a
totality. A contemporary example would be the Belt and Road
Project launched by China to absorb its rapidly expanding
productive capacity.

The totality therefore has a material geographical presence and
extension and, judging from this last passage, may spawn multiple
smaller totalities as settler colonies that may ultimately grow (as
did the United States) to challenge the hegemony of the originating constellation of surplus accumulation. This too is a theme
which recurs several times in the *Grundrisse*. In Marx's time, that
totality was generally confined to Britain, Western Europe and the
United States, with tendrils of settler colonies and merchant capitalist operations in noncapitalist economies that were captured by

often abusive practices of the merchant capitalists and their imperial backers.

The totality, as it developed in the United States, was different
from the economic totality as it was developed in Britain. Marx
does not take any of this very far, but the door is opened to integrate Arrighi's account of *The Long Twentieth Century: Money,
Power and the Origins of Our Times*[1] into Marx's account. In
Arrighi's work, the growth of the global economy is partitioned
and segmented into slowly transforming blocs of economic and
political powers with a shifting locus of hegemony over time. The
center of power shifted from the Italian city-states toward the Low
Countries in the seventeenth century, to Britain in the nineteenth
century, and then to the United States in the latter half of the twentieth century, and there are signs today of a hegemonic shift toward
East Asia centered on China. We see in this historical geography
competing totalities in formation and in competition, but woven
together by intricate flows of capital from one place to another. The
obvious unit in the organization of these flows is the state, which
only came to be conceptualized as a national economy (as opposed
to an independent entity) from the 1920s onward, and moved
from an ideal and conceptual status to a real economy as policymakers and state officials sought to shape the distinctive form of
the totality where they lived and worked through the applications
of government policies with respect to taxation, balances of
payments and regulatory regimes, all caught up in geopolitical
rivalries.

The borders and boundaries of a totality in formation and transformation are not secure. It can be expanding geographically. It
could be colonizing spaces. The appropriate analogy for Marx's
conception is that of an open and evolving ecosystem, the concept
of which was formulated in the latter half of the nineteenth century.
Marx seems not to have been aware of it. Had he known, he might

---

1 Giovanni Arrighi, *The Long Twentieth Century: Money, Power and the
Origins of Our Times* (London: Verso, 1994).

well have depicted the totality as a complex and perpetually evolving ecosystem accommodating multiple species (divisions of labor) in interaction, which can be expanding and growing, transforming and mutating, changing internally in all sorts of ways. The totality, I repeat, is not something that is fixed and it is not something that is predesigned. It is something that is constantly in the process of evolution. Furthermore, a variety of totalities (economic ecosystems) can coexist, all of them in interaction with each other. For instance, there is the formation of the European Union, the history of which looks like a new totality in formation (but with Brexit reducing its reach). How, for example, was production and distribution and so on organized through the European Union and to what degree did it then have to start establishing borders around itself. Should it stretch into Turkey? Would Algeria or Egypt be admitted? The zone where the European Union goes up against Russia is deeply troubled. So the totality does not have a fixed territorial designation.

Global capital currently operates with macro-alliances in regional power blocs, such as NAFTA, MERCOSUR, the Trans Pacific Partnership (from which Trump withdrew) and the Asian co-prosperity sphere. I have elsewhere proposed to look at global capital through the lens of different, unstable but recognizable regional value regimes (which mirror the more obvious currency regimes in world capitalism). Marx here briefly appears open to such a mode of thinking before reverting to a more singular mode of analysis.

Marx here briefly makes space for some brief reflections on how the market, "which appears as an abstract quality at the beginning of economics, takes on total shapes," culminating in an extensive list of types of market for grain, tea, sugar, raw materials, metals (copper, iron, tin, zinc, etc.), drug and dyes, wool and cotton and so on. The main point appears to be that the concept of the market as an abstraction in economic theory is manifested as an incredible diversity of material forms functioning as use-value. Most interesting, however, are the initial comments on the nature of money markets, which include "the discount market . . . the loan market; hence money trade, bullion market . . . the market in all interest-bearing bills; state funds, and the share market." It is not hard to divine the drift of Marx's thinking here. The concreteness of the astonishing diversity of markets of all sorts (use-values), gives rise to the concrete abstractions of the market in which exchange-value mediates relations between all commodities, and the yet-to-be-defined value theory becomes the central theoretical category. Marx incidentally notes "the concentration of the money market in a chief location within a country, while the other markets are distributed according to the division of labour; although here, too, great concentration in the capital city, if the latter is at the same time a port of export" (280).

THE LABOR QUESTION

Marx transitions on pages 282–3 into a deeper discussion of the positionality of the laborer in relation to capital. After a passing but dismissive mention of the labor furnished by the capitalist himself, Marx turns to the question of how the value of labor-power, as a commodity, might be determined. His answer is "only by the amount of objectified labour contained in it; hence, here, by the amount of labour required to reproduce the worker himself" (282). The use-value that the laborer offers, the capacity to labor, depends on the bodily reproduction of the laborer and the wage must therefore be sufficient for that purpose. "Like every individual subject within circulation, the worker is the owner of a use value; he exchanges this for money, for the general form of wealth, but only in order to exchange this again for commodities considered as the objects of his immediate consumption, as a means of satisfying his needs" (283). So what kinds of needs might the worker have? "The sphere of his consumption is not qualitatively restricted, only quantitatively." Once the workers have the money, they cannot be stopped from buying whatever they want. They are free as consumers. The only restraint is the lack of enough exchange-value to buy up everything they may want and desire (as well as need). "The sphere of his consumption is not qualitatively restrictive, only quantitatively. This distinguishes him from the slave, serf, etc." (283).

> This much, however, can even now be mentioned in passing, namely that the relative restriction on the sphere of workers' consumption . . . gives them as consumers . . . an entirely different importance as agents of production from that which they possessed e.g. in antiquity or in the Middle Ages . . . the worker receives the equivalent in the form of money, the form of general wealth, he is in this exchange an equal vis-à-vis the capitalist, like every other party in exchange; at least, so he *seems*. (283)

Worker consumption is an important component of effective demand. But what is essential is that "the purpose of the exchange for him is the satisfaction of his need" (284). "What he obtains from the exchange is therefore not exchange value, not wealth, but a means of subsistence, objects for the preservation of his life, the satisfaction of his needs in general, physical, social etc." (284). It could also be that the worker's objective is to acquire exchange-value—wealth—that can be stored. This involves sacrificing "substantial satisfaction" and engaging with "*self-denial*, saving, cutting corners in his consumption so as to withdraw less from circulation than he puts *goods* into it. This is the only possible form of enriching oneself which is posited by circulation itself." The worker could deny himself rest and in myriad ways increase his industriousness.

But the result is capital's increasing demand "for industriousness and also for *saving, self-denial*" on the part of workers (285). Society today makes the paradoxical demand that "he for whom the object of exchange is subsistence should deny himself, not he for whom it is wealth. The illusion that the capitalists in fact practised 'self-denial'—and became capitalists thereby . . . has been abandoned by all modern economists of sound judgement. The workers are supposed to save, and much bustle is made with savings banks etc." (285). This has nothing to do with any concern for the distribution of wealth. It is merely meant to ensure "that in their old age, or in the case of illness or crises etc., they do not become a burden on the poorhouses, on the state, or on the proceeds of begging (in a word, so that they become a burden on the working class itself and not on the capitalists . . .)." The result would be the degradation of the worker "to the level of the Irish, the level of wage labour where the most animal minimum of needs and subsistence appears to him as the sole object and purpose of his exchange with capital" (285).

Marx is not very kind to the Irish in his early writings. He later changed his position. He recognized that the problem was not the Irish and their culture but capital's manipulation of the Irish in a politics of divide-and-rule against the working class. Class solidarity required agitation for better living and working conditions for the Irish. There is an interesting parallel with the role of Puerto Ricans in the United States after 1945. Both the Irish and the Puerto Ricans could freely move to the metropole, where capital put them to work with the clear objective of depressing the wage rate. Much the same scurrilous things were typically said about both groups in terms of their cultural habits and expectations.

For the working class as a whole, "the maximum of industriousness" and "the minimum of consumption" was the rule. "The maximum of his self-denial and of his moneymaking . . . could lead to nothing else than that he would receive for the maximum of his labour a minimum of wages" (286). Furthermore, "if they all save, then a general reduction of wages will bring them back to earth again; for general savings would show the capitalist that their wages are in general too high." The capitalists in fact demand that "the workers should save enough at the times when business is good to be able to more or less live in the bad times." In other words, "they should always hold to a minimum of life's pleasure and make crises easier to bear for the capitalists etc. Maintain themselves as pure labouring machines and as far as possible pay their own wear and tear." The neoliberal ethic, it seems, was as omnipresent in Marx's time as it is in our own.

> Quite apart from the sheer brutalization to which this would lead—and such brutalization itself would make it impossible even to strive for wealth . . . and the worker's participation in the higher, even cultural satisfactions, the agitation for his own interests, newspaper subscriptions, attending lectures, educating his children, developing his taste etc., his only share of civilization that distinguishes him from the slave, is economically only possible by widening the spheres of his pleasure at the time when business is good, where saving is to a certain degree possible. (287)

Even if his savings "surpass the piggy-bank amounts," they are then vulnerable to appropriation by the state or capital such that it seems as if he engages with maximum exertion in order to save "*for* capital and not for himself."

Incidentally, "each capitalist does demand that his workers should save, but only *his own*, because they stand towards him as workers, but by no means the remaining *world of workers*, for these stand towards him as consumers. In spite of all 'pious' speeches he therefore searches for means to spur them on to consumption, to give his wares new charms, to inspire them with new needs by constant chatter" (287). This is typical bourgeois hypocrisy. One wonders what Marx would have said after an evening of watching TV and being saturated and seduced with ads for all manner of enticing products, while receiving a parsimonious and precarious wage.

The demands of "hypocritical bourgeois philanthropy" turned out to be self-contradictory and thus to prove precisely what they were supposed to refute, namely that, in the exchanges between the worker and capital, the worker finds himself in the relation of simple circulation, hence obtains, not wealth, but only subsistence,

use-values for immediate consumption. But this fails to acknowledge what the laborer actually does in the course of exchange, a
question that is revealed by the various proposals for profit-shar-
ing (288). This leads Marx into some intricate argumentation as to
the content of the exchange between capital and labor. Profit-
sharing "presupposes labour which is not capital, and presupposes
that labour has become its opposite—not-labour. In order to
become capital, it itself presupposes labour as not-capital as against
capital." But if we look at what labor does as a use-value, then labor
"would confront capital not as labour, not as not-capital but as
capital. But capital, too, cannot confront capital if it does not
confront labour, since capital is only capital as not-labour; in this
contradictory relation" (288). "As capital it can posit itself only by
positing labour as not-capital, as pure use value." The free laborer
"has no value." Indeed, "his valuelessness and devaluation is the
presupposition of capital." The worker is "a person who is something for himself *apart from his* labour, and who alienates his life
expression only as a means towards his own life." Industrial capital
and capital in general "cannot exist" if the worker as such has
exchange-value. The only thing that matters for capital is the use-
value of the worker's capacity to labor.

The purpose of this somewhat abstract argumentation appears
to be the establishment of the intricate threads through which
capital and labor are bound together. In other words, the exchange
between capital and labor is not like all other forms of commodity
exchange in the market, because it involves the interpenetration of
capital and labor such that they both define and complete the other
through the exchange. This has implications for the nature of the
exchange.

The laborer here is depicted as a person with wants, needs, and
desires embedded in the prevailing conditions of life and culture.
What the workers might want, might try to acquire in the process
of class struggle is an open question. We should never forget that
the worker is "a person who is something for himself apart from
his labour" (289). Alienated labor is for the worker a means to an

end, the reproduction of their life. Marx does not elaborate upon this theme, but in the history of capital, the capacity of the working classes to make themselves a life in the sphere of family and social reproduction has been an important antidote to the alienation of their labor in the labor process. Later analysts have discussed the role of compensatory consumerism in relation to alienated labor, and in this brief intervention Marx opens the way to incorporate such potentialities into the investigation.

The danger, however, is that we join "the whitewashing syco-phants of bourgeois economics" who consider "the worker to owe a debt to capital for the fact that he is alive at all, and can repeat certain life processes every day as soon as he has eaten and slept enough" (293). After twenty years of giving over their labor capac-ity to capital for minimum reward and effectively barred from the accumulation of wealth, the capacity to "*squander his dosages of vital force as much as possible, without interruption*" is surely exhausted. The struggle over the Ten Hours' Bill, which proposed to limit the length of the working day, is indicative of capital's intent (294). The worker only ever receives "subsistence . . . *never the general form of wealth.*" Labor ends up existing as "*absolute poverty*: poverty not as shortage, but as total exclusion of objective wealth" (295). In fact, the positionality of capital vis-à-vis labor within the circulation process, as already noted, is fundamentally different. For example, "the worker who exchanges his commodity goes through the form C–M–M–C" in which the exchange of use-values is what matters, whereas capital represents M–C–C–M in which the only thing that can matter is the quantitative increase of M (295). In this section of the *Grundrisse*, almost every possible inner relation has been held up for scrutiny. It is clear that the exchange between capital and labor is qualitatively different from all other forms of market exchange.

The "contradictory statements that labour is *absolute poverty as object*, on one side, and is, on the other side, the *general possibility* of wealth as subject and as activity, are reciprocally determined and follow from the essence of labour, such as it is *presupposed* by capital as its contradiction and its contradictory being, and such as it, in turn, presupposes capital" (296). The "essence" to which Marx appeals in this formulation is the "not *objectified labour, not-value*, conceived *positively*, or as a negativity in relation to itself, is the *not-objectified*, hence non-objective, i.e. subjective existence of labour itself." What we are witnessing, in other words, is the triumph of subject over object, process over thing. "Labour not as an object, but as activity, not as itself *value*, but as the *living source* of value" (296).

Meanwhile, we are left to contemplate what Marx dubs "the essence of labour" as set up in this section. It is, he writes, "not at all contradictory . . . that labour is *absolute poverty as object*, on one side, and is, on the other side, the *general possibility* of wealth as subject and as activity." It is important to remember, however, that the labor that capital confronts "is not this or another labour, but *labour pure and simple*, abstract labour; absolutely indifferent to its particular *specificity*, but capable of all specificities." Thus, "capital *as such* is indifferent to every particularity of its substance, and exists not only as the totality of the same but also as the abstraction from all its particularities, the labour which confronts it likewise subjectively has the same totality and abstraction in itself." While this was not true of guild and craft labor, in the capitalist mode "capital can come into relation with every *specific* labour; it confronts the *totality* of all labours . . . and the particular one it confronts at a given time is an accidental matter" (296–7). The worker likewise "is absolutely indifferent to the specificity of his labour; it has no interest for him as such, but only in as much as it is . . . a use value for capital. It is therefore his economic character that he is the carrier of labour as such . . . in opposition to the capitalist" (297). This economic relation "develops more purely and adequately in proportion as labour loses all the characteristics of art; as its particular skill becomes something more and more abstract, and as it becomes something more abstract and irrelevant, and as it becomes more and more *purely abstract activity*, a purely mechanical activity." This capital–labor relation "becomes real only with the development of a particular *material mode of production* and of a particular stage in the development of the industrial *productive forces*" (297). The practice of laboring lacks meaning.

This alerts us to the question that still has to be addressed, which is exactly how labor that is "the living source of value" is used in production. "We now come to the second side of the process. The exchange between capital or capitalist and the worker is now finished . . . We now proceed to the relation of capital to labour as capital's use value" (297). This labor is not objectified. It is "the possibility of values, and, as activity, the positing of value. As against capital, labour is the merely abstract form, the mere possibility of value-positing activity, which exists only as a capacity, as a resource in the bodiliness of the worker" (298). There is an opening here to accommodate contemporary biopolitical interpretations. "But when it is made into a real activity through contact with capital . . . then it becomes a really value-positing, productive activity." The result: "capital itself becomes a process. Labour is the yeast thrown into it, which starts it fermenting." But the inputs into the process are constituted as objectified labor, and they are of two sorts, "that of the *raw material*" and "that of the *instrument of labour*, the objective means which subjective activity inserts between itself as an object, as its conductor" (299). "The substance of value . . . is objectified labour," produced through the connection of living labor with raw materials and instruments of labor. The latter may be found "freely in nature" and appropriated as such.

After brief consideration of the use-values that money can procure for capital, Marx concludes: "Thus: the raw material is consumed by being changed, formed by labour, and the instrument of labour is consumed by being used up in this process, worn out. On the other hand, labour also is consumed by being employed" (300). But "labour is not only consumed, but also at the same time fixed, converted from the form of activity into the form of the object." In other words, "the change from activity to being" creates a product. "All three moments of the process, the material, the instrument, and labour coincide." But "the moments of the process of production which have been consumed to form the product are simultaneously reproduced in it. The whole process therefore appears as productive consumption." This is an important concept in Marx's theory. It contrasts with final consumption, where commodities drop out of sight. With productive consumption the objectified conditions for future production are actively produced and sustained. "This *form-giving* activity consumes the object and consumes itself ... only in its subjective form as activity."

Marx then submits a summary statement on the results "so far obtained ... *Firstly*: the appropriation, absorption of labour by capital ... brings capital into ferment, and makes it into a process, *process of production*, in whose totality it relates to itself not only as objectified by living labour, but also, because objectified, [as] mere *object* of labour." This is another way of discussing the relation between process and thing, between the objectifications accomplished by the subjectivity of living labor. Second, within circulation, commodity and money are indifferent to their specific forms since both are "expressions of exchange value, and differed only as general and particular exchange value." Given Marx's assumption of the equivalence of value and exchange-value, the most important thing is the continuous circulation and accumulation of value. "In the process of production, capital distinguishes itself as form from itself as substance. It is both aspects at once and at the same time the relation of both to one another." The form is labor process; the substance is thing. Third, what Marx calls "the *material* moment" divides into raw material and means of production, both of which may be objectifications of prior labor. But labor is indifferent and necessarily views them as material elements necessary for production to proceed.

This paves the way for the central topic of the next section, which concerns how the use-value of labor power is consumed in the process of production:

To the extent to which we have examined the process so far, capital in its being-for-itself, i.e. the capitalist, does not enter at all. It is not the capitalist who is consumed by labour as raw material and instrument of labour. And it is not the capitalist who does this consuming but rather labour. Thus the process of the production of capital does not appear as the process of the production of capital, but as the process of production in general, and capital's *distinction from labour* appears only in the material character of *raw material* and *instrument of labour*. (303)

This is important because socialists

sometimes say, we need capital, but not the capitalist. Then capital appears as a pure thing, not as a relation of production which, reflected in itself, is precisely the capitalist. I may well separate capital from a given individual capitalist, and it can be transferred to another. But, in losing capital, he loses the quality of being a capitalist. Thus capital is indeed separable from an individual capitalist, but not from *the* capitalist, who, as such, confronts *the* worker. Thus also the individual worker can cease to be the being-for-itself of labour; he may inherit or steal money etc. (303–4)

The internal relations between alien capital and alien labor have here been subjected to microanalytic inspection. This opens up a fertile terrain for far deeper and broader investigation of the roots of contemporary alienations and the loss of meaning at the core of the ever-expanding and ever complexifying totality of capital's social relations networked together within the world market.

4

The Production of Capital
Pages 304–70

Marx opens his argument in this section with the following observation: "If at the end of the process of production, which was begun with the presuppositions of capital, capital appears to have vanished as a formal relation, then this can have taken place only because the invisible threads which draw it through the process have been overlooked" (304). Marx evidently intends to expose and follow these "overlooked invisible threads." It is helpful, however, to settle up front on what "invisible" might mean. This is made very clear in a later statement. The economists

> do not conceive capital in its *specific character as form*, as a *relation of production* reflected into itself, but think only about its material substance, raw material etc. But these material elements do not make capital into capital. Then, however, they recall that capital is also in another respect a *value*, that is, something *immaterial*, something indifferent to its material consistency. Thus, Say: "*Capital is always an immaterial essence*, because it is not material which makes capital, but the *value* of this material, a value which has nothing corporeal about it." (309)

When Marx uses the terms "form" and "formal" with respect to capital it is always in this noncorporeal sense.

Let us be clear. Marx, who is elsewhere critical of Say (particularly Say's law), is here agreeing with him. I also earlier noted that Marx's conception of value as exchange-value (arising out of some sort of fusion of labor inputs and market prices) hobbles his analysis in the *Grundrisse*, but here the concept of value has evolved to become much closer to the formulation in *Capital*, i.e., value is distinct and separable from exchange-value. What is at stake is the relation between the materiality of the tangible processes and all the things involved in commodity production and exchange, on the one hand, and the immateriality of the social relation that puts value on these processes and things, on the other. Economists have an obvious preference for the tangible, the material, and the measurable, but Marx is signaling that it is the social relations, which are immaterial but objective, that anchor the concept of capital. As human beings we are, of course, material flesh and blood, but the intangibles of persona, image, charisma and reputation are often far more important. Indeed, contemporary economics has recently had to deal with this problem directly, since the valuation of corporations is now dominated by intangibles such as reputation and name recognition. What is the value of the Nike logo and reputation?

The notion of "invisible threads" requires explication. It is particularly important around the question of what value is and how it might be represented and determined. In *Capital*, Marx asserts that value is immaterial but objective (he even calls it a "phantom objectivity"), which is entirely consistent with the position he will adopt here. This contests the popular view of Marx as a purely physical materialist. If he were, then how could he accord such importance to the immaterial and the invisible threads? The answer is that Marx is not a natural scientific materialist but a historical materialist, for whom human behaviors, beliefs, thoughts and ideologies are just as important to human action as physical materialities. But it is also true to say that the immaterialist elements remain just that until they are materialized physically. We can have lots of immaterial thoughts and imaginary projects, but only some of them become real.

As is well known, Marx's theory of value is controversial and has been subject to many competing interpretations. It may be helpful here to parse those different interpretations in the light of certain "invisible threads." The two threads that Marx has already identified are (1) the relation of value to labor time (of some sort), and (2) its relation to prices achieved in the market. In earlier sections, Marx paid more attention to value in the market (while denying that value could be created through market operations), but in this section he pays almost exclusive attention to labor time (of some sort) as the creative moment in the production of value. In both cases, however, the material interpretation gives way to the invisible threads of abstract labor (socially necessary labor time) and abstract price (the average or so-called "natural" price, as opposed to actual prices). Some take the view that the only invisible thread that matters is the relation to labor, since it is clear that value cannot be created in circulation. But Marx on several occasions signals that value depends on both value creation in production and the realization of value in the market. The contradictory unity between production and market realization lies at the heart of the value theory. If nobody wants a product in the market, then it has no value, no matter how much labor is involved in its production. In this section, however, Marx pays far more attention to the creation of value in the labor process than to its realization in the market. It is often assumed, for purposes of analysis, that all commodities trade at their values (which they obviously do not). This assumption permits the analysis of production while ignoring the impact of market processes. There is nothing wrong in doing so, but there is something very wrong in concluding that realization in the market is irrelevant, simply because Marx has ruled it out by assumption in the course of a particular investigation.

However one looks at it, social relations are crucial. Imagine somebody digging a ditch. You could describe in great detail the energy expended by the digger, the tools used, the depth of the ditch, how long it takes to dig, and so on. And you can measure and record all these physical things. At the end of the day, this will not tell you what you really want to know. The person digging could be a wage laborer, a slave, a prisoner doing forced labor, a willing participant in collective labor, a dedicated member of an anarchist or feminist commune, a socialist worker, some insane aristocrat who takes exercise by digging ditches and filling them again. You may get some hints of which of these is operative by a study of the physical conditions (an overseer with a whip tells us something), but to really find out we have to investigate. For Marx, the most important thing is to establish the social relation embodied in the physical action. He has already tentatively differentiated, for example, between wage labor employed by capital (productive) and the same wage labor exchanged against revenues (unproductive).

There can be no socialist revolution, no anticapitalist movement that does not address the criticality of the "invisible threads" that constitute the dominant social class relations. Attached to the social relation (as we also saw in the case of the doctrines of equality, freedom and reciprocity that arose in relation to market exchange) are modes of thought, modes of activity, forms of organization, institutional arrangements, legal structures, ideologies and all the rest of it. But at the heart of it, Marx is saying, look carefully at the social relations. This is what the invisible threads are about. Just because you cannot see capital at work in the labor process, and you cannot tell from examining it physically what the dominant social relation might be, that does not mean the social relation is unimportant. Social relations are always going to be critical. This is one of Marx's central contributions. Presumably, ditches will need to be dug under socialism, so the latter is not defined by abolition of the former. It is the social relation behind it that will matter.

If the social relationship does not change, then something that started out as a socialist enterprise slides back into a capitalistic mode of operation. An interesting example would of course be something like the Israeli kibbutz, set up initially under a completely different set of socialist relations. Over the years, these became more and more compatible with a capitalist social order. Henri Lefebvre once defined "heterotopia" as a space in which something radically different could happen that could survive for a while before being reabsorbed into the dominant praxis. This is a good description of what happened to the kibbutz, to the recuperated factories in Argentina, to worker-controled collectives like Mondragon. The socialist content gradually dissipates in the face of the dominant social relations. The world of capital is littered with a history of heterotopic anticapitalist experiments of the sort that Lefebvre describes. If they fail, then it is almost invariably because of the breakdown of social relations.

Socialists often dream of changing the physical world in some way: creating more commodities to distribute more equally. But Marx's argument is that changing the social relations is crucial to revolutionary action. What then is the social relation expressed in the value theory? This is absolutely central to what capital and its distinctive value theory is about. It obviously will be a class relation, that between capital and labor. But what invisible threads exist within this class relation? It is important to read the subsequent text in the light of this question.

The "first result" in Marx's investigation is that "capital becomes the process of production through the incorporation of labour into capital; initially, however, it becomes the *material* process of . . . production in general, so that the process of production of capital is not distinct from the material processes of production as such. Its formal character is completely extinguished." What this means is that "the *labour process posited prior to value, as point of departure* . . . is common to all forms of production." But it "here reappears *again within capital,* as a process which proceeds within its substance and forms its content" (304). In other words, the insertion of capital into long-standing labor processes is initially hidden, but later reappears as the form and content of capital begin to take control. The physical character of the labor process, common to all modes of production, may be unchanged, but now it is capital, rather than products and commodities, that is produced under the social conditions of laboring. In addition, the labor process is used by capital to preserve and modify itself.

At this point, we need to address the lengthy footnote on pages 305–6. Here, Marx takes up once more Adam Smith's distinction between productive and unproductive labor. Marx will not here settle the question, but he does advance some tentative ideas. He takes up Smith's dictum that "productive labour is only that which produces capital." He then cites Nassau William Senior concerning the "crazy" situation to which this leads in which "the piano maker is a *productive worker*, but not the *piano player*, although obviously the piano would be absurd without the piano player." Marx accepts that "this is exactly the case. The piano maker reproduces *capital*, the pianist only exchanges his labour for revenue." The paid pianist who entertains an audience certainly produces something, "but that does not make it *productive labour*." Only that labor is productive that "produces capital." The labor that does not do this is "unproductive labour." It is, however, the case that "production [e.g. tobacco] for unproductive consumption" (in which the commodity literally goes up in smoke) is productive. Marx concludes by supporting Malthus's view that productive labor is that which "directly augments his master's wealth." This is all somewhat confusing. Plainly, the promoter who sponsors a piano player to perform in a concert from which the promoter will take most of the profits after paying a fee to the pianist places the piano player in the category of productive laborer. Later in the text, Marx confirms this view (328). "Actors are productive workers, not in so far as they produce a play, but in so far as they increase their employer's wealth." That same piano player performing the same music in the drawing room of a wealthy patron is unproductive. There is also a difference between the piano producer who handcrafts a singular product and a factory in China producing pianos for sale as commodities. Marx is moving toward a definition in which the immaterial social relations shape the definition of productive labor as opposed to the material conditions.

Following the first invisible thread, we see that "as *use value,* labour exists only *for capital* and is itself the use value of capital," while capital appears "as that which reproduces and increases its value, is autonomous exchange value (money)" (305). The workers give up their capacity to create wealth and value to capital in return for exchange-value (money). Their use-value is not available to them. Their exchange-value, like that of any other commodity, is set by supply and demand or "by the cost of production, the amount of objectified labour, by means of which the labouring capacity of the worker has been produced and which he therefore obtains for it, as its equivalent" (306). The value of labor power is fixed by the value of the commodities needed for the reproduction of that labor power at a given standard of living. That value is presupposed. Capital buys labor power "as living labour, as the general productive force of wealth; activity which increases wealth. It is clear, therefore, that the worker cannot become *rich* in this exchange, since . . . he surrenders its *creative power,* like Esau his birthright for a mess of pottage. Rather, he necessarily impoverishes himself . . . because the creative power of his labour establishes itself as the power of capital, as an *alien power* confronting him." The upshot is that "*real* labour, *comes* to confront the worker as an *alien power;* capital, inversely, realizes itself through the *appropriation of alien labour*" (307).

There are some noteworthy things about these formulations. To begin with, the emphasis upon process rather than things is notable, as is his tentative solution to the conundrum of why those who produce the wealth receive a mere mess of pottage for it. Marx also reaffirms the view that the relation between capital and labor is alien on both sides (see 266). The appropriation of the creative powers of labor by capital extends to all those means whereby the productivity of labor might be advanced.

All the progress of civilization, or in other words, every increase in the *powers of social production* . . . in the *productive powers of labour itself*—such as results from science, inventions, division and combination of labour, improved means of communication, creation of the world market, machinery etc.—enriches, not the worker, but rather *capital*; hence it only magnifies again the power dominating over labour; increases only the productive power of capital. Since capital is the antithesis of the worker, this merely increases the *objective power* standing over labour. (308)

Labor creates capital and the capitalist, and it is capital and the capitalist who have the power to dominate labor. The more productive the labor, the greater the power of capital's domination. This is the relevant social relation here. "Labour itself is *productive only* if absorbed into capital, where capital forms the basis of production, and where the capitalist is, therefore in command of production. The productivity of labour becomes a productive force of capital" (308). How to follow up on this invisible thread is the question.

Those who demonstrate that the productive force ascribed to capital is a *displacement*, a *transposition of the productive force* of labour, forget precisely that capital itself is essentially this *displacement, this transposition*, and that wage labour as such presupposes capital, so that, from its standpoint as well, capital is this *transubstantiation*, the necessary process of positing its own powers as *alien* to the worker. Therefore, the demand that wage labour be continued but capital suspended is self-contradictory, self-dissolving. (308–9)

This has not, alas, stopped communist regimes from preserving wage labor while loudly and proudly proclaiming the end of capital. Here is one of the most signal and profound problems facing any move toward socialism. The labor process, which existed prior to capitalism, is now construed as dominated by capital and therefore a vehicle for confirming the primacy of the intertwining social relation between alienated capital and alienated labor. How to liberate the labor process from this now dominant social relation is the problem. This invisible thread clearly needs some further unraveling. Marx attempts to do so by way of the positive commentary, already cited, regarding Say's characterization of the immaterial "essence" versus the material definition of capital.

Capital as "capital in general" does not descend to earth out of an idealist sky. We are, says Marx, "present at the process of its becoming. This dialectical process of its becoming is only the ideal expression of the real movement through which capital comes into being. The later relations are to be regarded as developments coming out of this germ. But it is necessary to establish the specific form in which it is posited at a *certain* point. Otherwise, confusion arises" (310). I suspect Marx is signaling here that capital looks very different in its early stages of "becoming," when the merchant, financial and landed versions of capital played prominent roles. He will later offer commentaries upon the distinctive theoretical formulations that arise—such as the physiocrats supported by landed capital and the mercantilism of the merchants and financiers. What Marx elsewhere refers to as these "antediluvian" forms of capital produced a very different kind of social world from the industrial form that later came to dominate.

From the standpoint of the "formal specificity" of capital in general, "this process is a *process of self-realization*. Self-realization includes preservation of the prior value as well as its multiplication." He continues: "Value enters as subject. Labour is purposeful activity" (311). It works up and transforms materials to create new use-values, use-values for others. At the same time, higher exchange-value (profit) must be created. The fate of the simple commodity in circulation is problematic. It may or may not be realized in money form (312). Its "higher exchange value in circulation cannot originate out of circulation itself, in which . . . only equivalents are exchanged. Therefore, if it comes out of circulation as a higher exchange value, it must have entered into it as such." The contradiction between the constraints of equivalence in the market and the necessity for capital to expand looms.

"Capital as a form consists not of objects of labour and labour, but rather of values, and still, more precisely, of prices." Marx once more fails to liberate the concept of value from exchange-values (prices). "The fact that its value-elements have various substances in common during the production process does not affect their character as values; they are not changed thereby. If, out of the form of unrest—of the process—at the end of the process, they again condense themselves into a resting, objective form, in the product, then this, too, is merely a change of the material in relation to value and does not alter the latter" (312). The process of value circulation proceeds through the transformation of things (raw materials, commodities, labor processes, money). "True, the substances as such have been destroyed, but they have not been made into nothing, but rather into a substance with another form." But what, exactly, is this "substance"? To identify the "substance" of value is the challenge. The commodity disappears, but its value is preserved in money form. "The value of the product can therefore only = the sum of the values which were materialized in the specific material elements of the process, i.e. raw material, instrument of labour . . . and labour itself" (312). In conventional Marxist notation, this would amount to C (the value of the raw material and means of production input) + V (the value of the labor power input). All of these material elements are used up (or partially so with respect to the instruments of labor) in the labor process even as the value in motion is preserved.

The different modes in which the values existed [prior to production] were a pure semblance; value itself formed the constantly self-identical essence within their disappearance. Regarded as a value, the product has in this respect not become *product* but rather remained identical, unchanged value, which merely exists in a different mode, which is, however, irrelevant to it and which can be exchanged for money . . . The price of the product is equal to these costs of production, i.e. = to the sum of

the prices of the commodities consumed in the production
process [C+V].

In other words "the production process in its material aspect has
been irrelevant to value; that value has remained identical with
itself and has merely taken on another mode of existence, become
materialized in another substance and form (the form of the
substance is irrelevant to the economic form, to value as such)"
(313). This is an important step in the argument. Marx here recognizes that value flows through the circulation process taking on
different material forms, thus sustaining its own reproduction.
Marx furthermore recognizes that value seemingly has some independent form or "substance." The definition of capital as value in
motion is in formation. But the content (substance) of value
remains opaque.

It is therefore important to recall that capital is centered on
value, and that value is immaterial but objective. Value is the invisible thread which maintains itself throughout the whole circulation process, though it is still the case that Marx is conceptualizing
the achievement of value in exchange-value form. Value assumes
the commodity form; then the production form; then the produced
commodity form; before finally returning to the money form from
whence it came. But although value assumes these different material guises, it is itself indifferent to any of them.

If exchange cannot create value, then the production process
has not only to create new value, but also to preserve the value that
already exists. Marx's formulation is constant capital plus variable
capital, C+V; the value of the raw materials and means of production plus the value of labor power. Those values have to be
preserved, even though the produced commodity, which is for a
time the bearer of those exchange-values, ultimately disappears
from circulation because it is eaten or used up or whatever. So, the
use-value is consumed, but the value is maintained. A hamburger
has a value, but when it is eaten it is the use-value, not the value,
that is consumed.

We cannot understand this dynamic without understanding the circulation process, because what the circulation process does is to take capital from the production process, into the commodity form, which is then taken to market, where it is sold for money. After it is sold for the money, the commodity drops out of circulation, unless it is one of those commodities that comes back into production (e.g., the machinery to be used in productive consumption). Marx then sets out the first of innumerable (and somewhat tedious) arithmetic examples (calculated in thalers, a silver currency common in German states at that time), of what a capitalist production schema looks like on the ground. "Original capital = 100 (e.g. raw material = 50; labour = 40; instrument = 10) + 5% interest + 5% profit." The interest and the profit constitute a "surplus value," which has yet to be explained (315). Marx first flirts with the idea that the surplus-value might represent the "labour of superintendence" of capital. He rejects this on the grounds that capital entails being able to live "as a not-worker" (317). He next takes up the idea that it is compensation for "the risks of production." These risks, Marx concedes, are real enough. For example, "the constantly ongoing devaluation of capital, resulting from the increase in the force of production, has to be compensated." Such devaluations (e.g., from technological obsolescence) will be very important to the theory later on but are here summarily dismissed.

THE ORIGINS OF SURPLUS-VALUE

Having cleared the decks, Marx sets out to explain where the surplus-value might come from, of how capital "can create values greater than those with which it began" (318). We are finally approaching the mystery of surplus-value production.

Marx first examines the question of interest. What happens when a capitalist borrows money and pays interest? Should that not be regarded as "a direct production cost"? For this to happen requires, however, that capital itself becomes a commodity, albeit a commodity "specifically distinct from all other commodities" (318). Capital surpluses seeking interest-bearing opportunities must already exist, and capital itself has already become commodified on capital's own terms. The use-value of capital as a commodity (usually in money form) is that it can be deployed to produce surplus-value. But interest derives from surplus-value already produced. As such, it cannot explain where surplus-value comes from. Perhaps the surplus-value can be imported from outside by robbery or some other form of appropriation? Marx thus briefly takes up the question of original or primitive accumulation (319). There are various ways, legal and illegal, that the initial capital can come into being: thievery, robbery, cheating, extortion and the like, and various ways that labor can be separated from the land as the primary means of production: enclosure, evictions, dispossession and the like. While these were all important in the origins and history of capital, they cannot, in Marx's view, sustain the circulation and continuous expansion of capital in the long run, even if what I like to call "accumulation by dispossession" remains an important feature of capital until today (something that Marx did not envisage but did not rule out either).

Having briefly surveyed and rejected the most prominent ideas among the political economists for explaining where profit comes from, Marx finally gets around to stating his own distinctive theory of surplus-value. Unfortunately, Marx surrounds his theoretical breakthrough with so many caveats and elucidations that it is hard to distinguish the core of his argument. He states:

> *The surplus value which capital has at the end of the production process*—a surplus value which, as a higher price of the product, is realized only in circulation, but, like all prices, is realized in it by already being ideally *presupposed* to it, determined before they enter into it—signifies, expressed in accord with the general concept of exchange value, that the labour time objectified in the product—or amount of labour (expressed passively, the

magnitude of labour appears as an amount of space; but expressed in motion, it is measurable only in time)—is greater than that which is present in the original components of capital. This, in turn, is possible only if the labour objectified in the price of labour is smaller than the living labour time purchased with it. (321)

My first response to reading this is to complain about the total disregard for trying to communicate the essence of his most signal concept—that of surplus-value—to any kind of public. I then have to remember that this is Marx talking to himself. But behind the confusing presentation lies an important conceptual point. The exchange of labor capacity with capital is a very special kind of exchange. In the standard form, the participants part company after the exchange and may never see each other again. With capital and labor, however, the bonds—the invisible threads—continue to play a role as each side completes itself in their relation to their other.

Simplifying (which Marx can on occasion do brilliantly, unlike in his presentation here), capital purchases labor power in the market at an (exchange-) value fixed by the (exchange-) value of the commodities needed to reproduce the laborer and her dependents at a given standard of living. This purchase does not violate in any way the equality of exchange principle that supposedly regulates market exchange. The capitalist puts the laborer to work in a labor process that creates (exchange) value and does so in such a way as to ensure that the (exchange) value that labor produces in commodity form is greater than the (exchange) value of the labor power purchased as a commodity. The profit (surplus-value) is realized by a sale in the market that entails the producer proposing an "ideal" sale price, which may (or may not) be accepted by the purchaser in practice, but we can assume that the commodity exchanges at its value (devaluation is ruled out). The core feature in this account is the difference between the (exchange-) value that labor receives and the (exchange-) value that labor creates (and which is realized in the market). I have spelled this out in (exchange-) value terms. This works out just as well as the value formulation that Marx deploys in *Capital*.

Marx then modifies his initial arithmetic formulation of the production process, which focused on C+V, to add in the surplus (exchange-) value, S. which labor produces free for capital (321). Henceforth, the analysis will be based on C+V+S.

In commenting on this formulation, Marx notes that "if the capitalist has paid the worker a price = one working day, and the worker's working day adds only one working day to the raw material and the instrument, then the capitalist would merely have exchanged exchange value in one form for exchange value in another. He would not have acted as capital" (321–2). Some economists actually embrace this possibility to show that capital and worker exist as a partnership, but Marx shows that in such a situation the capitalist's capital would soon be "eaten up" and the workers would inherit the earth. "If one day's work were necessary in order to keep one worker alive for one day, then capital would not exist . . . If, however, only half a working day is necessary in order to keep one worker alive one whole day, then the surplus value . . . is self-evident" (324). Marx therefore concludes that "the only thing that can make him into a capitalist is not exchange, but rather a process through which he obtains *objectified labour time*, i.e. *value*, without exchange. Half the working day costs capital nothing; it thus obtains a value for which it has given no equivalent." Surplus-value can never be created in circulation, through acts of exchange. "It has to arise from the production process itself" (324).

"The great historic quality of capital is to create this *surplus labour*, superfluous labour from the standpoint of mere use-value, mere subsistence; and its historic destiny is fulfilled as soon as, on one side, there has been such a development of needs that surplus labour above and beyond necessity has itself become a general need arising out of individual needs themselves" (325). This is the sort of commentary that makes the *Grundrisse* so surprising and enriching. The theory of surplus-value is contingent upon the creation and production of new wants, needs and desires, as we will later see (see also Figure 2). The cultural shifts implied in this formulation are staggering both in content and form. But it also implies on the other side, "the severe discipline of capital, acting on succeeding generations" to produce "general industriousness as the general property of the new species" (325). This new form of society cannot be created or survive without the production of new kinds of human beings and a new kind of worker. This is the kind of finding that Gramsci makes so central in his essay "Americanism and Fordism."[1] Finally, "the development of the productive powers of labour, which capital incessantly whips onward with its unlimited mania for wealth" produces a stage of society in which "the possession and preservation of general wealth require a lesser labour time of society as a whole, and where the labouring society relates scientifically to the process of its progressive reproduction ... in a constantly greater abundance." The mix of teleological vision and of technological utopianism, from the perspective of 1858, is stunning, particularly when we look back from where we are now. Teleological and utopian it may be, but it is astonishingly close to our contemporary reality, more than a century and a half later.

> Capital's ceaseless striving toward the general form of wealth drives labour beyond the limits of its natural paltriness, and thus creates the material elements for the development of the rich individuality, which is as all-sided in its production as in its consumption, and whose labour also therefore appears no longer as labour, but as the full development of activity itself, in which natural necessity in its direct form has disappeared; because a historically created need is taking the place of a natural one. This is why capital is productive; i.e., an essential relation for the development of the social productive forces. It ceases to exist as such only where the development of these

---

1 In Antonio Gramsci, *Selections from the Prison Notebooks*, trans. Quintin Hoare and Geoffrey Nowell-Smith (London: Lawrence & Wishart, 1971), 558–622.

productive forces themselves encounters its barrier in capital itself. (325)

Present all of this to any far-seeing Silicon Valley entrepreneur and he or she will get both the picture and the argument directly, though the solutions may well be substantially different. But Marx for his part adds a strange coda. He appends to this broadly positive but problematic account an equally problematic report in *The Times* of 1857 of "the cry of outrage" from a West Indian plantation owner who was requesting the reintroduction of slavery on the following grounds. The free blacks of Jamaica

> content themselves with producing only what is strictly necessary for their own consumption ... and regard loafing (indulgence and idleness) as the real luxury good ... [They] do not care a damn for the sugar and the fixed capital invested in the plantations, but rather observe the planters' impending bankruptcy with an ironic grin of malicious pleasure ... They have ceased to be slaves, but not in order to become wage labourers, but, instead, self-sustaining peasants working for their own consumption. As far as they are concerned, capital does not exist as capital, because autonomous wealth as such can exist only either on the basis of *direct* forced labour, slavery, or *indirect* forced labour, *wage labour*. Wealth confronts direct forced labour not as capital, but rather as a *relation of domination*; thus the relation of domination is the only thing reproduced on this basis, for which wealth itself has value only as gratification, not as wealth itself, and which can therefore never create *general industriousness*. (326)

Marx promises to write about this later, but I cannot say whether he ever did, nor can I say with any certainty what he might have said. I can speculate on one angle. Marx is not critical of industriousness per se. But he is scathing in his criticism of industriousness when presented as a form of bourgeois virtue visited upon the working classes for the sole benefit of capital. He is also a strong advocate for free time ("loafing") as the greatest form of wealth to which humanity might aspire. His son-in-law Paul Lafargue wrote a compelling tract on *The Right to Be Lazy* (echoed in Bertrand Russell's famous piece "In Praise of Idleness").[1] Capital is the enemy of free time and the quest for free time is a serious threat to capital. The West Indian plantation owner is plainly terrified of those who seek it or possess it. Industriousness, Marx seems to say, is only worth it if it delivers free time. But this is pure speculation on my part.

MARX ON HIS PRECURSORS

So back to the main topic, which is Marx's theory of surplus-value. Marx searches among his precursors to see how close they came to identifying where surplus-value (profit) might come from. Marx was curious as to why Ricardo in particular failed to see the importance of surplus-value as Marx understands it. To be sure, Ricardo "well understands that the creation of surplus value is the presupposition of capital" (326), but the only systematic source he saw for its expansion lay outside of capital circulation in population growth (327). The internal mechanisms of surplus-value production within the circulation of capital eluded him.

The Physiocrats—an influential eighteenth-century school of French economists—likewise had difficulty "grasping capital, the self-realization of value, hence the surplus value created by capital in the act of production." Marx clearly has a soft-spot for the Physiocrats. He appreciates that they were the first school of economists to attempt a systematic theorization of what capital might be about, and the questions they posed were foundational for all later work. "They are the fathers of modern economics" and "they also understand that the creation of surplus value by wage labour is the self-realization . . . of capital" (328). They were understandably misled, however, by their absorption in the concrete conditions of

---

1   Paul Lafargue, *The Right of Be Lazy* (New York: Charles Kerr, 1883).

production of their time. They held that "only that labour can be productive which takes place ... where the natural force of the instrument of labour tangibly permits the labourer to produce more value than he consumes. Surplus value therefore does not arise from labour as such, but rather from the natural forces which labour uses and conducts—agriculture." In the agricultural sphere "human labour has only to conduct the chemical processes ... and in part also to promote them mechanically ... in order to obtain the surplus" (329). In the period when the Physiocratic view was strongest, most manufacturing activity was conducted in small workshops. The factory system did not yet exist. And the small workshops were largely attached to meeting the consumption desires of the aristocracy. If you visit the Château in Versailles, you will see the kinds of beautiful things they made. This kind of labor was considered parasitic by the Physiocrats. Saint-Simon, a utopian socialist who Marx held in high regard, later changed that. He saw capitalist entrepreneurs and their workers as jointly defining the productive sector against the parasitism of the landed aristocracy, the church and the state. Marx clearly appreciated the class analysis for what it was in both cases. He also appreciated some of their analytical techniques. One of the Physiocratic theorists, Quesnay, produced a "tableau économique" to depict the circulation of values in society as a whole. Marx was inspired by it and adapted it in his highly innovative study of capital's reproduction schemas in Volume II of *Capital*.

Adam Smith recognized that labor was "in principle the source of value, likewise of wealth, but actually labour too posits surplus value only in so far as in the division of labour the surplus appears as just as much a gift of nature, a natural force of society, as the soil with the Physiocrats." While Marx will deny that the surplus-value is attributable to the gifts of nature, the question of how to incorporate "gifts of nature" into the analysis is here left unanswered (330). Adam Smith ends up with a tautological account in which the surplus-value is presupposed "in the clumsiest fashion. The capitalist does not want to give the use of his capital for nothing; the landowner, similarly, does not want to give land and soil over to production for nothing. They want something in return," profit and rent. But these "are only *deductions* from wages, arbitrarily wrested by force in the historical process by capital and landed property, and justified *by law*, not economically" (330). In Marx's view, "wages are actually the *only economically* justifiable because necessary element of production costs." Profit and rent are facts of distribution. Smith, by contrast, vacillates on the theory of value to present it on occasion as an addition of wages, profit and ground rent (thus matching the categories of land, labor and capital so familiar to conventional economics).

"The exact development of the concept of capital," Marx concludes, "[is] necessary, since it [is] the fundamental concept of modern economics, just as capital itself . . . [is] the foundation of bourgeois society." Only when we are armed with this, can we hope to "bring out all the contradictions of bourgeois production, as well as the boundary where it drives beyond itself" (331).

But Marx, having tracked down the origin of surplus-value, exhibits a certain nervousness that this may be viewed as "the exact development of the concept of capital." He fades back into his more dialectical and relational mode in the subsequent passage. "Bourgeois wealth, is always expressed to the highest power as exchange value, where it is posited as *mediator*, as the mediation of the extremes of exchange and use value themselves." This assertion would be easier to understand if the first "exchange value" was replaced by "value" in its *Capital* meaning. It would then position "value" as a mediator between use-value and exchange-value. "This intermediary situation always appears as the *economic* relation in its completeness, because it comprises the opposed poles . . . because the movement, or the relation, which *originally* appears as mediatory between the extremes necessarily develops dialectically to where it appears as mediation with itself, as the subject for whom the extremes are merely its moments." Thus "does industrial capital appear as producer as against the merchant, who appears as circulation . . . At the same time, mercantile capital is itself in turn the mediator between production (industrial capital) and circulation (the consuming public) or between exchange value and use value" (332). He then continues: "Similarly within commerce itself: the wholesaler as mediator between manufacture and retailer, or between manufacture and agriculturalist, or between different manufactures … And in turn, in the same way, the commodity brokers as against the wholesalers. Then the banker as against the industrialists and merchants; the joint-stock company as against simple production; the financier as mediator between the state and bourgeois society." I cite this longish passage to illustrate how Marx, as he probes more deeply into capital's diversified and complex ecosystemic totality, cannot be squeezed into any simple conceptual definition of capital. It is, in short, all over the place in the multiple connotations of that phrase. It cannot be pinned down. Yet Marx is prepared to assert that "*capital* is *direct unity* of product and money or, better, production and circulation … and its development consists of positing and suspending itself as this unity" which "at first appears in capital as something *simple*," even as it is constantly destabilizing itself and assuming different guises (332–3). Another way of putting this is to say that capital is a flow coursing through different qualitative moments while quantitatively reproducing and growing itself.

RELATIVE SURPLUS-VALUE

Marx then works through arithmetic examples of how surplus-value production works and discovers something of great significance. If it takes half a day for the laborer to produce the value equivalent to that of the commodities required for her own reproduction, then the impact of increasing the productivity of labor would be to reduce the hours of necessary labor needed to produce the use-values required (to, say, a quarter of the working day), and so increase the hours of surplus-value production for the benefit of capital. "The increased productive force of his labour, to the extent it is a shortening of the time required to replace the labour objectified in him (for use value, subsistence), appears as a lengthening of the time he works for the realization of capital" (335). The whole process derives from the simple fact that driving the value of labor power down produces more surplus-value for capital. Clearly, the value of labor-power is attached to a certain length of the working day (absolute surplus-value), which can itself be extended to yield more surplus-value for capital. The capitalist has a compelling interest in finding ways to work the laborer harder, over longer hours, and at lower wages. Maximizing the production and appropriation of surplus-value is capital's reason for being.

Marx here discovers the simple version of the principle of relative surplus-value that dominates the argument in Volume I of *Capital*. As wage goods get cheaper, thanks to the rising productivity of labor, so the value of labor power declines, leaving more surplus-value for capital. This helps explain something about the persona of the capitalist:

> As representative of the general form of wealth—money—capital is the endless and limitless drive to go beyond its limiting barrier. Every boundary is and has to be a barrier for it. Else it would cease to be capital . . . If ever it perceived a certain boundary not as a barrier, but became comfortable within it as a boundary, it would itself have declined from exchange value to use value, from the general form of wealth to a specific, substantial mode of the same. Capital as such creates a specific surplus value because it cannot create an infinite one all at once; but it is the constant movement to create more of the same. The quantitative boundary of the surplus value appears to it as a mere natural barrier, as a necessity which it constantly tries to violate and beyond which it constantly seeks to go. (334–5)

This dynamic of endless accumulation accompanied by an ever-rising productivity of labor is one of the key features that defines capital's nature. This is the source of major contradictions which have grown and intensified rather than lessened over time.

In working through various arithmetic representations over the many pages that follow, Marx does recognize some internal checks upon the impact of transformations in the productive forces upon surplus-value production. "The larger the surplus value of capital *before the increase of productive force* . . . or, the smaller the fractional part of the working day which forms the equivalent of the worker . . . the smaller is the increase in surplus value which capital obtains from the increase of productive force" (340). He also had already noted that the impacts of such increases varied a great deal from country to country and from sector to sector, depending (to use a later formulation) on the value composition of capital (the ratio of C to V). Its internal barrier "always remains the relation between the fractional part of the day that expresses *necessary labour*, and the entire working day."

The next twenty pages or so of text (340–64) are taken up for the most part with exploring the implications of different arithmetic configurations of the C+V+S formulation. Since I find this part of the text tedious and not very enlightening, I propose to skip most of it, with the exception of the following brilliant, felicitous phrase which breaks up the tedium: "Labour," Marx asserts, "is the living, form-giving fire." This is what anchors the production of surplus-value no matter under what conditions. This form-giving fire not only produces new value but it also preserves and reanimates pre-existing values as a free gift to capital along with the surplus labor for which capital pays nothing. Yet it is also "the transitoriness of things, their temporality, as their formation by living time. In the simple production process—leaving aside the realization process—the transitoriness of the forms of things is used to posit their usefulness" (361).

In invoking the "transitoriness of things," Marx is introducing a subject of considerable moment in our contemporary world. It is living labor which maintains the value of the previous labor materialized in the component parts of capital used up in the production process. Living labor preserves the previously existing value of capital. "This preserving force of labour therefore appears as the self-preserving force of capital . . . [It] *makes instrument and material in the production process* into the body of its soul and thereby resurrects them from the dead" (364). This preservation does not entail any increase in the amount of labor. The preservation of the value of past labor is something that occurs on the side. It is a free gift that the laborer gives to capital in addition to creating surplus-value (365).

Capital, Marx insists, is not natural. But it has a nature driven by its internalized abstractions. This is the phantom-like objectivity which constitutes its driving force, and the result is endless expansion and limitless accumulation, to which the planet has to accommodate, come what may. While there are clear limits and inhibitors to the endless accumulation of production capacity and commodity output, there are no limits to monetary expansions. The expansion of the money supply and of credit has been phenomenal in recent times. The total global debt (personal, corporate and state) now amounts to $85,000 for every woman, man and child on planet earth and there is no concern for its redemption. For every debt there is, of course, a credit. Are you a net creditor or a net debtor? There used to be a time when policymakers worried about the debt-to-GDP ratio. If a country went above 70 or 80 percent, that was considered to be really dangerous. The IMF disciplined Mexico and a whole raft of other countries in the 1980s because they had too much debt relative to their GDP. The global debt right now in relationship to global GDP is something like 230 or 240 percent. And this is what we call leaping over barriers. The Federal Reserve Bank of St. Louis is an excellent source of data on matters of this sort. Graphs of indebtedness and world money supply indicate exponential growth of indebtedness and the money supply over the last half-century.

This is, presumably, the kind of "leaping over barriers" that Marx has in mind. It is in the nature of capital, Marx seems to be saying in 1858, to do things of this sort. This is what the system, driven by abstractions, "naturally" does. Toward the end of the section we are here examining, Marx makes another trenchant but somewhat scary observation:

> *Money*, then, in so far as it now already *in itself* exists as capital, is therefore simply *a claim on future* (new) labour. It exists, objectively, merely as *money*. Surplus value, the new growth of *objectified labour*, to the extent that it exists for itself, is *money*; but now, it is money which *in itself* is already capital; and, as such, it is a *claim on new labour*. Here, capital already no longer enters into relation with ongoing labour, but with future labour. And it no longer appears ... as money, which is merely the abstract form of general wealth, but as a claim on the real possibility of general wealth—labour capacity, and more precisely, *labour capacity in the process of becoming*... Like the creditor of the state, every capitalist with his newly gained value possesses a claim on future labour, and, by means of the appropriation of ongoing labour has already at the same time appropriated future labour. (367)

The invisible thread that Marx is following here is that which binds capital to labor in and around the labor process. And to the degree that that invisible thread, that phantom-like objectivity, continues and strengthens, so it becomes dominant and foundational within capital's totality. But labor is dominated by capital, even though labor creates capital. In a sense, labor is therefore a victim of its own creation. The Frankenstein myth has a real basis, and the horrors it produces are daily visible in the factories of the world. Marx wants working people to understand the origins of their alienations and their discontents. He wants them to understand their role in the making of capital, their creative force in this construction. Withdraw your labor and capital dies. The problem is that, if you cease to labor, in the long run you are dead as well.

5

Production and Realization
Pages 373–458

It useful when reading Marx to have a cognitive map of where we have been and where we might go. In his "Introduction," Marx examines how bourgeois political economy handles relations between production, distribution, exchange, consumption, realization and the like within the economy. Marx suggests that classical political economy misses something because it does not have a concept of totality. It views these categories as independent and autonomous entities that interact with each other. Marx instead proposes a concept of the totality and its moments in order to understand the internal relations between production, realization, distribution, etc. We are encouraged to believe that a better understanding of capital might lie through a study of capital as a continuous process—a flow—within a totality constituted by different moments connected by a variety of intersecting and mutually supportive circulation processes.

The totality is not simply an idea. But we need to get a proper representation of it. Marx's mission is to try to represent it as correctly as possible in the realm of ideas. However, the totality is not created by ideas. Ideas do not get imposed upon it. The totality is something that grows. As it grows, the dominant conception of it may become a material force affecting its evolution. The relation between the totality and the idea of it is dialectical rather than monocausal. If, for example, an idea takes hold that the totality should be constructed according to principles of free trade, then the economic system is affected if not shaped accordingly. The ruling ideas of a ruling class are therefore important. In seeking to understand its evolution on the ground (which is where the impact of any dominant idea of it has to be felt), Marx, in effect, appeals to the analogy of an organic and dynamic ecosystem. Such a totality has many different facets (e.g., divisions of labor and class factions) interacting within it. It is also a historical product in constant evolution. We need to come to terms with the historical process that brings the totality into being, to understand how the moments (along with the idea of it) interact with each other and thereby reshape it and how it evolves over time and space. It then follows that how the totality is represented in the world of thought must also be in continuous evolution. We have to keep pace in the realm of ideas with what is happening on the ground. This is historical materialism in action.

Marx begins this task with considerations concerning money, which leads him back into his obsessive critique of Proudhon. His aim is to refute the idea that the totality could go socialist by revolutionizing the monetary system. Marx spends a lot of time disabusing us of that "crazy" idea. In the process, he does something significant. There are, he concedes, many roles that money can perform in the social process. But money used as capital is a very specific role and an aspect of the totality that requires close study. We need to look at the circulation of money as capital (money capital).

This leads Marx into the first and most obvious definition of capital as money being used to make more money. Not all money is capital, but capital is money used in a certain way. It is the use that defines capital and not its being money. Capital is not, as classical political economy typically construed it, a "thing" (a distinctive factor of production) introduced into the labor process.

Capital, says Marx, is a process and not a thing. It is a process in which the activities of production in the workplace and circulation in the market are taken together (see Figure 2). This process is continuous. But it takes the form of a spiral rather than a cycle. The spiral takes over because if capital is money that is used to make more money, then the requirement that there be "more" money capital at the end of the day than at the beginning means the totality has to be in a state of continuous and endless expansion in order to survive.

So capital is defined as a process, which is in continuous expansion, dedicated to endless accumulation. This endlessness is attached to the desire of capitalists to accumulate more and more wealth. There is a subjective, psychological aspect to this, which Marx touches upon. More and more money is converted into money capital and launched into circulation to make more money. But the requirement of continuous expansion poses a very serious problem. The market, if it is to conform to its rules of formation, is characterized by an exchange of equivalents. How can a system which is based on equivalence of exchange actually expand and grow? Where does the growth come from? The answer resides in the theory of surplus-value, which focusses on production, not circulation in the market.

The opening to Notebook IV of the *Grundrisse* seeks to reassure us that the "highly irksome" calculations that dominated the previous forty pages "will not delay us further" (373). Marx then plunges into a dozen or so pages of even more irksome calculations. The intent, it seems, is to investigate in arithmetical form the relations between surplus-value and surplus labor time, the impact of technological changes on the rate of surplus-value, the distinction between absolute and relative surplus-value, and finally to append a few comments on the changing rate of profit (which will be featured later). "It is now time to finish," he announces on page 386, "with the question of the value resulting from the growth of the productive forces." We need to return, he writes, "to the point where we last broke off" (which was page 353). I propose, therefore, to bracket off pages 353 to 387 as a diversion from the main argument and not a particularly enlightening one at that, though Marx certainly consolidates his (and potentially our) understandings of the topics listed above.

Marx returns to his central theme with the observation that "an increase in productivity increases the *surplus value*, although it does not increase the absolute amount of exchange values" (387). This is a seemingly obvious point that popular understandings get wrong. A million workers working ten hours a day generate a certain amount of value. If the productivity of those workers doubles, then the total value produced is not affected. The total value only increases when either the number of workers or the hours worked increases. With increasing productivity, the mass of the individual items (use-values) produced doubles and the value of each individual item is halved. If the value of the use-values required to reproduce labor power at a given standard of living is cut in half, then the value of labor power can be cut in half (presuming the standard of living in use-value terms remains constant). This releases more labor time for the production of surplus-value. While Marx does not make the point, the implication is that, under conditions of strong technological change, the surplus-value appropriated by capital can be rising rapidly at the same time that the material standard of living (measured in use-values) of the workers may be rising. Since 1850, there have been many periods and places where workers and capital have shared in the benefits of rising productivity. This has been a potent source historically for garnering popular acceptance or even active support for capitalism on the part of some segments of the working class. If some affluent workers live in a suburban house with a car in the driveway and a house full of household gadgets, then why militate for socialism? The neoliberal politics instituted after 1980 stands out, however, for being a general period in which most workers have received little or no benefit from significant technological change. The benefits have mainly accrued to capital or the top 1 percent. Profits to capital have soared as the share of labor in national income has declined dramatically in almost all advanced capitalist countries, even as the standard of living of labor (as measured in use-values, e.g., household and electronic gadgets) has risen somewhat.

Marx actually returns to his arithmetic mode for several pages in order to prove that "an increase in the productivity of labour means nothing more than that the same capital creates the same value with less labour, or that less labour creates the same product with less capital. That less necessary labour produces more surplus labour" (388). The question of time allocation within production emerges step by step, leading Marx to the following conclusion: "Just as capital on one side creates surplus labour, surplus labour is at the same time equally the presupposition of the existence of capital. The whole development of wealth rests on the creation of disposable time" (398). The idea that wealth is measured in disposable time as opposed to monetary or some other form of power is important. It implies that a hallmark of socialism is a proper distribution of wealth measured as disposable time. Under the regime of capital, disposable time is converted into surplus labor time. This thought seems to galvanize Marx to abandon the dull and restrictive perspective of accountancy that has dominated the last fifty or so pages and to take on the aura of an inspirational and visionary interpreter of capital's past, present and future history. He notes, to start with, that the relation between necessary and superfluous labor time changes historically and varies with the form of development. Initially, only surpluses were exchanged. Wants and needs were also few, so necessary labor time was limited. But with capital, the surrender of surplus labor time became mandatory for access to the necessary labor time that allowed for the reproduction of the laborer. What is necessary also changes, as we shall see, with the development of capital.

Marx then shows that it is a law or tendency of capital "to create as much labour as possible; just as it is equally its tendency to reduce necessary labour to a minimum. It is therefore equally a tendency of capital to increase the labouring population, as well as constantly to posit a part of it as surplus population" (399). Here the relation between population growth and the accumulation of capital as well as the role of a relative surplus population (or industrial reserve army, as it is termed in *Capital*) are placed on the agenda. "It is equally a tendency of capital to make human labour (relatively) superfluous, so as to drive it, as human labour, towards infinity." What exactly this might mean is unclear. But if "value is nothing but objectified labour" and surplus labor is objectified labor beyond that required for necessary labor, then capital has to produce more and more surplus, and this it can only do if it multiplies the number of laborers employed. The other tactic focuses on the working day. "But the working day—time itself regarded as space—is *many working days alongside one another.*" The more laborers are brought together the more surplus can be extracted. "This is why capital solicits the increase of population . . . The increase of population is a *natural force* of labour, for which nothing is paid" (399–400). It is also the case that, with the decline in necessary labor, the cost of the reproduction of labor power declines (which may explain the decline of the wage share in national income already noted). "Hence the tendency of capital simultaneously to increase the *labouring population* as well as to reduce constantly its *necessary* part (constantly to posit a part of it as reserve). And the increase of population itself the chief means for reducing the necessary part" (400–1).

Marx does not too often venture into the demographic aspects of capital accumulation, but when he does so he makes clear that it is both important and worthy of serious critical discussion. "Here already lie, then, all the contradictions which modern population theory expresses as such, but does not grasp" (401). In Marx's time, Malthus was the dominant figure in population theory, and he infuriated Marx with his insistence that poverty was a product of overpopulation due to the proclivity of the poor to reproduce. Marx shows convincingly that it is a product of capital no matter what the state of reproduction. The implication is not that demographic conditions have no relevance (indeed, increase of population is a necessity for reasons already stated), but that capital makes use of (and even promotes) demographic conditions in ways advantageous to surplus-value extraction and formation of an industrial reserve army. It is striking in our own neoliberal times, for example, that the global wage labor force has grown from 2 billion to 3 billion while the surplus-value has been captured by a smaller and smaller number of capitalists. During this time, the figure of the disposable and precarious low-paid laborer has come to dominate on the world stage.

Clearly, there is much more to be said about demographic conditions than Marx advances. In the 1960s, for example, governments in the advanced capitalist countries responded to labor shortages and rising working-class power by sponsoring immigration. The Germans turned to Turkey, the French to North Africa, the Swedes to Yugoslavia and the British to their former colonies, and the USA liberalized its immigration policies in 1965 to abolish European-oriented immigration quotas in favor of worldwide recruitment of both skilled and unskilled labor. Increasing (white) working-class resentment of immigration was one long-lasting consequence. In France, for example, some members of the Communist Party migrated to support of the National Front because of immigration policies. And after 1980, China entered dramatically into the field of low-wage, labor-intensive production, in which its massive labor surpluses were critical for surplus-value production compared to those countries, such as Japan and Italy, where problems of zero population growth, an aging population and hostility to immigration hindered capital accumulation. China's one-child population policy, instituted in 1980, has now produced problems of shrinking labor supply and an aging population, to which China has responded by (ineffectively) dropping the one-child policy and shifting emphasis from labor-intensive to capital-intensive production.

These issues are felt even at the household level. My grandmother, daughter of an agricultural laborer and a strong supporter of the Labour Party, argued that the working-class family should have no more than one child. To have more would be to breed one's own competition (what Marx calls a free gift to capital). I was a second child (an accident!). My grandmother was furious, called my mother "a dirty little slut" and totally boycotted us for ten years. Ironically, she and I became close allies thereafter, and I learned a lot politically from her. When I heard about the one-child policy in China I fancied the Communist Party had been talking with my grandmother, even though their rationale was totally different! In any case, it is hard to analyze contemporary economic conditions and politics (particularly with respect to immigration) without careful consideration of the gaping contradictions arising from the relation between demographics and capital. The fact that some fifty or more countries in the world now have population growth rates close to, if not below, zero is highly significant.

In Marx's time, there was, however, a more pressing problem. In a footnote, he notes that "the creation of surplus labour on the one side corresponds to the creation of minus-labour, relative idleness (or *not-productive* labour at best)." A whole army of workers "live not from capital but from revenue." Marx is rather contemptuous of this "service class" constituted by "paupers, flunkeys and lickspittles" along with "a whole train of retainers." It contrasts with his representations of the working class proper. But the existence of disposable time also permits the "creation of time for the production of science, art etc." The development of wealth exists at the intersection between the not-labor largely required for control over labor and the surplus labor actively engaged in the production of surplus-value. For Marx, however, only industrial labor matters. Which leads him to evoke ironically Malthus's "demand for surplus idlers, consuming without producing, or the necessity of waste, luxury and lavish spending etc." (401–2). This is, interestingly, a precursor to the analysis that follows.

Marx now turns his attention to the relation between the production and realization of values and surplus-values. This is, I think, one of the more crucial arguments advanced in the

Grundrisse, and I shall be at some pains to emphasize it for reasons that will soon become apparent.

"We have now seen how, in the realization process, capital has (1) maintained its value by means of exchange . . . with living labour; (2) increased, created a surplus value. There now appears, as the result of this unity of the process of production and the process of realization, the product of the process, i.e. capital itself, emerging as product from the process whose presupposition it was" (401–2). I take this to say that capital is itself the product of the coming together—the unity—of processes of production and realization in the realms of both production and the market. This is in itself an important claim that will subsequently be built upon. The commodity that emerges from production, whose value only exists ideally in the form of an asking price, has "to realize itself" in "the exchange process" as value in money form. Hence (3) "Looked at precisely . . . the *realization process* of capital—and money becomes capital only through the realization process— appears at the same time as its *devaluation process,* its demonetization" (402). This seems to throw the monkey wrench of devaluation into the whole process of circulation and accumulation of capital. But Marx pulls back from any analysis of "the constant devaluation of existing capital" on the grounds that "it does not belong here." Instead, "the *devaluation* being dealt with here is this, that capital has made the transition from the form of money into the form of a *commodity* . . . which has a certain price, which is to be realized" in the market.

> In its money form it existed as *value.* It now *exists* as product, and only ideally as a price; but not as *value* as such. In order to *realize* itself . . . it would first have to make the transition from the form of money into that of use values . . . but it would thereby lose the *form* of value; and it now has to enter anew into circulation in order to posit this form of general wealth anew. (403)

Marx is simply saying that in the transition from M–C (production) to C–M, value (which Marx associates with exchange-value) gets hidden except when it can be tangibly measured in money form, which is at the beginning and end of this sequence. This commentary derives in part from Marx's continuing persistence in equating value with exchange-value (the latter being firmly rooted in the money form).

REALIZATION AND DEVALUATION

"The capitalist now enters the process of circulation not simply as one engaged in exchange, but as *producer*, and the others engaged in exchange are, relative to him, *consumers*. They must exchange money in order to obtain his commodity for their consumption, while he exchanges his product to obtain their money" (403). Suppose this process breaks down: "then the capitalist's money has been transformed into a worthless product, and has not only not gained a new value, but also lost its original value. But whether this is so or not, in any case devaluation forms one moment of the realization process" (403). And this occurs in two respects. First, by increasing absolute labor time; and secondly, by decreasing "the relative, necessary labour time" (402).

There is thus a devaluation deriving from the increasing diminution of the labor content, which cheapens commodities. Elaborating, he says that "one part of the capital on hand is constantly devalued owing to a decrease in the cost of production at which it can be *reproduced*." The fact that this is all so very obvious makes it all the stranger that Marx's theory of value and his concept of capital are so often presented and used as if devaluation and realization in the market neither exist nor matter as persistent problems. "While capital is reproduced as value and new value in the production process, it is at the same time posited as *not-value*, as something which first has to be *realized as value by means of exchange*." It is almost as if the value of capital which is knowable at the start in the money form gets submerged in the opaque forms of commodity production, only to be resurrected when it returns to the money form through sale in the market.

"The three processes of which capital forms the unity are external" (by which Marx means external to and therefore independent of each other); "they are separate in time and space. As such, the transition from one into the other, i.e. their unity as regards the individual capitalists, is accidental." But "this inner unity must necessarily maintain itself to the extent that the whole of production rests on capital, and it must therefore realize all the necessary moments of its self-formation, and must contain these determinants necessary to make these moments real" (403).

He then elaborates on this idea. "In the production process" the question of realization appears as a relation between "objectified labour to living labour." Here Marx is using the term "realization" to depict what happens in production rather than in the market. This is what will later be referred to as "productive consumption"—investment in new productive capacity. But realization also "appears dependent on circulation" (what is referred to elsewhere as final consumption). "Inside the production process, realization appeared totally identical with the production of surplus labour . . . and hence appeared to have no *bounds*" except those "posited within it as *barriers* to be forcibly overcome" but "there now appear barriers to it which lie *outside* it" (404). The commodity must be a use-value to somebody somewhere. The "first barrier" is therefore "*consumption itself—the need for it.*" The state of wants, needs and desires (see Figure 2) becomes critical. "Secondly, there has to be an equivalent for it." Need backed by ability to pay becomes crucial. But since capital is perpetually creating new value, then "it seems indeed as if no equivalent were available for it" (405). Capital, when entering circulation, "appears to encounter a barrier in the available magnitude of *consumption—of consumption capacity.*" This barrier is intensified because use-value "does not have the boundlessness of value . . . Given objects can be consumed as objects of need only up to a certain level." But capital also "seems

to encounter a barrier in the magnitude of *available equivalents*"—
"effective demand" as we would now term it. "The surplus value . . .
requires a surplus equivalent. This now appears as a second barrier"
(405).

Marx has already shown that there is no force within circulation
to produce renewal, let alone expansion of value. It is now the
production process that "appears to be in a fix" because of barriers
in circulation. Marx concludes that "these . . . are the contradictions which present themselves of their own accord to a simple,
objective, non-partisan view . . . All the contradictions of circulation come to life again in a new form" (406).

"The main point here—where we are concerned with the general
concept of capital—is that it is this *unity of production and realization*, not *immediately* but only as a *process*, which is linked to
certain conditions, and, as it appeared, *external* conditions" (407).
Marx's insistence that this is "the main point" cannot be overemphasized. It gives the lie immediately to the frequently expressed
view that conditions of consumption, and therefore of realization,
should be relegated to some add-on to the study of production.
While Marx does not specify them, I take it that the external
conditions he has in mind are those of the state of wants, needs
and desires, along with cultural preferences in addition to all those
societal features that govern the state of effective demand.

THE WORLD MARKET AND CONSUMERISM

The creation of absolute surplus-value, for example, "is conditional
upon . . . a constant expansion of the sphere of circulation. The
surplus value created at one point requires the creation of surplus
value at *another* point." A constantly widening sphere of circulation is thus a necessary condition for the survival of capital. As a
result, "the tendency to create the *world market* is directly given in
the concept of capital itself" (408). What Marx seems to be asserting here is that the contradiction of need and effective demand in

the market can be resolved by surplus-value being generated at one point, creating a demand for surplus-value being generated somewhere else. Surplus-value production chases across the world in search of more surplus-value production opening up. The contradictions are absorbed within the constant expansion of the world market, but at the price of commerce evolving from the opportunistic buying of surpluses here for marketing somewhere else to an essentially all-embracing networked global activity derived from the expansion of production itself.

> On the other side, the production of *relative surplus value*, i.e. production of surplus value based on the increase and development of the productive forces, requires the production of new consumption; requires that the consuming circle within circulation expands as did the productive circle previously. Firstly quantitative expansion of existing consumption; secondly: creation of new needs by propagating existing ones in a wide circle; *thirdly*, production of *new* needs and discovery and creation of new use-values. In other words, so that the surplus labour gained does not remain a merely quantitative surplus, but rather constantly increases the circle of qualitative differences within labour.

The capital and labour set free by technological change allows for the creation of a "new qualitatively different branch of production" which "satisfies and brings forth a new need" (408–9). "The value of the old industry is preserved by the creation of the fund for a new one in which the relation of capital and labour posits itself in a *new* form" (409). The history of capital is very much about the creation of new wants, needs and desires.

This speaks to the revolutionary qualities of the capitalist mode of production:

> Hence exploration of all of nature in order to discover new, useful qualities in things; universal exchange of the products of

all alien climates and lands; new (artificial) preparation of natural objects, by which they are given new use values. The exploration of the earth in all directions, to discover new things of use as well as new useful qualities of the old; such as new qualities of them as raw materials etc.; the development, hence, of the natural sciences to their highest point; likewise the discovery, creation and satisfaction of new needs arising from society itself; the cultivation of all the qualities of the social human being, production of the same in a form as rich as possible in needs, because rich in qualities and relations—production of this being as the most total and universal possible social product, for, in order to take gratification in a many-sided way, he must be capable of many pleasures, hence cultured to a high degree.

This is all "a condition of production founded on capital" (409). The revolutionary potentialities of this are staggering in their implications.

But he is not done with this yet. "The creation of new branches of production" along with rapid transformations in divisions of labor create a new world "to which a constantly expanding and constantly enriched system of needs corresponds."

Thus capital creates the bourgeois society, and the universal appropriation of nature as well as of the social bond itself by the members of society. Hence the great civilizing influence of capital; its production of a stage of society in comparison to which all earlier ones appear as mere *local developments* of humanity and as *nature-idolatry*. For the first time, nature becomes purely an object for humankind, purely a matter of utility; ceases to be recognized as a power for itself; and the theoretical discovery of its autonomous laws appears merely as a ruse so as to subjugate it under human needs, whether as an object of consumption or as a means of production. In accord with this tendency, capital drives beyond national barriers and prejudices as much as beyond nature worship, as well as all traditional, confined,

complacent, encrusted satisfactions of present needs, and repro-
ductions of old ways of life. It is destructive towards all of this,
and constantly revolutionizes it, tearing down all the barriers
which hem in the development of the forces of production, the
expansion of needs, the all-sided development of production,
and the exploitation and exchange of natural and mental forces.
(409–10)

This is all presented with positive connotations of the creative
historical role capital has played in human history. We will return
to consider the implications of this later on (see pages 222–32).
The supposed "civilizing influence" that Marx seems to celebrate in
these pages has a far darker side, as we will later see.

In the wake of these astonishing pronouncements of global
import, Marx returns to consider how the contradictions he had
identified pan out. He knows that capital views every limit "as a
barrier" and seeks to get ideally beyond it. He also knows that
"production moves in contradictions which are constantly overcome but just as constantly posited" and that "the universality
towards which [capital] irresistibly strives encounters barriers in
its own nature, which will, at a certain stage of its development,
allow it to be recognized as being itself the greatest barrier . . . and
will drive towards its own suspension" (410). This hopeful futuris-
tic view (hopeful at least from Marx's viewpoint, though not at all
from the standpoint of capital) is bolstered by an appeal to Ricardo,
who was "heedless of the barriers of consumption" or of barriers in
circulation. He grasped "the positive essence of capital more
correctly and deeply than those who, like Sismondi, emphasized
the barriers of consumption."

This opens up the whole controversy over whether capital is
liable to crises of overproduction. The controversy "revolves
around the point whether the process of realization of capital
within production directly posits its realization in circulation,
whether its realization posited in the *production process* is its *real
realization*" (411). Ricardo concedes that the conditions of

exchange have a role, but mainly an accidental rather than a systematic one. Unfortunately, in Marx's view, Ricardo and his school "never understood the really *modern crises*." If this is so, the immediate question is whether or not Ricardo's dismissal of circulation problems has something to do with this failure? Sismondi, for his part, emphasized the barriers of circulation and advocated protections. He failed to appreciate the essential qualities of production. This brings Marx back to his critique of Say's law, in which "allegedly there is no general overproduction, but merely overproduction of one or a few articles, as against underproduction of others" (412). Marx considers this whole line of argument "childish."

What the Say faction forgot is that production capital is not interested in use-values but value and surplus-value. It is an illusion that the production that does not meet the test of realization is attributable to a shortage of money (which is Proudhon's basic position). Or, in another version, it is said that since "*production and consumption* are the *same from the social standpoint*" an excess or disproportion between the two "can never take place" (412). Marx concurs with Malthus and Sismondi (who the Ricardians referred to as "the general glut theorists"). While it is obvious that the workers' consumption is "in no way a *sufficient* consumption for the capitalist," productive consumption ("of machines, coal, oil, required buildings etc.") is also in no way identical with production. With the Say faction, "the moment of realization is here simply thrown out entirely" and, while there are good grounds, at least according to Ricardo, to view production as the essential moment, this does not mean the conditions of realization can be ignored. Marx emphasizes, instead, "the disharmony and hence the contradiction—in a general crisis of overproduction the contradiction is not between the different kinds of productive capital, but between industrial and loanable capital" (413). This is a somewhat surprising assertion, particularly since Marx has so far ignored the category of loanable capital. I suspect that what Marx understood about the crisis unfolding around him in

1857–58 directed his attention to commercial and financial matters and that he is simply making a gesture toward work that remains to be done. But it is also the case that the contradictions within the field of circulation produce the necessity for the deployment of credit and the circulation of interest-bearing capital.

A further disruptive element is then introduced. "In competition this inner tendency of capital appears as a compulsion exercised over it by *alien capital*, which drives it forward beyond the correct proportion, with a constant *march, march!*" Note the importance here of this condition of "the correct proportion" of the different inputs into capitalist production. Classical political economy understood competition simply as negation of the feudal system, based on "monopolies, the guild system, legal regulations etc." For Marx, however, "conceptually, *competition* is nothing other than the inner *nature of capital*, its essential character, appearing and realized as the reciprocal interaction of many capitals with one another, the inner tendency of external necessity." This is a significant assertion. Since it is placed in brackets in Marx's text and crops up in more detail later, I will refrain from any further detailed discussion of it. Its main role at this point is to explain why "capital is just as much the constant positing as the suspension of *proportionate production*," particularly by the "creation of surplus values and the increase of productive forces." The phrase "proportionate production" refers to the supply of necessary inputs from many capitalists to support a given production process. It contains the potentiality of crises of disproportionality, though Marx does not develop that idea here.

Clearly there are many aspects of the relation between production and circulation that have yet to be analyzed and clarified. But even at this preliminary point, "the simple concept of capital has to contain its civilizing tendencies etc. *in themselves*; they must not, as in the economics books until now, appear merely as external consequences." If only the economics texts of today would observe this injunction, while also paying attention to "the contradictions which are . . . already latent within it" (414).

Marx then sketches, in a rather abstract depiction, where he is at in his investigation of production and realization. "So far in the realization process, we have only the indifference" (e.g., on questions of use-value) "of the individual moments towards one another; that they determine each other internally and search for each other externally; but they may or may not find each other, balance each other, correspond to each other. The inner necessity of moments which belong together, and their indifferent, independent existence towards one another, are already a foundation of contradictions." What Marx seems to be saying is that the different moments within the realization process are autonomous, independent yet also integral and correlated with each other. This is rather like saying that if I choose to breathe deeply for the benefit of my lungs, this may or may not have an effect on my digestion, even though both lungs and stomach are foundational and integral for my body functioning as a totality.

"Still, we are by no means finished. The contradiction between production and realization—of which capital, by its concept, is the unity—has to be grasped more intrinsically than merely as the indifferent, seemingly reciprocally independent appearance of the individual moments of the process, or rather of the totality of the processes" (414–15). The contradictory unity of production and realization within the totality, as Marx has conceptualized it, is a central and foundational feature in the theory of capital. To be sure, the role of production is, in some sense, more essential because that is where surplus-value originates, where it is created, but value and surplus-value exist only potentially and remain so until realized through sale in the market and all that that requires (including, for example, the participation of merchant capitalists).

"To approach the matter more closely: *First of all, there is a limit, not inherent to production generally, but to production founded on capital.*" Marx sees the limit as twofold. To begin with there are inherent limits. (1) necessary labor depends on existing labor capacity and the wage level; (2) surplus-value limits surplus labor time; (3) the transformation into money may be constricted by lack of effective demand; (4) the search for exchange-value may restrict the production of use-values (wealth). But these limits are confronted with the general tendency of capital to expand. "Hence overproduction" and "general devaluation" in response to capital's tendency to drive beyond all barriers. "Capital, at the same time, [is] thereby faced with the task of launching its attempt anew from a higher level of the development of productive forces, with each time greater collapse *as capital*. Clear, therefore, that the higher the development of capital, the more it appears as barrier to production—hence also to consumption—besides the other contradictions which make it appear as burdensome barrier to production and intercourse" (416).

The pressures of crisis tendencies may be relieved, however, by developments within the credit system (as already mentioned) and through foreign trade (416–17). While Ricardo may have been correct to depict the production process as the "essence" of capital, there is an enormous amount going on in the field of circulation as the search to realize the value through sale in the market intensifies. Not only does capital have to expand to encompass the production of the world market and to open up wholly new lines of production, but it also entails appeals to expand foreign trade or resort to an expansion of the credit system to realize the value and the surplus-value that have been produced. We here have early hints of what I have elsewhere referred to as a "spatial fix" (geographical expansion) to counter the endemic tendencies toward overproduction or to absorb the overaccumulation of capital in particular places and times.

Marx then approvingly cites Malthus to the effect that "the *wealth* of a country depends partly upon the *quantity of produce* obtained by its labour" along with "an *adaptation of this quantity to the wants and powers of the existing population*," concluding with the observation that "the powers of production are only called fully into motion by the unchecked demand for all that is produced" (418). This materializes "on the one hand by constantly new branches of industry (and *reciprocal* expansion of the old), by means of which the old obtain new markets, etc. Production indeed itself creates demand, in that it employs more workers . . . but the demand created by the productive labourer himself can never be an *adequate* demand." Therefore, profit presumes "*a demand exterior to that of the labourer who has produced it.*"

"The point here," Marx notes, "is not yet to develop overproduction specifically, but only the predisposition to it." We must also "omit here any regard for the other possessing and consuming etc. classes which do not produce but live from their revenue . . . We can consider them only partly (but better along with *accumulation*) in so far as they are most important for the historic formation of capital" (418). If Marx is serious on this point, then not only do we have to rewrite the history of capital to incorporate their role (whoever they are) but we need also to question to what degree contemporary capitalism incorporates "possessing and consuming classes" that play distinctive roles not only economically but also with respect to class formation and political orientation. This is not the only place where Marx mentions such classes, without, however, much elaboration. Recent writings on rentier capitalism suggest that such classes (not including a landowning class, which Marx usually does separate out) may have a continuing presence and distinctive roles in capital's political economy. The clergy and religious leaders could well fit in with this designation. So, for that matter, would state employees.

Marx does, however, look more closely at the role of the workers as consumers. To each capitalist, the total mass of all workers, with the exception of his own workers, are regarded as consumers, possessors of exchange-values (wages), money that they exchange for commodities. "They form a proportionately very great part—although not so great as generally imagined—of all consumers. The greater this number . . . the greater the sphere of exchange for capital" (419). Wage workers thus "form an independent centre of circulation" (an idea to which we will later return). Every capitalist has an interest in reducing wages and thereby limiting the consumption of his own workers. But he "would like the workers of *other* capitalists to be the greatest consumers possible of *his own* commodity" (420). While Marx agrees with Malthus that "the *demand of the labourer himself can never be an adequate demand*," it is still the case that the worker confronts capital "as consumer and possessor of exchange values and that in the form of the *possessor of money* . . . he becomes a simple centre of circulation—one of its infinitely many centres, in which his specificity of worker is extinguished" (420–1).

"On the one side, this demand which production itself posits drives it" (the workers' demand) forward, while on "the other side, if the demand *exterior to the demand of the labourer himself* disappears or shrinks up, then the collapse occurs" (420). In a crisis, however, "capital itself then regards the *demand by the worker*" (wages) "not as a gain but as a loss" thus reasserting the power of the "*immanent relation*" between alien capital and alien labor. Austerity is often presented as the antidote to economic distress, but, more often than not, it deepens the distress. Competition between capitals acts to enforce conformity (e.g., austerity measures) but working-class consumption may still play a significant role in realization. But that significant role is not a class role. It is the role of buyers and sellers. The workers go into the marketplace with their wages, but they are simply one set of buyers among many. At certain points in their lives, they will behave like buyers. This may have a profound effect on class consciousness. If there is going to be a struggle against monopoly pharmaceutical pricing, for example, it is not going to be a working-class struggle in the narrow sense, even as it certainly qualifies as an anticapitalist struggle. The workers will contribute to the struggle as buyers. All buyers who need those drugs are going to be participating, no matter what their class position in relation to production. For the workers, this implies a different positionality to that assumed in production: hence Marx's use of the term "extinguished" with respect to their class role.

In spite of these diversions, capital's forcing of the workers beyond necessary labor to surplus labor is the only way for capital to be realized in both production and circulation. "By its nature, therefore, it posits a *barrier* to labour and value creation, in contradiction to its tendency to expand them boundlessly. And in as much as it both posits a barrier *specific* to itself and on the other side equally drives over and beyond *every* barrier, it is the living contradiction" (421). There are factors that limit the boundless and limitless thirst for surplus-value. From the perspective of production these would be the length of the working day and the potential of an actually existing working population. But here we encounter the limits set by the necessity for proportionality in the exchanges among the capitalists and the limits of final consumption (including, but not confined to, that of the working class).

A couple of footnotes are here inserted that have some significance (as is often the case with Marx's footnotes). Production itself creates demand "for raw material, semi-finished goods, machinery, means of communication, and for auxiliary materials, such as dyes, coal, grease, soap, etc." The essence of capital is to drive beyond the correct exchange proportionalities between multiple producers and to drive up against the barriers of indirect and final demand. "The *correct* (imaginary) proportion in which [the producers] must exchange with one another in order to realize themselves at the ends as capital lies *outside* their relation to one another." To this Marx adds an interesting insight. "Since value forms the foundation of capital, and since it therefore necessarily exists only through exchange for *counter-value*, it thus necessarily repels itself from itself." This "reciprocal repulsion between capitals is already contained in capital as realized exchange value" (421). It is characteristic of Marx to see what often looks like an external disruption as being realized through internalized relations. The theory of capital as value already internalizes counter-value, non-value and anti-value in its very heart. The external forces of crisis formation trigger (sometimes, Marx comments, "explosively") the internal vulnerabilities.

While labor capacity is an important center of exchange, it is just as essential "to restrict the worker's consumption to the amount necessary to reproduce his labour capacity and to reduce necessary labour to the minimum." This adds "a new barrier to the sphere of exchange" which emphasizes "the tendency of capital to relate to every limit on its self-realization as to a barrier. The boundless enlargement of its value—boundless creation of value—therefore absolutely identical here with the positing of barriers to the sphere of exchange, i.e. the possibility of realization—the realization of the value posited in the production process" (422). Put as simply as possible: the maximization of surplus-value through the reduction of necessary labor reduces the market for realization through the restraint this imposes on working-class consumption.

The same issue arises with regard to revolutions in the productive forces. Relative surplus-value decreases necessary labor time, hence the worker's exchange capacity. But "*the mass of products grows*" along with "the difficult of realizing the labour time contained in them—because the demands made on consumption rise." Marx here recognizes that there is a necessary relation between realization and devaluation: "In one and the same moment, [capital] posits the values on hand in circulation . . . as the . . . necessary barrier to its value-creation; on the other hand, its productivity as the only creatrix of values. It therefore drives constantly on the one side towards its own devaluation, on the other side towards the obstruction of the productive forces, and of labour which objectifies itself in values" (423).

It is interesting to note Marx's appeal to the concept of devaluation in the analysis. To be sure, he is only concerned here to insist on devaluation as a basic moment alongside the preservation of value and the production of surplus-value in the essence of what capital is about. This is a sign of an inherent weakness and potent vulnerability within capital itself. In what follows, we will have plenty of opportunities to identify what might prey upon those vulnerabilities and thereby have a role in crisis formation. The constant devaluation of existing capital consequent upon technological changes underpinning the devaluation of the production apparatuses of whole cities (like Detroit or Sheffield in the 1980s) is yet to be considered. But devaluation is a major concern in the theory of capital that Marx is building.

While the essence of capital may reside in production (as Ricardo insisted), it has no existence outside of the vast problem of realization in the market. It is through the latter that we get to understand, furthermore, the complex of forces creating new wants, needs and desires, the conquest of the world market, and a whole host of other implications such as the role of merchant capital and the credit system, with which we have to grapple in seeking to theorize the dynamics of a capitalist mode of production.

Up until now, we have followed Marx's text step-by-step. Once we had gotten through the multiple forms and functions of monetary circulation, we sought to elucidate the concept of capital, locked in mortal embrace with alienated labor, each striving to realize itself in the other. But the struggle between them is largely conceptualized as occurring at the point of production. Marx's next step is to analyze the positionality of labor in relationship to circulation as a whole. This highlights the problem of labor's role in the realization of values in the market.

Marx uses this term "realization" in a variety of ways and contexts. At certain points, he will talk about realization through production, which is different from realization in the market. The value of the money form of capital is transformed into and "realized" in the value of the commodities brought together in an act of production (the first box in Figure 2). These values are "realized" in the labor process, which reproduces values and adds a surplus-value in the act of production. The value of the produced commodity is then "realized" in money form through sale in the market. Each of the transformations that occur at the different moments of the circulation process as a whole (as depicted in Figure 2) is a moment of realization. But when I use the term "realization" I refer exclusively to realization in the market, unless specified otherwise. This is so because Marx converges on the formulation of value created in production and realized in the market as central to his analysis. Value is the contradictory unity between production and realization. In the next few pages the multiple uses of the term will be very much in evidence. The employed laborer receives a money wage, which circulates as a revenue at labor's disposal. This money is used to buy the commodities that labor needs (and labor made) in order to reproduce itself. The money wages flow back into the circulation of capital as part of aggregate market demand. This constitutes a mini-circulation process (or what Marx will later examine as a "small circulation process") embedded within the larger circulation process of capital in general.

The class relation between capital and labor at the point of production is foundational for Marx's theorization of class and class struggle. When the worker goes into the market to buy wage goods, the worker then sheds the identity of worker and becomes instead a buyer. As buyers, workers have to confront the practices of capitalists as sellers. If the sellers are cheaters or monopolists, then they may steal back as much of the money as they can from the hard-earned wages of the worker. This moment is not constituted by Marx as a class relation. It is a relation between buyers and sellers. Workers are not alone in their struggles against sellers. Pretty much everyone is caught up contesting what Marx and Engels referred to in the *Communist Manifesto* as "secondary forms of exploitation" practiced by the corporations, the shopkeepers, the credit institutions or the landlords. The configuration of social struggles starts to look rather different from this perspective. At several points in the *Grundrisse*, Marx emphasizes how the character of the worker dissolves as we move from the positionality of production to the positionality of realization in the market. This is what he depicted on pages 420–1.

The ability of the worker to participate as buyer and consumer is limited. The ability to perform necessary labor time (to earn the wage) depends on the capacity of the laborer to produce surplus-value for capital. Only when "capital forces the workers beyond necessary labour to surplus labour" does capital "realize itself, and produce surplus value. But on the other hand, it posits necessary labour only *to the extent* and *in so far as* it [performs] surplus labour . . . *realizable as surplus value.*" This is "the living contradiction" which grounds the analysis to come (421). What happens, for example, when there are insufficient buyers in the market such that the opportunity to perform surplus labor for capital is lacking? If there is no market, then the commodities already produced will have no value. The labor expended on them will be socially unnecessary as opposed to socially necessary.

Is overproduction therefore possible? (424). Marx answers in the affirmative, but insists that "overproduction takes place in connection with realization [in the market], not otherwise." He emphatically rejects Say's law and everybody who has anything to do with it. Proudhon was one of those, so Marx spends several pages refuting Proudhon's thesis of systemic overproduction due to the fact that "the worker cannot buy back his own product." Proudhon "certainly hears the bells ringing, but never knows where." All sorts of things can happen in the price sphere, of course, including "*fraud* [and] *reciprocal chicanery*" in which "one party can win in exchange what the other loses" (433). But this has nothing to do with surplus-value production and appropriation as Marx theorizes it.

An odd aside on page 434 is, however, worth noting. Marx considers the appearance of overproduction in ancient Rome along with other imperial regimes. In such cases, he suggests, the issue was not overproduction but insane "*over-consumption*" and its turn toward the "monstrous and the bizarre." It was this and not overproduction which "led to the downfall of the old system of states." Marx does not here discuss overconsumption under capitalism, but I sometimes wonder if global capital is not destined to collapse under a similar weight of monstrous and bizarre consumerism. I look, for example, at Hudson Yards in New York and think that that is insane consumption, almost as bad as what we see in the crazy urbanization of the Gulf States. The Covid-19 pandemic has radically curbed this kind of consumption, particularly that of the insane and monstrous tourist variety. We will see if it makes a comeback. But clearly its negative effects are everywhere apparent and worthy of critical study.

Marx's own focus shifts (435) to surplus goods in the market that cannot be sold at their value. The only option then is to sell off the goods below their value. This diminishes the profit. The result could be multiple sectors of zero profit due to overproduction. This does not necessarily mean that the rate of profit in general falls. The falling rate of profit is discussed at length and in depth in Volume III of *Capital*. But he already had this question in his mind in 1858. He comes back to it in some detail later in the *Grundrisse*, so I will delay full consideration of it until then. All he says here is that "the general rate cannot fall" simply because of overproduction of particular commodities. It can fall "only if the proportion of surplus labour to necessary labour falls *relatively*." This can occur only "if the part of capital which exchanges for living labour is very small compared to that which exchanges for machinery and raw material. The general rate of profit can fall in that case, even though absolute surplus labour rises" (435). In other words, any increase in the rate of exploitation of living labor power may be offset by reductions in the number of laborers employed, due to the adoption of labor-saving innovations (revolutions in the productive forces).

"With that," says Marx, "we come to another point," which, it turns out, is of major importance. "A *general rate of profit* . . . is possible only if the rate of profit in one branch of business is too high and in another too low" and if "a part of the surplus value—which corresponds to surplus labour—is transferred from one capitalist to another." "The capitalist class . . . distributes the total surplus value so that . . . it [shares in it] evenly in accordance with the *size* of its capital, instead of in accordance with the surplus values actually created by the capitals in the various branches of business" (435–6). The equalization of the rate of profit through competition redistributes surplus-value from firms, sectors and even whole nations engaging in labor-intensive forms of production to firms, sectors and nations engaging in capital-intensive forms of production. This important thesis is taken up in detail in Volume III of *Capital*. The redistribution follows the rule: from each capital according to the labor it employs and to each capital according to the total capital it advances. Marx humorously dubs this elsewhere as "capitalist communism." The theoretical statement of this rule is followed by several pages (435–43) of tedious arithmetic calculations showing the redistributions between five different capitals of different labor intensity.

This arithmetic inquiry produces one important insight. "General overproduction would take place, not because relatively *too little* had been produced of the commodities consumed by the workers or too little of those consumed by the capitalists, but because too much of *both* had been produced—not too much *for consumption*, but too much to retain *the correct relation between consumption and realization*, too much for realization" (443). The focus is then on the contradictory unity between the creation of value in production and the realization of value in the market and the disruptive impact on that relation due to technological changes (revolutions in the productive forces).

From this point on, Marx converges more and more on dissecting the various relations between the different components that enter into the production and realization of capital. The ratio of capital laid out on means of production relative to that laid out on the purchase of labor power (later called the value composition of capital) affects the redistributions of surplus-value achieved through the equalization of the rate of profit. "At a given point in the development of the productive forces ... a fixed relation becomes established" between "raw material, machinery, necessary labour, surplus labour." But the inputs (of raw materials and machinery) are independently produced by autonomous independent capitals (443). These different components have to be brought together in the right ratios, not through planning, but through the anarchy of market exchange. The "inner necessity" that binds them all together to create a unity within the totality only "becomes *manifest* in the crisis, which puts a forcible end to their seeming indifference towards each other" (444). The surplus labor for its part also divides into that which supports capitalist consumption and that part which returns to the role of capital (e.g., reinvestment) (443). "If the surplus value were simply consumed, then capital would not have realized itself as capital, and not produced itself as *capital*, i.e. as value which produces value" (444). How the surplus-value is used becomes a critical question.

The purpose of the somewhat convoluted numerical examples (444–6) seems to be to demonstrate how prices and values can and do diverge from each other in the market. The depreciation of prices realized in the market by one firm because of lack of demand can, however, be compensated for by a depreciation in prices of its inputs for the same reasons, thus stabilizing profits and relative value relations. But in a general crisis all commodity values can suffer devaluation. Note, however, the distinction that arises (446) between the terms "devaluation" (the loss of value measured by labor input) and "depreciation" (which refers to falling market prices) and "destruction" (which refers to physical loss of use-values [e.g., the decay of unused machinery or produce that rots in the supermarket]). These distinctions can be very important. For example, technological changes can devalue existing machinery without in any way affecting the physical use-value of that machinery in production. "In a crisis—a general depreciation of prices—there occurs up to a certain moment a *general devaluation* or *destruction of capital.*" But this almost invariably "coincides with . . . a general growth of the *productive forces*" which produces "a decrease of the existing value of raw materials, machines, labour capacity." The disruptive impacts of technological and organizational change are again invoked. "A sudden general increase in the forces of production would relatively devalue all the *present values* which labour objectifies at the lower stages of the productive forces, and hence would destroy present capital as well as present labouring capacity" (446).

Marx begins the next sequence of his analysis with the observation that "exchange does not change the inner characteristics of

realization; but it projects them to the outside; gives them a reciprocally independent form, and thereby lets their unity exist merely
as an inner necessity, which must therefore come forcibly to the
surface in crises." In a peasant economy, production and realization are internalized within the household. The peasants eat what
they produce. When exchange becomes generalized, the relationship between production and realization is externalized and mediated by the arbitrariness and anarchy of what happens in the
market. This is a typical Marx move. Recall how the commodity
internalizes an antithesis between use-value and exchange-value,
which gets externalized in the act of exchange, which in turn gives
rise to the money form as a medium to facilitate exchange and
ultimately as an independent expression or representation of value.
This then leads to the recognition that value could not be found
without the existence of money as its representation.

When peasants start to trade surpluses, part of their production is measured by the realization of their surplus in money
form. In a capitalist economy, production and realization are
understood as entirely separate moments (although many will
eat produce they grow in their own backyards as a sideline). The
autonomy of the two moments within the regime of capital introduces a moment of devaluation in between the production and
realization of value. "The essence of capital" comprises the
"devaluation of capital in the production process, as well as the
suspension of devaluation and the creation of the conditions for
the realization of capital" (447). A moment of devaluation exists
at every moment of the circulation process, but we only become
aware of it at times of general crisis, when the otherwise salving
effect of suspension of devaluation (through, for example, sale in
the market) fails to materialize. The full realization of value in
the market is, however, a necessary precondition for the realization of capital as capital (i.e., as money capital). "Capital is thus
now posited as money again, and money therefore posited in the
new aspect of *realized capital*, not merely as realized price of the
commodity" (447–8).

This realization of capital in money form through a sale in the market invites us to a reprise of money in its different forms of measure of value, medium of circulation (performing the role of circulating capital) and as an independent commodity in the form of self-sufficient value, which can be used to produce surplus-value (449). It is "capital in this *general form*" which "accumulates in banks or is distributed through them . . . in accordance with the needs of production" (449). Through loans, this general capital also

forms a level between the different countries. If it is therefore e.g. a law of capital in general that, in order to realize itself, it must posit itself doubly and must realize itself in this double form, then e.g. the capital of a particular nation which represents capital *par excellence* in antithesis to another will have to lend itself out to a third nation in order to be able to realize itself. This double positing, this relating to self as to an alien, becomes damn real in this case. (449–50)

So what does this mean? When capitalists come to the end of the production process and sell commodities in the market, they end up with money in their pocket. They then face a choice as to how that money can be used. They can lend it out to somebody else in return for interest, or they can plough it back into production to get more surplus-value. This is the double character of what a capitalist does. The capitalist sees two rates of return: the profit rate derived from surplus-value production and the interest rate derived from lending the money out (even to themselves). The capitalist assumes two personas and acts accordingly. This doubling is externalized if the capitalist is working with borrowed capital. They then pay out interest to the lender and retain profit for themselves. At the macro level, what initially appeared as external presuppositions are internalized within the circulation system and "now appear as moments of the motion of capital itself" (450).

It is at this point also, that we encounter money "in transition from its role as [exchange] value to its role as capital." This transition rests upon the unity of production and realization in the market. What happens in effect is that "all moments which confronted living labour capacity, and employed it as *alien external powers*, and which consumed it under *certain conditions independent of itself*, are now posited as *its own product and result*" (451). The capitalist system increasingly becomes self-replicating.

Notice the movement that occurs in Marx's argument. We began with the externalization of realization in the market as a separate and autonomous moment in relation to production but ended up with "the surplus product in its totality" appearing as "*surplus capital*" or as "independent exchange value [loan capital]" being used to create even more capital. The totality that is capital is here in plain formation. But this totality, Marx insists, is wholly created out of surplus labor, albeit broken into the proportionate fragments of constant and variable capital at the moment of reinvestment. But "the fact that instrument and necessaries were on hand in the amounts which made it possible for living labour to realize itself not only as *necessary* but also as *surplus* labour . . . appeared as an act of capital" (452). In other words, the necessary preconditions and presuppositions for the further production of surplus-value are no longer located outside of the totality but are internalized and produced within its circulation process by capital itself.

UNIVERSAL ALIENATION AND THE
REPRODUCTION OF THE CLASS RELATION

This prompts an astonishingly dense conceptual passage which is impossible to summarize, if only because of the intensity of its reasoning and its language. It is almost as if the capitalist serpent slithers into the body of the totality, burrowing and churning its way until everything within the totality is turned upside down and inside out into an alienated and evil version of itself. I quote here the single sentence that goes on for half a page or so in language worthy of James Joyce:

> The independent, for-itself existence, of value *vis-à-vis* living labour capacity—hence its existence as capital—the objective self-sufficient indifference, the *alien quality* of the objective conditions of labour *vis-à-vis* living labour capacity, which goes so far that these conditions confront the person of the worker in the person of the capitalist—as personification with its own will and interest—this absolute *divorce, separation* of property, i.e. of the objective conditions of labour from living labour capacity— that they confront him as *alien property*, as the reality of other juridical persons, as the absolute realm of *their* will—and that labour therefore, on the other side, appears as *alien labour* opposed to the value personified in the capitalist, or the conditions of labour—this absolute separation between property and labour, between living labour capacity and the conditions of its realization, between objectified and living labour, between value and value-creating activity—hence also the alien quality of the content of labour for the worker himself—this divorce now likewise appears as a product of labour itself, as objectification of its own moments. (452)

There you have the condensation of Marx's theory of the relation between production and realization in a single sentence!

Everything becomes internalized within the totality within this historical dynamic. This internalization forms the basis for a self-sustaining and self-replicating productive system. Once labor is incorporated into this system, it cannot walk away—divorce itself—from it, even as it is alienated from its own capacities and powers. The workers require, in order to live, necessary labor, but they have to produce surplus-value in order to be allowed to perform the labor necessary for their own reproduction. In so doing, they produce both capital and the capitalist. The worker is then confronted by capital as "an alien, commanding personification." Labor produces the capitalist who is the instrument of its own domination and repression.

The result is that "the worker emerges . . . rather poorer from the process than he entered . . . He has produced not only the alien wealth and his own poverty, but also the . . . independent, self-sufficient wealth [which] draws new vital spirits into itself and realizes itself anew," i.e., that of capital (453). "All this," says Marx, "arose from the act of exchange," in which he, the laborer, made the fatal forced error of exchanging "his living labour capacity for an amount of objectified labour." Unfortunately for him, this objectified labor, these external conditions of his being (e.g., the wage goods that facilitate his own reproduction) and the "independent externality" of these objective conditions "now appear as . . . *his own product*, as his own self-objectification as well as the objectification of himself as a power independent of himself, which moreover rules over him, rules over him through his own actions" (453). The laborer reproduces herself at the same time as she reproduces capital and the capitalist.

One of the themes I have always found interesting in reading Marx is how we humans so often produce the conditions and even instruments of our own domination. Here we have his Exhibit A of this principle at work. Labor produces capital, the primary agent of its own repression and domination. This is the source that assures the production and reproduction of the laborer's abject poverty. In this theorization (which, incidentally, reveals the source of the Ricardian socialists' moral dilemma of how labor, which is the source of all value, can be so ill-rewarded), the concept and practice of alienation plays a critical role. "In surplus value, all moments are products of alien labour," and, to top it all, "the objective conditions of labour now appear as labour's product" (453).

So, "while capital thus appears as the product of labour, so does the product of labour likewise appear as capital—no longer as a simple product, nor as an exchangeable commodity, but as *capital*; objectified labour as mastery, command over living labour" (453).

Notice that objectified labor (in the hands of the capitalist) now seemingly commands living labor. The laborers are the bearers of living labor. They are the ones who are dominated by capital. But capital is not living labor; capital is objectified surplus-value. "The product of labour appears as *alien property*, as a mode of existence confronting living labour as independent, as *value* in its being for itself; the product of labour, objectified labour, has been endowed by living labour with a soul of its own" (454). This notion of the soul within objectified labor, the product of an alien power, is a gesture, I suspect, toward the figure of Frankenstein.

"As a consequence," he says at the end of page 454, "of the production process, the possibilities resting in living labour's own womb exist outside it as realities—but as *realities alien* to it, which form wealth in opposition to it." Labor is giving birth to capital, but giving birth to a monstrous child that dominates it. He lists the elements of this in some detail on page 455, then offers this summary:

> It here becomes evident that labour itself progressively extends and gives an ever wider and fuller existence to the objective world of wealth as a power alien to labour, so that, relative to the values created or to the real conditions of value-creation, the penurious subjectivity of living labour capacity forms an ever more glaring contrast. The greater the extent to which labour objectifies itself, the greater becomes the objective world of values, which stands opposite as . . . alien property. With the creation of surplus capital, labour places itself under the compulsion to create yet further surplus capital.

I here sympathize with all those who find this argument and this language intimidating, if not impenetrable, and cast at an unbearable level of conceptual abstraction. But I would remind you that these are notes that Marx is making to himself. And it is unquestionable that Marx has here reached the point where, as we like to say, "it all comes together," in a theory of universal alienation. He is getting closer to the center of the maelstrom of the interrelations, collisions and contradictions that define the essence of capital. These passages bear careful study and thought. This takes time and patience. These pages are critical not only to the reading of the *Grundrisse* but to understanding the true nature, the essence of the capitalist beast which we have to confront every day of our lives.

Marx concludes by considering how all this looks "from the standpoint of capital" (456). This is easier to grasp and to summarize. The capitalist lays out funds to cover the values of raw materials and labor power. But after the commodity is produced and its value is realized in the market, all of that value laid out is returned to the capitalist. If the value of the commodity is realized in the market, then the net outlay is zero. But the capitalist also appropriates a surplus-value. The whole operation rests on the appropriation of alien labor capacity from the worker. The capitalist can then claim a right of a private property to the whole value.

"Finally," Marx says, "the result of the process of production and realization is, above all, the reproduction and new production of the *relation of capital and labour itself*, of *capitalist and worker*." The reproduction of the class relation is, he suggests, "an even more important result of the process than its material results." Marx's preference for prioritizing the social over the physical material relation comes to the fore. "Within this process, the worker produces himself as labour capacity, as well as the capital confronting him, while at the same time the capitalist produces himself as capital as well as the living labour capacity confronting him. Each reproduces itself, by reproducing its other, its negation. The capitalist produces labour as alien; labour produces the product as alien. The capitalist produces the worker, and the worker the capitalist" (458). With that, this vital section of Marx's presentation comes to a close.

6

Capital's Becoming:
Past, Present and Future
Pages 459–71

Marx's theoretical explorations in the previous pages culminated in a depiction of capital as a working totality, in which the presuppositions and preconditions for the further expansion of surplus labor and hence surplus-value production, are internalized and produced by capital itself. But Marx is a historical materialist and is faithful to his calling. In order to complete the analysis, he evidently felt impelled to investigate the historical and geographical processes that not only promoted the rise of capital to dominance but also secured the conditions required for its sustained reproduction as a totality. Marx here offers a rare glimpse into how such an inquiry into the history of capital's formation should be conducted (459).

"The conditions and presuppositions of the *becoming*, of the *arising* of capital presuppose precisely that it is not yet in being, but merely in *becoming*; they therefore disappear as real capital arises." Thus, while the use of money as capital presupposes an initial accumulation of money acquired as "a not-capitalist", its use produces surplus-value, and hence money capital as its own presupposition. "These presuppositions, which originally appeared as conditions of its own becoming—and hence could not spring from its *action as capital*—now appear as results of its own realization . . . *not as conditions of its arising, but as results of its presence*" (460). In this way, capital produces the conditions of its own reproduction.

Marx repeatedly asserts that capital and value are historical constructs. He needs to say something about how this construction came about. His theoretical stance is clear. Imagine, initially, no circulation of capital, then build its representation moment by moment until the circulation process as a whole (e.g., Figure 2) comes clearly into view. This is what he has done in the preceding pages. The question then arises as to whether or not this logical exercise mirrors the history. All of what we have been talking about is based upon "historic presuppositions, which . . . are past and gone, and hence belong to the *history of its formation*" (459). So what then do we need to know about this history? "Conditions and presuppositions of the *becoming*, of the *arising*, of capital, presuppose precisely that it is not yet in being but merely in *becoming*; they therefore disappear as real capital arises." This disappearing act has to be investigated. "While the process in which money or value for-itself originally becomes capital presupposes on the part of the capitalist an accumulation [of money], perhaps by means of savings garnered from products and values" arising out of labor "undertaken as a *not-capitalist* . . . the presuppositions under which money becomes capital appear as given, external *presuppositions*." They are not yet internalized. What this means is that "as soon as capital has become capital as such, it creates its own presuppositions." The preconditions for production and circulation of capital are actively produced by capital itself. This entails a whole set of transformations. An examination of contemporary realities exhibits traces of what these were.

Consider the existence of a hoard of money. People have long hoarded gold or other valuables and precious metals, and they continue to do so, but it "is transformed into capital only by means of the exploitation of labour" in the course of circulation. "The bourgeois economists who regard capital as an eternal and *natural*, not historical, form of production then attempt . . . to legitimize it again by formulating the conditions of its becoming as the conditions of contemporary realization." They present "the moments in which the capitalist still appropriates as not-capitalist—because he is still becoming—as the very conditions in which he appropriates *as capitalist*" (460). They seek to make it appear as if the capitalist system is entirely natural. An act of thievery or robbery in the market is mistaken for the legal and legitimate appropriation of surplus-value through the legal exploitation of living labor in production under the juridical conditions of private property and exchange. Conversely, the fact that merchant capital procures a profit by buying cheap and selling dear is used to mask the true origins of surplus-value in capital's exploitation of living labor in production. The myth that capital is produced through exchange is conveniently propagated to shield the fact that its true origin lies in the exploitation of living labor in production.

To see this does not require that we "write the *real history of the relations of production*." It is "a correct grasp of the present" which provides "the key to the understanding of the past." This "correct view" likewise points to the potential suspension of present forms and "foreshadowings of the future." While Marx does not invoke the figure here, the question of how the "emancipated labourer" might use such an insight is clearly implied. "Just as, on one side, the pre-bourgeois phases appear as *merely historical* . . . so do the contemporary conditions of production likewise appear as engaged in *suspending themselves* and hence in positing the *historic presuppositions* for a new state of society" (461).

Marx elsewhere noted, and I think this is relevant here, that no society can build an alternative if the elements for that alternative are not already present and within the grasp of that existing society. If that is so, then the study of how one society morphed into another is going to be helpful. The study of the rise of capital should provide clues as to how to transcend capital and chart a way to socialism and communism. Marx elaborates on these thoughts in somewhat mysterious ways:

If we initially examine the relation such as it has become, value having become capital . . . so that living labour appears as a mere means to realize objectified, dead labour, to penetrate it with an animating soul while losing its own soul to it—and having produced, as the end-product, alien wealth on one side and [on the other,] the penury which is living labour capacity's sole possession—then the matter is simply this, that the process itself, in and by itself, posits the real objective conditions of living labour (namely, material in which to realize itself, instrument with which to realize itself, and the necessaries with which to stoke the flame of living labour capacity, to protect it from being extinguished, to supply its vital processes with the necessary fuels) and posits them as alien, independent existences. (461)

The dense language to which Marx resorts here requires a lot of parsing. Note well, however, the implications of the phrase "value having become capital," for what it says about both value and capital. The "objective conditions for production" include plant and machinery, raw materials and partially finished products and energy; in short, adequate means of production. These commodities have to be purchased in the market, presumably at their value (price?). A precondition for the functioning of capital is that such commodities already exist and can be found and purchased in the market. They form the means of production whose value stands to be recuperated through the making of new commodities to be sold at their value on the market. But these means of production—the objective conditions—are dead labor (things). They can in themselves create no new value. The recuperation of their value depends upon the application of living labor capacity—here defined as "the subjective condition" of production. But the living subject—the laborer—can reproduce herself only through the performance of necessary labor using the objective conditions. And she does so only on the condition—imposed by capital—that she also produce a surplus-value for capital. The workers need access to the objective conditions in order to reproduce their own lives. In this sense, the objective conditions dominate the subjective. But the production and reproduction of capital depends upon the mobilization of living labor capacity (the subjective agent). "The objective conditions of living labour appear as *separated, independent* values opposite living labour capacity as subjective being, which therefore appears to them only as a value of *another* kind, not as value, but different from them, as use-value. Once this separation" of objective from subjective conditions "is given, the production process can only produce it anew, reproduce it, and reproduce it on an expanded scale" (462).

This is simplistic in its meaning while complex in its articulation. But Marx is showing that capital and value are produced and reproduced through simple material operations. He also shows wage labor as labor divorced from control over the means of production. This may seem (and indeed is) banal, but it is exactly such a banal material condition of lack of direct access to the means of production that makes it impossible for labor to become emancipated and truly free. When we track back the origin of capital's domination over the material means of production, it lies, of course, in the power to accumulate enough money capital to purchase and thereby control the material means and conditions of production that labor needs to produce and gain a livelihood.

The importance of the argument that follows cannot be overemphasized. "The objective conditions of living labour capacity are presupposed as having an existence independent of it, as the objectivity of a subject distinct from living labour capacity and standing independently over against it." Behind the mass of means of production that constitute the objective conditions for production there looms the shadowy figure of the capitalist pulling the strings. The expansion of the objective conditions then appears "as the wealth of an alien subject indifferently and independently standing over against labour capacity." What is produced and reproduced "is not only the . . . objective conditions of living labour, *but also their presence as independent values, i.e. values belonging to an alien subject, confronting this living labour capacity.*" This "alien subject" lacks a name. But now, "the objective conditions of labour attain a subjective existence *vis-à-vis* living labour capacity—capital turns into capitalist" (462). Finally, the culprit is named. The "alien subject" is capital. Notice Marx's tactic here. He refuses to name "capital" before its time. That time is the moment of becoming of the capitalist.

The image I have of this process starts with an individual who has a lot of money in her pockets (acquired somehow) and who is just wandering aimlessly around on the edge of town. She sees a bunch of laborers just sitting around and shooting the breeze along with some tools and piles of raw materials. Just for a lark, she hires the laborers, buys up the raw materials and tools and puts them all to work in the production of a commodity that is then sold in the market. She finds she gets back more money that she laid out. This seems to be a pretty good bargain. So she decides to go out to the edge of town and do it all over again. This time, she is purposive. It is at this point that she becomes (takes on the persona of) a capitalist.

The living laborer cannot but become aware of the power relation that puts capital in command over the objective conditions that labor requires to be able to work.

> The recognition of the products as its own, and the judgement that its [the labourer's] separation from the conditions of its realization is improper—forcibly imposed—is an enormous [advance in] awareness, itself the product of the mode of production resting on capital, and as much the knell to its doom as, with the slave's awareness that he *cannot be the property of another*, with his consciousness of himself as a person, the existence of slavery becomes a merely artificial, vegetative existence, and ceases to be able to prevail as the basis of production. (463)

Capital, by virtue of its ownership and control over the means of production, is the great barrier—recognized as such—to the ambitions of emancipated labor.

This has to be the high point of appeal in the *Grundrisse*, if not in all of Marx's writings, to the theory of labor's alienation as the cutting edge of political revolt. Capital is not only named but recognized. Marx appeals to the politics that comes from recognition and of awareness. Labor's consciousness of its own position and condition is the foundation for such a politics. Making laborers aware and conscious of their condition is an essential precursor to anticapitalist politics.

This process emphasizes how living labor appears as separated and independent, and how the values attached to the means of production form opposite its capacity to labor. These values initially appear as use-values, but the value that Marx works with is that produced by capital. Once upon a time, we may infer, there was a value theory that was not produced by capital. Individual actors and laborers grappled with such values in some noncapitalist way. This was the theory of use-value, not the value associated with necessary labor time, but a value that derives from and relates to the production of useful objects and things. This is the value theory which arose through the proliferation of noncapitalist market exchange.

The precapitalist notion of value had to be supplanted by the value theory of capital. This prompts us to think about the transition to a socialist theory of value. By correctly dissecting what is happening around us under the laws of motion of capital, we become much more aware and conscious of what alternative possibilities might be and why some such transformation in value theory is necessary or even inevitable. This is something Marx raises, albeit obliquely, when he talks about the way in which the product appears to labor, "as a combination of alien material, alien instrument and alien labour—as *alien property*, and why, after production, [labour] has become poorer by the life forces expended, but otherwise begins the drudgery anew, existing as a mere subjective labor capacity separated from the conditions of its life" (462–3). This is what happens to laborers as they become separated (alienated) from the objective conditions of their own life. And this is what the capitalist theory of value encompasses and what the laborer at some point recognizes and resists.

"However," Marx goes on to say, "if we consider the original relation, before the entry of money into the self-realization process,"
that is, before this whole system got going, "then various conditions
appear which have to have arisen, or been given historically, for
money to become capital and labour to become capital-positing."
The condition is "capital-creating labour, wage labour." This kind of
labor requires (1) the separation of living labor capacity as a subjective existence from the objective conditions of living labor as well as
from the means of existence; (2) the existence of value in the form of
objectified labor presented as an accumulation of the use-values
required for production; (3) the circulation of money through
exchange sufficient to buy alien labor; and (4) "the side representing
the objective conditions of labour in the form of independent values
for-themselves—must present itself as *value*, and must regard the
positing of value, self-realization, money-making, as the ultimate
purpose—not direct consumption or the creation of use value"
(463–4). Notice, once again, that it is capital that is value-making
and value-defining. This is the point at which capital's theory of
value begins to crystallize. This is the moment of its becoming. The
conditions of "equality and freedom" and free-market exchange
must already be established, however, in the labor market.

By correctly dissecting what is happening around us under the
laws of motion of capital, we become much more aware of what alternative possibilities might be. "The conditions under which the relation appears at the origin, or which appear as the historic presuppositions of its becoming, reveal . . . on the one side, dissolution of lower
forms of living labour; on the other, dissolution of happier forms of
the same" (464). Among the former, it is vital that slavery and serfdom have been suspended and that "living labour capacity belongs to
itself," and that labor "has disposition over the expenditure of its
forces, through exchange." The conditions of "equality and freedom"
must already be established in the labor market. What the free worker
sells is a "particular expenditure of force to a particular capitalist,
whom he confronts as an independent *individual*" (464). This is not,
however, "his relation to the existence of capital as capital, i.e. to the

capitalist class." Unlike the slave and the serf, "the totality of the free worker's labour capacity appears to him as his property ... over which he, as subject, exercises domination, and which he maintains by expending it" (465). What the worker sells to capital is not labor or even labor power, but laboring capacity, which ultimately translates into the capacity to produce surplus-value for capital.

Capital-creating labor has to be distinguished, however, "from other forms of labour for day-wages, etc." "The exchange of objectified labour for living labour does not yet constitute either capital on one side or wage labour on the other. The entire class of so-called *services*, from the bootblack up to the king falls into this category. Likewise, the free day-labourer . . ." (465). There is a vast army of such free day laborers available (and Marx spells out a number of examples) that supply a good or a service for some sort of monetary remuneration. But none of this is capital-making. The soldier, for example, "exchanges the performance of his services not for *capital* but for the revenue of the state" (468). The point, however, is that for capital to form and to take over the organization of production there had to be a preexisting "free" labor force that could easily be converted into the wage labor—the capacity to labor—that capital craves and needs. The mass of labor already exchanging against revenues constitutes such a force.

The importance of this stratum in the population carries over into "bourgeois society itself," where "all exchange of personal services for revenue—including labour for personal consumption, cooking, sewing etc., garden work etc., up to and including All the unproductive classes, civil servants, physicians, lawyers, scholars etc.—belongs under this rubric, within this category . . . All these workers, from the least to the highest, obtain for themselves a share of the surplus product, of the capitalists' *revenue*." To be sure, all those who provide such services create a use-value of some sort for their clients in return for money value. It is they who may well convert their role to that of capital over time—"the emancipated serf becomes . . . the capitalist" (468). But "with the presupposition of capital as the dominant power, all these relations become more or less *dishonoured*." "In periods of the dissolution of *pre-bourgeois* relations, there sporadically occur free workers whose services are bought for purposes not of consumption, but of *production* . . . only of *direct* use values, not of *values* . . . wherever these free workers increase in number . . . there the old mode of production— commune, patriarchal, feudal, etc.—is in the process of dissolution, and the elements of real wage labour are in preparation."

There are three points to be made about this account of the transition in the role of wage labor with the rise of capital to dominance. The first is that, while there had to be an abundance of a "class" of unproductive "free labourers" available for conversion from the role of service-providing to that of capital-producing wage labor, the form of the precapitalist social formation might vary considerably, with important carryover effects (e.g., the perpetuation of patriarchy). The second is that the "unproductive class" of laborers living by exchange against revenues does not and cannot disappear. Its continuing role requires rather more consideration than Marx and subsequent analysts typically give to it. Third, the account of original or primitive accumulation which Marx provides makes it seem as if the violent dispossession of access to the means of production was critical for the formation of wage labor, whereas here we see a broad preparatory process that paved the way for a possible peaceable conversion from revenue-seeking to capital-producing employment rather than a violent dispossession of, say, the peasantry.

We end up finally with some observations on how "property relations or laws" enter in. "For example, the fact that surplus labour is posited as surplus value of capital means that the worker does not appropriate the product of his own labour; that it appears to him as *alien property*." This is the first law of bourgeois property and rests on the identity of laboring capacity with alien property. The second law is an inversion of the first; "property as negation of the alien quality of alien labour." The latter is best understood as property by seizure of alienated labor. Labor is not, furthermore, isolated but "a combination of labours—whose individual component parts are alien to one another, so that the overall process as a totality is *not* the *work* of the individual worker." The combination of the labor involved (the detail divisions of labor within the corporation) is imposed by "an alien will and an alien intelligence" (that of capital). This is materially manifest through "the *objective unity* of the *machinery*, of fixed capital, which, as *animated monster*, objectifies the scientific idea." Hence, "just as the worker relates to the product of his labour as an alien thing, so does he relate to the combination of labour as an alien combination, as well as to his own labour as an expression of his life, which, although it belongs to him, is alien to him and coerced from him" (470).

"Capital thus represents both labour and its product as negated individualized labour and hence the negated property of the individual worker. Capital is the existence of social labour." It is the collective organization of divisions of labor within the corporation that matters. It "appears as the predominant subject and owner of *alien labour*, and its relation is itself as complete a contradiction as is that of wage labour." This difference between social and combined labor on the one hand (e.g., in the factory) and individualized labor (e.g., artisan production) on the other will return to haunt the analysis later on in the text.

Thus endeth, as they say, the first lesson on how to investigate the becoming of capital with historical materialist tools.

PRECAPITALIST ECONOMIC FORMATIONS

The next forty-five pages are taken up with Marx's attempt to reconstruct the history of precapitalist economic formations with an eye to understanding the circumstances of the becoming of capital to dominance. This section was translated and presented to English-speaking readers in 1965 with an excellent introduction—worth reading to this day—by the eminent Marxist historian Eric Hobsbawm.[1] As he points

---

1 Karl Marx, *Pre-capitalist Economic Formations*, ed. Eric Hobsbawm, trans. Jack Cohen (New York: International Publishers, 1965).

out, Marx (and Engels) did not have available to them the extensive historical investigations into global economic history that have accumulated since their times. Furthermore, their own historical investigations were limited by their other commitments. Under these circumstances, it is astonishing how much they did accomplish. This derives from their historical materialist method (honed in the study of capital's becoming, as we have seen). This also allowed them to laser in on the central questions that needed to be addressed about the past. They were, in short, prepared to sift through the mass of detail already available to them in, for example, the legal texts of classical scholars (which Marx was familiar with from his early doctoral research) and a mass of (sometimes questionable) anthropological and historical writings to synthesize some understanding of how precapitalist economic formations functioned. Nevertheless, there were many areas of economic history that remained in the shadows. For example, Marx raises the later much-contested idea of a distinctive oriental despotism as an Asiatic mode of production. This is but one of several unsupported (and some would argue unsupportable) shortcuts that Marx uses to organize his investigations. In reading these materials, therefore, the issue of whether Marx got it all right is not the point. What stands out is his method of inquiry and ability (and preparedness) to tentatively sketch in the shadowy outlines of the ecosystemic totalities that human societies have managed to construct in different places and times prior to the rise to dominance of capital. The fact that capital was itself rooted in and built upon this prior history is taken for granted.

We begin, however, with a conundrum. In *The Critique of Political Economy*, which was published in German in 1859 and was therefore written around the same time (if you can believe it!) as the prolific writings of the *Grundrisse*, Marx ventured the following periodization of world history, prefaced, however, with some general observations on how political-economic transitions typically occur:

> No social order is ever destroyed before all the productive forces
> for which it is sufficient have been developed, and new superior

relations of production never replace older ones before the material conditions for their existence have matured within the framework of the old society. Mankind thus inevitably sets itself only such tasks as it is able to solve, since closer examination will always show that the problem itself arises only when the material conditions for its solution are already present or at least in the course of formation. In broad outline, the Asiatic, the ancient, feudal and modern bourgeois modes of production may be designated as epochs marking progress in the economic development of society. The bourgeois mode of production is the last antagonistic form of the social process of production—antagonistic not in the sense of individual antagonism but of an antagonism that emanates from an individuals' social conditions of existence—but the productive forces developing within bourgeois society create also the material conditions for a solution of this antagonism.[1]

What is strange about this statement is not the incisive if cryptic summary of the principles of progressive social evolution, but the epochal designations of Asiatic, ancient, feudal and bourgeois modes of production. Such designations are not supported, as Hobsbawm also points out, anywhere else in Marx's work (with the exception of *The German Ideology*, in shadowy form), and they can be reconstructed only with great difficulty in the more nuanced presentation of historical and geographical transformations in the *Grundrisse*. Furthermore, the teleological linearity of "progress" (with its pointer to the communism to come) in the *Critique* gets muffled if not extinguished in the *Grundrisse*. The impression created in the latter is of an evolutionary process that is far more contingent and differentiated by place, culture and time. This section of the text needs to be read against the background of this conundrum.

---

1 Karl Marx, *A Contribution to the Critique of Political Economy*, ed. Maurice Dobb, trans. S. W. Ryazanskaya (New York: International Publishers, 1970), 21.

"One of the historic presuppositions of capital," Marx begins by observing, "is free labour" exchangeable for money and separated "from the means of labour and the material for labour." This presumes "release of the worker from the soil as his natural workshop—hence dissolution of small, free landed property as well as of communal landownership resting on the oriental commune." In these prior forms "the natural unity of labour with its material" is achieved and "the individual relates to himself as proprietor, as master of the conditions of his reality" (471). Individuals relate to others as "co-proprietors" depending on whether their situation derives "from the community or from the individual families which constitute the commune." They relate to each other not as workers but as proprietors. Their aim "is not the *creation of value*" but the "sustenance of the individual proprietor and of his family, as well as of the total community" (472). The labor theory of value has no function or purpose in situations of this kind.

In this first form of landed property, a "spontaneous" form of community arises, comprising "family, and the family extended as a clan, or through intermarriage between families, or combination of clans." When the pastoral version of this gives way to the settled version, this community will likely be modified depending on "various external, climatic, geographic, physical etc. conditions" as well as according to "their clan character." But it is the clan community that presupposes *the communal appropriation . . . and utilization of the land.*" Furthermore, the communality "of blood, language, customs" shapes the objective conditions of their life. But above all, "the earth is the great workshop, the arsenal that furnishes both means and material of labour, as well as the seat, the *base* of the community. People relate naïvely to it as the *property of the community*, of the community producing and reproducing itself in living labour. Each individual conducts himself only as a link, as a member of this community as *proprietor or possessor*" (472). The distinction between proprietorship (e.g., private or common ownership) and possession (usufruct, the right to use the land) is important.

Such a mode of production rests on a direct metabolic relation with nature. The conditions of labor are not themselves the product of labor but appear as "natural or divine." With such a land-relation as its foundation, labor can be realized "in very different ways" (472). This is an important concession on Marx's part. It affects, for example, how we might interpret this famous statement, immediately preceding the passage already cited from the *Critique of Political Economy*:

> Changes in the economic foundation lead sooner or later to the transformation of the whole immense superstructure. In studying such transformations it is always necessary to distinguish between the material transformation of the economic conditions of production, which can be determined with the precision of natural science, and the legal, political, religious, artistic or philosophic—in short, ideological forms in which men become conscious of this conflict and fight it out. Just as one does not judge an individual by what he thinks about himself, so one cannot judge such a period of transformation by its consciousness, but, on the contrary, this consciousness must be explained from the contradictions of material life, from the conflict existing between the social forces of production and the relations of production.[1]

This statement of the so-called base-superstructure thesis has often been interpreted as economic determinism. But the fact that the material conditions can be determined with the precision of natural science, whereas the power of legal, religious, artistic and philosophic thought cannot does not automatically confer more power of determination to the material as opposed to the immaterial conditions. The presentation here in the *Grundrisse* is much more dialectical, fluid and contingent than that proposed in the vulgar physical determinist reading. But Marx is also conceding that

---

1 Ibid.

the same material and social conditions can give rise to a variety of legal and religious institutions and modes of thought (philosophies). But none of this occurs outside of the realm of our material experience of being in the world, and that experience is itself mediated through our history. There is a continuity here with the approach taken earlier, in which the relation between material conditions and immaterial political subjectivities (e.g., around the discussion of money and market exchange) was opened up for inspection.

The immediate problem for Marx was the obvious fact that the decentralized, communal, clan-like structures visible in many parts of the world were overlain in Asia (and in China in particular) with a "unity realized in the form of the despot, the father of the many communities" to which individuals were subservient (472–3). "The surplus product . . . automatically belongs to this highest unity. Amidst oriental despotism and the propertylessness which seems legally to exist there, this clan or communal property exists in fact as the foundation, created mostly by a combination of manufactures and agriculture within the small commune, which thus becomes altogether self-sustaining, and contains all the conditions of reproduction and surplus production within itself" (473). In the Asiatic case, as Marx understood it, much of the surplus was taken as tribute and common labor "for the exaltation of the unity, partly of the real despot, partly of the imagined clan-being, the god." A hierarchical structure (an imperial system) arises, of despot supported by tribute, and organized communes comprised of peasant families and others as producing entities concerned with self-reproduction.

There is a disputatious history concerning the conceptual relevance of an Asiatic mode of production. The political consequences have been serious. If prerevolutionary China was feudal, then the principal enemy of the emancipation of the peasantry was the landlord class organized as war-lords. If the main enemy and the main form of political oppressive power was the imperial state and its mandarin bureaucracy, then this defined a very different political task. In the 1930s, Stalin mandated the first position within the world communist movement, and Mao waged a revolutionary struggle against the landlord class largely on that political basis. Dissidents, most notably Karl Wittfogel (author of *Oriental Despotism*) depicted the state-oriented communism that arose after 1949 as a continuation of rather than a break with a centralized repressive imperial tradition rendered necessary because of the large-scale public works required to manage water use and irrigation in a semi-arid environment. This spurious environmental determinist thesis of distinctive, politically centralized "hydraulic civilizations" has since been largely discredited. Even in China, it turns out that large-scale water management did not necessarily require the bureaucratic centralization of state power to work.

The organization of labor may continue on a communal basis, even as it "vegetates" as individuals go about their appointed tasks in reproducing the existing system. But, within this precapitalist world, tentative steps are taken to appropriate communal labor for more significant tasks within a framework of social relations such as villeinage or the more formal structures of "lordly dominium" that could be found in Mexico, Peru, or India, culminating in "a more despotic or more democratic form of this community system" (473). Note how Marx here appears to postulate a historical political alternative between despotic and democratic forms. But Marx then changes tack. "The communal conditions of real appropriation" (e.g., irrigation works and transport systems) "then appear as the work of the higher unity—of the despotic regime hovering over the little communes." It is in this context too, that weak city formation makes its first appearance in relation to trade or as administrative and religious centers of surplus consumption (474).

The second form which Marx identifies—"and like the first it has essential modifications brought about locally, historically etc. . . . also assumes the *community* as its first presupposition" but "presupposes as base not the countryside, but the town as an already created seat (centre) of the rural population (owners of land)." "The earth in itself—regardless of the obstacles it may place in the way of working it . . . offers no resistance [to attempts] to relate to it as the inorganic nature of the living individual, as his workshop, as the means and object of labour and the means of life for the subject" (474). The main threat to the reproduction of the commune is rivalry from other communes, so that war, defensive fortifications and the like shape the mode of life in distinctive ways. The basis of "this bellicose organization" lies in "the concentration of residences in the town," presumably for defence and security reasons. Hierarchical forms of clan and class organization entail the separation out of communal property and communal functions in the public realm from private property such that "the individual can become a *private proprietor* of land and soil—of a particular plot—whose particular cultivation falls to him and his family. The commune—as state—is . . . the relation of these free and equal private proprietors to one another, their bond against the outside" (475). The communes rest on "working landed proprietors" and "small-owning peasants" whose independence "rests on their mutual relations as commune members." The intimate relation to the soil is "mediated" by "the being of the state." This is, we should note, one of the few passages where Marx touches upon state formation as a concrete precursor to and variant within the rise of capital.

The survival of such a community depends on "the preservation of equality among its free self-sustaining peasants, and their own labour as the condition of the survival of their property" (476). This means that "the individual is placed in such conditions of earning his living as to make not the acquiring of wealth his object, but self-sustenance." This, in turn, implies that "the survival of the commune is the reproduction of all of its members as self-sustaining peasants, whose surplus time belongs precisely to the commune, the work of war etc." Again, the labor theory of value has no relevance. In the Germanic version, which Marx examines at some length, the commune member is not "co-possessor of the communal property," as in the oriental form. Communal property prevails but the individual can have private possession without private property (477). This recurring distinction between property and possession is important. It persists into our own times. In contemporary China, for example, individuals have rights of possession on the land, but the state retains ownership.

Marx identifies two different organizational principles—those of "*ancestry* or *locality*"—upon which "the ancient states" were founded. "The ancestral clans preceded the locality clans in time and are almost everywhere pushed aside by the latter" (478). How the territoriality of the commune or state is constructed raises major questions which are not elaborated on here. Nor does Marx take up here the logic and significance of colonial conquest and empire building to economic life. It is interesting to note Marx's belief in the trend toward more territorial forms of organization over time. However, the rise of the state form is, alas, not subjected to any detailed scrutiny.

Several themes are enunciated in these pages, which echo throughout this study of precapitalist social formations. The form of social relations (in the family, the clan or as opposing classes) rests upon a process of "becoming" that is perpetually opening the way to future possibilities, even as capital itself in embryo so often blocks the transitions to that which it renders possible. There is the question of how to understand the metabolic relation to nature both as a universal principle and as a specific modality given the conditions prevailing within a given mode of production. We will take up this question in some detail shortly. But this relation to nature and the land is mediated through property relations, through diverse legal and political structures embedded in communal forms such as the commune, the city, the state or some other specific social structure within the public realm (the *ager publicus*). Urbanization and the town–country (urban–rural) relation also have to be interrogated and addressed:

> The history of classical antiquity is the history of cities, but of cities founded on landed property and on agriculture; Asiatic history is a kind of indifferent unity of town and countryside (the really large cities must be regarded here merely as royal

camps, as works of artifice ... erected over the economic
construction proper); the Middle Ages (Germanic period)
begins with the land as the seat of history, whose further development then moves forward in the contradiction between town
and countryside; the modern [age] is the urbanization of the
countryside, not the ruralization of the city as in antiquity. (479)

The rise of urbanization plays a key role in the changing structures of social relations and political forms. "With its coming-
together in the city, the commune possesses an economic existence as such; the city's mere *presence*, as such, distinguishes it from
a mere multiplicity of independent houses. The whole, here,
consists not merely of its parts. It is a kind of independent organ-
ism." It would then follow that if the town and the city are independent organisms within the capitalist mode of production (itself
construed as an organic or ecosystemic totality), then the laws of
growth and integration governing urbanization will have an
important role to play. While Marx does not venture too far down
this line of inquiry, the general contemporary acceptance of the
role that urbanization and city formation played in the transition
from feudalism to capitalism accords with Marx's observation. In
the Germanic case, the commune "appears as a *coming-together* . . .
not as a *being-together*, as a unification made up of independent
subjects, landed proprietors, and not as a unity. The commune
therefore does not in fact exist as a state or political body" (483).
Marx is here making a very important point. The state and the city
are constituted differently, and to this day there is not only difference but frequent conflict between them within the mode of
production as a totality. New York City is not the United States and
vice versa.

In the case of urbanization, Marx argues, "individual property
does not appear mediated by the commune; rather, the existence
of the commune and of communal property appear as mediated"
through the relations "of independent subjects to one another. The
economic totality is, at bottom, contained in each individual

household, which forms an independent centre of production for itself." In this Germanic world, "the totality is the individual residence, which itself appears as only a small dot on the land belonging to it." There then follow a couple of pages of detailed discussion of the various forms of private property and communal powers and obligations even as, in the Germanic case, "urban citizenship resolves itself economically into the simple form that the agriculturist [is a] resident of a city . . . not citizen of a state" (484). "The main point here is this: In all these forms—in which landed property and agriculture form the basis of the economic order, and where the economic aim is . . . the production of use values," then "social reproduction" entails "appropriation" of land, soil and nature. It is at this point that Marx shifts away from the questions of urbanization that he began with to consider in some detail the role of the metabolic relation to nature. Since this is a theme of some importance in contemporary Marxism, I here examine the general stance that Marx assumes with respect to this question.

THE MASTERY OF AND METABOLIC RELATION TO NATURE

There is frequent mention in these pages of how we might best understand the metabolic relation to nature. Was Marx anthropocentric in his formulations? The answer is yes, clearly so. Given his principled historical materialism he cannot be anything but. He often resorted to a language of domination and mastery over nature and was committed to overcoming "nature idolatory" in any form. This was a common stance in his time, and Darwin was his lodestar. While his language seems at times insensitive and objectionable given contemporary sensibilities, it is important to recognize what Marx meant by it. He was far from believing that the metabolic relation to nature was unproblematic. He recognized the unintended consequences of human action were everywhere apparent, and that mastery did not mean a total disregard for nature in itself, but a responsibility to sustain and work with the laws of nature. Mastery through a sophisticated scientific understanding of natural law is critical to the perpetuation of human life. The eradication of smallpox and the total control of other catastrophic viruses is, for example, from Marx's perspective, neither pernicious nor unduly arrogant. In Marx's time, the control of cholera was a pressing problem in both Paris and London.

There are different forms and degrees of anthropocentrism. As usual in these situations, we need to distinguish between Marx's own views (which sometimes remain obscure) and the views he is attributing to capital given its practices and statements of its ruling ideas. Historically, the productivist views of many Marxists during the Stalin era led to a cavalier, utilitarian and uncaring approach to nature and environmental questions, with some disastrous results in the communist world. The revolt of many in the Frankfurt School against the domination of nature thesis opened the way toward a far more responsible and integrated view of how the metabolic relation to nature should be approached both in theory and in practice. But as late as the 1970s, there were many currents in Marxist thinking that were hostile to building environmental and ecological perspectives into Marxist theory and practice. A commitment to do so does not entail the total rejection of anthropocentrism. While we can write beautiful tracts on "thinking like a mountain" or "like a stream" (as the anarchist geographer Elisée Reclus did so effectively in the nineteenth century) or espouse principles of "deep ecology," it is impossible to avoid the fact that it is human beings who are doing the imagining, the thinking and the communicating. As Wittgenstein once said in relation to his theory of language games, "if lions could speak we could not understand what they say." It is in this context that the passages that take up the question of the metabolic relation to nature in the *Grundrisse* offer an opportunity for purposive reflection.

In precapitalist formations, we are dealing with "the unity of living and active humanity with the natural, inorganic conditions of their metabolic exchange with nature, and hence their appropriation of nature." This is not what requires explanation. Rather, it is "the *separation* between these inorganic conditions of human existence" and human activity that calls for explanation, and this arises, Marx argues, "only in the relation of wage labour and capital." The separation of nature from culture in thought and concept is, in short, a historical product of the rise of capital (489). "Nature becomes purely an object for humankind, purely a matter of utility; ceases to be recognized as a power for itself; and the theoretical discovery of its autonomous laws appears merely as a ruse so as to subjugate it under human needs, whether as an object of consumption or as a means of production" (409). This is not Marx's normative view, but a representation of what capital does.

In his earlier discussion of communal structures, Marx noted the specific way in which "the earth in itself—regardless of the obstacles it may place in the way of working it, really appropriating it—offers no resistance to [attempts] to relate to it as the inorganic nature of the living individual, as his workshop, as the means and object of labour and the means of life for the subject" (474). The term "inorganic nature" is frequently used and calls for elucidation. Marx appears to mean by it all of those appropriations from the natural world external to human labor. It does not refer to that aspect of nature that is physical and dead rather than biological and alive. Another way to understand this is to accept precapitalist understandings of nature, in ways broadly consistent with many contemporary Indigenous views, as alive and inseparable from the human life process, as an integral rather than separable part of social and ecological life. Capital, by way of contrast, objectifies all of nature as dead and treats it as a separable world containing manipulable features of utility for human use. It is ultimately commodifiable and is incorporated as a property right subject to appropriation and therefore monetizable as land rent. The result is an alienated relation to nature, an unwelcome product of capital's becoming.

The agriculturalist "appropriates" the "natural conditions of labour, of the *earth* as the original instrument of labour as well as its workshop and repository of raw materials. The individual relates simply to the objective conditions of labour as being his;

[relates] to them as the inorganic nature of his subjectivity" which "does not itself appear as a *product* of labour, but is already there as *nature*" (485). The individual relates to this as a sensuous being evolving in response to a life process "instantly mediated by the naturally arisen, spontaneous, more or less historically developed and modified presence of the individual as *member of a commune*." The relation "to the earth as property is always mediated through the occupation of the land and soil." Hence "the individual can never appear here in the dot-like isolation" presumed by the liberal theory of the "mere free worker." The different forms of communal organization intersect with "climate, physical make-up of the land and soil, the physically determined mode of its exploitation" along with wars, "migrations, historic experiences etc." These determine the fruits of labor in specific instances (486). Under conditions of slavery and serfdom,

> this separation [between nature and culture] does not take place; rather, one part of society is treated by the other as merely an inorganic and natural condition of its own reproduction. The slave stands in no relation whatsoever to the objective conditions of his labour; rather labour itself, both in the form of the slave and in that of the serf, is classified as an inorganic condition of production, along with other natural beings, such as cattle, as an accessory of the earth. In other words: the original conditions of production appear as natural presuppositions, natural conditions of the producer's existence just as his living body . . . appears as the presupposition of his self.

This very important passage firstly reaffirms that the distinction which arises between nature and culture is a product of the historic separation of capital from labor. At the same time, it also explains how the treatment of Indigenous, colonized and occupied populations along with serfs and slaves as "natural" creatures rather than "human" beings ends up bifurcating the capitalist social world (with obvious and often disastrous racial consequences).

> These *natural conditions of existence*, to which he relates as to
> his own inorganic body, are themselves double. (1) of a subjec-
> tive, and (2) of an objective nature. He finds himself a member
> of a family, clan, tribe, etc.—which then, in a historic process of
> intermixture and antithesis with others, takes on a different
> shape; and, as such a member, he relates to a specific nature (say,
> here, still earth, land, soil) as his own inorganic being, as a
> condition of his own production and reproduction. (490)

Marx thus seeks to reintegrate on the basis of historical inquiry some
alternative meaning into a contemporary world by viewing nature as
part of our own inorganic being. It is part of us. It is not something
outside of us to be merely dominated. This earlier position on page
410 and the argument on page 488 and onward is the creation by
Marx of broad, sweeping arguments about our positionality in relation to nature. It is about meaning, recognition and consciousness as
well as material connection and necessary appropriation.

There can be, at the end of the day, no separation between us and
nature. It is this arbitrarily imposed separation that fosters the environmental dangers we now face. The appropriation of natural forces
and powers underpins and presumes some sort of property rights—
not necessarily private or individualized property rights, but collective and common property agreements through which the metabolic
relation of nature is mediated and regulated. Meanwhile, human
beings assiduously work to transform their natural world into what
Marx elsewhere refers to as a "second nature." But, as Marx more
specifically argues in *Capital*, we cannot change the natural world
without changing ourselves. Nor can we change ourselves without
changing the natural world around us. It is, after all, our inorganic
body. Here he is simply content to point out that "the full development of human mastery over the forces of nature" is inseparable (for
good or for ill) from mastery "of humanity's own nature" (488).

Some of the insights that come out of this section of the
Grundrisse on the different modes of production refer briefly to
colonization. But surprisingly, the roles of colonialism (including

of the settler variety) and imperialism are ignored. Marx briefly discusses wars and conquest, communal defense of territory, along with slavery. But he also talks about the dissolution of preceding social relations, and this will become a major theme. When money comes in, for example, it dissolves preexisting social relations. Part of what we are looking at here is the possibility of reconstructing relationality to nature, social relations, and also, at the same time, becoming aware and becoming conscious of the ways in which labor is producing not only capital but the capitalist class which returns to dominate the worker. Labor constructs the agency and instruments of its own domination (including that of nature) in the form of capital, in the persona of the capitalist. This sets the stage for an emancipatory project of negation, first in its bourgeois and ultimately in its socialistic form.

THE DISSOLUTION OF PREEXISTING SOCIAL RELATIONS

As the text unfolds the issue increasingly arises as to how, exactly, capital might root itself in the different prior modes of production (or particular elements therein) at the same time as it converts or transcends prominent features in those prior modes of production into forms adequate to capital. The most obvious example is the conversion of money forms with their multiple functions and long and complex histories into money capital and the rise of banking as a prime instrument of this conversion. Another example is the existence of wage labor in relation to revenues that could easily be diverted into wage labor to produce capital. While it is vital to acknowledge the hybridity of different modes along with significant geographical variations that have arisen across time and space, these transitions (and they were certainly plural) had to be sufficiently concordant as to make ultimate fusion into a global system of capital accumulation possible (a process arguably only now reaching its conclusion). This issue is broached on page 495 with the help of one word—"dissolution." But dissolution of what?

> The original unity between a particular form of community (clan) and the corresponding property in nature . . . has its living reality in a specific *mode of production* itself, a mode which appears both as a relation between the individuals, and as their specific active relation to inorganic nature, a specific mode of working (which is always family labour, often communal labour). The community itself appears as the first great force of production; particular kinds of production conditions (e.g. stock-breeding, agriculture), develop particular modes of production and particular forces of production, subjective, appearing as qualities of individuals, as well as objective [ones]. In the last analysis, their community, as well as the property based on it, resolves itself into a specific stage in the development of the productive forces of working subjects— to which correspond their specific relations amongst one another and towards nature. (495)

This form of society reproduces itself up until a certain point. Then it "turns into dissolution."

The next twenty pages of the text are devoted to the study of dissolution. The first step may seem somewhat peculiar. "Human beings become individuals only through the process of history," Marx declares. Humans appear originally "as *species-being . . . clan being, herd animal*—although in no way whatever as a [person] in the political sense." The rise of capital "dissolves" this "herd-like existence" and renders it "superfluous." In bourgeois society, the worker stands alone, individuated subjectively in the context of a "true community," which the worker "tries to make a meal of, and which makes a meal of him" (496). The bourgeois community "presupposes its subjects [as individuals] in a specific objective unity with their conditions of production." The latter are perpetually being revolutionized. "The development of the forces of production dissolves these forms, and their dissolution is itself a development of the human productive forces."

The rise of capital "presupposes a process of history which dissolves the forms in which the worker is a proprietor, or in which the proprietor works" (497). This is followed by a short-list of the dissolutions requisite for to the needs of an emergent capital. (1) "*Dissolution* of the relations to the earth—land and soil—as natural condition of production"; (2) "*Dissolution of the relations* in which he appears as *proprietor of the instrument*(s)" of production (e.g., the artisan labor typical of medieval cities); (3) Dissolution of the worker's control over "the means of consumption" and of "the consumption fund" (the means of consumption); (4) "*Dissolution* . . . of the relations in which the workers themselves, the *living labour capacities* themselves, still belong *directly among the objective conditions of production*" (i.e., the conditions of slavery and serfdom). These are the "historic presuppositions needed before the worker can be found as a free worker, as . . . purely subjective labour capacity confronting the objective conditions of production as his *not-property*, as *alien property*, as *value* for itself, as capital" (498). This, for the laborer, entails

> the negation of the situation in which the working individual relates to land and soil, to the earth, as his own . . . Posited in the most original form, it means relating to the earth as proprietor, and finding raw material and instrument on hand, as well as the necessaries of life created not by labour but by the earth itself. Once this relation is reproduced, secondary instruments and the fruits of the earth created through labour itself appear as included with landed property in its primitive form.

The tentative transition to capital began upon the land, but "this historic situation is thus first of all negated as a full property relation, in the worker's relation to the conditions of labour as capital" (498–9).

This "dissolution" of the worker's relation to the land has obvious consequences (not least the alienated relation of labor to nature). It sets the stage for the conceptual separation between nature and culture that bedevils our current mental conceptions of the world, making it difficult to confront and control (let alone internalize) severe environmental stresses and disruptions. The rise of capital entails a revolutionary transformation in the metabolic relation to nature. Mastery and domination of culture over nature displaces the concordance and integration of life forms which to this day ground much Indigenous thought and practices. The second transition liberates the free worker as "purely subjective labour capacity" that confronts the objective conditions of production "as *alien property*", as value for itself, "as capital." This requires transcending the forms of capitalism created during the manufacturing period, in which artisanal labor with particular and sometimes guild organizational skills was empowered, even as it was increasingly mobilized to satisfy capital's quest for surplus-value. The laborer's relation to the instruments of labor is dissolved.

What follows is a detailed inquiry into the way in which successive dissolutions and reconfigurations in social practices enabled the rise of capital to dominance. On page 514, he arrives at an interim conclusion: "The true nature of capital emerges only at the *end of the second cycle* . . . Production originally appeared to lie beyond circulation, and circulation beyond production. The circulation of capital—circulation posited as the circulation of capital—spans both moments. Production appears in it as the conclusion and the point of departure of circulation, and vice versa."

What does Marx mean by this? What does the invocation of "the end of the second cycle" have to do with it? Consider the depiction of the completed circulation process of capital in Figure 2. We there see the different moments of production, circulation, consumption, social reproduction, distribution, etc., all linked together systemically to enable a continuous process (which eventually becomes a spiral) of capital accumulation. Figure 2 presupposes that the value that is in motion has gone around the circuit not just once but twice, thrice, in an ongoing continuous process of accumulation. Capital is defined, recall, as value in motion. The value is realized and preserved only when it keeps moving through the different moments (speeding up, expanding and accelerating). It can be tagged and named as capital only when we see it moving through the cycle for the second time. Thereafter, it becomes self-perpetuating. What the intervening pages (495–514) describe is how the different moments are brought into a distinctive relation to each other. In a peasant economy, for example, production and consumption are confined to the peasant holding. Circulation in the market is of no consequence (except for occasional trading of unneeded surpluses). Production and circulation are not connected, while production and consumption are indistinguishable (they are not separate moments). Similarly, traders and usurers may actively circulate money, but in a way that has nothing directly to do with production activities on the peasant plot or even within the largely self-sufficient peasant community. Money, on the other hand, circulates according to its own laws of motion (as described in the opening chapter of the *Grundrisse*). This has nothing to do with how money might circulate as capital. Marx holds that the "true nature of capital" entails the connecting together of these separate and different moments into a coherent system of the sort depicted in Figure 2. Once these connections have been made in practice, then production is both a product and a point of departure in relation to circulation and production and consumption as separable acts. The money that becomes money capital clearly originates in circulation (505), but its use changes. "What enables money wealth to become capital is the encounter, on one side, with free workers; and on the other side, with the necessaries and materials etc., which previously were in one way or another the *property* of the masses who are now object-less, and are also *free* and purchasable." In other words, money could be used as capital only when there was a preexisting labor market in which "free" workers needed to trade their capacity to labor in order to live, along with a commodity market in which there were sufficient means of production available for purchase. The fact that money could become money capital had nothing to do with the inherent qualities of money and everything to do with the existence of free markets for labor capacity along with markets to buy objective means of production. How the laborers became "free" is a long story which Marx endeavours to relate in some detail in these pages. I leave these details to the reader, but the linking together of the different moments depicted in Figure 2 into a coherent system was historically a messy business, entailing many false starts, partial breakthroughs, concrete struggles and some violent uprisings. "Dissolutions" (which are, by the way, ongoing) are stressful and difficult at the same time as they often create the potentiality for emancipations and liberatory politics, which Marx does not shy away from embracing. The social relations that had to be forged for the systemic circulation and reproduction of capital were not easily achieved. But once the system was set in motion, its evolutionary spiral became the motor for world history.

I shall refrain from attempting any systematic representation of Marx's exposition. But it is useful to highlight some of the qualities of Marx's thinking, since these inform his whole approach to the historical origins of capital throughout the *Grundrisse*, as well as in his other works. By extension, the account he offers should surely influence both his and our thinking about how the transition to socialism might be accomplished.

"The same process which divorced a mass of individuals from their previous relations to the *objective conditions of labour*, relations which were, in one way or another, affirmative, negated these relations, and thereby transformed these individuals into *free* workers, [also] freed . . . land and soil, raw material, necessaries of life, instruments of labour, money, or all of these—from their *previous state of attachment* to the individuals now separated from them" (503). This breakup and negation of the previously "affirmative" relations between these different elements prepared the ground for the entry of capital:

> In truth, the *period of the dissolution* of the earlier modes of production and modes of the workers relation to the objective conditions of labour *is at the same time a period* in which *monetary wealth* on the one side *has* already developed to a certain extent, and on the other side grows and expands rapidly through

the same circumstances as accelerate the above dissolution. It [money] is itself one of the agencies of that dissolution, while at the same time that dissolution is the condition of its transformation into capital. But the *mere presence of monetary wealth*, and even the achievement of a kind of supremacy on its part, is in no way sufficient for this *dissolution into capital* to happen . . . Capital does not create the objective conditions of labour. Rather, its *original formation* is that, through the historic process of the dissolution of the old mode of production, value existing as money-wealth is enabled, on one side, *to buy* the objective conditions of labour; on the other side, to exchange money for the *living labour* of the workers who have been set free. All these moments are present; their divorce is a historic process, a process of dissolution, and it is *the latter* which enables money to transform itself into *capital*. (506–7)

Marx here notes that when

the great English landowners dismissed their retainers . . . [and] their tenants chased off their smaller cottagers etc., then, firstly, a mass of living labour powers were thrown upon the *labour market*, a mass which was free in the double sense, free from the old relations of clientship, bondage and servitude, and secondly free of all belongings and possessions . . . *free of all property*; dependent on the sale of its labour capacity or on begging, vagabondage or robbery as its only source of income. (508)

An important quality of Marx's presentation is that, while he will be adamant in denying the triggering role of this or that moment in the transition process as being critical, he does not deny the active role of each and every moment in contributing to the long-drawn-out process of transition from feudalism to capitalism. For example, he denies the significance of the mere presence of monetary wealth and mocks the idea that some huge accumulation of hoarded money kick-started the whole transition

(506). It was something else that "enabled" the transformation in the use of money into money capital. But disposable surplus money was needed to "enable" that access to means of production which "money neither *created* nor *stockpiled*" (507). Furthermore, "while money wealth neither invented nor fabricated the spinning wheel and the loom," it was not long before the spinner and the weaver "came under the command of money wealth" (508). Moreover, "when the formation of capital had reached a certain level, monetary wealth could place itself as mediator between the objective conditions of life, thus liberated, and the liberated but also *homeless* and *empty-handed* labour powers, and buy the latter with the former." Thereafter, money acquired an independent role with all manner of consequences for the circulation of capital. In taking these positions, Marx builds upon his general analysis of the role of monetary circulation as laid out in the first chapter of the *Grundrisse*.

The distinctive method that Marx deploys in creating this account of the dissolutions and dispossessions that occurred in the transition from feudalism might best be termed a "method of moments." It reads like history as economic and social bricolage. Processes of dissolution here, there and everywhere open multiple pathways toward the piecemeal rise of capital. Capital did not originate by way of a linear process. It is a coming together, a coevolution, engineered through a troubled concordance of multiple forces. There is no magic bullet explanation of the rise of capital. Instead, there are multiple forces such as monetization, the rise of science and technology, new forms of belief, the invention of new productive apparatuses and the like, all of which create possibilities. Capital emerges from the shadows (it can then and only then be named as such) only when all of those possibilities come together, or as Marx puts it in the introduction to the *Grundrisse*, when we leave the "chaotic conception of the whole" behind and arrive at "a rich totality of many determinations and relations" in which "the concrete is the concrete because it is the concentration of many determinations, hence unity of the diverse" (100).

Marx identifies certain moments (such as the production of the free laborer) as key nodes in relation to other moments within an existing totality (say that of feudalism) and sets a social process (in this case capital accumulation *in potentia*) into motion that step-by-step promotes the creation of an alternative totality—that of capital. We see how different moments enable, restrain or regulate how other moments do or do not perform in ways adequate to the dynamic needs of the new totality that is in the course of its "becoming." Blockages and barriers produce crises, while in other instances runaway growth arises out of strong dynamic and mutually supportive interactions between multiple enabling forces coming together, sometimes contingently in space and time. In other instances, the enfeebling and exhaustion of older possibilities restrains the overall movement, resulting in stagnation and ultimately ossification. We see blocked transitions all over the place. Then comes the hollowing out, the dissolution of key elements that have blocked the path to a radical transition in the preexisting totality and a repurposing of its moments into a different configuration. In this account there are, plainly, key and compelling moments and strong relations of mutual enabling of social change. But there is, equally plainly, no single string to be pulled that will accomplish anything other than some minor perturbation in the constellation of forces that constitute an existing system.

Marx's deployment of the "method of moments" to unpack how capital rose to dominance on the back of precapitalist modes of production prompts us to imagine how this same method might usefully be deployed to map out the transition from capitalism to a radically different mode of production, more adequate to the material, social and cultural needs of the world's populations and enabled to ward off ecological collapses and stabilize environmental conditions. Such a revolutionary project will entail a panoply of dissolutions and dispossessions, many of which, if Marx's thinking is any guide, should already be happening. There should be some signs of the elements of a new political and economic order already in place. The problem is how difficult it is to see them even though they stare us in the face.

For example, Marx suggests later on in the *Grundrisse* (705–6) that the capitalist theory and law of value is threatened by technological advances that render labor less and less socially necessary. Artificial intelligence certainly threatens such an eventuality. Many Marxists fear this because the value theory anchors their thinking. Without value theory, they would be lost. I prefer to take it as a sign that an alternative theory of value is already potentially within our grasp. "Production based on exchange value breaks down, and the direct, material production process is stripped of the form of penury and antithesis." It becomes possible to create wealth independent "of the labour time employed on it." The problem is that capital "wants to use labour time as the measuring rod for the giant social forces thereby created, and to confine them within the limits required to maintain the already created value as value." During the Covid-19 pandemic, the so-called monopoly powers of the FAANG group (Facebook, Amazon, Apple, Netflix, Google) grew immensely worldwide (while employing relatively little labor), single-handedly propping up stock market values and centralizing and conferring quantities of money wealth on the controlling classes never before seen in the history of capital. In a rational society, all of these monopolistic organizations would be publicly regulated or controlled in the public interest. The capitalist market provision of basic needs such as food and shelter, health care and education, transport and communications could easily be abolished and replaced by public provision systems oriented to social needs (a shadowy version of which already exists in the voluntary delivery of free food to at least a fifth of all US families that now in 2022 live in conditions of food insecurity and chronic poverty). The threat of global famines in the midst of agricultural surpluses is real. Add to this the memory that the "free labourer" was not created in a day and that, while the exchange of that free labor against and within the flow of revenues means one thing, it is the exchange against capital that currently sets the norm for wage rates. The abolition of that norm in an expansive public sector will be a critical step toward reducing social inequality and freeing the exchange of wage labor against revenues from its capitalist chains.

But, as Marx also repeatedly shows, the forces that block transitions rarely fade away without major struggles, and the potential for social movements seeking radical change to go up cul-de-sacs is omnipresent. Revolutionary change is neither instantaneous nor of a particular moment, but a long-drawn-out process occurring over decades if not whole centuries. It is this never-ending conflict between the magical instantaneous transcendence that seems so possible at moments of revolution and the long-drawn-out and tedious transformations in the trenches of daily life required to restructure the daily practices of both production and social reproduction that Marx had to confront when writing about the Paris Commune.

> The Commune intended to abolish that class property which makes the labour of the many the wealth of the few. It aimed at the expropriation of the expropriators. It wanted to make individual property a truth by transforming the means of production, land, and capital, now chiefly the means of enslaving and exploiting labour, into mere instruments of free and associated labour. But this is communism, "impossible" communism! . . .
>
> The working class did not expect miracles from the Commune. They have no ready-made utopias to introduce *par décret du peuple*. They know that in order to work out their own emancipation, and along with it that higher form to which present society is irresistibly trending by its own economical agencies, they will have to pass through long struggles, through a series of historic processes, transforming circumstances and men. They have no ideals to realize, but to set free the elements of the new society with which old collapsing bourgeois society itself is pregnant.[1]

---

1 Karl Marx, "The Civil War in France," in *The First International and After* (London: Verso, 2010), 213.

While there is no single path to be taken, there can be critical moments. But such events, like the storming of the Bastille and the subsequent periodic uprisings in France (1830, 1848, 1871) throughout the nineteenth century, the Russian, Chinese and Cuban revolutions and significant movements like the so-called "pink tide" that flooded and then ebbed through Latin America, only to show signs of flooding again; the Arab Spring movements (which stretched from Tunisia to the Ukraine); the multiple urban uprisings and protest movements, occurring all around the world—all these signal the desire for and the existence of a radical possibility for economic and social changes. These are all portents and signs, but if the critical moment is not embedded in a movement of radical transformation deep in the trenches and daily practices of society, while addressing a radical restructuring of social relations, then the momentum is lost and the political moment is not seized.

In *The Enigma of Capital*, I drew upon Marx's formulations and practices in Volume I of *Capital* to capture the seven interactive moments within the totality of capital that condition and surround the expanding flow of capital. These were technological and organizational change (the evolution of productive forces); the dynamics of the metabolic relation to nature; the shifting structures of social relations in the population; the actual labor processes of production and circulation; the practices of social reproduction and the qualities of everyday life; the institutional arrangements of property, the law and the state apparatus; and, finally, the mental conceptions (both good and common senses, as Gramsci would describe them). Some Marxist thinkers promote transformations in the productive forces as the primary agent of social change, while others prefer to focus on social (class) relations. My argument is that lasting systemic changes require transformations and dissolutions across all seven moments in dynamic supportive concordance with each other, even while accepting uneven development, stiffening or crumbling oppositions and not a little frictional recalcitrance from one place to another. These are the sorts of things we should be looking at as we study this text. Marx frequently assumes an antagonistic posture toward utopianism. But hidden in the complex folds of the *Grundrisse* there are passages expressive of utopian longing and desire, even in the midst of material restraints and political barriers. From this derives a covert theory of revolutionary transformation. The latter needs to be better worked out and instantiated in political practices.

MARX'S DOUBLE CONSCIOUSNESS

In the *Grundrisse,* Marx provides two seemingly antagonistic visions of the role and significance of capital in the history of humanity. In the first, he builds a laudatory account and up-beat assessment of how, through its penchant for creative destruction and technological revolutions, capital can bring us to the edge of a new form of society, a civilization in which the human species can flourish as never before. I cite the passage at length:

> Capital creates the bourgeois society, and the universal appropriation of nature as well as of the social bond itself by the members of society. Hence the great civilizing influence of capital; its production of a stage of society in comparison to which all earlier ones appear as mere *local developments* of humanity and as *nature-idolatry*. For the first time, nature becomes purely an object for humankind, purely a matter of utility; ceases to be recognized as a power for itself; and the theoretical discovery of its autonomous laws appears merely as a ruse, so as to subjugate it under human needs, whether as an object of consumption or as a means of production. In accord with this tendency, capital drives beyond national barriers and prejudices as much as beyond nature worship, as well as all traditional, confined, complacent, encrusted satisfactions of present needs, and reproductions of old ways of life. It is destructive towards all of this, and constantly revolutionizes it, tearing down all the barriers which hem in the

development of the forces of production, the expansion of needs, the all-sided development of production and the exploitation and exchange of natural and mental forces. (409–10)

On page 488, in the midst of his attempt to reconstruct the various precapitalist modes of production, Marx offers some rather different reflections on how the history of humanity has unfolded with the rise of capital. Here the role of capital is primarily that of a barrier to a rosy future rather than a creative civilizing force:

The old view, in which the human being appears as the aim of production, regardless of his limited national, religious, political character, seems to be very lofty when contrasted to the modern world, where production appears as the aim of mankind and wealth as the aim of production. In fact, however, when the limited bourgeois form is stripped away, what is wealth other than the universality of individual needs, capacities, pleasures, productive forces etc., created through universal exchange? The full development of human mastery over the forces of nature, those of so-called nature, as well as of humanity's own nature? The absolute working-out of his creative potentialities, with no presupposition other than the previous historic development, which makes this totality of development, i.e. the development of all human powers as such the end in itself, not as measured on a *predetermined yardstick*? Where he does not reproduce himself in one specificity, but produces his totality? Strives not to remain something he has become, but is in the absolute movement of becoming? In bourgeois economics—and in the epoch of production to which it corresponds—this complete working-out of the human content appears as a complete emptying-out, this universal objectification as total alienation, and the tearing-down of all limited, one-sided aims as sacrifice of the human end-in-itself to an entirely external end. This is why the childish world of antiquity appears on one side as loftier. On the other side, it really is loftier in all matters where closed shapes, forms

and given limits are sought for. It is satisfaction from a limited
standpoint; while the modern gives no satisfaction; or, where it
appears satisfied with itself, it is vulgar. (488)

It is tempting to view the clash between these two statements as
contrasting the utopian vision of capital and the bourgeoisie as to
their historical role with Marx's dystopian account of what they
have actually accomplished on the ground. I think it would be
profoundly mistaken to interpret it thus. To begin with, there is
nothing in the context of either statement to support such an interpretation. There are also plenty of other passages in the *Grundrisse*
and elsewhere where Marx expresses admiration for the historical
achievements of capital and the bourgeoisie. These set the stage, he
typically argues, for socialist revolution at the same time as they
free us from the constraints of precapitalist modes of thought and
being. The laudatory account (in the first quote) is immediately
followed, however, by the prospect that the internal contradictions
of capital will frustrate the full realization of capital's noble goals.
The vision and goals, in short, are fine, but capital has to transcend
its internal contradictions to realize them. In the second quote,
however, the vision itself is compromised: it is seen to be corrupted,
empty and meaningless from the very start and its achievements at
best vulgar. The complete working out of the human content would
entail, under such conditions, the transcendence and transformation of all that capital and the bourgeoisie have achieved.
Furthermore, something important gets lost in the often brutal
transcendence of precapitalist modes of thinking and being.

It seems likely that Marx internalized both visions within his
mode of thought. I propose, therefore, to interpret the two quotes
as a manifestation of Marx's "double consciousness," or as he terms
it, "double positing." Marx's primary example of double positing is
the way land, labor and capital are viewed as facts of production,
while rent, wages and profit are treated as facts of distribution.
From this standpoint, the suggestion that production takes prece-
dence over distribution makes no sense. Both quotes are true, and

between equal truths, as Hegel taught Marx in his theory of tragedy, "force decides." The evil genius of capital is that it produces and endlessly manipulates this double consciousness. Marx's evocation of it is, therefore, a mirror of the net of confusions that capital casts over our mental conceptions of the world. If, as Marx argues in *Capital*, what separates the worst of architects from the best of bees is that the architect erects a structure in their imagination before materializing it on the ground, then the presuppositions that shape our mental conceptions are foundational in guiding our actions. Critical awareness of this problem is vital to revolutionary action.

Marx was thoroughly immersed in the external and the internal contradictions of capital. Neither he nor we can claim a transcendent position in relationship to these contradictions. Marx likely internalized them within his very being (as, I maintain, do we all). He was powerfully and permanently marked by the contradiction between his bourgeois origins and education and his revolutionary desires. The *Grundrisse*, in part, documents his struggle to free himself from dominant bourgeois interpretations even as he appreciates the achievements of capital in freeing him and us from medieval and precapitalist religious conceptions of the world. But the *Grundrisse* also documents the danger of a meaningless outcome to that struggle. This sort of double consciousness is not uncommon within the ranks of that radicalized bourgeoisie which has played such a major role in both shaping and leading revolutionary movements throughout history. For this reason, I find it helpful to think more deeply about the contradictions captured by these two seemingly opposed statements. This may tell us something important about the many ambivalences that inevitably color any socialist project and perhaps help us understand how and why so many well-meaning socialist projects turn barbaric in the course of their implementation.

There is a lot going on in these two distinctive statements. The second is full of question marks while the first is not. The second lists unfulfillable potentialities, while the first sees no immediate barriers to fulfillment save capital's internal contradictions. It is interesting to sit back and think about which of these two worlds we currently inhabit. In practice, we find ourselves perpetually negotiating between these two depictions of creative and emancipatory possibilities, which are cut across by demonic and self-destructive threats.

We live in a perpetual state of "double consciousness." This should not be surprising. Throughout Marx's work, affirmation is inextricably related to negation. It is also possible that this contrast derives from what the *Stanford Dictionary on Philosophy*, in an interesting entry on Du Bois's articulation of the theory of double consciousness, calls "the European romantic opposition," to be found in both Goethe and Hegel, "between an innate human affinity for the transcendent and a pragmatic 'materialism' grounded in a utilitarian attitude to life, to mundane needs and commercial enterprise."[1] It was "this anti-bourgeois romanticism," the *Stanford Dictionary* entry suggests, that formed the "figurative background" for Du Bois's adoption of the term "double consciousness." Marx was deeply familiar, of course, with both Hegel's and Goethe's positions, and in his youth, as evidenced from his notebooks, he was attracted to rather gothic forms of "anti-bourgeois romanticism." He also took from Hegel the insight that tragedy is not the outcome of struggle between right and wrong but the inevitable outcome of a conflict between two equal rights.

In *The Economic and Philosophical Manuscripts of 1844*, Marx had advanced the concept of humanity as a "species being" struggling to emancipate itself from the alienations largely imposed by capital. Many hold that Marx subsequently abandoned these postulates as too tainted by humanist idealism and transcendental romanticism. Althusser, for one, vigorously condemned both "species being" and "alienation" as unscientific concepts that should be expelled from the Marxist lexicon. But in these passages

---

1   John P. Pittman, "Double Consciousness," *The Stanford Encyclopedia of Philosophy* (Summer 2016 Edition), ed. Edward N. Zalta, plato.stanford.edu.

in the *Grundrisse*, it seems that the concept of species being is being revived (explicitly so on page 496) to acknowledge how social evolution "moves in contradictions which are constantly overcome but just as constantly posited." The two contrasting statements jointly point to how the "universality towards which [capital] irresistibly strives encounters barriers in its own nature." There is an attempt here to come to terms with what the human species has achieved and what it might have lost in relation to, for example, the world of antiquity.

Taken together, the two statements also say something about the future: there is no idealist or romanticist resolution (such as a perfected utopian communism). Marx almost certainly gave up on that idea. There is no stable harmonious endpoint for human evolution, only the prospect of a continuous unfolding of contradictions between our collective capacities and our desires on the one hand and the desecrated and vulgar nature of the world we actually produce on the other. The permanent revolution of Trotsky and uninterrupted revolution of Mao lie on the horizon. The two quotes are not mutually exclusive, but simply two sides of the profoundly contradictory nature of the project of humanity, in our time largely held captive by capital, as it claims to seek material well-being, an unalienated existence, deep sociocultural satisfactions and profound meanings in the face of its own banal materialist laws of motion which point in an entirely different direction.

This tension is internalized in the aesthetic traditions of a bourgeois culture that perpetually seeks some reconciliation between capital's vulgar despoliation of the world and the desire for reenchantment in the relation to nature, along with attempts to recuperate and appropriate for current monetized consumption the loftier products of humanity's history. The great bourgeois philanthropist builds a sumptuous art museum to exhibit classical treasures. The owner of the dark satanic mill retires to a country estate that is so immaculately landscaped as to become an icon in national culture, access to which on weekends is now duly monetized. The working-class version of this search for natural beauty in the midst of the crassness of British industrialism is the rose bush in the tiny front yard and the breeding of homing pigeons.

The "loftier," if childish, sensibilities and satisfactions achievable in the ancient world contrast with the "emptying out" of all meaning as the singular achievement of capitalist modernity, accompanied by the narcissisms of a contemporary philosophy, rooted in the reductionist individualism implied in the Cartesian dictum that "I think therefore I am" (an invitation to mental bedlam if ever there was one), to which Marx sensibly replies that you had better eat dinner first.

This is not the place to ruminate at any length as to what this double consciousness might mean for the play of political subjectivities in our times. But it is surely insightful and incisive to see that Marx, even in his day, recognized the tension between the incredible achievements of capital—its science and technology, its innovative organizational forms, its monstrous productive capacities and its sophisticated strategies to contain, even manage its own contradictions to its own advantage, on the one hand, and its vulgar banalities, its slavish and sometimes deadly obedience to its own laws of motion, its pathological worship of money as the only wealth, its destructive and sometimes deadly powers unleashed socially, environmentally, militarily and politically in the crass need to reproduce an ever-narrowing form of class power and greater and greater concentrations of wealth.

It was laudable, for example, that Big Pharma in general and Purdue in particular developed pain-killing medications for terminal cancer patients. Less laudable was Purdue's insistence on broadening its market by making oxycontin available to anyone who experiences chronic pain, stating that the drug was nonaddictive as certified by a (corrupted) government authority, while lining the coffers of political representatives to deregulate—by congressional consensus vote and Obama's presidential approval— the widespread use of a supposedly controlled substance. With the help of corrupt doctors and pharmacies, Purdue made billions and the Sackler family became one of the wealthiest in the world,

seeking social redemption by becoming one of the largest supporters of the arts in the United States. Over a dozen or so years, nearly
half a million US citizens died from overdoses in an opioid
epidemic that was almost as lethal as the Covid-19 pandemic.
When charged with malpractice, Purdue and the Sacklers paid a
trivial (for them) fine of close to a billion dollars while admitting
no wrongdoing. Big Pharma then partially retrieved its reputation
by producing a vaccine for Covid in record time (with a vast
subsidy from the public coffers and the exclusionary right to the
patents they filed under their corporate name). The media treated
the pandemic (from China!) as frontline news but relegated discussion of the equally deadly homegrown opioid epidemic to the back
pages (except when in the later stages of the epidemic the fentanyl
that came illegally from China was dubbed the main culprit).
Widespread vaccine skepticism now understandably is concentrated in opioid country. And this is the context in which the
struggle for a "complete working out of the human content" is
supposed to be ongoing.

What Marx seeks to map for us is a better understanding of the
forces at work with which we have to do battle, all the while recognizing that the double consciousness he encounters, both within
himself and in society at large, haunts all of us in some form or
other at every turn.

The politics of this double consciousness calls for some comment.
So let me close with an example. I will call Marx's first characterization of capital's progressive role as Model 1 and the critical questions of alienation, loss of meaning and emptiness as Model 2. The
example I will use is Andean socialism in general, and Ecuador in
particular, over the last couple of decades. The first round of the
2021 election for president in Ecuador produced three viable candi-
dates. Andrés Arauz emanated from the progressive left tradition
established by Rafael Correa, who had been president from 2007 to
2017. The neoliberal Opus Dei business candidate Guillermo Lasso
came a distant second. A close third behind him was Yaku Pérez,
who   had   Indigenous   backing   through   the   Pachakutik

(plurinational) movement. In the runoff, many leftist outsiders presumed that the Indigenous candidate would endorse and support Arauz, much as the Indigenous organizations had initially supported Correa and the rewriting of the Ecuadorian constitution in 2008. That new constitution declared Ecuador to be a plurinational state that acknowledged both the rights of nature and the rights of Indigenous populations. Bolivia adopted a similar constitution a year later. These were landmark, even revolutionary, transformations in bourgeois constitutionality that went beyond the constitutions that rested on the foundational but empty market logic of equality, freedom and reciprocity in exchange. But once securely in power, Correa pursued a left politics (Model 1) that sought to take all that was positive from the bourgeois tradition and reshape Ecuador's nature and people to facilitate a left developmentalism. This attempted and achieved some degree of economic redistribution while breaking from incorporation in the global system of US hegemony (at the expense, however, of relying upon China). But in so doing, Correa increasingly went against his Indigenous base (though he sought to incorporate Indigenous leaders into the state apparatus). He marginalised CONNAI (the Confederation of Indigenous Nationalities of Ecuador), abandoned all modes of Indigenous thinking (*Pachamama, sumac kawsay*, and even *buen vivir*), repressed and jailed the leaders of the more militant environmental organizations, such as Acción Ecológica, attacked the ecofeminists, abandoned the Yasuni initiative that sought to protect one of the most diverse ecologies in Amazonia, and opened up Ecuador to expanded oil and mineral extractivism (using the army to ride roughshod over Indigenous protests in southern Ecuador, which resulted in the deaths of three Indigenous leaders). This "complete working out of the human content" increasingly appeared (Model 2) as "a complete emptying out," and "this universal objectification" of nature and culture "as total alienation," which explains why the Indigenous view (with its emphasis upon a dialectical relation to nature) increasingly appeared to many (including demographics beyond the Indigenous) as far "loftier in all matters" though limited and circumscribed in scale, compared to the results of the Correa program, which "gives no satisfaction; or, where it appears satisfied with itself, it is vulgar."

This helps to explain why some major thinkers and leaders in the Indigenous tradition balked at supporting Arauz, claiming they had suffered more at the hands of left developmentalism than at the hands of the neoliberal oligarchy. The same tensions between Model 1 and 2 thinking are observable in Bolivia, where Evo Morales adopted an expanded left developmentalism and extractivism at the cost of support from some of his Indigenous base. This contributed to the right-wing coup against him. But Luis Arce, the current president who came to power in Bolivia through support from Morales's socialist party, was a successful finance minister much praised by the IMF during the Morales years. For both Arauz and Arce, the tension within the double consciousness that Marx depicts houses a critical contradiction that they must find some way to address. Arauz lost the runoff election by five percentage points. While there are doubtless many reasons why (including all kinds of dirty tricks by his opponent) the lack of enthusiasm from the Indigenous base was surely prominent among them. Some 16 percent of the electorate cast null votes. The outcome has been catastrophic for the socialist left as the right mounts (in true Opus Dei fashion) a vendetta against Arauz and his supporters. But it is important to learn the lesson and recognize the limits of left developmentalism. It is insufficient in itself. In the Andean case, Indigenous rights, traditions and meanings call for respect, not dismissal as archaic residues from the past. It is worth recalling that Sandinista developmentalism, as applied to the Indigenous Miskitu populations of the Pacific coast in Nicaragua, opened the door to the CIA-supported "Contra" movement in the 1980s that proved so troublesome both to the course of the now-failed socialist Sandinista Revolution and to the Reagan administration in the USA (in the form of the Iran-Contra scandal). Failure to understand and work creatively with the tensions arising out of double consciousness of the sort that Marx describes has been costly for socialist movements.

Problems can be solved, but contradictions, such as double consciousness, never go away. The answer is not to abandon left developmentalism as a stepping stone to socialism but to create spaces and opportunities within that rejigged developmentalism to permit the search for meaning, for unalienated sociality and physicality, to become immersed in the metabolic relation to nature, to open struggles for the "complete working out of the human content." Revolution, like almost everything else that we do, requires some mix of inspiration, perspiration and long-term patience to work creatively with the dialectics of the primary contradictions and the double consciousness that inevitably haunts political positions. Getting the balance right, even if only for a time, is critical for socialism to have some future and not lapse, as it sometimes has, into its own distinctive form of barbarism. The double consciousness portrayed in Marx's two presentations needs to be taken to heart politically if the anticapitalist struggle is to flourish.

7

The Space and Time of Turnover and the Realization of Capital
Pages 516–84

Marx's mission, up to this point, has been to define what capital is and how we should understand the concept of capital theoretically and historically. His interim conclusions are succinctly summarized in his opening remarks on page 516:

"The capitalist himself is the point of departure and of return. He exchanges money for the conditions of production, produces, realizes the product, i.e. transforms it into money, and then begins the process anew" (see Figure 2).

> The circulation of capital constantly ignites itself anew, divides into its different moments, and is a *perpetuum mobile* . . . In its circulation, capital expands itself and its path, and the speed or slowness of its circulation itself forms one of its intrinsic moments. It becomes qualitatively altered in circulation and the totality of the moments of its circulation [note the use of "totality" here] are themselves the moments of its production—its reproduction as well as its new production. (516)

Furthermore, "the circulation of capital is at the same time its becoming, its growth, its vital process." Marx then resorts to an analogy to which I have previously on occasion appealed. "If anything needed to be compared with the circulation of the blood, it was not the formal circulation of money, but the content-filled circulation of capital." This is so because "the circulation of money itself now appears as determined by the circulation of capital" (517). This echoes a frequent theme in Marx's work. Money (like landed property and wage labor) existed before capital (this we examined in chapter 2). But the capitalist form of money (like the capitalist forms of wage labor and landed property) eventually dominates to be an integral moment in what Marx calls "the inner structure" of capital in circulation.

While Marx's focus remains on production, he now needs to look at how production integrates with circulation as a whole. How long, for example, does capital remain within the sphere of production versus circulation in the market? (517). This depends on "the development of the productive forces" (518). "The speed with which it can repeat the production process anew is . . . determined by the development of the productive forces in all other branches of industry. This becomes quite clear if one supposes the same capital to produce its own raw materials, instruments and final products." In practice, a capitalist relies on other capitalists for the supply of inputs. If one capitalist speeds up, that will require the others to do so also. "The length of time during which capital remains in the phase of the production process becomes itself a moment of circulation, if we presuppose *various* capitals."

Be careful here, because Marx uses "circulation" in two different senses throughout the *Grundrisse*, and he usually fails to alert us as to which. He refers to the circulation process of capital as a whole (in which case, production is a moment within overall circulation), while elsewhere "circulation" refers to everything that goes on outside the production process (particularly circulation in the market but also through the fragmentations of distribution). Here he is concerned with time spent on the market up until the value is realized in money form (518). Marx has already presented "the law of substitution of velocity for mass, and mass for velocity" in the case of money circulation (chapter 2). This law also holds in production. Profit can be increased by increasing the velocity or augmenting the mass. This raises the intriguing question as to whether velocity constitutes "a moment of value determination . . . independently of labour, not arising directly but originating in circulation itself" (519). This would go against Marx's general view that value can arise only in production and not in circulation. That possibility is here left open.

What to do when different capitals have different turnover times? In agriculture, for example, many crops come in once a year, and that is the turnover time. In other lines of production, the turnover time can be much longer or shorter. Milk, for example, is produced on a daily basis, but a pear tree takes a long time to mature. The turnover time in pear production in agriculture is thus different from the turnover time of wheat production or milk production. There are multiple turnover times in different spheres of production. This poses the problem of coordinating all these different turnover times. For instance, the turnover time in the production of cotton cloth is continuous. But, if the cotton crop is harvested only once a year, there is a problem. How does capital negotiate and reconcile these different turnover times both materially and financially?

This leads into yet another problem. There are phases in production when nothing much happens (no useful labor is applied). The main labor inputs in growing wheat occur during planting and harvesting and there is a lot of dead time in between with only occasional applications of labor (519). In any production process, Marx observes, there will be moments when nothing is happening. Wine takes years to mature in the bottle. This entails a loss of value or "devaluation." If capital is defined as value in motion, then if there is no motion there is loss of value. Moments and phases of devaluation, Marx shows, are integral to the overall circulation of capital.

This is one of many tantalizing insights in the *Grundrisse* where something is brought up which is of great potential importance but the implications of which are left dangling. Devaluation is clearly a crucial concept. Here, Marx appears to be saying that it is in the nature of capitalist production processes that there are many moments or phases of devaluation. This makes sense. If capital is value in motion, then any interruption or even pause in the motion, for whatever reason, entails a temporary devaluation until the movement resumes, in which case the value gets resurrected to rejoin the mass of value in motion. A crisis can then arise not out of devaluation per se, because that is going on all the time according to this conception. Instead, it will arise because of the inability or failure to resurrect the capital in time, to resume the motion and to revalue the capital within a certain span of time. Elsewhere, Marx comments that crises do not occur because commodities cannot be sold but because they cannot be sold in time. Stagnation in the market is a sign of crisis.

This explains why, as Marx frequently asserts, the continuity of capital flow has to be a crucial property of capital. It is a property that needs to be reasserted as much as possible at whatever cost. Otherwise, devaluation occurs, possibly on a massive scale. Unfortunately, Marx himself failed to follow up on this point. A coherent study of devaluation in relation to crisis theory would have been invaluable.

The duration of the production process of capital is one thing, but there is also the duration of the circulation process on the market. How long does it take from producing the finished cotton cloth to getting it to market and receiving the money for it? The cotton cloth may stay on the market for some time before it can be sold. Just after harvest time there may be a glut of raw cotton to make the cloth, while just before harvest there may be a scarcity. There is also the problem of different turnover times in industries supplying intermediate products. Marx mentions the case of the hand-spinning industry at the end of the eighteenth century, which was incapable of supplying the raw material for weaving, which led in turn to the invention of the spinning machine.

How do all the different temporalities of production and circulation fit together both physically and materially, on the one hand,

and financially and in money and value-flow terms, on the other? There are, Marx suggests, "four moments" in the turnover process. These are (1) the duration of the production process; (2) the duration of going to market for conversion into money; (3) the time needed to buy all the means of production; and (4) the time needed to get labor back on the job in production (520–1).

But the time it takes to get the product to market encounters complications. It depends on "the *greater distance of the market in space* and hence the delayed return. The longer time required by Capital A to realize itself will be due here to the greatest spatial distance it has to travel after the production process in order to exchange" (521). Why cannot "the product produced for China be regarded [as] completed, only when it has reached the Chinese market? Its realization costs would rise by the costs of transport from England to China." "The costs of production would resolve into the labour time objectified in the direct production process, [plus] the labour time contained in transport" (522). So, does transport add value?

Marx's answer is affirmative. The product is not finished until it is actually at the marketplace. The fact that you make it in place A is not necessarily the end of the product. It is not completed until it has gone from point A where it is made to point B where it is going to be sold. The cost of transportation adds to the value of the commodity (522). While Marx is clear enough, this does lead to some confusion. Marx's general argument is that value cannot be created in circulation (narrowly defined). Merchant capitalists and retailers do not create value even though their contribution may be necessary. But this does not apply to transport to market. If the merchants arrange and produce the transportation, then they add value to the commodity. A certain amount of value is created during the process of circulation, provided it produces change of location. Otherwise the value that merchants command or appropriate in their own right is a deduction out of the value which was created in production. Merchants take commodities off the hands of the direct producers at a discounted value and then seek to market them at their value. The advantage for the direct producers is that selling their products on to the merchants at a discounted value puts sufficient money in their pockets to renew their production process now, as opposed to waiting weeks or months for the product to be sold to its final consumer. Transport and communications and movement over space are different. Can surplus-value be extracted from transportation? Marx again answers in the affirmative, provided that the transport service is organized capitalistically through the employment of wage labor. No surplus-value is extracted if I just pay a carter a fee to deliver a piano to a client. But if I call a moving company and pay the company who sends a team of wage laborers to move my goods to another location, then the conditions are right for surplus-value production and appropriation. Laborers will be paid the value of their labor power, and the value of the change of location will be greater than the value of their labor power. Hence the surplus-value. But notice that this value is not a material thing but stems from change of location!

Surplus-value can be extracted from the transport and communications industries. This applies not only to the outputs but also to the inputs into production. It makes no difference "whether I extract metals from mines, or take commodities to the site of their consumption, both movements are equally spatial" (523). Change of location is value-producing no matter where it occurs. It then follows that improvement of the means of transport or communication falls into the category of the development of the productive forces of capital. Technological changes in the transport and communications sector have been hugely important in the history of capital. How many innovations in the history of capital are simply about revolutionizing the ability to create change of location? The degree to which transportation and change of location are judged to be productive of value is a major finding, foundational for understanding the historical geography of capital:

The more production comes to a rest on exchange value, hence on exchange, the more important do the physical conditions of exchange—the means of communication and transport—become for the costs of circulation. Capital by its nature drives beyond every spatial barrier. Thus the creation of the physical conditions of exchange—of the means of communication and transport—the annihilation of space by time—becomes an extraordinary necessity for it. Only in so far as the direct product can be realized in distant markets in mass quantities in proportion to reductions in the transport costs, and only in so far as at the same time the means of communication and transport themselves can yield spheres of realization for labour, driven by capital; only in so far as commercial traffic takes place in massive volume—in which more than necessary labour is replaced—only to that extent is the production of cheap means of communication and transport a condition for production based on capital, and promoted by it *for that reason*. (524–5)

There is an interesting phrase here, which I have often used in my own work: "the annihilation of space by time." I have always found this phrase a bit odd. It suggests that time actually annihilates space. I have often wondered if this is the correct translation. It turns out that that it is not. The proper translation, I have been told, is "the annihilation of space *through* time." We will see yet another translation shortly.

It is the "annihilation of space *through* time" because socially necessary labor time is the measure of value. The big question is not the measure of space itself but the time taken or the cost incurred to traverse that space. Shortening this time or reducing the cost is what many technological revolutions are all about. This explains why it is that production based on capital is so attached to the annihilation of space through time, the perpetual search to reduce the time or the cost of a move from A to B. This also explains why so many of the innovations in the history of capital are about reducing space to less and less time or cost of movement. Space is, from capital's viewpoint a critical barrier to be overcome. The historical rise of containerization from the 1960s onward is a great example of how this is done. Sea routes are favored, of course, by trading peoples, while "highways originally fall to the community, later for a long period to the governments, as pure deductions from production" (525).

ON ROAD BUILDING

This triggers an extended digression about the roads that facilitate the overcoming of spatial barriers. Who builds the road? What is its purpose and so on? (525). Does the capitalist or the state build the road, and if the former, how is its value realized when the buying and selling of a road does not fit well with the general rules of commodity production? "First, strip off what is puzzling about the road," Marx advises, "which arises from its nature as fixed capital. Imagine that the road could be sold at once, like a coat or a ton of iron." Note here the characterization of the nature of the road as a form of fixed capital. This will ultimately be decisive. Marx then goes into a lengthy discussion on the economics of road building. This is not simply about road building, however; Marx is actually opening up the whole question of the production and use of physical infrastructure—the production of space—in relation to capital accumulation. Who is going to be responsible for producing this infrastructure? What is its role? Do roads actually produce value or create conditions in which value can be created by, say, trucks taking commodities to market using the road? Is it possible for roads to be built by capital? (The answer today would be yes, in the form of toll roads and bridges.) And then the question arises as to who needs the road and by what means is the need for a road communicated in such a way that a road actually gets built.

These passages do not address, let alone solve, all the relevant questions about the production of physical infrastructure, of the built environment, of urbanization, and the like. But I find it interesting that Marx had in mind a framework for asking such questions. I will come back to this issue later.

Physical infrastructure absorbs a considerable concentration of raw materials and productive capacity. This can be achieved through the agency of the state or through the concentration and centralization of capital. Joint-stock companies to build the railroads and ancillary infrastructure were emerging in Marx's lifetime. But who needs the road and for what purposes? And in what way might capital respond to this need in ways that do "not interfere in laying the foundations of the theory of value through objectified labour time" (526). The question then becomes "can the capitalist realize the road, can he realize its value through exchange?" Suppose the value is not realized but the road is built "because it is a necessary use value." In this case, it has to be built and paid for whether through corvée or taxes. "But it is built only because it is a necessary use value for the commune." The building of it takes raw materials but also labor. "But to the extent that it is necessary for the commune, and for each individual as its *member*, what he performs is not surplus labour, but a part of his *necessary* labour, the labour necessary for him to reproduce himself as a *commune member* and hence to reproduce the community, which is itself a general condition of his productive activity" (526). This is one of the rare occasions where Marx discusses the question of collective labor performed for a collective purpose. What he describes is almost exactly what happens in, say, indigenous *communas* in the Andes where *mingas*, levies of labor for collective purposes, are foundational for the reproduction of the *communa*. On this basis it becomes possible to imagine all labor as collectively organized such that "one individual would have to spend e.g. so much time for agriculture, so much for industry, so much for trade, so much for making instruments, so much, to return to our subject, for road building . . . All these necessities resolve into so much labour time which must be directed towards different aims and expended in particular activities." Much then depends on labor capacities and productive forces. Only when activity is mediated through exchange-value does capital enter in with its divisions of labor organized in relation to needs. But "needs are produced just as are products and the different kinds of work skills." To be sure, "increases and decreases do take place" but "the greater the extent to which historic needs—needs created by production itself, social needs . . . are posited as *necessary*, the higher the level to which real wealth has become developed." Marx then resorts to a familiar refrain: "Regarded *materially*, wealth consists only in the manifold variety of needs" (527).

But needs proliferate. If, for example, scientific agriculture "requires machinery, chemical fertilizer acquired through exchange, seeds from distant countries etc., and if rural, patriar-chal manufacture has already vanished . . . then the machine-making factory, external trade, crafts etc. appear as *needs* for agri-culture. Perhaps guano can be procured for it only through the export of silk goods. Then, the manufacture of silk no longer appears as a luxury industry, but as a necessary industry for agri-culture" (527). This "whole complex set of interconnections" pulls industry away from its natural grounds to found it on the general context of evolving divisions of labor, rendering what was "previ-ously superfluous" into a "historically created necessity." It is inter-esting that, even when Marx was writing, the whole problem of supply chains and commodity chains across the world market would be so plainly visible. "The general foundation of all indus-tries comes to be general exchange itself, the world market, and hence the totality" (again, mark the appeal to this concept) of the activities, intercourse, needs etc. of which it is made up" (528).

Here we have an important digression on commodity chains within a digression about road building! But "now back to our road." Marx recognizes that infrastructure of this sort requires a considerable concentration of labor power, and that historically this meant slavery or some other unification of powers for "forced construction and compulsory public works." Capital, however, "effects the same concentration in *another* way." "A special class of road-workers may form, employed by the state." Construction work, he concedes, is special, but he does not go on to analyze it in detail. Can capital itself become concentrated enough or large enough in scale to undertake this work? "For the capitalist to undertake road building as a business, at his expense, various conditions are required, which all amount to this, that the mode of production based on capital is already developed to its highest stage. *Firstly, large* [-scale] *capital* is itself presupposed, . . . in order that he may be able to undertake work of such dimensions and of such slow turnover, [and hence] realization" (529–30). This implies *"share-capital."* Second, "[the project] must bring *interest*, but not necessarily *profit."* The distinction between profit and interest is an important point which has some substantial implications (to which we will later return). It arises particularly in relation to fixed capital formation and, even more particularly, as we shall see, in relation to fixed capital of an independent kind. This is an issue that is largely ignored in the literature. Third, the volume of traffic should be sufficient so that "the road pays for itself." This presumes that the "use of the road is *worth* that much exchange value for the producers, or supplies a productive force for which they can pay that much." What Marx has in mind here is a toll road of some kind which could pay for itself, depending on the volume of the traffic and the pricing. *"Fourthly*: A portion of idle wealth which can lay out its revenues for these articles of locomotion." In other words, the production of roads could become a means to absorb surplus and overaccumulated capital—the interstate highway system of the 1960s in the USA is a good example. This is another matter to which we must perforce return.

These are the conditions required to make large-scale infrastructure projects viable for capital. Over the last fifty years or so, larger and larger projects have been financed by capital. A good example is the Channel Tunnel between Britain and France, which was privately financed by a consortium of banks. It seemed at the time that there was a clear need for it, given Britain's then role in the development of the European Union.

Marx has his own example. "The first railway between Liverpool and Manchester had become a necessity of production for the Liverpool cotton brokers and even more for the Manchester manufacturers ... Capital as such ... will produce roads only when the production of roads has become a necessity for the producers, especially for productive capital itself; a condition for the capitalist's *profit-making*" (530), as was most obviously the case for the cotton mills of Manchester and for the merchants in Liverpool. For all of this to happen, there must be plenty of surplus (idle) productive capacity around mobilizable into a form (such as a joint-stock company) seeking only interest. Plainly, a falling rate of interest combined with an increasing mass of surplus money capital will form a particularly favorable environment for such works to be undertaken. But the other presupposition is that "the volume of traffic [be] sufficient, and the barrier formed by the lack of means of communication sufficiently felt as such, to allow the capitalist to realize the value of the road (in instalments over time)" (530). Marx concludes:

> All *general conditions* of *production* such as roads, canals, etc., whether they facilitate circulation or even make it possible at all or whether they increase the force of production ... presuppose, in order to be undertaken by capital instead of by the government, ... the highest development of production founded on capital. The separation of *public works* from the state, and their migration into the domain of works undertaken by capital itself, indicates the degree to which the real community has constituted itself in the form of capital. A country, e.g the United States, may feel the need for railways in connection with production; nevertheless, the direct advantage arising from them for production may be too small for the investment to appear as anything but *sunk capital*. Then capital shifts the burden on to the shoulders of the state. (531)

Marx then adds a further interesting observation. "Capital undertakes only *advantageous* undertakings, advantageous in its sense. True, it also speculates unsoundly, and, as we shall see, *must do so.*" Why it must do so calls for elucidation, but this will come later. Capital undertakes investments "which do not pay, and which pay only as soon as they have become to a certain degree *devalued.* Hence the many undertakings where the first *investment* is sunk and lost, the first entrepreneurs go bankrupt—and begin to realize themselves only at second or third hand, where the invested capital has become smaller owing to *devaluation*" (531). The initial investors go bankrupt, making way for a second wave of capitalists who pick up the use-value of these investments for almost nothing and put them to work to make a handsome profit. This sequence happens again and again in the production of built environments.

But there is another angle to all of this. "The road itself may so increase the force of production that it creates new traffic which then makes the road profitable." Investments in the built environment can either address an existing demand or seek to stimulate or even create a demand. A great deal of capital investment in the built environment looks to create the demand. But if the demand does not materialize, the investors then go bankrupt. Hence the speculative nature of such investments.

The London Underground system was a classic case, and this would be my example. Large amounts of capital were mobilized from the United States in the early 1900s to build the Underground system in London. The initial rate of return was too low and the investments could not pay off in time. The initial companies went bankrupt, and wealthy families, many from Maryland, by the way, lost their money. But the tunnels had been built, and the second wave of investors bought them up later for almost nothing and rapidly completed a profitable Underground system.

Marx at this point closes off this important digression dealing with infrastructure investments, how they're mobilized, whether they are mobilized by the state, how the need is expressed and what the need is about and how needs are met or created. "The result of our digression is . . . that the production of the means of communication, of the physical conditions of circulation, is put into the category of the production of fixed capital" (533). Investment in the built environment "does not constitute a special case." The rules of fixed capital formation are going to be applied but in a certain way. But what does open up is "the prospect . . . *of a specific relation of capital to the communal, general conditions of social production*, as distinct from the conditions of a *particular capital* and its *particular production* process."

THE SPACE AND TIME OF CAPITAL

After this digression, Marx returns to the question of how "*circulation proceeds in space and time*." He restates the point that "economically considered, the spatial condition, the bringing of the product to the market, belongs to the production process itself. The product is really finished only when it is on the market" (533). The reduction of the costs and time of circulation and the falling away of barriers to realization belong to the development of the forces of production by capital. The time taken to get the product to market belongs to the cost of production. "Quite different is the time which generally passes before the commodity makes its transition into money." This, says Marx, "is pure loss" (535). This creates an accounting nightmare. A merchant who stocks an inventory of goods in preparation for Christmas sales is losing value by the day because the commodities are not being sold in time. But if that same merchant takes time and incurs costs (hiring wage laborers) to transport the commodities to village markets, then the merchant adds value to the commodities!

Marx writes:

> It is clear that circulation appears as an essential process of capital. The production process cannot be begun anew before the transformation of the commodity into money. The *constant continuity* of the process, the unobstructed and fluid transition of value from one form into the other, or from one phase of the

process into the next, appears as a fundamental condition for the production based on capital to a much greater degree than for all earlier forms of production. (535)

As we saw earlier in the discussion of devaluation, the continuity of production and movement is a vital feature, and its maintenance through circulation is critical. The rationalization of the spatial network of transport and communication becomes imperative.

How the circulation process proceeds, how transport and communications work, how change of location is set up, how all the different turnover times are related, these features are all integrated into Marx's account of the space-time economy of capital. Relations between these different features and the general dynamics of accumulation can become both complex and tangled. A lot can go wrong. New forms of capital have to be invented to deal with these problems. "The suspension of this chance element by capital itself is *credit*." We are way ahead of ourselves here and, if Marx is true to form, he will delay any detailed consideration of the credit system until much later. But he obviously feels obliged to mention it here because of its role in synthesizing and standardizing the multiple differential turnover times of capital and coordinating the creation of a spatial economy adequate to capital. If the interest rate is 5 percent per year, the performance of all forms of production and circulation across space and time can be measured against this standard. Recall that investment in this sphere depends on the circulation of interest-bearing capital and that the quest for profit has no direct role.

Borrowing and lending have been around for a very long time, and "usury is even the oldest of the antediluvian forms of capital." However, "borrowing and lending no more constitute *credit* than working constitutes *industrial labour* or *free wage labour*. And credit as an essential, developed relation of production appears *historically* only in circulation based on capital or on wage labour" (535). This view contradicts the ideas popularized in David

Graeber's *Debt: The First Five Thousand Years*, in which the continuity of the debt relation from ancient Sumer to the present is presumed. This is yet another example of Marx recognizing that an ancient practice and economic form gets revolutionized when it is taken up and absorbed into the orbit of capital.

If, as Marx here insists, the "foundation of the necessity of credit" lies in "the direct nature of the production process," then another popular view, that financial operations and the credit system are entirely parasitic on value creation, also must be rejected. It is particularly in relation to the formation of the space-time economy of capital that we can see the relevance of the capitalist form of the credit system most conspicuously at work.

CAPITAL AS VALUE IN PROCESS: A REPRISE

At this point, Marx reverts to his initial description of the circulation of capital as a whole (Figure 2):

> Capital is now posited . . . as not merely sustaining itself formally but as *realizing itself as value*, as value relating to itself as value in every one of the moments of its metamorphosis, in which it appears at one time as money, at another time as commodity, then again as exchange value, then again as use value. The passage from one moment to the other appears as a particular process, but each of these processes is the transition to the other. Capital is thus posited as value-in-process, which is capital in every moment. It is thus posited as . . . circulating from one form into the next. The point of return is at the same time the point of departure and vice versa—namely the *capitalist*. All capital is originally circulating capital, product of circulation, as well as producing circulation, tracing in this way its own course. (536)

A version of this course is represented in Figure 2.

We are now back to capital as value in process, as value in motion, as a process of circulation. As such, it passes through different moments. Production is critical, but so too is realization in the market. The inner relation between production and realization emerges as a key focal point in the analysis of value in motion. Marx next returns to the spatiality inherent in this relation.

> Capital travels in order to go from one of these forms into the other ... in specific *amounts of time* (even spatial distance reduces itself to time; the important thing e.g. is not the market's distance in space, but the speed—the amount of time—with which it can be reached), by that much the velocity of circulation, the *time* in which it is accomplished, is a determinant of how many products can be produced in a given period of time; how often capital can be realized in a given period of time; how often it can *reproduce* and *multiply* its value. Thus a moment enters *into value determination* which indeed does not come out of the direct relation of labour to capital. (538)

This is a stunning modification of Marx's value theory. As far as I know, this is the only place where Marx considers it. He continues:

> The frequency with which the same capital can repeat the production process (creation of new value) in a given period of time is evidently a condition not posited directly by the production process itself. Thus, while circulation does not itself produce a moment of *value determination*, for that lies exclusively in labour, its speed does determine the speed with which the production process is repeated, values are created—thus, if not *values*, at least to a certain extent the mass of values. Namely, the values and surplus values posited by the production process, multiplied by the number of repetitions of the production process in a given period of time ... Thus, in addition to the

labour time realized in production , the *circulation time* of capital enters in as a moment of value creation—of productive
labour time itself. (538)

This seeming amendment of Marx's value theory calls for some
commentary. First, Marx has not consolidated his understanding
of value theory in the *Grundrisse*, and much of what he writes
about value is ambivalent and tentative. These passages could
therefore be dismissed as exploratory, only to be later abandoned
in the "mature" work of *Capital*. Against that, the substantive
content of Marx's study of spatio-temporality in the creation of
value and surplus-value would also have to be abandoned, because
Marx's logical exposition points inexorably toward the kind of
conclusions that Marx is here reaching. Accelerating the turnover
of capital means increasing value creation simply by moving faster
back into production. If I employ labor for twelve hours in a day,
and I then change to a twenty-four-hour shift system, then I double
the daily value I create.

We may here learn something from the history of bourgeois
economics. Conventional economic theory became more and
more a-spatial from the mid-nineteenth century onward.
Economic theorists in the neoclassical tradition increasingly
formulated their propositions as if all economic activity occurred
on the head of a pin. Alfred Marshall was probably the last conventional economist to recognize the importance of agglomeration
economies in leading to industrial concentrations of small firms in
production districts. When Koopmans and Beckmann tried to
introduce locational pricing and behaviors into their modeling of
economic activity, they could find no equilibrium prices, which in
bourgeois economics are the holy grail of economic theorizing.
They were so concerned about the disruptive implications of their
findings for general theory that they delayed publication of the
results. In spite of Paul Krugman's later valiant efforts to deal with
the problem of spatiality in the context of international trade, the
prevalence of a-spatial theorizing in economics has not been

challenged. The failure to theorize production beyond the head of a pin may account for the substantive failures of bourgeois economic theory to cope with the realities of economic life.

But here is Marx encountering the same problem. If we take the spatio-temporality of capital flow seriously, as Marx plainly does, at least in these passages, then the simple version of the labor theory of value is inadequate. We either transform the value theory accordingly or stick to the formulation of value as a-spatial socially necessary labor time as laid out in Volume I of *Capital*. If we do the latter, then we abstract from spatio-temporal concerns and conceptualize capital as if it operates on the head of a pin. There may be tactical reasons for doing this in Volume I of *Capital*, but the study of turnover times, working periods, velocity and speedup in Volume II, to say nothing of the thorny issue of value creation through transport and communications, point in a very different direction. These formulations in the *Grundrisse* lay a theoretical groundwork for a more thorough understanding of these topics.

But there is a contradiction here. "The circulation time of capital appears as the *time of devaluation*" (538). It is "not a positive value-creating element" and it "determines value only in so far as it appears as a *natural barrier* to the realization of labour time" (539). Circulation in itself does not contribute to value formation, but speedup and accelerating turnover time in circulation do. These latter drive a desire to reduce circulation time to as close to zero as possible. This helps explain certain twists in consumerism in recent years as capital flows into the production of events, spectacles and experiences that have an instantaneous consumption time and are locationally specific (even when they are broadcast far and wide). If capital concentrated on the production of long-lived consumer items, it would long ago have run out of a viable market.

Circulation time "*appears as a barrier to the productivity of labour* = an increase in necessary labour time = a decrease in surplus labour time = a decrease in surplus-value = an obstruction, a barrier to the self-realization process of capital." Thus,

> while capital must on one side strive to tear down every spatial
> barrier to intercourse, i.e. to exchange, and conquer the whole
> earth for its market, it strives on the other side to annihilate this
> space with time, i.e. to reduce to a minimum the time spent in
> motion from one place to another. The more developed the
> capital, therefore, the more extensive the market over which it
> circulates, which forms the spatial orbit of its circulation, the
> more does it strive simultaneously for an even greater extension
> of the market and for greater annihilation of space by time.
> (539)

Capital simultaneously produces time-space compression and
time-space expansion of the spatial range over which it operates.

THE UNIVERSALIZING TENDENCY OF CAPITAL

The abolition of spatial barriers, the reduction of the frictions of
distance and the substitution of spatial relations by temporal relations form but one aspect of what Marx refers to as "the universal-
izing tendency of capital" (540). This is what capital always does
and has been doing from its very inception. "Although limited by
its very nature, [capital] strives towards the universal development
of the forces of production, and thus becomes a presupposition of
a new mode of production, which is founded not on the development of the forces of production for the purposes of reproducing
or at most expanding a given condition, but where the free, unob-
structed, progressive and universal development of the forces of
production is itself the presupposition of society and hence of its
reproduction, where advance beyond the point of departure is the
only presupposition. This tendency—which capital possesses, but
which at the same time, since capital is a limited form of production, contradicts it and hence drives it towards dissolution—distinguishes capital from all earlier modes of production." This is, of
course, Marx reiterating his frequently stated theme that the

technological revolutions to which capital gives rise create a potential basis for the transition to socialism.

This broaches the question of how transitions from one mode of production to another might occur. "All previous forms of society . . . foundered on the development of wealth," Marx declares. "Those thinkers of antiquity who were possessed of consciousness therefore directly denounced wealth as the dissolution of the community. The feudal system, for its part, foundered on urban industry, trade, modern agriculture (even as a result of individual inventions like gunpowder and the printing press)." These material transformations produced concomitant shifts in social relations, institutions, relations to nature, science, and even in "the character, outlook etc. of the individuals." From an idealist perspective, it would then seem as if "the dissolution of a given form of consciousness sufficed to kill a whole epoch" (541). Would it were so! But this is not how Marx sees it. "In reality, this barrier to consciousness corresponds to a *definite degree of development of the forces of material production* and hence of wealth." The highest development of this material basis corresponds to the "richest development of the individuals." Earlier forms of community were purposed to the task of "*reproduction of specific conditions of production* and of the individuals, both singly and in their social groupings and relations—as living carriers of these conditions." But capital is disruptive of all that:

Capital posits the *production of wealth* itself and hence the universal development of the productive forces, the constant overthrow of its prevailing presuppositions, as the presupposition of its reproduction. Value excludes no use value; i.e. includes no particular kind of consumption etc., of intercourse etc., as absolute condition; and likewise every degree of the development of the social forces of production, of intercourse, of knowledge etc. appears to it only as a barrier which it strives to overpower. Its own presupposition—value—is posited as product, not as a loftier presupposition hovering over

> production. The barrier to *capital* is that this entire develop-
> ment proceeds in a contradictory way . . . The working out of
> the productive forces, of general wealth etc., knowledge etc.,
> appears in such a way that the working individual *alienates*
> himself; relates to the conditions brought out of him by his
> labour as those not of his *own* but of an *alien wealth* and of his
> own poverty. (542)

What is at stake here is "not an ideal or imagined universality of
the individual, but the universality of his real and ideal relations.
Hence also the grasping of his own history as a *process*, and the
recognition of nature . . . as his real body" (542).

Notice here that value is understood as a product of history and
nature and not an ideal superimposed from heaven, dropped from
the sky, or conjured up in the feverish brain of some human visionary. Also note that we all live under the imperative to grasp our
own history as a lived material process rather than as the earthly
realization of some higher-order moral or ethical imperative.
Finally, we are reminded that the production and circulation of
capital rests upon an interactive metabolic relation to nature that is
itself in constant evolution and modification in the context of
constantly evolving spatio-temporal relations.

Throughout, however, Marx again and again reasserts his
commitment to the idea that we should understand our lives as a
process, that we are not born saints or sinners, and that we derive
our consciousness and political subjectivity from the experience of
living a material life of certain qualities. To understand the nature
of our life process is to understand where we get our ideas from
and who we are. He then goes on to insist that the dialectic of our
positionality in relation to nature is important. But "the richest
development of the individuals" rest on "the *highest development of
the forces of production*" (541).

"If we now return to the *circulation time* of capital, then its
abbreviation (except for development in the means of communication and transport required to bring the product to market) . . .

[means] in part the *creation* of a continuous and hence an ever more extensive market" (542). This double movement toward a simultaneous expansion and compression of space relations arises within the logic of capital circulation itself. "Production based on capital originally came out of circulation; we now see that it posits circulation as its own condition, and likewise the production process in its immediacy as moment of the circulation process, as well as the circulation process as one phase of the production process in its totality." While there are, as we have already seen, all manner of problems deriving from the different circulation times of different commodities (which culminates in the "impulse" for the development of credit), the outstanding relation is simply that "the circulation of capital *realizes value* while living labour [in production] *creates value*" (543).

It follows that "the total realization of capital in a given epoch, is determined not simply by the new value which it creates in the production process" but rather by this surplus-value "multiplied by the number which expresses how often the production process of capital can be repeated in a given period of time" (544). There follow some intricate arguments concerning the role of velocity in enhancing production with the aim of refuting those "circulation artists" who believe that capital accumulation can in itself be enhanced by augmenting the velocity of circulation without reference to structures of production and even more nefariously by resort to tricks of credit.

"Capital exists as capital only in so far as it passes through the phases of circulation, the various moments of its transformation, in order to be able to begin the production process anew, and these phases are phases of its realization—but at the same time, as we saw, of its *devaluation*. As long as capital remains frozen in the form of the finished product, it cannot be active as capital, it is *negated* capital" (546). How long a fully produced automobile sits on the dealer's lot before it is sold is an important economic issue. If its realization process is delayed, then its value in process is partially negated. This inflicts a loss for capital, a relative loss of its value, for its value is sensitive to conditions within the realization process. This loss of capital arises because "time passes by unseized," time during which it could have been appropriating alien and surplus labor. The dialectical relation between production and realization in the market is foundational for the overall circulation of capital.

Marx points to the inevitability of devaluation within the flow of value and so converts it into a systemic liability within the totality. Furthermore, this explains the drive to ensure that, in the capitalist mode of production, time shall under no circumstances pass by unseized. But the concept of negated capital stands, and it is not hard to see how the crises of the 1930s and, say, 2007–8 produced a plethora not so much of surplus capital but of negated capital. A few pages later, Marx refers to capital "lying fallow" in the production apparatus, a break in the continuity of flow that is often necessary and which can on occasion constitute a *"general barrier* to capital's realization" (548). Obviously, Marx is here sketching in the beginnings of an argument. Much work will need to be done to bring this argument to completion, if, of course, it is deemed important to do so. It is, sadly, a reflection of the paucity of thinking among Marxist economists (and I will include myself in this criticism) that we have not sought to explore the possibilities inherent in these suggestive formulations.

Interestingly, this intervention is followed by another that has garnered more attention in the literature because it is elaborated upon by Marx in the chapter on the "Equalization of the Rate of Profit" in Volume III of *Capital*. Marx simply points out that "the distribution of surplus labour among the capitals takes place not in proportion to the surplus labour time achieved by the individual capital but in proportion to the *total surplus labour* which the totality of capitals achieved, and hence a higher value-creation can be attributed to the *individual capital* than is directly explicable from its *particular* exploitation of labour power" (547). What Marx is referring to here (and he does so again on page 761) is how the equalization of the profit rate under competition redistributes surplus-value from labor-intensive to capital-intensive firms, sectors, regions or places/states. Marx is incorrect to call this a form of value creation, even though it may appear as such. It is better described as lopsided appropriation and distribution. Capital-intensive firms, sectors and states receive more surplus-value than they produce, and labor-intensive firms (nations) receive less surplus-value than they produce. The rule is: from each capital according to the labor they employ and to each capital according to the total value they advance. It is interesting that Marx was well aware of this general issue as early as 1858. This is what happens through the competitive equalization of the rate of profit. The breakdown of the Bretton Woods system, in which national economies were protected to some degree from the equalization of the rate of profit, led to a far more competitive international system that redistributed surplus-value from labor-intensive sectors, corporations and economies (such as China and Bangladesh) to capital-intensive sectors, corporations and economies (such as the USA).

The metaphor of commodity capital as butterfly (548–9) is suggestive. "[Capital] must spend some time as a cocoon before it can take off as a butterfly." In writing about the different geographical mobilities of capital, I would say that production capital is the cocoon, commodity capital is the caterpillar and money/finance capital is the butterfly form. This last form can flit around the world and alight for a while, wherever it wants. This is much in evidence in contemporary finance capitalism. Until recently, commodities were harder to move, while production was clearly the least mobile form of capital. In our times, however, these distinctions are less clear cut.

The next forty-four pages are taken up with close readings and analyses of classical political economy (Ricardo, Malthus and other minor figures such as Carey and Rossi). Marx learns a great deal by reviewing this literature, but I leave this aside in favor of concentrating only on those passages where Marx is clearly developing and enunciating his own views. This is one of the few places where Marx takes Malthus seriously, so if you want to deepen your appreciation of how Marx interrogated classical political economy and built a lot of his theory out of that interrogation, this is not a bad place to begin.

There is one topic that does crop up in the subsequent pages which is worthy of consideration. That is the role of competition (552). In his outlines for future work, Marx sometimes proposed a whole book on competition, but he never got around to it. His views on it are scattered and not always consistent (being composed at different times). In an aside during his critique of Ricardo's presentation of the laws of motion of capital, Marx asserts that "competition generally, this essential locomotive force of the bourgeois economy, does not establish [capital's] laws, but is rather their executor" (552). Unlimited competition (like value) is something that is produced, not given or presupposed. "Competition, therefore does not *explain* these laws; rather, it lets them be *seen*, but does not produce them." The laws of motion of capital have to be explained a different way.

We have seen some of that work already, in the examination of space and temporality and the building of infrastructure. If we want to explain how infrastructure gets built, then competition comes into the story. This raises an interesting question, which I think to some degree Marx begs in much of his work: if competition, the enforcer, goes to sleep at the controls and capital lapses (as it all too often does) into monopolistic practices, what happens to the laws of motion as Marx depicts them? Without "the coercive laws of competition" there would, for example, be little compulsion behind technological change."This means, in other words, nothing other than that the laws of capital are completely realized only within *unlimited competition* and *industrial production*" (559). This Ricardian principle in turn reveals something important about Marx's proposed theory of capital. He wants to know what happens under conditions of unlimited competition and industrial production. What happens when you have oligopoly or monopoly or what happens when you are not simply dealing with industrial production but also with, say, real estate development is pushed to one side.

How would capital evolve on the basis of unlimited competition and industrial production, presupposing "its immanent laws enter completely into reality." It would first "have to be shown how this *unlimited competition* and *industrial production* are conditions of the realization of capital, conditions which it must itself little by little produce (instead of the hypothesis appearing here as merely that of the theoretician, who places free competition and the productive mode of capital's existence . . . as imaginary presuppositions of capital for the sake of purity.)" (560). This is a difficult claim to sustain. The assumption of unlimited competition and industrial production is an abstraction, but maybe it is concrete enough to mirror the realities somewhat, and maybe as capital evolves and matures so the reality will more and more conform to the theoretical claim.

It is here relevant to ask to what degree conditions approaching unlimited competition have ever prevailed in the history of capitalism. Under the Bretton Woods Agreement of 1944, for example, international competition was circumscribed by a framework that conceded considerable autonomy to individual states with respect to fiscal policies and labor laws within a framework of international capital controls. Competition occurred within states but was limited between states. As a result, the Big Three auto companies in Detroit were considered the paradigm case of monopoly capitalism at work in the 1960s because they (and their labor forces) were insulated from foreign competition. From the 1970s onward the Bretton Woods system was abandoned along with capital controls, and international competition intensified (the monopoly power of Detroit wilted in the face of competition from the Japanese and German auto companies). But in Ricardo's theoretical framework, the conditions of intensifying competition would be "little by little produced" as capitalism matured. In other words, the conditions presupposed have been in the process of becoming more true. This does not prove that the theory is adequate, however, except in the sense that the general trajectory of the neoliberal counterrevolution has been in almost all aspects a return to the competitive conditions that Marx was encountering when writing *Capital*. The teleological assumption that capital would inevitably move into more and more competitive formations is not justified. The history seems to be more characterized by alternating phases of exaggerated and sometimes "ruinous" competition on the one side and overwhelming monopoly power on the other. Since 2007–8 there has been a strong resurgence, for example, of monopoly power in many sectors of the global economy.

The question of competition recurs throughout the *Grundrisse*. On pages 649–52, for example, it is taken up in some stunningly critical detail. I think it is worth consolidating Marx's views on the matter here. Marx begins by noting that the removal of barriers to trade and the whole politics of laissez-faire and laissez-passer, which had consumed Physiocratic thinking in the eighteenth century, had led to the "even greater absurdity" of seeing the economy as determined by "the collision of unfettered individuals who are determined only by their own interests—as the mutual attraction and repulsion of free individuals, and hence as the absolute mode of existence of free individuality in the sphere of consumption and exchange" (649). To this Marx responds: "Nothing can be more mistaken."

While the barriers imposed by earlier modes of production and exchange were broken down, the freedoms it liberated were limited and constrained. "*Free competition* is the relation of capital to itself as another capital, i.e. the real conduct of capital as capital." This means that "it is not individuals who are set free by free competition; it is, rather, capital which is set free" (650).

As long as the capitalist mode of production prevails, "the movement of individuals within the pure conditions of capital appears as their freedom . . . Free competition is the real development of capital . . . The reciprocal compulsion which the capitals within it practise upon one another, on labour, etc. (the competition between workers is only another form of the competition among capitals) is the *free*, at the same time the *real* development of wealth as capital." It was for this reason that the political economists, most notably Ricardo, postulated the existence of free competition as the basis for establishing their version of the laws of motion of capital. The closer a society approached a condition of free competition, the more closely the society adhered to the laws of motion Ricardo derived. When capital was weak, the more it relied "on the crutches of past modes of production," but "as soon as it feels strong, it throws away the crutches, and moves in accordance with its own laws" (651).

"Competition is nothing more than the way in which the many capitals force the inherent determinants of capital upon one another and upon themselves." Hence "the insipidity of the view that free competition is the ultimate development of human freedom; and that the negation of free competition = the negation of individual freedom and of social production founded on individual freedom." This kind of individual freedom entails "the most complete subjugation of individuality" under the objective social conditions imposed by capital (652).

"The analysis of what free competition really is, is the only rational reply to the middle-class prophets who laud it to the skies or to the socialists who damn it to hell . . . The assertion that free competition = the ultimate form of the development of the forces of production and human freedom means nothing other than that middle-class rule is the culmination of world history." This sentiment was most explicitly expressed in Fukuyama's triumphal declaration in 1992 of "the end of history."

But there is a crack in this argument. As soon as capital becomes conscious of the fact that it is itself a barrier to its own further development, "it seeks refuge in forms which, by restricting free competition, seem to make the rule of capital more perfect, but are at the same time the heralds of its dissolution and of the dissolution of the mode of production resting on it" (649).

8

Turnover Times and the Circulation of Labor Capacity
Pages 584–678

Marx does not have some straight-line argument that gets us to a conclusion as to how best conceptualize the economy of capital as a totality. The *Grundrisse* does not work that way as a text, even though it does have an underlying structure. Rather, Marx probes hither and thither until he homes in on a foundational idea of how perhaps to better conceptualize the totality within which capital and labor have their being. Different pieces of the puzzle get put into place at different times.

In the pages we are here considering, the key insight comes on page 678, in the section entitled the "Threefold character, or mode, of circulation." In it, Marx disaggregates the flows that constitute a capitalist totality into three distinctive circulatory systems: the circulation system in general, as depicted in Figure 2; what he calls "small-scale circulation," which depicts how the laborer as a person circulates while playing a variety of distinctive roles (Figure 1); and "large-scale" circulation, which deals with the distinctive mode of circulation of fixed capital and the consumption fund (Figure 3). It will later turn out that there are more than three forms of circulation to be considered, but at this point Marx isolates just these three for detailed consideration.

Disaggregating processes in this way is a familiar research strategy in many arenas of inquiry. For instance, the human body can be and in medical research is frequently represented in terms of the different circulation processes within it. But the organic analogy that Marx had in mind is plainly not that of the human body, even though he occasionally cites a possible analogy between the circulation of value and the circulation of the blood. Marx's thinking, as we have seen, is more evolutionary and ecosystemic, though he did not articulate it as such (in part because the concept of an ecosystem was not available to him—it only came into use in the 1930s, although the scientific concept of "ecology" was introduced by the German scientist Ernst Haeckel in 1866). But it is at this point in the *Grundrisse* that Marx comes up with the novel and, in my view, critically insightful way of examining the different circulatory systems that work together to constitute a capitalist totality.

Marx emerges from his detailed analyses of Ricardo, Malthus and others on page 584 with consideration of a quote from John Wade, in which it is claimed that "labour is the agency by which capital is made *productive of wage, profit, or revenue.*" Marx disputes this formulation. "All productive powers of labour" appear, he says, "as the *productive power of capital*" and "all social powers of production are productive powers of capital." Or, put another way, "the collective power of labour, its character as social labour, is therefore the *collective power* of capital." In fact, "all social powers of production are powers of capital." The association of the workers, "as it appears in the factory, is . . . not posited by them but by capital. Their combination is not *their* being, but the *being* . . . of capital." While the act of laboring lies exclusively with the worker, its social form and economic effects are defined and designed entirely by capital. The individual worker even "relates to his own combination and cooperation with other workers as *alien*, as modes of capital's effectiveness." Marx here positions the worker as a person, as an individual, in relation to capital, which mobilizes his alienated labor for purposes of surplus-value production. The laborer is a mere bearer of the capacity to sell labor capacity as a commodity. Beyond that, Marx suggests, labor has no agency. The active subject is capital. Laboring and working can be found, of course, in all modes of production. But under the rule and domination of capital, the form and qualities of the laboring experience are unique and special to this mode of production. The laborers themselves would not and possibly could not have come up with the factory system as a mode of organization. The best that they could and did do was to help build the manufacturing system that arose in late feudalism and which rested on their knowledge and skills. Competitive industrial capitalism turns the circulation and accumulation of capital into capital's signature product.

Both the manufacturing system and the generalized industrial factory system are products of capital. In the manufacturing system "the mass of (accumulated) workers must be large in relation to the amount of capital" even as the workers are in command of their tools. In the factory system, "the communal spirit of labour is transferred to the machine." Or, "the principle of developed capital is precisely to make special skill superfluous, and to make manual work, directly physical labour, generally superfluous both as skill and as muscular exertion; to transfer skill, rather, into the dead forces of nature," i.e., into the machine (587). The long-term consequences of this in the history of capital are important to note. Even mainstream accounts of neoliberalism acknowledge the continuing disempowerment of labor to be a key objective. These tendencies of capital were abundantly clear to Marx in 1858!

The result is an inversion of agency under capital's rule. All value may derive from labor, but it is capital that calls the shots. How this inversion took place is speculatively examined as capital increasingly colonized preexisting labor practices and incorporated labor into production under a variety of different conditions—both formal and real subsumptions under the power of capital. This colonization of precapitalist labor processes by capital implies the increasing concentration and, ultimately, centralization of capital itself. "Capital does indeed exist from the outset as One or Unity as opposed to the workers as Many" (590).

The argument on pages 588–9 is particularly hard to parse. The concentration of workers—the Many—has to be big enough to produce a surplus that will ground profit at the same time as it creates enough surplus and surplus-value to reinvest in further expansion. In the course of this analysis, Marx suggests that there is some reason to distinguish between absolute and relative forms of surplus-value. It seems that Marx is putting down some early markers as to how the theory of surplus-value will work in relation to conditions of laboring. "Only capital," he says "has subjugated historical progress to the service of wealth" (590). Remember, however, that back on page 488, Marx talked about wealth and how the bourgeois definition of wealth (which is presumably what is at stake here) is hollowed out and has no meaning. If wealth is measured in terms of free time, then plainly capital has no interest in subjugating society to that. Capital absorbs free time as surplus-value. It is also worth revisiting Marx's argument back on page 541, where he forcefully argues that the highest development of the forces of production corresponds to the potential for the richest possible individual development.

There is a big difference between saying we want a society where wealth as money is everywhere in evidence, which is the kind of society that capital builds, and adopting Marx's view of wealth as the maximum of free disposable time, creating the possibility for the richest individual development. The latter cannot be achieved under repressive conditions of wage labor, of debt peonage, and the general alienation of whole segments of the population from both the experience of work and cultural life. Even in bourgeois society, Marx comments, the subjugation of everything to the wealth requirement diminishes "historical development, political development, art, science, etc. [which] take place in higher circles over their heads" (589).

Capital creates a world out of the pursuit of monetary wealth, where some people are astonishingly wealthy, because of the increasing impoverishment of the laborer. The poverty of the worker grounds the production of wealth for capital. This plainly does not allow for the full development of the individual in general and certainly not of the workers in particular. Certain individuals may flourish, but that is not for everyone.

What Marx seems to be posing here is a grand contradiction between a bourgeois mode of production, which, in itself, is about the development of the productive forces and endless capital accumulation, versus the construction of a universalism which is potentially progressive, covering basic needs in the minimum of time, such that all individuals can freely explore their own potentialities in any way they like. This is the alternative possibility that casts a shadow across the analysis even as it is not explicitly laid out. But here, too, we come back to the temporality of all of this, the speedup of everything which is not necessarily beneficial to the exploration of alternative possibilities. In fact, speedup and the drive for faster and faster turnovers and modes of consumption have created a world based on instant gratification and experiential forms of consumerism, all of which frustrate searches for a rational, contemplative alternative.

Marx then diverts us into an examination of Rossi's theory of wages. While wage payments come out of capital, exactly what the wages are for is a matter of controversy. The payment could be construed as a return for laborers' participation in a joint productive enterprise with capital. This seemingly peculiar perspective probably derived from Saint-Simon, who divided society into productive and unproductive (parasitic) classes. Capital and workers jointly formed the productive class, while state and religious functionaries, landed aristocrats, lawyers and judges, military officers etc., along with feudal retainers and lumpen elements, were the parasites. Marx respected Saint-Simon, and there are passages where Marx seems to follow some of his thinking. Here Marx does take from Rossi the idea that wages once paid circulate as a form of revenue and that they play an important role in the formation of what Marx calls a "consumption fund" (for example, working-class savings that might fund some transition to working-class homeownership). "In the hand of the worker, the wage is no longer a wage, but a consumption fund" (594). These ideas (not elaborated upon but not rejected either) are later incorporated in the "small-scale circulation" associated with the multiple roles of the wage laborer.

The distinction between "wages as forming a part of capital and at the same time the worker's revenue" then paves the way to quickly consider profit and interest. The rate of profit, which Marx knows from his reading of Ricardo is likely to fall, is "the percentage upon the value of the advances" (595). Those advances of money capital have to cover the wages of necessary labor along with the purchase of materials and machines. "Profit is only a secondary, derivative and transformed form of the surplus value." It is "the bourgeois form, in which the traces of its origin are extinguished." We see the profit but not the surplus-value from which it is derived.

"If raw material and instrument cost nothing, as in some extractive industries" such as "metal and coal mining, fishing, hunting, lumbering in virgin forests etc.) then they also add absolutely nothing to the value of production." This is a very important though controversial point, for there are some in the Marxist camp who want to insist that "nature" contributes value to production. But Marx clearly does not accept that view, which does not mean that the extractions contributed by the extractive industries are irrelevant (he will later term them "free gifts of nature"). For capital, nature has no inherent value. It is just there to be used.

If raw materials and instruments are incapable of adding value, then surplus-value rests on a relation between necessary labor (the value required for the reproduction of labor power) and the surplus-value appropriated by capital. This was what Ricardo failed to see. He therefore lacked the "insight that the bourgeois system of equivalents turns into appropriation without equivalent." Unable to "get to the bottom of the creation of surplus value" he could not explain "the continuing decline in the rate of profit." This left him with his only option, which was to explain the falling rate of profit by rising wages (hence the frequent description of the so-called "profit squeeze" theory of crisis formation as a Ricardian rather than Marxist formulation). From Ricardo's perspective, "a rise in wages is *harmful* [to labour] because it hinders accumulation" (596). This idea was widely accepted in workers' circles in Britain in Marx's time. Rising wages would mean less job creation. Marx was fiercely opposed to this view. "When competition permits the worker to bargain and to argue with the capitalists, he measures his demands against the capitalists' profit and demands a certain share of the surplus value created by him ... Further, in the struggle between the two classes—which necessarily arises with the development of the working class—the measurement of the distance between them ... becomes decisively important." The result is that "the *semblance of exchange* vanishes" and it then becomes obvious that "the worker receives as wages ... what is only a part of his own labour" (597). The processes of commodity exchange, with their emphasis upon equivalence, do not regulate what happens in labor markets, as bourgeois theorists typically assert.

The raw fact of wage rate determination through class struggle, Marx argues, "enters into the consciousness of the workers as well as of the capitalists" (597). Marx does not often open up the question of class consciousness. His phrasing here is interesting. It suggests that class consciousness arises out of class experiences and material practices and not the other way around. If Marx is true to his colors, as evidenced elsewhere, he would then go on to say that class consciousness, once established, has the capacity to become a material force in capitalist history, but only if continuously sustained by material class practices. The hollowing out of class consciousness by the failure to maintain class practices is unfortunately all too familiar in the history of capital. Nevertheless, the emergence of class consciousness on the part of both capital and labor "shows by itself that the mode of production founded on capital had, by this time, taken on a form more and more adequate to its nature" (597).

This phrase, "adequate to its nature," is also important. We will encounter it again and again in what follows. What is "adequate to capital's nature" is one of the critical questions that Marx poses throughout the *Grundrisse*.

Marx then turns for inspiration (and provocation) to the work of Reverend Thomas Chalmers, whose views were obnoxious but illuminating. Chalmers makes clear, for example, what Marx considers the correct view that "the aim of producing capital is *never use value*" (600). Chalmers also sought to analyze the "whole *circulation* process" as an "economic cycle." The world of trade, Chalmers wrote, "may be conceived to revolve in what we shall call an economic cycle, which accomplishes one revolution by business coming round again, through its successive transactions, to the point from which it set out." Marx eagerly takes up this cyclical vision.

His first move is to revisit the question of differential turnover times. This depends "not only on the longer or shorter labour time required to complete the article (e.g. canal building etc.), but also . . . on the interruptions of the work which are due to the nature of the work itself, where on the one hand capital lies fallow, and, on the other, labour stands still" (602).

> The constancy of the production process here does not coincide with the continuity [required for] the labour process. This is one moment of the difference. *Secondly*: the product generally requires a longer time to be *completed*, to be put into its finished state; this is the total duration of the production process, regardless of whether interruptions take place in the operations of labour or not . . . *Thirdly*: after the product is finished, it may be necessary for it to lie idle for some time, during which it needs relatively little labour in order to be left in the care of natural processes.

Wine maturation is an example. "*Fourthly*: a longer time to be brought to market, because destined for a more distant market . . . *Fifthly*: The shorter or longer period of the total return of a capital . . . in so far as it is determined by the relation of fixed capital and circulating capital" (603). This is a key moment in the text when the question of the relation between fixed and circulating capital enters the picture.

Value is created only when living labor is being applied. "The *difference* of time required to complete the products of agriculture, and of other species of labour, is the main cause of the great dependence of the agriculturalists. They cannot bring their commodities to market in less time than a year. For that whole period they are obliged to borrow from the shoemaker, the tailor, the smith" (603). This sort of problem will later specifically set the stage for consideration of the role of the credit system in dealing with problems of differential production and turnover times. But "the total capital's period of reproduction within the cycle is determined by the total process, circulation included." From now on, the analysis must go beyond production to consider circulation in the market.

A DIGRESSION

Pages 603–18 constitute a digression. It begins with some general observations on the conditions of labor, passes through a thorough debunking of Malthus's theory of population before taking up Adam Smith's theories of labor and of value and finally closing out with a commentary on John Stuart Mill.

Marx does not often take up the demographic basis for the accumulation of capital, in part, one suspects, because the specter of Malthus, who had put forward a "false and childish" universal theory, based in nature, in which an exponential growth of population butts up against an arithmetic growth in agricultural productivity and land capacity. The rapidly increasing gap between the two growth curves (in Malthus's view) produces overpopulation and mass impoverishment, and invites positive checks to further population growth through famine, disease, starvation and war. The tendency toward overpopulation is for Malthus a universal natural law and therefore irreversible. It was validated, in his view, by the miserable condition of the lower classes in Britain. Here, as well as in chapter 25 of Volume I of *Capital*, Marx vigorously rebuts Malthus. Under capitalism, the production of poverty and of an industrial reserve army are solely due to capital. There is, says Marx, no way they could be attributed to human nature. They were and are a product of capital's own distinctive nature, and Marx shows precisely why and how this must be so.

Marx makes his own position clear, though he does engage in dialectical word games that make it hard to summarize his thinking in plain English. "Maximum growth of population—of living labour capacities" is, Marx concedes, "a fundamental condition" for a mode of production founded on capital (608). This is a rare admission in Marx's work. It seems to imply some sort of relation between endless accumulation and endless population growth. In addition to the "labour necessary for production—there should be a *surplus population*, which does not work." The role of this surplus population is not to consume (as Malthus proposed). It is exclusively concerned with regulating the supply of "*labour capacities*."

Here comes the tricky bit in Marx's argument. Labor is desperately concerned to perform necessary labor (the labor needed to produce the value equivalent of the commodities the workers require to reproduce themselves). But the capitalist denies the workers access to produce necessary labor unless they perform surplus labor for the capitalist. "Labour capacity can perform its necessary labour only if its surplus labour has value for capital," which includes the realization of its value in the market. "If this realizability is blocked" then the "necessary appears as superfluous" labor (609). Labor is "necessary only to the extent that it is the condition for the realization of capital." From the perspective of capital, it is the necessary labor performed by the laborer that is superfluous. The capitalist therefore has an interest in diminishing this superfluous labor by any means possible, including, of course, the mobilization of technological change. "The positing of a specific portion of labour capacities as superfluous ... is a necessary consequence of the growth of surplus labour relative to necessary. The decrease of relatively necessary labour" increases the superfluous laboring population. The result is the creation of a relative surplus population (or an industrial reserve army of the sort Marx describes in Volume I of *Capital*). This is a product of capital's distinctive nature. The overpopulation that arises under the rule of capital is produced by capital. It is not, as Malthus proposed, a result of natural law.

How does this superfluous population survive when deprived of access to necessary labor? "The worker is maintained as a living being through the mercy of others . . . Society in its fractional parts undertakes for Mr Capitalist the business of keeping his virtual instrument of labour—its wear and tear—intact as a reserve for later use. He [the capitalist] shifts a part of the reproduction costs of the working class off his own shoulders and thus pauperizes a part of the remaining population for his own profit" (610). In this way, surplus capital and surplus population intimately relate to each other. In later times, the state became broadly responsible for providing the means of survival for the industrial reserve army, in part because in times of war it came to be recognized that a malnourished and unhealthy population did not provide a good base for military recruitment. In the Franco–German conflict of 1870, the depleted and malnourished working and peasant classes of France were no match for the healthy and well-fed Prussian soldiers.

But the general principle stands. "The positing of surplus capital . . . requires a growing population in order to be set into motion" along with "a part of the population which is unemployed." Strange to read these words written in the dark winter of 1857 in the summer of 2020 in the United States, where 40 million or more workers condemned to the superfluity of unemployment increasingly depend on the mercy of others, as they draw upon unemployment benefits and line up at food banks, plead for free cooked meals and other forms of charity to stay alive. The mercy of others and the reluctant support from the neoliberal state is all they have.

For the capitalist, the pauperization which produces profit while off-loading costs of maintenance of the industrial reserve army continues to be good economics (for the capitalist).

Marx then offers some observations on Adam Smith's view that "in its historic forms as slave-labour, serf-labour, and wage-labour, labour always appears as repulsive, always as *external forced labour*; and not-labour, by contrast, as 'freedom, and happiness.'" The potentiality is there, however, for labor to become "attractive work, the individual's self-realization" which "in no way means that it becomes mere fun, mere amusement, as Fourier, with *grisette*-like naïveté, conceives it. Really free working, e.g. composing, is at the same time precisely the most damned seriousness, the most intense exertion" (611). This is the closest Marx comes to defining his conception of unalienated labor. For this to be so, requires social labor and a scientific approach in "regulating all the forces of nature" (612).

Even though all productive powers are those of capital, as Marx previously asserted, it is labor alone that produces: "it is the only *substance* of products as values. Its measure, labour time—presupposing equal intensity—is therefore the measure of values." Here Marx takes some further steps toward a purely labor theory of value. "Two things are only commensurable if they are of the *same nature*. Products can be measured with the measure of labour—labour time—only because they are, by their nature, *labour*" (613). They have no other features in common. "They exist as equals as long as they exist as activity. The latter is measured by time, which therefore also becomes the measure of objectified labour." "It is then found upon further examination that the values of products are measured not by the labour employed in them, but by the labour necessary for their production" (614). Marx is here coming close to recognizing socially necessary labor time as the way to define value. This goes firmly against all chatter by Adam Smith and others, made much of in these pages, that value has something to do with abstinence and sacrifice—a view that Marx mockingly rejects.

RETURN TO THE MAIN ARGUMENT

After passages laying out some of the ideas of John Stuart Mill, Marx declares his intention of "going back to our subject" (618). His first step is to explore two related topics. First, he returns to the question of circulation time, the circulation process, and the temporality of accumulation. He then opens up questions about the cost of circulation, which can be broken down "into costs of movement; costs to bring the product to market; [and the cost of] the labor time required to effect the transformation from one state [e.g., commodities] to the other [e.g., money]" (619). The accounting operation this requires leads to the creation of a special technical skill and "trade" of money management, e.g., bookkeepers, chartered accountants and auditors as we now know them.

The circulation of capital as a whole is embedded within the monetary circulation described in the first part of the *Grundrisse*. Recall that while all capital at some point takes on the money form, not all money is capital. Production (in the narrow sense) is just one moment within the overall circulation process of money as money, though it could also be said that production extends to the production of circulation (620). The more production is organized by capital the more the general circulation of money starts to dance to the tune of the needs of capital for realization in the market. It is useful here to remember Marx's language back on page 93 of the *Grundrisse* in which production and consumption are seen as each penetrating each other. The key passage is this:

> The total production process of capital includes both the circulation process proper and the actual production process. These form the two great sections of its movement, which appears as the totality of these two processes. On one side, labour time, on the other, circulation time. And the whole of the movement appears as unity of labour time and circulation time, as unity of production and circulation. The unity itself is motion, process. Capital appears as this unity-in-process of production and

circulation, a unity which can be regarded both as the totality of the process of its production, as well as the specific completion of *one* turnover of the capital, *one* movement returning into itself. (620)

Capital is understood as this totality of movement, with circulation time being narrowly defined as movement taking place in the market in contrast to production. Capital "as the subject predominant over the different phases of this movement, as value sustaining and multiplying itself in it, as the subject of these metamorphoses proceeding in a circular course—as a spiral, as an expanding circle—capital is *circulating capital*. Circulating capital is therefore initially not a *particular* form of capital but is rather *capital* itself."

From now on, we think of circulation as the total movement within which the spiral form dominates. Value flows from one material form (moment) to another—a movement which Marx calls the "metamorphoses" (changes of form) of capital. What counts is the motion through the different moments. But while "*circulating capital . . .* is the process of going from one phase into the other, it is at the same time, within each phase . . . restricted to a particular form, which is the negation of itself as the subject of the whole movement. Therefore, capital in each of its particular phases is the negation of itself" (620). As "the subject moving through all phases, as the moving unity, the unity-in-process of circulation and production, capital is *circulating* capital; capital as restricted into any of these phases . . . is *fixated* capital, *tied-down* capital. As circulating capital it fixates itself, and as fixated capital it circulates." As long as capital remains in commodity or money form it cannot function as circulating capital and "as long as it remains in the production process it is not capable of circulating" and "as long as it cannot be brought to market, it is fixated as product." The conflict between stasis and motion stands out. Wherever capital is fixated it becomes "dormant" or "fallow" capital (621). The industrialist, for example, can only use that portion of the capital not already circulating in the market, while the merchant always has to maintain a reserve stock of commodities and the banker likewise has to operate with reserve requirements (to guard against a bank run). The volume of fixated capital required operates as a barrier to raising productivity and to further accumulation. This is one of the reasons why questions of temporality and turnover time return so frequently to haunt Marx's thinking.

A part of the national capital is always fixated in one of the phases through which capital has to move. Capital can "lie fallow, be fixated in the form of money, of value withdrawn from circulation. During crises—*after* the moment of panic—during the standstill of industry, money is immobilized in the hands of bankers, billbrokers etc." Money then "cries out for a field of employment where it may be realized as capital" (621). Capital, as the unity of circulation and production, is, at the same time, the division between them, and a division whose aspects are separated in space and time.

The amount of fixated capital is not itself fixed. But the fact that "the realization process appears at the same time as the devaluation process, contradicts the tendency of capital towards maximum realization" (622–3). Capital, by its nature, is "never completely occupied" but "always partially *fixated*, devalued, unproductive" (623). The level and degree of its occupation (fixation) varies with the economic cycle. A contemporary data point that reflects this is that of fixed capital utilization. When times are bad there are a lot of idle plants and machinery to be found. Capital, furthermore, "invents contrivances to abbreviate the phase of fixity" (623). In recent times, major strides have been made to develop "just-in-time" production systems to reduce the stock of inventories and release idle capital for productive uses. While "money suspends the barriers of barter only by generalizing them . . . so shall we see later that *credit* likewise suspends these barriers to the realization of capital only by raising them to their most general form, positing one period of overproduction and one of underproduction as two periods" (623). What is interesting about this remark is the movement in the text from the simple act of the time structures of production and circulation through the analysis of the circulation of fixated and ultimately fixed capital to invocation of the credit system. While Marx does not say it, the implication is that the circulation of capital, which encounters barriers to its own nature in the fixation of part of the disposable capital, ultimately turns into the circulation of fixed capital. But this in turn is facilitated by the emergence of the credit system as a crucial feature in the totality of capital's movement. The credit system and the circulation of interest-bearing capital, which Marx does not mention here, become central "contrivances" for resolving contradictions at one level while exaggerating the contradictions on a completely different scale at another level. As capital's nature has evolved, so it has become more and more reliant on and more and more obsessed with the contradictions residing within the credit system. But these contradictions have their origin in the distinction between fixated and circulating capital.

Marx's immediate purpose is to introduce us to the relation between the circulating and fixed aspects of the same capital. This topic dominates in the subsequent pages. Here however, he shows how fixed capital exists in embryo as fixated capital within the circulation of capital itself. It is not imposed from outside. It emerges organically within the totality of capital circulation. Fixated capital is the embryonic form. Fixed capital is its mature externalized manifestation.

Circulation, as we have already seen in the previous section, is not a costless enterprise. Labor time is taken up by the circulation process of capital. But "the *costs of circulation* as such, do not add anything to the value of the product, are not value positing costs, regardless of how much labour they may involve. They are merely *deductions from the created* value" (624). This is a cardinal principle in Marx's theorizing. There are, however, some exceptions (such as transport costs) and some caveats, to be explained shortly. But Marx is adamant: "The *costs of circulation* as such *do not posit value*, they are *costs of the realization of values*—deductions from them" (625).

We now need to consider some of the problems that attach to circulation times and turnover times (626). *"The circulation of capital is the change in forms by means of which value passes through the different phases."* The time and costs involved in this process belong to "the *production costs of circulation."* Marx then considers the process of continuous renewal of production through repeated circulations of capital through production. "The retransformation of money into capital . . . depends . . . on its *circulation time"* (in the market) as distinct from "its production time." Hence

> the repetition of the production process . . . is determined by circulation time, which is equal to the velocity of circulation. The more rapid the circulation, the shorter the circulation time, the more often can the same capital repeat the production process. Hence, in a specific cycle of turnovers of capital, the sum of values created by it (hence surplus values as well . . .) is *directly proportional to the* [production] *time and inversely proportional to the circulation time.* (627)

A long circulation time inhibits production of value.

Note that circulation time here refers to time on the market and not the time of the total capital circulation. "Hence, to the extent that circulation time determines the total mass of production time in a given period of time . . . to that extent is it itself a moment of production, or rather appears as a limit of production." This signals a major departure from the simple thesis that value arises solely in the moment of production. "This is the nature of capital, of production founded on capital, that circulation time becomes a determinant moment for . . . the creation of value. The independence of labour [production] time is thereby negated, and the production process is itself posited as determined by exchange" (628). This, to put it mildly, seemingly contradicts the view that value creation rests solely on what happens in the moment of production, independent of conditions of circulation in the market. I think the best way to present this is to say that barriers to circulation in the market diminish the capacity for realization, and that this in turn inhibits production. It then follows that transcendence of the barriers to realization in the market will open the way to an expansion of value production. This point was established earlier, but Marx sees fit to remind us of it here. Marx is right to challenge the supposed independence of the production of value and surplus-value from realization. But he is doing so without abandoning the view that all value is created in production. As he says elsewhere: value is created in production and realized in the market.

This leads Marx to some interesting conclusions. "The maximum realization of capital, is also the maximum continuity of the production process." If circulation time is posited as zero, "then, the conditions under which capital produces, its restriction by circulation time . . . are suspended." Therefore, "it is the necessary tendency of capital to strive to equate circulation time to 0; i.e. to suspend itself, since it is capital itself alone which posits circulation time as a determinant moment of production time" (629). Circulation time inhibits the production of value which, if it is released, allows for greater production of value and surplus-value. While value cannot be created in circulation, the capacity to appropriate and realize it can be expanded by increasing the velocity of circulation, by being slicker and faster in the marketplace. While the relationship between necessary and surplus labor time may remain the same, the number of times you go through a production process depends on circulation time. "It seems, therefore, that the magnitude of the capital can be replaced by the velocity of turnover, and the velocity of turnover by the magnitude of capital. This is how it comes to appear as though circulation time were in itself productive" (630).

Over the next few pages, Marx examines some specific examples only to show that "*circulation without circulation time*—i.e. the transition of capital from one phase to the next at the speed of thought" would ensure the "renewal of the production process with its termination" (631). He reasserts "that circulation . . . cannot increase the value of circulating commodities. Therefore, if labour time is required to undertake this operation" and "if circulation entails costs, and if circulation time costs labour time, then this is a deduction from . . . circulating values; their devaluation by the amount of the circulation costs" (632).

This opens the way to examine what Marx calls the *"faux frais de production"* (the necessary costs of production). These necessary costs act as a drag upon the motion of capital. The drive to reduce these necessary costs and to increase the productivity of the labor engaged in this activity does not add to value. It does, however, reduce the negation of created values and the deductions from value taken by the merchants (633). In general, Marx concludes, circulation time in the market is of interest only in "its relation—as barrier, negation—to the production time of capital" (634).

Transportation is, however, a different matter.

> In so far as trade brings a product to market, it gives it a new form. True, all it does is change the location. But the mode of transformation does not concern us. It gives the product a new use value (and this holds right down to and including the retail grocer, who weighs, measures, wraps the product and thus gives it a form for consumption), and this new use value costs labour time, is at the same time exchange value. Bringing to market is part of the production process itself. The product is a commodity, is in circulation only when it is on the market. (635)

Capital accumulation is sensitive to the negative effects of circulation time. This helps to explain certain things like the pressure to rationalize circulation costs and times in the market, the creation of just-in-time systems, inventory reduction strategies, the tendency to reduce reserves and diminish the volume of fixated capital. But going too far in these directions increases vulnerabilities. If there is an interruption in the commodity flow or a hiccup in the value chain of the sort that occurred during the Covid-19 pandemic, then the result will be devaluation. The tension between maintaining adequate reserves for emergencies and keeping capital as fluid and disposable as possible never goes away. Furthermore, the power of labor to disrupt is sensitive to inventory levels. When Margaret Thatcher forced the coal miners to strike, she first ensured that all the power stations had sufficient reserves of coal to stay in production for several months. In intricate commodity chain structures, on the other hand, a strike at one component factory can bring the whole system down almost with "the speed of thought."

If capital is value in motion, then the motion has to be maintained and if possible accelerated through the fixated states. Marx approvingly cites the economist Storch: "The nation whose capital circulates with a proper speed, so as to return several times a year to him who set it in motion, is in the same situation as the labourer of the happy climates who can raise three or four harvests in succession from the same soil in one year." Storch went on to emphasize the importance of the "means for the abbreviation and acceleration of circulation: (1) the separating-out of a class of workers occupied exclusively with trade; (2) ease of transport; (3) currency; (4) credit" (637). The credit system becomes critical to the continuity of circulation. It is not, therefore, parasitic. It smooths out and accelerates turnover times.

There then follow three of four pages of intricate and difficult-to-interpret argument. Here is how I interpret them. Consider a simple act in which someone buys a sewing machine. The material content of that act (something that always concerns Marx) is that money has been used as a medium of circulation to transfer a property right over the sewing machine from one juridical person to another. There is nothing in the act itself to tell us if this is an act of capital or not. It could, after all, simply be my grandmother wanting to make some new curtains. We will only know if this act contributes to capital after we have followed the use of the machine and established that it was used to produce something through hiring labor, that the resultant product was sold on the market as a commodity, and—here is the crucial point—the money procured from the sale was used to promote yet another turnover cycle of production. Under these conditions, the buying of the sewing machine can, retrospectively, be seen as a first moment in the chain of moments that make up capital circulation and accumulation. There is no way to say definitively we are dealing with capital from the detailed examination of any one moment. The definition of capital rests on the totality of the circulation process through all the moments and, in addition, to the repetition of that flow over continuous repetitive cycles (which morph into a spiral). Marx had earlier argued that there is nothing interesting to be said about circulation in the market when it comes to value creation. But now he is saying that capital is defined by this circulation process as a whole, a total process in which production is but one moment. While the meaning of circulation in the market is not interesting, the meaning of the circulation process as a whole is of critical significance. It is only in relation to this circulation process that the contribution of the particular moments can be understood:

> Circulation is not merely an external operation for capital. Just as it only becomes capital through the production process . . . so does it become retransformed into the pure *form* of value . . . only through the first act of circulation; while the repetition of this act . . . is made possible only through the second act of circulation, which exists of the exchange of money for the conditions of production and forms the introduction to the act of production. Circulation therefore belongs *within* the concept of capital. (638)

I earlier alluded to the confusion in the *Grundrisse* between the two senses of circulation. But here we learn why the confusion exists and how we have to work with it. In what follows, the definition of capital as value in motion and the emergence of the circulation and accumulation of capital as a totality, as the object of investigation, lies in the forefront of the analysis. This is how capital "self-immortalizes" and "self-multiplies" itself. "Capital is, therefore, essentially *circulating capital*" (639). Value cannot be created through circulation in the market. But the reduction of barriers to circulation in the market opens the path to the further expansion of value and surplus-value in production; hence, as we have seen, the persistent illusion that value can be created through circulation.

Within the circulation process as a whole, the distinction between production and circulation in the market reemerges as significant for a very particular reason. "While in the workshop of the production process capital appears as proprietor and master, in respect to circulation, it appears as dependent and determined by social connections" (639). Within the production process, the capitalists exercise quasi-total control. But, beyond that they are subject to the anarchy of the market. They are subject to the vagaries of wants, needs and desires in the marketplace. They are not in control. The circulation process as a whole has two spheres, one of which is within the tight control of capital. In the other, the capitalists are subject to the whims of consumer desires.

In practice, however, the direct producers will not probably confront that problem. They will not sell direct into the market but sell to an intermediary, such as a wholesale or retail merchant. "This much is clear," Marx says on 639, "that consumption need not enter into its circle [i.e. the circulation process] *directly*. The actual circulation of capital, as we shall see later, is still circulation between dealers and dealers. The circulation between dealers and consumers, identical with the retail trade, is a second circle." Hence the circulation of capital in general can go forward without any direct and immediate link to consumption. The secondary orbit takes care of that. The simultaneity of the activity within this secondary orbit becomes an important feature. Many producers trade their commodities to department stores (like Walmart). That is where the link to the consumer is forged.

With respect to the specific use-values and the specific labor involved in commodity production, Marx proffers the opinion that "the most fundamental of these production processes is that through which the body produces its necessary metabolism, i.e. creates the necessaries of life in the physiological sense" (640). This is an important point. The use-values Marx is here referring to are elsewhere characterized as "wage goods," i.e., that specific bundle of commodities which capital produces and which the laborers and their dependents need to survive and reproduce. The value of these goods fixes the value of labor capacity as a commodity in the market. But it is interesting that at this point in his thinking, Marx also seems to have in mind what he calls the "small circulation" of labor capacity. This focuses on how the reproduction of labor capacity is integrated into the general circulation and accumulation of capital. We now take up this topic in greater detail, leaving the circulation of fixed capital, which Marx begins to probe here (640–73), for consideration in the next chapter.

THE SMALL-SCALE CIRCULATION OF LABOR POWER

"The process of exchange between capital and labour capacity" has been a recurrent theme throughout the *Grundrisse*. "What precisely distinguishes capital from the master–servant relation," Marx had earlier observed, "is that the *worker* confronts him as consumer and possessor of exchange values, and that in the form of the *possessor of money*, in the form of money he becomes a simple centre of circulation—one of its infinitely many centres, in which his specificity as worker is extinguished" (420–1).

In these few pages (673–9), Marx seeks to consolidate seemingly disparate themes into a single conception of a circulation process based on the selling and buying of "labour capacity." Small-scale circulation is "the part of capital which is paid out as wages, exchanged for labouring capacity" (Figure 1). This circulation process delivers labor capacity as a use-value to the capitalist in return for a money wage which can be used to purchase the commodities (use-values) needed for working persons to reproduce themselves (and their dependents) at a given standard of living at their site of social reproduction. Within the framework of small-scale circulation, Marx suggests that "capital constantly expels itself as objectified labour," presumably in the form of commodities ready for consumption, "in order to assimilate living labour power, its life's breath" (676). When workers consume and reproduce themselves, they do so as living labor capacity. Their reproduction is itself a condition for capital and "*therefore the worker's consumption also appears as the reproduction not of capital directly, but of the [class] relations under which alone it is capital.*" If, in short, laborers did not reproduce themselves, then there would be no labor power for capital to hire. Consequently, "*living labour capacity belongs just as much among capital's conditions of existence as do raw material and instrument. Thus, [capital] reproduces itself doubly, in its own form, [and] in the worker's consumption, but only to the extent that it reproduces him as living labour capacity.* Capital, therefore, calls this consumption productive consumption—productive not in so far as it reproduces the individual, but rather individuals as labour capacities" (676). The consumerism of the workers and the payment of wages exists in a certain relation to the general circulation of capital even as it exists within the "small circulation" we are here concerned with. "The payment of wages is an act of circulation which proceeds simultaneously with and alongside the act of production" (676). Or, as Sismondi says: "The worker consumes his wages unreproductively, but the capitalist consumes them productively, since he gets labour in the exchange, which reproduces the wages and more than the wages . . . in so far as capital is a relation, and, specifically, a relation to living labour capacity, [to that extent] worker's consumption reproduces this relation." Capital therefore "reproduces itself doubly, as value through purchase of labour . . . and as a relation through the worker's consumption, which reproduces him as labour capacity exchangeable for capital—wages as part of capital" (676–7). The general outline of this circulation process is of the following sort:

> Capital pays wages e.g. weekly; the worker takes his wages to the grocer etc.; the latter directly or indirectly deposits them with the banker; and the following week the manufacturer takes them from the banker again, in order to distribute them among the same workers again, etc. and so forth . . . This circulation is a condition of the production process and thereby of the circulation process as well . . . hence it is itself conditional upon capital passing through the various moments of its metamorphosis *outside* the production process. (677)

It is in this sense that we can say that capital is indirectly embodied in the worker at the same time as capital subsumes the worker. The reproduction of capital is therefore "itself conditional upon capital passing through the various moments of its metamorphosis *outside* the production process" (677).

Marx does not lay out the distinctive moments within the circulation of labor capacity "*outside* the production process." Nor does he examine in any detail their consequences for the condition of capital–labor relations. In what follows, I will venture well beyond Marx's text and speculate freely on the subjective and political consequences of the circulation of labor capacity. The framework (Figure 1) is that of a continuous flow in the supply of labor capacity from the site of social reproduction, passing through the labor market and the labor process, culminating in a brief moment of command over the money power (given by the wage) that can be used to buy the commodities needed to sustain workers and their dependents back in their place of social reproduction. There are five distinctive moments within this circulation process, which simultaneously guarantees the reproduction of the laborer and the capitalist alongside the class relation between them. Consider, then, the five distinctive moments in this continuous flow.

(1) The worker leaves home and enters a labor market in search of a position. The worker has one commodity to offer, the capacity to labor. In this moment, the worker takes on the

persona of commodity seller in competition with many others. The demand for labor capacity is constantly shifting both qualitatively and quantitatively with the technological evolution of divisions and specializations of labor. The quantitative and qualitative aspects of the commodity each worker has for sale are relevant to its price and to the competitive success of particular sellers. Sellers will seek to differentiate the commodity they have for sale from that of others. Labor market conditions vary greatly: segmentations in the supply of labor, cultural preferences along with biases due to gender, ethnicity, religion, race, and the like may enter in. Immigrant groups often colonize certain job types and collectively organize to bring new immigrants preferentially into the labor market. Workers experience the labor market, in all of its complexity, as sellers or groups (ethnic, racial, gendered, etc.) in competition with other sellers (individuals or groups). This market is typically fragmented, segmented and fractured along all manner of socio-political lines. The experience of the labor market is not automatically conducive to a political subjectivity based on class consciousness, even though there are clear class consequences (e.g., fixing the value of labor power).

(2) Once hired (hopefully in a secure position), the worker passes through the gates (sometimes metaphorical) into the place of employment. There, they put their capacity to labor at the disposal of the capitalist, who makes all the decisions on what is to be produced, where and how. Workers, as Marx emphasizes, experience the labor process as alienated labor, collectively working under the supervision of capital. The material experience varies greatly, of course, from industry to industry and from employer to employer, as well as from one part of the world to another. But the role of mobilizing labor capacity under the domination of capital is the embodiment of the class relation, which is the focus of much of Marx's writing on the theory of capital. "The use

value of labour capacity, as value, is itself the value-creating force; the substance of value, and the value-increasing substance" (674). Or, more prosaically, the use-value of labor power "exists as the worker's specific, productive activity; it is his vitality itself, directed toward a specific purpose and hence expressing itself in a specific form" (260). The detailed divisions of labor usually found in employment situations may reflect and confirm the segmentations that arise in labor markets. In the US steel industry in the 1960s, for example, the dirtiest and most dangerous jobs were typically assigned to African Americans and Puerto Ricans, and women only arrived on the scene in the 1970s. But the political subjectivity of class domination, repression and exploitation is so strong in this experiential world as to make it the paradigmatic home of class consciousness formation.

(3) At the end of the working day (or week or month), the worker will receive a wage, usually in money form, as a form of revenue. The wage never touches production. It flows in the form of variable capital in a parallel stream to the labor process. What wage workers do with their money is their own business. The capitalists self-servingly urge them to save (by denial of consumption) in order to cover their needs at times of distress and provide for their old age. "The demand for industriousness and also for *saving, self-denial*, is made not upon the capitalists but on the workers, and namely by the capitalists" (285). In this way, they will not place any financial burden on capital or state institutions. Hence the proliferation of savings and piggy banks to be put at the disposal of the working class. But if everyone is in a position to save, then the capitalists will doubtless conclude that wages are too high. Workers may also borrow, either from the pawnbroker, from some financial institution or, in our time, by maxing out on credit cards. In spite of elaborate capitalist-inspired schemes and scams to

dispossess the worker of their new-found wealth and restrain their freedom of consumer choice, nothing can take away from them the elation that this moment of freedom of monetary control and consumer choice (however ephemeral and paltry) brings to the worker's life. Some workers may put aside enough money over time to start their own business (a frequent ambition among immigrant groups in the United States).

(4) In practice, the worker will usually be desperate to acquire the commodities needed to sustain a daily life (or more likely lives). At this moment in the circulation process, workers function as buyers of commodities (which they have produced) from the capitalist, who takes on the role of seller (usually as merchant capitalist). Workers can express their wants, needs and desires (subject to their ability to pay) in a variety of ways in the marketplace. They may even feed their aspirations to a better life by (as Marx noted), subscribing to newspapers and joining educational clubs. But the social relation that dominates is that between buyers and sellers. It is here that their identity as worker "is extinguished." The working person exercises the same rights and privileges and suffers the same anguishes as any buyer. Situations arise in which some privileged workers may achieve a superior standard of living; the so-called "affluent white workers" of the 1960s (with a suburban house and two cars in the driveway) in the United States were an example. Problems in consumer markets can, for example, lead to common social struggle against monopoly pricing or price-gouging. Access to key features of consumption (such as housing) is not necessarily egalitarian. Discrimination (similar to that in labor markets) is widespread in many markets (e.g., everything from housing to food deserts in urban areas). Furthermore, the use of tax funds to support the social wage and public services funded by the state (e.g., education) is filtered through public policy

practices that are typically class- and often race-biased. The experience in this sphere is fragmented and only partially conducive to a clear class consciousness. But there is something else of vital importance here. The collective purchasing power of the working classes is a key aspect of aggregate effective demand in the economy. In the same way that individual capitalists repress the wages of their own employees while looking to the employees of others as potent consumers, so the aggregate fact that the effective demand of the working class cannot possibly exceed the total value and surplus-value produced does not deny that a collapse of working-class consumerism poses a huge threat to the continued accumulation of capital.

(5) Once back in the realm of the household or family, the worker (along with everybody else) needs a space in which to live. Everyone has to negotiate (unequally) with landed property over the extraction of rent (or its equivalent) for the privilege of occupying a space in which to live on planet Earth. Within this space, working people (and all others) take on the role of social reproduction of themselves as individuals, as collective entities (such as households and families) and as builders of social and community solidarities and state institutions (or their equivalent). This will be done in support of a particular and distinctive cultural mode of daily life. Again, workers are not alone in this realm of social action. Marx is frequently accused of neglecting questions of the social reproduction of labor power and, in many respects, the accusation is more than justified (as the vast subsequent literature on social reproduction, much of it by Marxist feminists, attests). But he does advance a theory of social reproduction from the standpoint of capital, and from this certain insights arise. What the overall circulation process of the capacity to labor reveals is the importance to social reproduction of producing workers with the right capacity to labor (in a particular

place and historical time) while also socializing inhabitants to be "adequate" consumers and to cultivate the requisite mix of wants, needs and desires to help stabilize effective demand in the market. The household is the site where cultures of consumerism are confirmed and where the discipline required for laboring might be acquired, in collaboration with public sectors of education and all sorts of institutions of cultural and religious education. This is not, I hasten to add, all that matters in the sphere of social reproduction, but it is one important component that arises out of the embedding of social reproduction within the circulation of capacity to labor in general. It takes a leap of conscious understanding to appreciate the class basis of much of what goes on in the moment of social reproduction (e.g., in schooling). It is also the case that the relation between activities in this sphere and what happens in the other moments is not a one-way relation. It is reciprocal and dialectical, not monocausal.

The working person must, perforce, relate to these different experiential worlds and the fragmentations they express. Some workers might succumb to the temptation of a compensatory consumerism, in which they are offered access to a cornucopia of cheap consumer goods as compensation for horrific alienations in production. Others may consent to alienated labor and exploitation in the hope that they be able to put sufficient money by to someday open a bodega or a coffee shop. Yet others may consent to everything in this circulation process provided they can create for themselves a meaningful family or household life at the site of social reproduction. Taking the kids to Little League games or music classes or just romping with them in the backyard may afford enough pride and pleasure to mask the miserable alienating experience of working for capital. The creation of a solidary and amicable neighborhood life has been, for many working-class populations, a compensatory joy that makes class struggle against capital in production seem a remote and even unnecessary engagement. Many of the active struggles we are now witnessing are over such matters as exploitation in the market (action against monopoly power and pricing of pharmaceutical products or housing, for example) and the perversions of the credit and mortgage debt system. Workplace struggles are just one form of many social struggles and by no means always the most immediately important. The deterioration of the qualities of neighborhood life and stresses within families, some of which can be traced back to deindustrialization and unemployment, now lie at the root of many working-class discontents and much political malaise.

The social experience and therefore typical forms of political subjectivity vary from moment to moment. Individualistic and cut-throat competition in labor markets typically marked by racial, ethnic, religious and gender discriminations in job access do not gel with the class solidarity that should supposedly dominate in labor processes. Neither of these gel with the roles of independent money manager and autonomous buyer of commodities—even under conditions of, for example, discrimination in housing markets. The conditions of social reproduction, furthermore, exist in a different constellation of social forces even as they touch upon labor capacity, consumer preferences, the cultures of daily life and the opening up of channels for political activism. As in any totality, the relations between the different moments are crucial. For example, the experience of class domination in production can promote a class-consciousness approach by participants in labor markets conducive to worker solidarities, rather than to ruinous inter-worker competition and sectional discriminations. The class consciousness of capitalists, on the other hand, leads them to insist upon flexibility and individualism in labor markets, and they do their level best to persuade the workers and the public at large that this arrangement will redound to the benefit of all. For this reason, debt relief packages served out by the IMF invariably insert a conditionality of increasing flexibility in labor markets. Class consciousness forged in the labor process can likewise lead to collective action against the depredations of landlords and the price gouging that occurs in consumer markets. Capitalists would also likely prefer it if workers brought into the workplace a culture of hostility to others (provided it does not impinge upon efficiency) so as to forestall collective worker organization. On the other hand, gender discriminations in social reproduction have spilled over with a vengeance into labor markets as well as into the social relations of production. But in all these last instances, the worker is not alone. Alliances within and between different social layers or identities in the population can be built to regulate and control, for example, housing rents or the prices of pharmaceuticals, while the principle of equality preached (though rarely practiced) in labor markets can play a role in modifying structures of social reproduction. This means that anticapitalist politics has a different social basis to that which has historically been attributed solely to the class relations of production.

If we apply the Marxist principle that political subjectivity rests ultimately upon material experiences, then workers perforce absorb the different experiences of seller, of productive if alienated laborer working under the command of capital, of money manager, of buyer of commodities and finally as member of some social group engaging in social reproduction. Only one of those experiential sites is directly involved in the production of class consciousness. To be sure, there is an indirect experience in the labor market where capital will seek to promote individual competition between laborers along with divisive segmentations such as those of race, gender, ethnicity and the like as a means to repress wages as a capitalist class strategy. Workers may actively promote those differentiations which redound to their own advantage (ethnic exclusions constructed by the workers themselves have been longstanding). Workers will likely carry with them prejudicial views on racial, gender, religious and other distinctions arising from the labor market experience throughout the other moments (especially within the labor process but also in social reproduction). Hence the significance in the United States of a white working class currently prone to beliefs of its supremacy.

It takes a leap of conscious understanding on the part of the worker to see the totality as a product of a capitalist mode of production and to hone their class consciousness around an understanding of that totality accordingly. It is exactly such a leap of conscious understanding that Marx probably hoped to provoke. This explains why it is that the concept of totality was so important for him. It helped as an aid to theory formation. But more importantly, it was from the perspective of the totality that the clearest conception and understanding of class positionality, class experience and class political strategy within the mode of production in general could flow.

9

The Power of Fixed Capital
Pages 640–701

On page 640, Marx declares a major shift of emphasis in his investigation. He wants to understand "the distinctions the economists draw between *fixed capital* and *circulating capital*." For the next hundred pages, this topic will dominate the inquiry, though punctuated with a few detours, some but not all of which are of considerable interest. The stage for this move is set by the conclusions to his earlier studies of turnover times and the role of "fixated" capital. The latent contradiction between the continuity of the capital flow principle and the problem that some capital inevitably becomes fixated in some state for some time lurks in the background. Marx recognized the vast amount of work that bourgeois political economists put into understanding relations between fixed and circulating capital and that these were foundational concepts for their thinking. Marx himself was edging toward constant and variable capital as his foundational concepts (briefly invoked on page 649, perhaps with the intention of reminding us of the alternative power of these other categories), since only through them could he explain the concept of surplus-value. To insist, as did Ricardo, that the focus should be on fixed and circulating capital explained why Ricardo and his school could not grasp the theory of surplus-value as the basis for profit.

But Marx also recognized, through his studies of turnover time and of fixated capital, that serious attention had to be paid to the fixed–circulating distinction. His starting point is arbitrary. Based on the rhythms of agricultural production "in the temperate zone (the home of capital)" in Marx's time, it follows that the year "has been adopted as the general period of time by which the sum of the turnovers of capital is calculated and measured; just as the *natural working day* provided such a natural unit as measure of labour time" (640). The implication is that the more the turnover time of some components of capital stretches beyond a year, the more we need a distinctive form of analysis to understand it.

This will become explicit on page 678, where Marx singles out fixed capital as one of three distinctive and autonomous circulation processes embedded in the totality of capital. The implication is that the circulation of fixed capital is independent and autonomous, even as it is subsumed within the overall logic of the totality of relations and processes that constitute a capitalist mode of production. Figure 3 depicts how it might look.

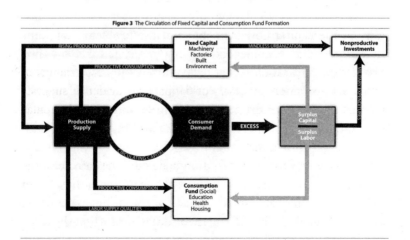

Figure 3 The Circulation of Fixed Capital and Consumption Fund Formation

For example, a falling rate of interest may be just as important as a falling rate of profit, while investments in fixed capital (particularly that of an independent kind in physical infrastructure, urbanization and the like) come to play a major role in capital accumulation in their own right. Fixed capital dances to a different drummer (with players drawn from the financial institutions) than circulating capital, where the industrial capitalist's search for profit holds sway. I introduce all of these prospective and speculative arguments here in order to stress the high stakes involved in the subsequent investigation. The question of fixed versus circulating capital is given far more airtime in the *Grundrisse* than anywhere else in Marx's writings.

On a personal note, I should add that given my interest in the role of urbanization in relation to capital accumulation, the textual materials covered in this section have been inspirational for me. As early as 1978, I published an article on "The Urban Process under Capitalism," inspired by the *Grundrisse*, where I identified a "secondary circuit of capital" constituted by flows of overaccumulating capital into fixed capital formation in general and into the built environment (including the consumption fund) in particular, especially during times of crisis. These flows depended heavily on the mobilization of the credit system or the state apparatus to engineer the shift from circulating to fixed capital. Look no further than the role of urbanization in China in 2008–9 for a clear example of the role of fixed capital formation through state credit–fueled urbanization in relation to the revival of a seriously endangered capital accumulation process worldwide. The evidence suggests that this massive switch from circulating to fixed capital circulation in China saved international capitalism from total collapse during those troubled years.

In introducing the topic of fixed capital, Marx makes some quite stunning prospective assertions. "In the calculation of profit, and even more of interest, we ... see the unity of circulation and production time ... Surplus value in connection with *circulating capital* obviously appears as profit, in distinction to *interest* as the surplus value in connection with *fixed capital*." While "profit and interest are both forms of surplus value" it seems that the relation between circulating and fixed capital rest on a separation between the circulation of interest-bearing capital and the circulation of profit-seeking capital. There is a "new moment which enters with the calculation of profit as distinct from surplus value" (640–1). This puts the relation between profit and interest at the center of the analysis. This is a startling if not troubling conceptual shift. To begin with, profit and surplus-value seem to be parting ways such that we can no longer be satisfied with the idea that profit is simply the money name of surplus-value. Second, the split of surplus-value into profit and interest seems now ready to play some sort of definitive role in relation to the split between fixed and circulating capital. These questions hang over Marx's subsequent discussion. But it takes many pages before we get close to any answers. From page 640, where Marx states this conceptual shift, until page 678, where he takes up fixed capital as one of the three basic circulation processes within the totality of capital, Marx mainly examines, without much commentary, the ruling ideas in bourgeois political economy (along with Proudhon's "obvious errors").

The distinction between fixed and circulating capital had a long history in the work of economists. The first few pages of Marx's review of the literature focus on the different ways in which circulating and fixed capital might be distinguished from each other. "Depending on whether *capital* is more or less *transitory*, hence *must be more or less frequently reproduced in a given time*, it is called *circulating or fixed capital*" (644). The one question of significance, which will be taken up again later, is how use-values might here enter in as an economic category (646). A review of Ricardo shows that the distinction between fixed and circulating capital is internalized within capitalist production processes and that it is impossible to get any fine-grained measure of the differentiation outside of an understanding of production time, labor time and the overall turnover time of capital. An added complication comes with the "different *degrees of durability*" and the "*relative durability of the relatively fixed*" (645).

It is perhaps this last point that provokes Marx into some further reflections on the general theme of turnover times in both production and circulation. "We have seen, then, that the surplus value a capital can posit in a given period of time is determined by the number of times the realization process can be repeated," and this is also constrained by circulation time ("realization" almost certainly refers here to the total turnover process including production). The latter "thus appears as time during which the ability of capital to reproduce itself ... is suspended" (658). "Circulation time is not time during which capital creates value, but rather during which it realizes the value created in the production process." It then follows that "the necessary tendency of capital is therefore *circulation without circulation time*, and this tendency is the necessary determinant of credit and capital's credit contrivances" (659).

Marx is making two points of major import here. To begin with, the reduction of circulation time (in the market) to zero is to capital's benefit, and the promotion of modes of consumption (such as all forms of spectacle) that have almost instantaneous turnover times is a latent tendency within capital. Instantaneous consumerism has expanded enormously in recent times. Second, the credit system arises in response to capital's need to circumvent the "suspension" of surplus-value production through the time taken for realization. "Credit creates new products of circulation" (a tendency strongly exhibited around us today) to facilitate the rapid if not instantaneous return of capital to surplus-value production well before the commodity has actually been sold. "The contradiction of labour time and circulation time contains the entire doctrine of credit," Marx concludes. This is one of those moments when we get a glimpse of an analysis to come rather than a present ambition to be pursued and nailed down. But it has been firmly established that capital contains both moments of production time and circulation time, and that the time which elapses between production and reproduction "is time which devalues capital" (663). Capital suffers when the continuity is disrupted—hence, the concern over turnover time. For capital, this is given by "the sum of circulation and production time." The obvious corollary comes several pages later. "Value, hence also surplus value, is not = to the time which the production phase lasts, but rather to the labour time, objectified and living, employed during this production phase" (669).

All this talk of circulation and turnover times diverts Marx from his declared pathway to deal with fixed capital in all of its complexity. Instead, Marx engages in an all-too-brief survey of certain different modes of circulation to be found within capital as a totality. It goes without saying that the passages that follow were a crucial key to unlocking some of the secrets of the *Grundrisse*'s structure. This is where he explicitly approaches the question of the threefold character, or mode, of circulation within the totality of capital. Since Marx backs into this discussion, I jump ahead to get the general conception and then come backwards into the depiction of some of the details.

"Regarded as a whole, circulation thus appears threefold: (1) the total process—the course of capital through its different moments," as it is depicted in Figure 2 (678). Then there is (2) small-scale circulation between capital and labor capacity (as discussed in the previous section and depicted in Figure 1); and (3) large-scale circulation, the movement of capital outside of the production phase, "where its time appears in antithesis to labour time, as circulation time." Instead of accelerating and speeding up, as typically happens with the case of circulating capital, fixed capital slows everything down. "The distinction between *fluid* and *fixed* capital is the product of this opposition between the capital engaged in the production phase and the capital which issues from it. Fixed is that which is fixated in the production process and is consumed within it; comes out of large-scale circulation, certainly, but does not return into it, and . . . circulates only in order to be consumed in, confined to, the consumption process" (Figure 3). Marx surely means productive rather than final consumption here and, in these statements, he is referring to the mode of consumption of machinery and plant which occurs within the production process (678).

After due consideration has been given to the "small-scale circulation" of labor capacity analyzed earlier, Marx returns to the main topic at hand, which is the distinctive circulatory form taken by fixed capital. Consider a sewing machine in a factory setting. It is being used as a means of production, but it is not consumed physically in the production process. There is a big difference between this and the raw cotton going into a textile factory and coming out as cotton cloth or a cotton shirt. At the end of the annual turnover period, the raw cotton is used up but the sewing machine is still there.

The second point about the machine is that it typically lasts for more than one turnover cycle. If the standard turnover time is one year, a sewing machine may be used for ten or fifteen years. Moreover, the machine remains in the possession of the capitalist during that time. It does not pass on into the possession of the final consumer, as does a cotton shirt. The big question is: how does the value of the machine circulate in the absence of any material transfer?

In the case of the raw cotton, there is no problem. Its value ends up in the shirt. But it does so because labor transfers the existing value (free of charge, it should be noted) from the raw cotton into that of the shirt. It is, in principle, possible to show and calculate how the value of the raw cotton gets re-created to reappear in the shirt. But how then does the value of the machine get re-created and in what sense does it reappear in the shirt?

If the machine lasts for ten or fifteen years, it presumably has the same or similar capacity at the end of ten years as it did at the beginning. There may be some deterioration with use, but the machine remains the same machine throughout. It is not as if bits of the machine fly off into the shirts over the ten years until there is no machine left. How is the value of the machine transferred into the cotton shirt? The obvious answer is that labor does it, by using the machine to make the shirt. The problem then is to show

how much of the value of the sewing machine (presumably purchased as a commodity on the market) is transferred by labor into the product each year. The easiest answer is to define a depreciation schedule in which the value of the sewing machine over a ten-year lifetime would transfer one-tenth of its total value into all of the shirts made during each year. Everything then rests on the lifetime of the machine, which is partly a physical and partly a social and economic determination.

The social determination of the machine's lifetime will eventually pose some acute problems. This is so because it entails an accounting procedure that lacks any material referent. It is not only machines which are like this. Consider, for example, the use of energy (e.g., electricity) in production. The energy is not transferred into the cotton, into the shirt, but it is used up in making the shirt. The energy is consumed on a continuous basis. But unlike the machine, there is none left over at the end of the year. The value of the energy used up during the production period is spread over all of the shirts made during a year. So fixed capital is not alone in being used but not physically transferred into the produced commodity. What is distinctive about the machine, however, is that it remains in production and is physically present as a use-value over many turnover cycles.

The value of the machine is initially given by the socially necessary labor time taken up in the making of the machine. That constitutes the value that has to be transferred to the product on an annual basis over the lifetime of the machine. What is the lifetime of the machine? It could be ten years, fifteen or even thirty years. Who knows? There are still machines from the nineteenth century being used. So how do we actually create this fiction of a steady value flow from the machine into the product during the production process? And what will we do about the fact that new, cheaper and more efficient machines are coming onto the market all of the time, thus devaluing the comparative worth of existing machines. For the moment, Marx seems happy to ignore this problem and to assume that the lifetime of the machine is fixed and known.

Fixed capital is typically consumed slowly. It is, in the first instance, construed as circulating capital which assumes a fixated form. But fixed capital is destined to be consumed as a means of production. It does not move freely. It is fixed and, for the most part, remains within the ownership of the capitalist throughout the lifetime of the machine (though there is a secondhand market), and it has this very peculiar way of circulating its value.

The rise of machine technology has a huge impact on how capital works. Its adoption and diffusion is impelled through intercapitalist competition, which probably accounts for Marx interrupting his investigation of fixed capital to insert his devastating critique of competitive individualism, which we reviewed earlier. But recall that "competition is nothing more than the way in which the many capitals force the inherent determinants of capital upon one another and upon themselves" (650–1). If I have a superior machine, I can drive you out of business unless you adopt a similar machine or get yourself an even better machine to drive me out of business. The result is a trend within capitalism, driven by the coercive laws of competition, to continuously increase labor productivity over time by perpetually seeking out more efficacious forms of fixed capital.

To the degree that machine technology becomes more significant, so the circulation of fixed capital becomes more and more dominant. The passages that follow on fixed capital and the general intellect constitute a high point of theorizing in the *Grundrisse*. There is some remarkable writing and insights into the nature of capital in these pages (680–711). There has also been not a little controversy over how to interpret some of the key concepts. It is wonderful stuff, beautifully written and quite startling in its potential implications. Its insights into the dynamics of a capitalist mode of production, it turns out, are deeply relevant to our own time.

The definition of fixed capital is that it "circulates as *value*" but that "it does not circulate as *use value*" (680). A sewing machine does not circulate as a use-value, but a portion of its value does circulate when it is used in the production process to facilitate the production of a commodity. But there is no material transfer from the machine into the commodity that is produced. The use-value of the machine is that it increases the productivity of the labor going into the production of the commodity. "As far as its material aspect is concerned, as a moment of the production process, *fixed capital* never leaves its boundaries; is not sold by its possessor; remains in his hand." Circumstances such as the secondhand market for machines and the leasing of fixed capital equipment on an annual basis are for the purposes of analysis ruled out. Fixed capital "circulates as capital only in its *formal aspect*" (680). That is, its value circulates but its material form does not. This leaves us with the problem of figuring out the rules of its value circulation without any material cues. Fixed capital "realizes itself as value only as long as it remains in the capitalist's hand as a use value . . . as long as it remains in the production process." It then follows that items are "*fixed capital* not because of the specific mode of their being, but rather because of their use. They become fixed capital as soon as they step into the production process. They are *fixed capital* as soon as they are posited as moments of the production process of capital" (681).

Think of sewing machines. One of the valued things in working-class households when I was a kid was having a sewing machine in the parlor. The women were very adept at using them to make the kids' clothes, curtains, or whatever. The sewing machines were not fixed capital because they were not used in the production of commodities. But let us suppose somebody came along and bought up all of the unused sewing machines in the parlors, set them out in their basement and hired people to make clothing. Then those sewing machines become fixed capital incorporated within a capitalist system of production. This, then, leaves a problem of how to establish the value of the sewing machines and how to allocate that value when used in production.

The entrepreneur may find the old machines inefficient and go out and buy a whole lot more. The machines are produced as circulating capital but converted into fixed capital when placed in the sweatshop. Maybe the sweatshop goes bankrupt. Then the sewing machines get taken out and maybe end up back in people's households, so that people can use them in a different kind of way. They are no longer fixed capital and they are devalued as far as capital is concerned.

Whether or not things are fixed capital depends, therefore, on their use. This explains why use-value returns to become such a key economic category. The amount and form of fixed capital in society can increase or diminish simply by changing the use of existing things. This is a mode of thinking that is very special to Marx but elicits grunts of consternation or exasperation among bourgeois economists, who lust after certainty and firm unquestionable data. It is frequently argued in conventional economics that increasing fixed capital formation in, for example, infrastructure is a necessary precursor to the "take-off" into economic growth. Walt Rostow, in his book *The Stages of Economic Growth*, showed that capitalist development in most countries entailed a vast surge in fixed-capital formation (at the expense of current consumption) to prepare the way for the "take-off" into growth. The problem was that there was no sign of this for Britain, which was the first to develop. The reason almost certainly was that fixed capital augmentation occurred not through raising the rate of fixed capital investment but by changing the uses of existing things. A parallel contemporary example arises when labor increasingly works at home, in which case special office space is rendered redundant and individuals convert a spare room into fixed capital. The spread of microfinance in peasant populations converts peasant huts into fixed capital, while former textile factories move from fixed capital to being part of the consumption fund when converted into condos. The flexibility of built structures in relation to fixed capital is important to note.

How, then, does fixed capital circulate?

[It] can enter into circulation as value . . . only to the extent that it passes away as use value in the production process. It passes,

as value, into the product—i.e. as labour time worked up or
stored up in it—in só far as it passes away in its independent
form as use value. In being used, it is used up, but in such a way
that its value is carried over from its form into the form of the
product. (681)

What is being envisaged here is a machine that deteriorates over
the years until it needs to be replaced with a new machine. Over
the lifetime of the machine, the value is steadily transferred to the
products on an annual basis to be eventually realized in the market.
If, however, "the machinery stands still, the iron rusts, the wood
rots—then of course its value passes away." It is, in short, devalued.
At the end of its lifetime, when the use-value is lacking but the
value has been recuperated, then the machine can be replaced.
"With fixed capital, circulation is determined by the time in which
it is consumed as use value, in its material presence, within the act
of production, i.e. by the period of time within which it must be
reproduced" (682). "The time in which it is consumed and in
which it must be reproduced in its form as use-value depends on
its relative durability." This turns out to be what Marx characterizes
as "a form-determining moment" in the circulation process (685).
"The necessary reproduction time of fixed capital, together with
the proportion of the total capital consisting of it, here modify,
therefore, the turnover time of the total capital, and thereby its
realization." The temporal effect is similar to that experienced
when capital has to seek realization in distant markets (685).

This is the primary peculiarity about the circulation of fixed
capital. It doesn't circulate in the way that other commodities do.
A machine is produced as a commodity and is bought in the
market as circulating capital in commodity form. It is then taken
inside of production as fixed capital and never comes out. It stays
there until it is used up. It is then replaced by another machine.

Marx is well aware that the value flow is an artifice of accounting.
The question of how fixed capital should be depreciated is a thorny
one, and Marx avoids it here. The valuation of fixed capital is a big

problem for bourgeois economics as well. There are a variety of conventions, standard procedures, taxation gimmicks and the like. But Marx avoids going into that here. In Volume II of *Capital* he spent considerable time studying the handbooks of the railroad system engineers to see how they devised depreciation schedules covering the rails, the sleepers, the rolling stock and so forth.

"The time in which [the fixed capital] is consumed and in which it must be reproduced depends on its relative durability" (685). The relative durability is, in part, a physical matter. Problems arise because different fixed capital items depreciate at different rates. In a house, for example, light bulbs may need replacing once a year but the roof should last sixty years. I have a printer which could function as fixed capital. But it requires print cartridges. The lifetime of the print cartridge is very different from the lifetime of the printer. The printer is relatively cheap. The ink cartridges are expensive and do not last very long. I suspect the company makes most of its money out of the cartridges while selling the printer at a loss. Most forms of fixed capital are made up of parts that decay and depreciate at widely disparate rates. Think of a delivery truck, for example.

Marx is well aware of this. "The return of its value," he says on page 686, will occur "in successive parts, whereas each part of circulating capital is exchanged in its entirety." The different lifetimes of the components "becomes important where the fixed capital appears not as a mere instrument of production within the production process, but rather as an independent form of capital, e.g. in the form of railways, canals, roads, aqueducts, improvements of the land, etc." (686).

Note here the introduction of the category of "fixed capital of an independent kind." This refers to the fixed capital that is often produced and used in common outside of direct production, such as the road discussed earlier in some detail, but also extending to physical infrastructure, the built environment and other physical assets that support capital accumulation. This does not encompass everything there is because the question of use returns to haunt the investigation. "A house can serve for production as well as for consumption; likewise all vehicles, a ship or a wagon, for pleasure outings as well as a means of transport, a street as a means of communication for production proper, as well as for taking walks." Joint uses are all too common. Marx decides not to pursue these features further here, since his main concern is with the role of fixed capital in relation to the immediate processes of production and realization. But he does inform us that the circulation of fixed capital of an independent kind will be taken up—note well— "when we study interest" (687). This, it will turn out, is one of the most fascinating aspects of fixed capital circulation.

Marx amuses himself somewhat by criticizing Ricardo, according to whom "a coffee pot would be fixed capital, but coffee circulating capital." Marx severely criticizes the crude materialism of the bourgeois economists, which led them to interpret social relations in terms of the natural qualitative and quantitative properties of things. These economists consequently grounded their theories in crude idealism, even fetishism, directly imputing social relations to things as inherent characteristics and thus mystifying them (687). To this Marx adds the insight that "the difficulty of defining a thing as fixed capital or circulating capital on the basis of its natural qualities has here, by way of exception, led the economists to the discovery that things in themselves are neither fixed nor circulating, hence not capital at all, any more than it is a natural quality of gold to be money" (687).

Fixed capital is used in the production process "as a means, and itself exists merely as an agency for the transformation of the raw material into the product" (691). It is, however, "a means of labour not only in regard to its material side, but also at the same time as a particular mode of the presence of capital, determined by its total process." Fixed capital evolves alongside the evolution of the capitalist mode of production taken as a totality. "Once adopted into the production process of capital, the means of labour passes through various metamorphoses, whose culmination is the *machine*, or rather, *an automatic system of machinery* ... set in motion by an automaton, a moving power that moves itself . . . consisting of many mechanical and intellectual organs, so that the workers themselves are cast merely as its conscious linkages" (692). This is a fantastic evocation (particularly since it was written in 1858) of the evolving qualities of capital's machine technologies. "In the machine, and even more in machinery as an automatic system, the use value, i.e. the material quality of the means of labour, is transformed into an existence adequate to fixed capital and to capital as such." Only through the development of fixed capital can the mode of production acquire a technological configuration "adequate to" capital's true nature.

Several times, in these pages, Marx elicits the idea of some thing or some process being "adequate to capital." There is, it seems, an evolutionary process at work which is forcing things and processes to conform and align with each other so that they become "adequate to capital." And it is not hard to identify the driving force behind all of these realignments. "The increase of the productive force of labour and the greatest possible negation of necessary labour is the necessary tendency of capital" (693). The competitive individualism of the sort that Marx so scathingly criticizes, animates this process (the coercive laws of competition, as he calls them in *Capital*). The irresistible impacts on the evolution of capitalism are then easier to comprehend. Capital is in the driver's seat of social evolution, constructing a new world conducive to its own reproduction under the laws enforced through competition. This is what the phrase "adequate to capital" represents.

The subsequent pages (692–712) take the whole question of the implications of fixed capital circulation to an entirely different level, generating some controversial and far-reaching claims as to the viability, for example, of the labor theory of value. To be honest, I am not entirely sure what to make of these claims. So I will, for the most part, simply present them. But I do have some preliminary observations that might be helpful in seeking an interpretation.

Up to this point, analysis has focused on the implications of machinery (with occasional mention of fixed capital of an independent kind). But Marx now transitions to consider the factory system, in particular the cotton mills of Manchester with which Engels was all too familiar. Marx focuses attention—and this characterization bears repeating, since it sets the stage for everything that follows—on "an *automatic system of machinery . . .* set in motion by an automaton, a moving power that moves itself . . . consisting of many mechanical and intellectual organs" (692). The laborer in a typical Fordist factory is a cog in the wheel of a social system organized by capital, so that science and intelligence are incorporated in the technology and organizational form. The worker becomes a machine-minder rather than a direct producer. Hitherto, productive labor has been conceptualized in relation to the individual, but now it has to be understood as social, a mass of workers organized together, which renders discussions of productive versus unproductive labor within the detail divisions of labor and hierarchies of managerial authority in the factory somewhat irrelevant. Today, this becomes even more problematic because a typical factory will not only subcontract many tasks (for example, cleaning and design) but its reliance upon supply chains often turns the last step in production (of an auto or a computer) into assembly rather than production. So when Marx says the traditional version of value theory does not work, he probably has considerations of this sort in mind. If value is social labor time, as represented by achieved average price in the market (as it is in the *Grundrisse*), then the question of whose labor really matters in a complex social organization becomes almost unanswerable.

Similarly, the reduction of the worker to a cog-in-the-wheel position underpins the sense of "helplessness" and powerlessness" of the worker in relation to capital. When Marx evokes the parlous condition of "individual" and "direct" labor, he is contrasting traditional labor with the social organization of labor in the factory. At the same time, the incredible increases in productivity achieved through the factory system lead to a general reduction in the overall demand for labor (unless there is a vast expansion of production to compensate), even as the factory system itself leads to the concentration of the laboring mass. This revolution in production technology and organization calls forth the need for a conceptual revolution of the sort that Marx seems to seek but not firmly achieve in these pages.

Marx does, however, achieve something extraordinary in the passages that follow. He focuses on those technological processes that are "adequate to capital," so that we see and feel them as an alien power that rules not only over the laborer but also over *us*. "In no way does the machine appear as the individual worker's means of labour." In fact, laboring "merely transmits the machine's work, the machine's action, on to the raw material—supervises it and guards against interruptions" (692). The worker becomes the supervisor of the machine, and the machine, in effect, does the work. What this implies, is that "it is the machine which possesses skill and strength in place of the worker; is itself the virtuoso, with a soul of its own in the mechanical laws acting through it" (693). The idea that the machine possesses a soul projects us into the realm of mythology. The labor process now appears as a living beast which "consumes coal, oil, etc. . . . just as the worker consumes food, to keep up its perpetual motion. The worker's activity, reduced to a mere abstraction of activity, is determined and regulated on all sides by the movement of the machinery and not the opposite." Small wonder that Marx was fascinated by stories of vampires and werewolves, and that Frankenstein's monster was a cultural icon of his day.

Capital mobilizes also the science which "does not exist in the worker's consciousness, but rather acts upon him through the machine as an alien power" (693). The workers are deprived of any formative material role in the shaping of production processes. Their knowledge structures, their understandings and their science, all derived from years of experience, are replaced with an alien science. What is embodied in the machine in terms of skill is not available to the worker's consciousness, but rather acts upon him through the machine as an alien power, as the power of the machine itself. How prescient this is in relation to the current expansion of artificial intelligence!

The result is "the appropriation of living labour by objectified labour," i.e., the machine. Such a revolutionary transformation in the form of the labor process within the capitalist totality has all manner of ramifications. "The production process has ceased to be a labour process in the sense of a process dominated by labour as its governing unity. Labour appears ... merely as a conscious organ, scattered among the individual living workers at numerous points of the mechanical system; subsumed under the total process for the machinery itself" (693). The result: "objectified labour," that is, the machine, "confronts living labour within the labour process itself as the power which rules it; a power which, as the appropriation of living labour, is the form of capital." The machine system, as Charlie Chaplin so brilliantly depicts in *Modern Times*, now dominates the worker. It even regulates the speed of work.

This is more than just simply turning living labor into an appendage of the machine. This is a machine technology that incorporates knowledge and understandings which are outside of the consciousness or ken of the worker. The result of this, Marx says on page 694, is that "the value-creating power of the individual labour capacity is an infinitesimal vanishing magnitude." Note that Marx is here referring to the position of the individual laborer in relation to the social labor that is involved in mass production with machine technology. The significance of social labor, on the other hand, is enhanced, while on the other, the value and the significance of the individual labor input declines to almost nothing. "The production in enormous mass quantities which is posited with machinery destroys every connection of the product with a direct need of the producer."

> In machinery, objectified labour itself appears not only in the form of product ... but in the form of the force of production itself. The development of the means of labour into machinery is not an accidental moment of capital, but is rather the historical reshaping of the traditional, inherited means of labour into a form adequate to capital. The accumulation of knowledge and

of skill, of the general productive forces of the social brain, is thus absorbed into capital, as opposed to labour, and hence appears as an attribute of capital, and more specifically of *fixed capital* . . . (694)

Artisan technology and consciousness were not adequate to capital. They had to be replaced by a machine technology. In machinery, furthermore, "knowledge appears as alien, external to him [the worker]; and living labour [as] subsumed under self-acting objectified labour. The worker appears as superfluous to the extent that his action is not determined by [capital's] requirements" (695).

This transformation was not constructed out of nothing. It entailed "the historical reshaping of the traditional inherited means of labour . . . The accumulation of knowledge and of skill, of the general productive forces of the social brain, is thus absorbed into capital, and more specifically of *fixed capital*." It then appears as if it is machinery that is "the most adequate form of *fixed capital*, and . . . [is] *the most adequate form of capital* as such" (694).

But here the analysis crashes into a contradiction. "In so far as fixed capital is condemned to an existence within the confines of a specific use value, it does not correspond to the concept of capital, which, as value, is indifferent to every specific form of use value and can adopt or shed any of them as equivalent incarnations." After all, fixed capital is entirely defined by its use, and uses are contingent and flexible. The problem with fixed capital is that it is fixed, whereas circulating capital is about fluidity, flexibility, transformation and motion. Fixed capital gums things up and holds things down. It is, therefore "*circulating capital* which appears as the adequate form of capital, and not fixed capital." Increasing reliance on fixed capital condemns capital to a sclerotic future.

Nevertheless,

in so far as machinery develops with the accumulation of society's science, of productive force generally, general social labour presents itself not in labour but in capital. The productive force

of society is measured in *fixed capital*, exists there in its objective form; and, inversely, the productive force of capital grows
with this general progress, which capital appropriates free of
charge . . . In machinery, knowledge appears as alien, external
to him; and living labour [as] subsumed under self-activating
objectified labour. (694–5)

As a result, "the worker appears as superfluous." Workers are
superfluous in a double sense. Their physical presence is less and
less needed. But in addition, their knowledge and skills stand for
nought in the face of the knowledge and skill embodied within
machine technology.

There is, however, a far deeper and concerning contradiction
posed here. Perhaps inspired by the fact that he is opening a new
notebook, Marx rushes pell-mell into its exposition on page 699.
"The full development of capital, therefore, takes place—or capital
has posited the mode of production corresponding to it—only
when the means of labour has not only taken the economic form
of *fixed capital*," but when "the entire production process appears
as not subsumed under the direct skilfulness of the worker, but
rather as the technological application of science." There is, hence,
"the tendency of capital to give production a scientific character;
direct [individual] labour [is] reduced to a mere moment of this
process." Thus "the quantitative extent and the effectiveness (intensity) to which capital is developed as fixed capital indicate the
general degree to which capital is developed as capital, as power
over living labour, and to which it has conquered the production
process as such" (699).

But he immediately adds a caveat.

While capital gives itself its adequate form . . . in the form of
machinery and other manifestations of fixed capital, such as
railways etc. (to which we shall return later), this in no way
means that this use value—machinery as such—is capital, or
that its existence as machinery is identical with its existence as

capital; any more than gold would cease to have use value as gold if it were no longer *money*. Machinery does not lose its use value as soon as it ceases to be capital. (699)

There is no identity between machinery and capital. The use-value of machinery will doubtless be critical for the noncapitalist organization of production under socialism. It does not follow that "subsumption under the social relation of capital is the most appropriate and ultimate social relation of production for the application of machinery." Marx demurs from the frequently voiced argument that socialism will always need capital because it will need machines to function. It may or may not need machines (I would hope that aircraft carriers would not be required), but under socialism the machines would not operate exclusively as vehicles for capital accumulation. They would no longer perform the functions of fixed capital. They would simply assist in producing the use-values socially needed to survive.

"To the degree that labour time . . . is posited by capital as the sole determinant element, to that degree does direct labour and its quantity disappear as the determinant principle of production." By "direct labour" Marx is again alluding to the figure of the individual (productive?) laborer as distinct from the social labor involved in mass production. Direct labor of this sort is reduced, both "quantitatively" and "qualitatively," as an "indispensable but subordinate moment, compared to general scientific labour, technological application of natural sciences, on one side, and to the general productive force arising from social combination in total production ["social labour"] on the other side" (700). It would thus seem that capital would be working toward "its own dissolution as the form dominating production."

This is, to put it mildly, a startling claim. Along with individual labor's declining capacity to create value to an "infinitesimal vanishing magnitude," it surely asserts that capitalism is on a trajectory that points to its own dissolution. When Marx does this sort of thing, I think it first useful to ask whether he is making absolute or contingent claims. The essence of the argument is that the introduction of machine technologies, impelled onward by the coercive laws of competition, results in the displacement of living labor (the measure of value) by fixed capital, the disempowerment of the individual productive laborer through the incorporation of science and technology into the mode of production, and the ultimate dissolution of capital as a mode of production. These claims are contingent. Marx early on signals that the regime of fixed capital circulation is not the most adequate form of capital, relative to the fluidity of circulating capital. He subsequently goes on to study the relation of fixed to circulating capital in the context of the totality of capital. Since circulating capital rests on the "micro-circulation" of labor capacity, and since circulating and fixed capital are integral to each other, then, plainly, the assertions concerning the displacement of labor capacity and the dissolution of capital are contingent on viewing fixed capital in isolation from other forms of circulation within the totality. These assertions will likely be modified, nuanced and perhaps even wholly counteracted when the intimate codependencies of fixed and circulating capital are better understood.

Consider, then, how Marx proceeds immediately after announcing the self-dissolution of capital:

> While, then, in one respect the transformation of the production process from the simple labour process into a scientific process ... appears as a quality of *fixed capital* in contrast to living labour; while individual labour as such has ceased altogether to appear as productive ... and while this elevation of direct labour into social labour appears as a reduction of individual labour to the level of helplessness in face of communality ... so does it now appear, in another respect, as a quality of *circulating capital*, to maintain labour in one branch of production by means of co-existing labour in another.

It is useful here to recall Marx's earlier characterization of circulating capital as the most adequate form of capital. In small-scale circulation (the circulation of labor capacity examined earlier), we encounter a whole set of processes and circumstances that contradict, in whole or in part, the conclusion as to the self-dissolution of capital and the reduction of the laborer to a position of irrelevance. But this does not mean that the troublesome issues Marx uncovers through his study of the effects of machine technology and fixed capital circulation in isolation are irrelevant.

Given current reliance on science and technology in the reproduction and accumulation of capital, it is of major relevance to see how Marx attempts to deal with this troublesome issue. Plainly, capitalism has not as yet dissolved itself, though it has undergone radical transformations, and from time to time there have been situations in which technological breakthroughs have occurred which have held out the prospect for the transformation to some kind of anticapitalist future. Today, with robotization and artificial intelligence, such a potentiality cannot be ruled out. If only for this reason, it makes sense to follow Marx in his inquiry as to what might validate his claim as to the self-dissolving character of a capitalism dominated by fixed capital as "the most adequate form of capital."

Fixed capital displaces and disempowers labor so as to render "necessary labour" increasingly irrelevant. This is problematic from the standpoint of labor's role in maintaining consumer demand. Furthermore, the question of productive labor can no longer be assessed at the individual level because it is now the "common labours which subordinate the forces of nature." What individual labor does may be reduced to a minuscule quality and vanishing magnitude. It is in the nature of capital to promote such an outcome. This certainly threatens, in the absence of any countervailing force, the dissolution of the capitalist mode of production.

The seriousness of this threat needs discussion. The fact that we are now confronting the role of artificial intelligence as the most "adequate form of capital" suggests that Marx was perhaps on to something, even accepting the one-sided approach to fixed capital formation that he is here exploring. One thing is, however, clear. The "helplessness" to which individual workers are reduced in the face of fixed capital, and by extension capital in general, has long been a potent barrier to the organization of class consciousness and class struggle, and Marx has tracked down where that feeling of helplessness comes from. It will doubtless be claimed that Marx's argument is technologically deterministic, but I think the best answer to that is: "So what?" If, after all, this is what is happening all around us, and if Marx has a coherent explanation of how and why it is happening, then we would be stupid not to listen to him. Furthermore, it is deterministic only in the sense that, once the rules of the game under a capitalist mode of production have been set in stone, then its subsequent evolution is predetermined. It is always possible to change the rules of the game or even to invent a totally different, socialist game. When Marx points to what he considers the "self-dissolving" character of capital's dynamic, he is inviting us to consider what the anticapitalist alternative might look like, while at the same time suggesting one potential endgame for capital, even if it is impossible to put a date on it.

So why is contemporary capital so assertive about and persistent in the pursuit of artificial intelligence? And why does the whole future of capital right now seem to rest on the development of that artificial intelligence? Marx's answer would surely be to say that this is what we should expect given capital's nature and its reckless pursuit of fixed capital formation as a primary means to disempower labor. Note here the importance of the disempowerment of labor as the aim. This certainly has implications for the relevance of the traditional (Ricardian) version of the labor theory of value. It poses the question as to whether or not there is a more relevant (Marxist) version of the labor theory of value that is "adequate to capital," under these new material conditions. In the same way that capital has a tendency to reduce circulation time to zero (as we have already shown), it also internalizes the tendency to drive necessary labor time to zero by the perpetual pursuit and deployment of labor-saving innovations. The rise of artificial intelligence is just one more step on an evolutionary path foretold long ago in capital's nature. And we should be clear that individual capitalists do not turn to AI because they want or desire it (indeed, a good many plainly fear it) but because competition coerces them into using it whether they desire it or not.

Marx back in 1858 dissected capital's nature and saw clearly the prospect of capital's ultimate self-dissolution thanks to the agency of fixed capital. That there was something dystopian about it was clearly recognized in British culture at that time, with Mary Shelley in the vanguard.

Perhaps for this reason, these passages in the *Grundrisse* have made it into bourgeois thought. Even Marx, it is said, understood that traditional forms of valuation could not be sustained and that intangibles along with reputational, immaterial and monetary valuations might displace the more traditional reliance on some material labor-based version of value theory. The debate within contemporary bourgeois economic theory with respect to value theory interestingly parallels a similar debate within Marxism. In bourgeois theory, however, we see a return to Ricardo's idealist version of the coffee pot and the coffee along with all the presumptions derived from definitions based on material physical facts without reference to social relations. The turn toward immaterial properties and intangibles in valuation theory, it is said, means that we are moving into a world of capitalism without capital. This, for Marx, would be considered a supreme example of idealist fetishism run amok. Where Marx himself takes the argument will be examined shortly.

There was a time when workers were in control of their means of production because they were the only ones who knew how to use them. The capitalists, apart from those who emerged from the ranks of the skilled workers, for the most part had neither the knowledge nor the skills to use their tools, so they had to hire workers who had the skills and the know-how. The skilled artisans (as opposed to the illiterate masses) possessed a form of power which capital could not break. The artisans were for the most part self-educated, literate autodidacts and independent thinkers, a class of workers who have proven again and again throughout history (and, yes, they still exist) to be the most perceptive critics and the least easily manipulated thinkers. Capitalist producers were faced with a form of power that they could not displace or even control. The capitalists early on sought out innovations to displace the monopoly power of the artisans and free thinkers. The aim was to reduce all forms of monopoly power possessed by labor and, if possible, turn the workers into zombies. The overt aim of the Taylorism movement at the end of the nineteenth century, for example, was to redesign labor processes so that they could be performed by a "trained gorilla." In Marx's time, the theorists of capital, such as Ure and Babbage (who Marx frequently relied upon for his information), were pursuing an analogous agenda. When asked why he was so obsessed with innovations in production technology, a prominent industrialist and inventor working in Second Empire Paris cited the disempowerment of the laborer as one of his key motivations.

Capital has always favored innovations that disempower and deskill the laborer. The paradox, of course, is that this has frequently been accomplished through the definition and opening up of new skills that exercise their own monopoly power, only for them in turn to be deskilled. This has gone on from the late eighteenth throughout the nineteenth century until the present day, passing through Taylorism to automation, robotization in manufacturing and now pointing toward artificial intelligence. This is what much of the history of class struggle has been about. This is one of the key things that capitalist science and technology is summoned to address. And that project, which Marx clearly saw in motion in 1858, has largely been successful. If contemporary capital, even before the pandemic, was already in deep trouble, it was almost certainly so because of its success in sidelining and undercutting the power and significance of labor.

The outcome has been a series of technological revolutions to perfect the machine technologies that Marx describes. And the consequences have been quite shocking. Consider, once more, the key passage on page 700:

> To the degree that labour time—the mere quantity of labour—is posited by capital as the sole determinant element, to that degree does direct labour and its quantity disappear as a determining principle of production—of the creation of use values—and is reduced both quantitatively, to a smaller proportion, and qualitatively, as an, of course, indispensable but subordinate moment, compared to general scientific labour, technological application of natural sciences, on one side, and to the general productive force arising from social combination in total production on the other side—a combination which appears as a natural fruit of social labour (although it is a historic product). Capital thus works towards its own dissolution as the form dominating production.

Notice, then, how Marx proceeds in what follows. "In one respect the transformation of the production process from the simple labour process into a scientific process, which subjugates the forces of nature and compels them to work in the service of human needs, appears as a quality of *fixed capital* in contrast to living labour." Individual labor "has ceased altogether to appear as productive" except and insofar as it has become collective and common. The introduction of science revolutionizes the metabolic relation to nature with all manner of consequences (not necessarily benign). At the same time, the productivity and skill of the individual laborer becomes irrelevant relative to the productivity of the collective mass. The "common labours which subordinate the forces of nature to themselves" are subsumed within the organized dynamics of the working mass. This reduces "individual labour to the level of helplessness in face of the communality represented by and concentrated in capital." The rise of fixed capital and scientific management emphasizes the importance of managing the working mass as opposed to dealing with working individuals. Marx is here anticipating the turn to Taylorism and scientific management made possible by the increasing reliance on machine technologies coupled with the increasing centralization of capital (the modern corporation). Assembly-line Fordism is prefigured.

Marx then considers, as we have already noted, how these revolutions in the circulation of fixed capital relate to the "small-scale" circulation of labor capacity. Traditional labor does not disappear. Though subordinate, it is still indispensable. But in what sense? "While individual labour as such has ceased altogether to appear as productive," it is "a quality of *circulating capital* to maintain labour in one branch of production by means of *co-existing labour* in another. In small-scale circulation, capital advances the worker the wages which the latter exchanges for products necessary for his consumption" (700). What this means is that capital gives the worker "claims on alien labour, in the form of money." "The worker's ability to engage in the exchange of substances necessary for his consumption during production appears as due to an attribute of the part of *circulating capital* which is paid to the worker." The exchange of wages against alien labor is not an exchange of substances but of money within the metabolism (totality) of capital. Capital is, in fact, rescued to some degree from the tendency toward its own dissolution by the way in which "all powers of labour are transposed into powers of capital; the productive power of labour into fixed capital . . . and in circulating capital, the fact that the worker himself has created the conditions for the repetition of his labour [by consuming at home], and that the exchange of this, his labour, is mediated by the co-existing labour of others . . . Capital in the form of circulating capital posits itself as mediator between the different workers" (701). In other words, the metabolic structure of capital and money flows means that self-compensating movements, such as the workers' demand for commodities produced by the circulation of labor capacity goes quite a way toward controlling the diminution effects of fixed capital deployment in the realm of production. I get the impression that production divides into two distinctive circulation processes: that of fixed capital, which eliminates labor and tends toward the dissolution of capital, and circulating capital, which preserves the traditional capital–labor relation. Nevertheless, the forces within the totality prevail. That is how I read the difficult passages on 700–1.

While labor operates as a collaborative working mass alongside the increasing core of scientists and technologists in the fixed capital–intensive sectors, individual workers in one line of labor-intensive production are connected to those in other lines through the circulating capital that supports the production of localized wage goods and services. This seems to imply a workforce partitioned between the working collective masses taken up with large-scale fixed capital and mechanization, on the one hand (e.g., in the dark satanic textile mills of Manchester or in the contemporary labyrinths of Amazon warehouses), and localized workers employed in many small-scale, labor-intensive firms (like the local baker or delivery worker) producing wage goods and services to support their own collective social reproduction, on the other. Partitions of this sort have been known to exist. Jim O'Connor, writing in the early 1970s, liked to differentiate between privileged and unionized workers in the monopoly sector (labor in the big auto companies, steel, transport equipment, consumer durables and the like) and the seriously exploited and precariously employed workers (mainly African American in O'Connor's time in the USA) in what he called the competitive sector. Marx maybe had something analogous in mind. He then has to confront the myth that machines can compensate for the demotion of labor by being themselves a source of value. His answer is no, machines do not produce value—but they add to value in two respects. First, "the value of the machine is going to be discounted into the value of the product" over the years of its use. Like any other form of constant capital, its value is transferred into the product by labor through use, but only in aliquot parts over several years. Second, it contributes to the production of surplus value "by enabling labour, through an increase of its productive power, to create a greater mass of the products required for the maintenance of living labour capacity in a shorter time" (701). In other words, machinery contributes to relative surplus-value production for capital. Machines which cannot create value are a source of relative surplus-value! Under the rule of capital, machine technology does nothing to lighten the load of the laborer and everything to fill the coffers of capital.

But "quite unintentionally" capital "reduces human labour, expenditure of energy, to a minimum. This will redound to the benefit of emancipated labour, and is the condition of its emancipation" (701). The "emancipated labourers" would presumably look to machine technologies and artificial intelligence to reduce their material burdens to a minimum and thus liberate their own time for other, more joyful and worthwhile, things (which is something that capital can never do). There is, it seems, an important role for machine technologies to play under socialism. As it is, the machine posits the laborer as dependent. But "it can be effective only with masses of workers, whose concentration relative to capital is one of its historic presuppositions . . . Machinery enters only where labour capacity is on hand in masses" (702). The transition from the individual to the mass of labor is a key moment in capital's evolution. If only for this reason it must also be a key moment to adjust our conceptualizations and our mental conceptions of the world that capital makes. It seems hard, however, to reconcile the requirement that there be "masses of workers" with the decline of labor's capacity to produce value to an "infinitesimal vanishing magnitude."

10

Fixed and Circulating Capital
Pages 702–41

Until now, "fixed capital and circulating capital appeared merely as different passing aspects of capital" (702). But "they have now hardened into two particular modes of its existence, and fixed capital appears separately alongside circulating capital." What began as an investigation into the fixations that derived from multiple turnover times of different components of production now "hardens" into the study of "two particular kinds of capital circulation." The consequences are substantial, as we shall see.

To begin with, "the greater the scale on which fixed capital develops . . . the more does the *continuity of the production process* or the constant flow of reproduction become an externally compelling condition for the mode of production founded on capital" (703). This is a hugely important principle that we ignore at our peril. Interruptions to the flow and breaks in continuity are deeply problematic for capital (as became obvious in the Covid pandemic crisis of 2020), and particularly so for fixed capital. The measures that capital takes to ensure continuity of flow are extensive and in themselves technologically sophisticated. Fixed capital has to be kept fully employed if it is to retain and realize its value. All sorts of strategies and tactics arise to do this. In *Capital*, for example,

Marx looks upon twenty-four-hour production with two twelve-hour shifts as a means to shorten the turnover time of the fixed capital. The more you can do that, the quicker the value of the fixed capital returns to its point of origin in monetized form. Increasing the intensity of the labor process and reducing the "porosity" of the working day (e.g., cutting breaks) are also tactics oriented to this goal. There are, therefore, all sorts of reasons why fixed capital does not lighten the load of labor. Employment conditions become even more repressive.

The spread of fixed capital depends on the development of large-scale industries which have the capacity to press all the sciences "into the service of capital; and when . . . [the] available machinery itself already provides great capabilities." It is at this point that "invention then becomes a business, and the application of science to direct production itself becomes a prospect which determines and solicits it" (704). This is the second great breakthrough principle enunciated in this section. As in the case of the "continuity principle," Marx seems content merely to put down a marker on an important potential topic without offering much direct justification for or elaboration upon its significance. It is left to us to speculate and elucidate what happens when invention becomes a business. It obviously implies a capitalist world in which self-perpetuating technological change is supplied no matter what the existing demand.

It is somewhat surprising that Marx, rightly renowned as a penetrating commentator on the role of technological and organizational change in the evolution of capitalism, showed so little interest in the how and the why of invention becoming a business. Inventions targeted to address a very particular problem within a specifically designated division of labor, such as water drainage from mines, turn out to be useful in all manner of other areas, such as building locomotives. It also turns out that many inventions arise out of the putting together of two formerly independent inventions, so that the more inventions there are, the more potential hybrid combinations become possible. This spiraling field of possibilities is animated by the absolute fetish belief in the inevitability and goodness of technological progress, deriving from the material fact that under conditions of competition, the more efficient and labor-repressive technologies and organizational forms almost invariably win out through superior profitability.

From this, it is easy to see why, as Marx again and again asserts, capitalism is and always will be a technologically revolutionary mode of production. It has successfully navigated multiple radical reconfigurations of its productive forces and seems set fair to continue to do so into the future, unless there is some radical overthrow or constraint put upon the powerful forces promoting technological and organizational dynamism.

Since the pivotal role of science and technology is so clearly asserted in the *Grundrisse*, and its consequences postulated as being so far-reaching, I feel it necessary and justifiable to broaden consideration somewhat, beyond what the text warrants. To begin with, it is useful to distinguish between (1) technology in the hardware sense of machines; (2) science and knowledge in the software sense of how a technology might be socially appropriated and used; and (3) organizational forms that encompass everything from the corporation to structures of cooperation and specialization down to specific strategies such as just-in-time production systems. Marx actually touches upon all three of these facets of technology and organizational form in his writings but chooses not to distinguish between them. In a sense, he was right to do so from the perspective of the totality, but contemporary approaches to the totality might necessitate consideration of these categories separately before putting them together. The question of what kind of organizational form or software is most adequate for today's capital is in the forefront of a lot of contemporary discussions in the bourgeois management literature.

When technological innovation becomes a business, the supply of new technologies and organizational forms surges ahead of the demand. Whole sectors, from machine technology, the various branches of engineering (genetics), electronics, the R&D arms of corporations (e.g., Big Pharma) to management consultants and mental health experts, become concerned with the production of generic technologies and organizational forms that can have all sorts of uses across all manner of different economic sectors. When invention becomes a business, it does so only in part because there is a persistent underlying demand for science and technology to be mobilized to increase labor productivity while disempowering the laborer. "Thus, the specific mode of working here appears directly as becoming transferred from the worker to capital in the form of the machine, and his own labour capacity devalued thereby. Hence the workers' struggle against machinery," as evidenced by the Luddite movement of machine-breaking in Marx's time. "What was the living worker's activity becomes the activity of the machine. Thus the appropriation of labour by capital confronts the worker in a coarsely sensuous form; capital absorbs labour into itself—'as though its body were by love possessed'" (704).

Marx is certainly not claiming that all science and technology is purposive in this one capitalistic sense. In the same way that he defines fixed capital by its use and not by its material form, so it is the appropriation and use of science and technology and its embedding in the fixed capital of production by capitalist entrepreneurs that Marx is isolating for consideration. A common mistake in reading these passages is to imagine that all knowledge, sciences and technologies contribute to value and surplus-value creation directly, and that we are now in a new era of cognitive capitalism, in which the production of knowledge is in itself a leading edge of capital accumulation. To this we would need to add the crucial role of the military in fostering new technological forms and products, particularly since 1945, in pursuit of geopolitical and military competitive advantages on the world stage. Even the internet, we should remind ourselves, originated within the military.

At this point in Marx's analysis, however, the only form of (scientific) knowledge that matters is that which affects the productivity of labor through incorporation into fixed capital. Astronomy and musicology do not pass muster. But, as we will later see, science and technology are not only concerned with how to produce something with the utmost efficiency and the least labor input. They are also concerned with product innovation and market expansion (as is most clearly seen in our era with electronics and pharmaceutical products), with the perfection of instruments of war, with building cities, dwellings, monuments and cultural landscapes, or just titillating and advancing human curiosities and sexual satisfactions. And some of this has implications for capital accumulation through market formation.

In practice, the role of science and technology in product innovation and development has been just as important to capital accumulation as its role in revolutionizing labor processes, though Marx unfortunately pays scant attention to this fact. Whatever can be made and marketed for whatever purpose is just as important a question as how best to make it. But Marx is very clear that it is only when "all the sciences have been pressed into the service of capital" that invention will become a distinct sphere of business. This, in turn, has an important impact upon the direction of technological and scientific research, as is more than obvious when we look at the sponsorships and activities dominating in the world's research universities. In the half-century after Marx wrote the *Grundrisse*, research universities and institutes were popping up all over the place in broad support of capital's agenda. In this the University of Berlin, under the leadership of William Humboldt, became a model research institution (copied from the 1870s onward in the United States) during the years when Marx was writing. But later, the research universities in the United States (from MIT to CalTech and Stanford) became major institutions for fostering the idea of research and development as an ongoing business organized as an adjunct to capital and the military.

"The exchange of living labour for objectified labour," in the form of fixed capital, "is the ultimate development of the *value-relation* and of production resting on value. Its presupposition is—and remains—the mass of direct labour time, the quantity of labour employed, as the determinant factor in the production of wealth" (704). Notice how the concept of the mass of direct labor—as opposed to that of the individual—enters into the argument. But "the creation of real wealth comes to depend less on labour time and on the amount of labour employed than on the power of the agencies set in motion during labour time whose 'powerful effectiveness' is itself in turn out of all proportion to the direct labour time spent on their production, but depends rather on the general state of science and the progress of technology, or the application of this science to production."

The application of science affects all spheres of production. Even agriculture "becomes merely the application of the science of material metabolism." The aggregate effect is that "real wealth manifests itself, rather—and large industry reveals this—in the monstrous disproportion between the labour-time applied, and its product." Labor is "reduced to a pure abstraction" such that it "no longer appears so much to be included within the production process." The human being "comes to relate more as watchman and regulator to the production process." The worker "inserts the process of nature, transformed into an industrial process, as a means between himself and inorganic nature, mastering it" (705). It is easiest to visualize Marx's meaning in the case of agriculture, even though it is plain that Marx is advancing this commentary as a universal prescription for how the labor process should unfold as it becomes more and more scientific in both its conception and its practice. The human qualities of the "material metabolism" of the production process are everywhere in evidence.

But the laborer is no longer the "chief actor" because "in this transformation, it is neither the direct human labour he himself performs, nor the time during which he works, but rather the appropriation of his own general productive power, his under-standing of nature and his mastery over it by virtue of his presence as a social body—it is, in a word, the development of the social individual which appears as the great foundation-stone of production and of wealth" (705). The "social individual" is exemplified by the skilled line engineer who knows how to keep the machinery humming and the automaton well fed with raw materials and intermediate inputs.

Marx here gives an added meaning to his earlier commentary on how we are increasingly ruled by abstractions rather than by people or even by laws in the legal sense, but by the economic laws of motion of capital itself. This insight is not, as I have already emphasized, unique to Marx. Adam Smith's invocation of the hidden hand of the market, as I have often noted, emphasizes this point. It then follows that, if we object to the idea of the mastery of nature, then it is to capital that we must address our discontents, for it is capital that perpetually seeks the mastery of nature no matter how double-edged the results might be. This doubtless contributes to that double consciousness earlier commented on. We may regret the alienation we feel from nature but, when the virus strikes, we appreciate the mastery we might be able to exercise even if it deepens the sense of alienation:

> The *theft of alien labour time on which the present wealth is based*, appears a miserable foundation in face of this new one, created by large-scale industry itself. As soon as labour in the direct form has ceased to be the great well-spring of wealth, labour time ceases and must cease to be its measure, and hence exchange value [must cease to be the measure] of use value. The *surplus labour of the mass* has ceased to be the condition for the development of general wealth, just as the *non-labour of the few*, for the development of the general powers of the human head. With that, production based on exchange value breaks down, and the direct, material production process is stripped of the form of penury and antithesis. (705)

This is, it seems, Marx telling us how the dissolution of capital might occur through its self-dissolving contradictions. Any variant of the labor theory of value is called into question. But as Marx more than once asserts, the path of socialism is paved with the intention to abolish the operation of the capitalist law of value. And here is capital unwittingly creating not only the preconditions but the likelihood for this.

"Capital itself is the moving contradiction, [in] that it presses to reduce labour time to a minimum, while it posits labour time, on the other side, as the sole measure and source of wealth. Hence it diminishes labour time in the necessary form so as to increase it in the superfluous form." In effect, Marx is saying that surrendering the surplus productivity of labor to capital is a conditionality for the worker to procure the value of their labor power, which is in any case perpetually subject to reduction by way of rising productivity in the wage goods sector:

> On the one side, then, [capital] calls to life all the powers of science and of nature, as of social combination and social inter-course, in order to make the creation of wealth independent (relatively) of the labour time employed on it. On the other side, it wants to use labour time as the measuring rod for the giant social forces thereby created, and confine them within the limits required to maintain the already created value as value. (706)

The result is an incredible contradiction. "Forces of production and social relations—two different sides of the development of the social individual—appear to capital as mere means, and are merely means for it to produce on its limited foundation. In fact, however, they are the material conditions to blow this foundation sky-high" (706).

This contradiction is so powerful that it could actually pave the way for socialist revolution and for the abolition of capital itself. Capital itself has brought the new technologies to a point where it would be feasible to revolutionize the society in such a way as to create an alternative social order. Marx sounds utopian in express-ing this belief. And he here interweaves a counternarrative of where "the emancipated labourer" might take things. He cites:

" 'Truly wealthy a nation, when the working day is 6, rather than 12 hours' " (706).[1] He has already established the importance of the "free development of individualities . . . and the general reduction of the necessary labour of society to a minimum, which then corresponds to the artistic, scientific etc. development of the individual in the time set free . . . 'Wealth is not command over surplus labour time . . . but rather *disposable time* outside that needed in direct production, for *every individual* and the whole society.' "[2] As he puts it in Volume III of *Capital*, the realm of freedom begins when the realm of necessity is left behind. Let capital take care of the realm of necessity and we socialists will realize the benefits. This, it turns out, was one of the key reasons why the young radicals around Deng Xiaoping argued for the capitalist turn in 1978 in China. That turn and the opening to capital would facilitate the creation of the productive capacity to facilitate the turn to socialism at some future date (currently set at 2049).

Marx concludes this opening of the door to a new society with a beautiful and inspiring panegyric to the role of fixed capital formation in human history:

Nature builds no machines, no locomotives, railways, electric telegraphs, self-acting mules etc. These are products of human industry; natural material transformed into organs of the human will over nature, or of human participation in nature. They are *organs of the human brain, created by the human hand*; the power of knowledge, objectified. The development of fixed capital indicates to what degree general social knowledge has become a *direct force of production*, and to what degree, hence, the conditions of the process of social life itself have come under the control of the general intellect and been transformed in

1 Anon., "The Source and Remedy of the National Difficulties, Deduced from Principles of Political Economy, in a Letter to Lord John Russell" (London: Rodwell and Martin, 1821).

2 Ibid.

accordance with it. To what degree the powers of social production have been produced, not only in the form of knowledge,
but also as immediate organs of social practice, of the real life
process. (706)

Much has been made in the recent literature of Marx's invocation of "the general intellect" in this passage. In my view, far too
many of the readings are idealist, in the sense that they evoke the
power of some ruling idea governing capital's evolution. It is sometimes presented as some abstract or even occult power—"the
general intellect"—which God-like rules over capital in mysterious ways, its wonders to perform. This is, however, the only place
I can find in the whole corpus of Marx's works where he uses this
term, though a couple of pages later he does refer to "the social
intellect" as "the precondition of the productive power of the
means of labour as developed into the automatic process" (709). It
seems rather presumptuous to base a whole interpretive school of
Marxist thought—that of cognitive capitalism—on this unique
concept, which is mentioned only once and at that in the
Grundrisse, which is by far Marx's most imaginative but also most
experimental work.

The historical materialist interpretation would be a dialectical
unfolding of the understandings of how and why those practices
work (or do not work) in the way they do. In this case, the general
intellect simply refers to the state of general and scientific knowledge and the unfolding of interpretive ideas at any particular
moment in time and space. The railway system engineers produced
manuals and eventually textbooks to guide future practices. The
Federal Reserve Bank has a hundred-year (or more) archive on
what to do and what might work in times of trouble in the market.
The "general intellect" should be understood as the vast array of
operational manuals and knowledge banks on hand that can be
used to plan and facilitate further capital accumulation and,
perhaps, the transition to socialism. It is not and never could be a
perfect reflection of the mass of experience accumulated

throughout the history of capitalism. The general intellect (like Gramsci's "common sense") is not always right and is not immune to corruption, ideological contamination and bowdlerization. Political economy itself evolved as William Petty, the Physiocrats and the Mercantilists sought to create knowledge banks helpful to statesmen and officials as they set commercial and industrial policies that they hoped would augment their material wealth and political power. Marx also aimed to augment this knowledge bank and plainly did so in major ways. Contemporary economics is a specialized sector of the general intellect, and it is fractious, often misleading and deliberately obfuscatory, even as it is subject to all manner of reality checks while predominantly reflecting, as Marx frequently noted, the ruling ideas of an often fractured ruling class.

Here Marx appears bent on probing into the contradictions in both the realm of practice and in the evolution of ruling ideas in order to pave the way for a socialist transition. Such a transition would require socialist manuals of practices "adequate to socialism," alongside intellectual critiques of what is right or wrong with the state of today's general intellect. In our own time, the general intellect is heavily infused with neoliberal pabulum and orthodoxies, for the simple reason that the ruling ideas of any social order are powerfully influenced by its ruling class. As Marx freely conceded on a number of occasions, ideas can become a material force (both good and bad from the standpoint of labor) in history, but only when they are rooted in and applied to material practices.

Let us go over what has happened in these few intense pages of text. There is a lot to be said about them. Marx manufactures some fantastic and imaginative arguments. Whatever you think about the actual theses, it is a brilliant and evocative piece of writing. Consider, for example, the question of the value theory. Up until this point in the *Grundrisse*, we have been working with a version of value theory that references individual laborers and the productive qualities of the work they do and the resultant exchange-value achieved in the market. We think of a cabinetmaker and we note the skill, the tools, the time involved, and we extrapolate from that the idea that a certain amount of value (understood as an immaterial but objective social measure) has been congealed in the furniture they made. A skilled cabinetmaker will congeal more value than an unskilled one, the boss will take a surplus-value without doing anything, while the salesperson will be recompensed for their effort in covering the necessary costs of circulation as a deduction out of the value produced. The person who sweeps out the workshop will be paid out of somebody else's revenues.

But Marx now switches from the working individual to the concept of the working mass of social labor. This becomes more important with the greater centralization of capital, the much higher concentration and proliferation of fixed capital, the organization of the factory system with its machine technology, and ultimately the conditions prevailing within the industrial city. It ultimately led to what we now generally refer to as Fordism. Think of the manufacture of my Apple computer by Foxconn, a Taiwanese firm, which until recently operated an industrial encampment of over 250,000 factory laborers (some reports say 400,000 in all) in Shenzhen, with branch plants all over China as well as across the world, and feeds of components back down a production chain to thousands of workers in multiple locations in China and other countries. Such a material situation calls for a whole new mode of analysis in which the qualities of the social mass of labor predominate over those of individuals. The value theory derived from individual laboring makes no sense in this situation. But capital still requires some socially meaningful measure by which to gauge its performance and to match its ambitions. Even in the face of all of this, however, it seems that the metabolic relations within the totality still hold, even as they may change their mode of functioning. This was what Gramsci grappled with in his signal essay "Americanism and Fordism."

The shift from the micro to the macro perspective has long been deeply problematic for bourgeois economics. The theory of the firm and the theory of a national macro-economy (the latter a creative fiction that began to form in the 1920s) do not integrate with each other. Here is Marx engaging in a transformative operation that takes him from the perspective of the individual to the perspective of collective social labor. In *Capital*, he conducts this operation in chapter 16, where he announces that he will thereafter deal with the collective as opposed to the individual laborer. This broadens the definition of value production, since everyone contributing to the factory production process is part of the productive enterprise no matter what work they do (e.g., even those sweeping the floors). But it simultaneously narrows it to only those laborers who work to produce surplus-value for the capitalist. This means that all wage work done in relation to the circulation of revenues (such as mowing somebody's lawn or helping renew a neighbor's roof for pay) is deemed irrelevant, which is exactly what Marx argues should be the case (as we saw earlier).

But Marx also argues that the advent of more and more sophisticated and powerful fixed capital reduces the collective labor input so radically as to make the old version of the value theory redundant. This is not an unfamiliar argument. When I present Marx's value theory as socially necessary labor time in Volume I of *Capital,* somebody invariably asks me what happens in an automated factory employing no labor. In Volume III of *Capital,* Marx answers the question. He envisages a situation in which a capitalist employs "no variable capital at all in his sphere of production, hence not a single worker." In such an unlikely situation, the capitalist "would have just as much an interest in the exploitation of the working class by capital and just as much derive his profit from unpaid surplus labour as would a capitalist who employed . . . only variable capital"; that is, only labor—an equally unlikely situation. This happens because the equalization of the profit rate through competition redistributes value from labor-intensive to capital-intensive enterprises, sectors and nations. This redistributive mechanism is mentioned earlier in the *Grundrisse,* although its details are omitted (435). The rule for the creation and appropriation of value and surplus-value is from each capital according to the labor they employ and to each capital according to the capital they advance. The capitalist who employs no labor receives the average rate of profit, as does the capitalist who employs only labor power and no fixed capital at all.

Consider a concrete example of this. The largest employers of labor in the USA around 1970 were General Motors, Ford and US Steel. Their labor forces then constituted the heart of the "affluent" unionized working class. But they have been dramatically reduced in numbers since (in the way that Marx describes) through scientific deployment of automation and robots. The biggest employers of labor in the USA until recently were McDonald's and the franchisees of Kentucky Fried Chicken, who make hamburgers and fried chicken (rather than cars) in a labor-intensive way, hiring a lot of precarious, for the most part non-unionized, low-wage labor. Over the last twenty years, there has been a huge increase in many parts of the world, including in the United States, of this sort of labor. When the shutdowns occurred through the Covid-19 pandemic, some 40 million people lost their jobs in the USA, at least 15 million of whom were employed in restaurants (paradoxically, the drive-through restaurants did very well!). On the other hand, Amazon's workforce grew by leaps and bounds. The equalization of the rate of profit that goes on between the capital-intensive sectors like General Motors and the restaurant sector (particularly the family restaurants) produces a transfer of value from the restaurant sector to the auto sector. This matches, by the way, the distinction that Marx earlier made between the highly capitalized fixed-capital world of big capital and the small-scale circulation capital serving the reproduction of labor power. But we now see this distinction between small- and large-scale circulation through a different lens. The small-scale circulation process subsidizes the large-scale circulation process, which employs less and less labor.

Today, the small-scale labor-intensive sectors cluster around the hospitality and entertainment industries. The whole labor structure of contemporary capital, particularly since 2008, has been bent to patronize and to develop these industries. Tourism expanded dramatically (from 800 million to 1.4 billion foreign visitors worldwide from 2007 to 2017), as did the staging of cultural, sporting and other forms of spectacle. What these industries sell is an experience that is monetized and instantaneously consumed (with a consumption circulation time close to zero). All of these industries came crashing down in 2020, however, as a result of the Covid-19 pandemic. While the auto industry sells a product that lasts a long time and adopts the strategy of increasing resort to fixed capital formation and labor saving, the tourist industry grows in exactly the opposite direction. And given the equalization of the rate of profit, tourism has been subsidizing the auto industry in the same way that Greece has been subsidizing Germany through value transfers set up by differentials in the productivity of capacity to labor. But tourism requires a fixed infrastructure of hotels (and now Airbnb), transport (airlines, car rentals, cruise liners) and communications, all of which were funded out of the circulation of interest-bearing capital rather than through the circulation of surplus-value seeking capital. The lack of use of these forms of fixed capital during the pandemic visited widespread devaluation. It remains to be seen if the tourist industry will recover to resuscitate the value of all this fixed capital. There is clearly a strong incentive to do so. In this way the value transfer to the high-tech sector can also be resumed.

Plainly, the contradictions within this situation are multiplying, along with the dangers of serious disruptions and collapses. We have to look no further than the impacts of the Covid pandemic, in which the entertainment and hospitality sectors took a direct hit, with huge implications for unemployment and, if Marx is correct, upon value and surplus-value production in a sector that is predominantly labor-intensive and hence a source of subsidy for the capital-intensive industries that constitute the heart of contemporary capitalism. During the pandemic, air travel was radically curtailed. Airlines were vital supports for labor-intensive tourism but required large-scale, long-term fixed-capital investments, not only in the planes but also in the airports and other infrastructure

which during the pandemic were largely unused and unremuner-
ated. The fixed capital could not easily be monetized or converted
to some other use (as earlier happened with the conversion of
textile mills into residential condos). A lot of contemporary fixed
capital is inflexible. Which is why Marx earlier concluded that
while fixed capital may "appear as the most adequate form of capital," its confinement to a particular and inflexible use-value renders
it a liability. It is, therefore, in practice "*circulating capital* which
appears as the most adequate form of capital and not fixed capital"
(694).

The *Grundrisse* is, however, the one place in all of Marx's writings where fixed capital gets a thorough going-over. To the degree
that invention becomes a business and the fixed capital that results
incorporates science and technology, so workers are displaced and
repositioned within the system of accumulation. Fixed capital
tends to reduce the significance of labor in certain sectors to such
a point that any theory of value based on individualized labor
appears less and less relevant. The politics of the class struggle
between labor and capital gets mediated or even transformed by
the arrival of science and technology as singular powers within the
production process. The circulation of labor capacity generates
alternative moments of struggle in which the worker's identity as
worker is extinguished in the immediate sense. This is a fascinating argument and one which is very relevant to the contemporary
question of how the advent of artificial intelligence will have an
impact on the capital–labor relation and the dynamics of capital
accumulation in the near future. At the same time, the rising
productivity of labor that fixed capital facilitates poses the problem of how to absorb the "monstrous" quantities of commodity
output produced with such little labor input.

Much of what follows from page 707 onward is taken up with
studying what happens as a consequence of Adam Smith's observation that "*every fixed capital comes originally from a circulating capital*, and needs to be continually maintained *by means of a circulating capital*" (728). Marx begins by observing that fixed capital in

itself does not produce direct objects of individual gratification nor "directly realizable exchange values." From this it follows that

> only when a certain degree of productivity has already been reached . . . can an increasingly large part be applied to the production of the means of production. This requires that society be able to wait; that a large part of the wealth created can be withdrawn . . . from immediate consumption . . . This requires a certain level of productivity and of relative overabundance, and, more specifically, a level directly related to the transformation of circulating capital into fixed capital.

This is a familiar argument. Deferred gratification with respect to today's consumption lays the foundation for tomorrow's productivity gains by way of fixed-capital investments that pay off sometimes long into the future by way of rising productivity. "The *magnitude of relative surplus labour . . . employed on the production of fixed capital depend[s] on the productivity of the labour time spent in the direct production of products.*" In other words, the more productive the circulating capital, the more capital can be siphoned off to flow into the production of fixed capital. But conversely, the productivity of the circulating capital depends on the deployment of the fixed capital. "*Surplus population . . .* as well as *surplus production*" is, therefore, a condition for fixed capital formation and circulation. "The *smaller* the direct fruits borne by *fixed capital*, the less it intervenes in the *direct production process*, the greater must be this relative *surplus population and surplus production*; thus, more to build railways, canals, aqueducts, telegraphs etc. than to build machinery" (707).

We have here a thumbnail sketch of a very important argument that in effect defines a specific long-run evolutionary law of motion within a capitalist mode of production. The rising productivity of labor that results from the deployment of fixed capital in support of circulating capital produces not only more surplus-value but a "monstrous" increase in commodity volume at the same time as it releases more and more labor from employment. In other words, a capitalist mode of production automatically creates in its everyday practices both the surplus product and the surplus population required for further fixed-capital formation. Fixed capital therefore continuously reproduces the conditions required for its further expansion, and it does so on an increasingly expanding scale. This expansion goes way beyond machinery to encompass investments in physical infrastructure of all kinds, in what Marx elsewhere refers to as "fixed capital of an independent kind," including that which is immobile and embedded in the land (e.g., railways, ports, hydroelectric projects and the built environment more generally). In the *longue durée*, this law of motion of perpetual expansion of the fixed capital, particularly of an independent kind, produces, for example, a huge increase in the scale and intensity of urbanization. The most recent huge scale of urbanization in China is incomparable with the kind of urbanization that Marx and Engels were familiar with in mid-nineteenth-century London and Manchester. Contrast urbanization in Second Empire Paris under Haussmann with the Robert Moses metropolitan-wide style of urbanization in the postwar period in the United States and today's global urbanization in Shanghai, Tokyo, the Gulf States, Barcelona, Lagos, São Paulo and the like, and you will see this long-run evolution dramatically displayed. What its future betokens should be a subject of deep concern. This circular and cumulative growth in fixed-capital formation, particularly of an independent kind, poses all manner of problems and dangers, far more so today than in Marx's time. Yet Marx is here giving us a way to understand how and why it is in the nature of capital to produce such problems and difficulties. The golden rule in such situations is that the only way to combat a bad situation is to go after the process that produced it, which is, of course, the ceaseless class-based production and appropriation of surplus-value at the expense of working people.

This growth of fixed capital does not occur smoothly. "Hence—a subject to which we will return later—in the constant under- and over-production of modern industry—constant fluctuations and convulsions arising from the disproportion, when sometimes too little, then again too much circulating capital is transformed into fixed capital" (708). Marx is here anticipating the production of investment cycles, "switching crises," urban property booms, etc. in the complex relations between fixed and circulating capital. He briefly appeals to this idea later (720).

As so often happens in the *Grundrisse*, Marx suddenly pivots away from this critical question to revisit the concept of wealth and its meaning. This is understandable given that one of the key roles of fixed capital is to increase the material wealth of a population. Almost certainly this turn was also provoked by his earlier citation of a Ricardian socialist shortly before in the text (706): "Truly wealthy a nation, when the working day is 6 rather than 12 hours. *Wealth* is not command over surplus labour time (real wealth), 'but rather, *disposable time* outside that needed in direct production, for *every individual* and the whole society.'"

Marx first takes up the effect of fixed capital in "*the creation of a large quantity of disposable time*" (708). This in principle opens up "room for the development of the individuals' full productive forces" while creating something Marx calls "not-labour time" albeit "free time, for a few." Capital's mobilization of art and science augments the capacity to produce wealth in the form of surplus labor time. It is, therefore, "instrumental in creating the means of social disposable time, in order to reduce labour time for the whole society to a diminishing minimum, and thus to free everyone's time for their own development." On the one hand, it creates disposable time for everyone, while on the other it converts it into surplus labor and surplus-value that can be (and regularly is) appropriated by the few as capital. It is interesting to note in the *Grundrisse* how often Marx parallels his investigations of how capital works with thoughts about how the socialist alternative might do things better. In this case, he urges that "the mass of workers must themselves appropriate their own surplus labour. Once they have done so—and *disposable time* thereby ceases to have an *antithetical* existence—then, on one side, necessary labour time will be measured by the needs of the social individual, and, on the other, the development of the power of social production will grow so rapidly that . . . *disposable time* will grow for all." Marx expands upon this hopeful utopian view. "Real wealth is the developed productive power of all individuals. The measure of wealth is then not any longer, in any way, labour time, but rather disposable time." This attractive alternative contrasts radically with actually existing labor time, which operates "as the measure of value" and that "posits wealth itself as founded on poverty," and on labor's "degradation therefore to mere worker, subsumption under labour." Reminding us that these oppositions intrude upon his account of fixed capital (the primary potential agent for creating disposable time) for a reason, Marx then notes that "*the most developed machinery thus forces the worker to work longer than the savage does, or than he himself did with the simplest, crudest tools*" (708–9). Fixed capital continuously denies its own potentiality under the social relations of capital!

"In the production process of large-scale industry," Marx argues, direct labor as such ceases to be the basis of production and "the conquest of the forces of nature by the social intellect is the precondition of the productive power of the means of labour as developed into the automatic process," which displaces "the labour of the individual." "*Thus the other basis of this mode of production falls away.*" Direct individual labor is subsumed within collective social labor supervising an automatic process (709). This was, it is worth noting, exactly the sort of thing that was being said about the automation of automobile production during the 1980s! The oscillation between utopian and dystopian perspectives in this section is, I have to say, remarkable. Yet another occasion illustrative of the state of double consciousness.

"To the degree that production aimed at the satisfaction of immediate need becomes more productive, a greater part of production can be directed towards . . . the production of means of production." In so far as the production of fixed capital is directed "not towards value as an immediate object, but rather towards value creation," so "it is in the production of *fixed capital that capital posits itself as end-in-itself* and appears active as capital, *to a higher power than it does in the production of circulating capital*" (710). Fixed capital becomes "the measuring rod *of the development* of wealth founded on the mode of production of capital." From this perspective, superficial impressions are not misleading: the impressive and daunting skylines of contemporary world cities attest to the wondrous powers of capital to create an iconic urban landscape of fixed capital in its own image.

The durability of fixed capital "must not be conceived as a purely physical quality." To be sure, the durability is not independent of technical qualities (such as the use of metals that last longer than wood) but is fundamentally set by the way "the instrument is destined to play the same role constantly in repeated processes of production." Its durability "is its existence as means of production" and "its duration is an increase of its productive force." Marx fails to note here the problems of accelerated obsolescence of fixed capital through the inventions of new, cheaper and more efficient machines. The lifetime of a machine is dependent upon these external conditions, which should be mentioned here. The only point of substance in Marx's presentation is the odd way in which the use of fixed capital dovetails with how "articles are thrown into the consumption fund" to be collectively consumed by individuals. The fixed capital of a textile factory may become part of the consumption fund when converted into condominiums. This fluidity, Marx suggests, "is connected with further determinations (renting rather than buying, interest etc.) with which we are not yet here concerned." When Marx makes such an observation, it simply signals a whole field of unfinished business to which we will need to pay attention as we seek to advance the analysis. There are many items that are rented rather than purchased (e.g., photocopiers and forklift trucks) and the extensive back and forth of items (such as houses) between fixed capital and the consumption fund is important to track.

But Marx then turns back to offer some further thoughts on the emancipation of labor (711). "The saving of labour time [is] equal to an increase of free time, i.e. time for the full development of the individual, which in turn reacts back upon the productive power of labour as itself the greatest productive power." This does not mean that labor can become play, "as Fourier would like." Indeed,

> free time—which is both idle time and time for higher activ-
> ity—has naturally transformed its possessor into a different
> subject, and he then enters into the direct production process as
> this different subject. This process is then both discipline, as
> regards the human being in the process of becoming; and, at the
> same time, practice, . . . experimental science, materially crea-
> tive and objectifying science, as regards the human being who
> has become, in whose head exists the accumulated knowledge
> of society.

The transformation of the political subject into an active and free agent is, by implication, a necessary movement in the transition to a world of emancipated labor.

Again we find expressed Marx's utopian belief in the possibilities immanent within emancipatory labor. The passage that follows is expressive of exactly such possibilities, with abundant reference to the famous thesis advanced in the *Communist Manifesto* that in bourgeois society all that is solid is destined to melt into air:

> As the system of bourgeois economy has developed for us only
> by degrees, so too its negation, which is its ultimate result . . .
> When we consider bourgeois society in the long view and as a
> whole, then the final result of the process of social production
> always appears as the society itself, i.e. the human being itself in
> its social relations. Everything that has a fixed form . . . appears
> as merely a moment, a vanishing moment, in this movement.
> The direct production process itself here appears only as a
> moment. The conditions and objectifications of the process are

themselves equally moments of it, and its only subjects are the individuals in mutual relationships, which they equally reproduce and produce anew. The constant process of their own movement, in which they renew themselves even as they renew the world of wealth they create. (712)

There then follows a longish excerpt from the writings of Robert Owen which are worth reading if only to get a sense of the intellectual and political environment in which Marx was writing. For example, Owen rails against the prospect that "the small masters will be increasingly displaced by those who possess great capitals, and that the former relatively happier equality among the producers must give way to the greatest inequality between master and worker, such as has never before occurred in the history of mankind" (713). In this regard, it is perhaps significant to note the continuing political exhortations as to the significance of small business to the US economy, while its pillage by big capital ceaselessly operates. There has also been plenty of adverse commentary on the fact that the ratio of CEO remuneration to the average wage of their employees has risen from 40 to 1 to more than 300 to 1 in the neoliberal era in the United States. When the Congress passed the Cares Act in April 2020 to protect small business from the collapse created by the Covid-19 pandemic, almost all of the benefits were gobbled up by big capital. What seem to us today to be quite radical formulations were often commonsensical propositions for much of the oppositional left in Marx's time. Owen was one of the most forceful writers in this tradition, who also was prepared to put his money where his mouth was in setting up worker cooperatives. Marx took Owen's ideas seriously and learned much from him, even as he never abandoned his own rigorously critical stance.

Fixed capital is a produced agent for increasing the productivity of labor. But this raises the question of how "natural agencies enter in, such as water, land (this notably), mines etc., which are appropriated, hence possess exchange value, and hence come as values into the calculation of production costs" (714). The thorny and controversial question of how to deal with what Marx elsewhere refers to as "the free gifts of nature" has to be addressed. Marx's first move is to say we cannot answer this question without considering landed property. But this "does not belong here yet" and will have to be left until later, even though it is a "historic presupposition" for capital. But he does leave us with one clue as to how to proceed. "Only the form of landed property—or of natural agencies as value-determining magnitudes—modified to correspond to capital belongs within the examination of the system of bourgeois economy." As with so many of his other categories, Marx is only concerned with them insofar as they refer to the distinctively capitalistic form (of landed property, debt or even alienated wage labor). At this point, he does not rule out the possibility that nature can contribute value. But he is also hinting that the flow of the free gifts of nature into the production system of capital is mediated through the ownership rights of landed property and the capacity of the landowners to extract rent. Market prices can be established even in the absence of value creation.

What is certain is that the rising productive force of capital generates an increasing demand for raw materials. "In the extractive industries, such as fishery, mining, labour merely consists in overpowering the obstacles in the way of the seizure and appropriation of the raw products or primary products." This is Marx touching upon what we now call "extractivism," as the initial raw material is simply taken out and appropriated from the earth. In agriculture, however, we have to accept that "the raw material is earth itself" (715).

He then inserts a seemingly important question: can land be regarded as a form of fixed capital? This question explains the transition from the built environment to the brief consideration of raw nature in this section. Fixed capital can, of course, be placed upon the land and embedded in the land. But categorizing the land as fixed capital in itself, he argues, is not a good idea, inconsistent entirely with his later considerations on differential land rent. To be sure, the land is commodified and can be traded in a land market. And water, mineral resources and all the rest can be extracted from the land and all of these items have a potential use-value (and exchange-value, i.e., price) for both production and consumption. But it is not a good idea to categorize the land itself (as opposed to structures placed upon or built into the land) as fixed capital.

Fixed capital has a material existence that lasts for a while. The lifetime of fixed capital is an issue. As a product of labor, it congeals value within itself, even though its "use value is to create new values." Hence "the stage of development reached by the mode of production based on capital . . . is measured by the existing scope of fixed capital." Finally, "in *fixed capital*, the social productivity of labour [is] posited as a property inherent in capital; *including the scientific power as well as the combination of social powers" (what I call the organizational form) "within the production process, and finally, the skill transposed from direct labour into the machine, into the dead productive force. In circulating capital*, by contrast, it is the exchange of labours, of the different branches of labour, their interlacing and system-forming quality, the co-existence of productive labour, which appear as property of capital" (715–16). Strange, that it is the dead labor of fixed capital that stands out as the measure of capital's advancement versus the living labor that toils away on a daily basis in the material underworld of circulating capital.

Circulating capital flows into immediate production and produces the goods that end up on our table or in the shop. Fixed capital lies behind productive activity and has a different logic of circulation. These two different logics of circulation have so far been presented separately. Marx now brings them more closely together. He first emphasizes the radical contrast in their turnover times. In the case of circulating capital, "the velocity of turnover time . . . substitutes for the magnitude of capital" (718). A small capital that turns over four times a year produces as much surplus-value as a much larger capital that turns over only once a year.

"*Since circulating capital is completely absorbed into circulation and returns from it as a whole, it follows that it is reproduced as capital as many times as it is realized as surplus value* or as surplus capital" (719). In contrast, "the larger is the part of the capital consisting as fixed capital" and the "more durable" it is and the "longer its reproduction time," the more must the part that is circulating repeat its turnovers. "Hence," Marx concludes, "the continuity of production becomes an external necessity for capital" (719). Marx circles back to the importance of continuity such that circulating capital has to keep circulating if the value of the fixed capital is to be realized over its lifetime.

This is another aspect of capital's laws of motion that assumes a critical position within Marx's theory of capital. "For circulating capital, *an interruption, if it does not last so long as to ruin its use value, is only an interruption in the creation of surplus value. But with fixed capital, the interruption* . . . is the destruction of its original value itself. Hence the continuity of the production process which corresponds to the concept of capital is posited as *conditio sin qua* [*non*] for its maintenance only with the development of fixed capital." To which Marx then adds "likewise the continuity and constant growth of consumption" (719). So far in the *Grundrisse*, we have not dealt much with the role of final consumption. But here it is explicitly pulled into the analysis as a distinctive moment within the totality that is required to validate the realization of the full value of the fixed capital over its lifetime (which can be many years).

All of this rests on the convention of a standard measure of capital turnover time of one year (even as some capitals turn over several times in that year) and a labor turnover time of a standard working day. But

the introduction of fixed capital changes this; and neither the turnover time of capital, nor the unit in which their number is measured, the year, henceforth appear as the measure of time for the motion of capital. This unit is now determined, rather, by the *reproduction time* required for fixed capital, and hence, the total circulation time it needs to enter into circulation as value, and to come back from it in the totality of its value. (720)

The fixed capital internalizes, as it were, its own temporality. If I am using a machine that has a lifetime of ten years, then my temporality is fixed by a ten-year time horizon. If the average lifetime of comparable machines is also ten years, then this produces a ten-year (perhaps staggered) investment cycle in the economy as a whole. "According to Babbage," Marx reports, "the average reproduction of machinery in England is 5 years." Marx argues that "the real one hence perhaps 10 years. There can be no doubt whatever that the cycle which has passed through since the development of fixed capital on a large scale at more or less 10-yearly intervals, is connected with this *total reproduction phase of capital*." During Marx's lifetime there was evidence for a ten-year speculative investment cycle. There were sharp crises in 1826, 1836, 1847–48, 1857–58 (when Marx was writing the *Grundrisse*). These business cycles coincided with waves of reinvestment and renewal in fixed capital, including that of an independent kind. The waves of reinvestment in new machines often entailed devaluation of the old, but Marx does not discuss this. He simply notes that "the industrial cycle of a number of years, divided into characteristic periods, epochs, is peculiar to large-scale industry" (721).

Nevertheless, it is important to recognize that fixed capital "does not itself circulate as a use value, but rather enters as value into the manufactured raw material . . . only to the extent it is used up as use value in the production process . . . *It returns fragmentarily over longer periods, while circulating capital circulates wholly in shorter periods . . . It returns in principle only to the extent that it transposes itself directly or indirectly into the product, hence into circulating capital*" (721). In other words, there is a flow of the value congealed in the fixed capital into circulating capital, thus connecting long-term and short-term turnovers on a piecemeal basis. Circulating capital is "ejected from the production process in the form of the product" whose use-value is totally consumed. With its realization in money form, both the value and the surplus-value are realized and "all conditions of reproduction [are] fulfilled" (721). "Fixed capital, by contrast, does not itself circulate as a use value, but rather enters as value into the manufactured raw material . . . or into the directly extracted raw material (mining etc.) only to the extent that it is used up as use value in the production process." Its value "only returns in a cycle of years which embraces a series of turnovers of circulating capital. It enters into the price of the product only in successive bits . . . *It returns fragmentarily over long periods*."

"This different kind of return of fixed and circulating capital will appear significant later as the difference between selling and renting, annuity, interest and profit, rent in its different forms, and profit" (722). This is a potentially significant but uninformative statement. It suggests a linkage between the coordinations and codeterminations operating in the differential circulation processes of fixed and circulating capital and the role that other distributive forms—such as interest, rent and financial instruments—more generally play within the capitalist mode of production as a totality.

Marx's point of entry into this complex problem emphasizes that "it is neither the circulating capital nor the fixed capital which create the profit, but rather the appropriation of alien labour." And this alien labor comes, of course, "from small-scale circulation." But the profit is realized "only through the entry of capital into circulation, hence only in its form as circulating capital, never in its form of fixed capital" (722). Fixed capital is vital for understanding the production of value but irrelevant to the process of realization of that value through a sale in the market.

But how does this work in the case of that form of fixed capital "in which it does not directly enter into the production process as machinery, but rather in railways, buildings, agricultural improvements, drainings etc., where . . . the realization of the value and surplus value contained in it appears in the form of an annuity, where interest represents the surplus value and the annuity the successive return of the value advanced" (723). Fixed capital in this case "is here sold not all at once, but as an annuity." What we are dealing with here is the case of what Marx elsewhere calls "fixed capital of an independent kind." The circulation of fixed capital in this case appears, as we shall shortly see, to have some relationship with the circulation of interest-bearing capital.

Some forms of fixed capital "figure initially as circulating capital, and become fixed capital only when they become fixed in the production process." The machine-makers are working as producers of circulating capital up until that moment when the manufacturer purchases the machine to function as fixed capital. "Likewise even houses, despite their immovability, are circulating capital for the building trade; for him who buys them to rent them out again or use them as buildings for production, they are fixed capital" (723).

It is at this point that, for some reason, Marx goes back to his foundational argument regarding the circulation of capital. "Productive capital becomes product, commodity, money, and is transformed back into the conditions of production." This is his base-line conception (Figure 2). "It remains capital in each of these forms, and it becomes capital only by realizing itself as such. So long as it remains in one of these phases, it is fixed as commodity capital, money capital, or industrial capital. But each of these phases forms only one moment of its movement, and in the form from which it must propel itself to pass over into another phase it ceases to be capital. If it rejects itself as commodity and becomes money, or vice versa, then it does not exist as capital in the rejected form" (724). It therefore "rejects each of the forms as its not-capital-being, so as to assume them again later." The key, as always, is that if capital is value in motion, then any stoppage in the motion means loss of capital, devaluation. This is a clear articulation of Marx's argument that capital (value) cannot exist outside of anti-capital (or "rejected capital") with its constant threat of devaluation through lack of movement. I think Marx feels the need to restate this point here in order to confront the problem of the lack of motion that always attaches in one way or another to fixed capital. The threat of devaluation is real. But there is another angle to be considered as well. "If capital is lent out as money, as land and soil, house, etc. then it becomes a commodity *as capital*, or the commodity put into circulation is *capital as capital.*"

This is the first time in the *Grundrisse* that we confront the way in which capital can itself become a commodity. He promises to expand upon this "in the next section." In the normal course of events, the producer-buyer

> successively and bit by bit pays for the wear and use of fixed capital, even though the latter does not enter into circulation as use value. But there are forms of fixed capital where he pays directly for its use value [without owning it]—as with means of communication, transport etc. In all these cases the fixed capital in fact never leaves the production process, as with railways etc. But while it serves for some as means of communication within the production process itself, to bring the product to market, and for the others as a means of consumption, as use value for holiday travel, etc. Regarded as a means of production, it distinguishes itself from machinery etc. here in that it is used by various capitals at the same time, as a common condition for their production and circulation. (725)

The direct producer does not have to buy the railway, but can pay for its use (along with many other users) whenever needed. In this case, the fixed capital is not "locked within a particular production process, but rather as the connecting artery of a mass of such production processes of particular capitals, who use it up only in [their] portions" (725). Access to fixed capital is then bought and used as an end in itself. Railways "or buildings rented for production, are *simultaneously* instruments of production, and are simultaneously realized by their seller as product, as capital."

Consider the example of building a railway line. It may take ten years to build (or three years, if you are in China), and during that time there is no revenue but there are a lot of costs. Capital has to be prepared to wait. But workers have to be fed, raw materials and energy purchased and a host of incidental expenses are incurred within the circulating capital in producing the fixed capital. All this occurs within the frame of circulating capital. But circulating capital is diminished as it flows into fixed capital, which initially returns nothing to circulating capital. It may be several years before any return is received.

For example, the interstate highway project in the United States during the 1950s and 1960s was not initially set up to increase productivity. It was set up for military security reasons and absorbed a vast amount of circulating capital. But it is now generally accepted that the money was not wasted. It improved the productivity of the US economy, partly by facilitating the annihilation of space through time. But fixed-capital investment can flow into megaprojects which don't do anything whatsoever to enhance productivity or even to enhance the qualities of the consumption fund. Local officials in particular suffer from edifice complexes: they long to create a megaproject that bears their name, no matter whether it makes any sense or not. The wasteful absorption of surplus labor and surplus capital ("bridges to nowhere") is not uncommon. Elsewhere, Marx notes how many long-term projects result in the bankruptcy of the first wave of investors, after which a second wave of investors sweeps in and buys up the unused and devalued use-values at fire-sale prices to launch a successful round of rapid capital accumulation with much reduced fixed-capital costs.

The point that Marx is making is that fixed capital increasingly becomes a social project in itself, particularly when it becomes fixed capital of an independent kind. "The important thing now is that the production of capital thus appears as the production in definite portions of circulating and fixed capital, so that capital itself produces its double way of circulating as fixed capital and circulating capital" (727). This leads us back to the Smithian start-ing point that "*every fixed capital comes originally from a circulat-ing capital*, and needs to be continually maintained by *means of a circulating capital*" (728). This return to Smith leads Marx into some reflections on the historical role of fixed capital formation (and its theoretical status) in the rise and maturation of a capitalist mode of production.

He points out, for example, that every circulating capital "comes originally from fixed capital. Without nets he can catch no fish; without a plough, till not fields; and without a hammer etc., drive no mines. If he uses even so little as a stone for a hammer etc., then this stone is certainly no circulating capital, no capital of any sort, but rather a means of labour" (734). But the place "where all capi-tal, circulating as well as fixed, not only originally but continually comes from is the appropriation of alien labour." This is, of course, the founding principle of Marx's theory of capital, and it is only within this frame that the complex relations between fixed and circulating capital can be understood. The reassertion of this prin-ciple, counter to the physical universalism of Smith, leads Marx to make an interesting side comment on what happens

> when an industrial people producing on the foundation of capi-tal, such as the English, e.g., exchange with the Chinese . . . then one sees right away that the Chinese do not therefore need to produce as capitalists. Within a single society, such as the English, the mode of production of capital develops in one branch of industry, while in another, e.g. agriculture, modes of production predominate which more or less antedate capital. Nevertheless, it is (1) its necessary tendency to conquer the mode of production in all respects, to bring them under the rule of capital . . . (2) as to external markets, capital imposes this propagation of its mode of production through international competition. Competition is the mode generally in which capi-tal secures the victory of its mode of production. (729–30)

This is the kind of statement that Marx is prone to, which generates a storm of protest from opponents, and even sympathetic critics alike, as being rank historical determinism (even though Marx calls it a "necessary tendency"). It constitutes, they say, a denial of human agency. From the perspective of how the world is in 2022, what Marx wrote in 1858 appears devastatingly and irrefutably accurate. If, as Marx insists, we are ruled by abstractions, then the only goal for human agency that makes sense is to attack the processes that produce the abstractions and render them irrelevant. But that is precisely what capitalist ideology and politics refuse to contemplate. It is, in any case, very hard to contemplate class struggle against abstractions.

Almost immediately after this instructive aside, Marx drops yet another theoretical bombshell into the discussion, although, of course, "it does not belong here yet." Since fixed capital is "realized only in part during the year, it presupposes only a *partial countervalue.*" By this, I think Marx means that the whole machine will be deployed every year, but that the monetary return on the use of the machine will be only a portion of its value in a given year. "It is paid for only in proportion to its wear." But even as "*it engages the production of subsequent years,* and, just as it contributes to the creation of a large revenue, it anticipates further labour as a counter-value." And here comes the startling insight. "The anticipation of future fruits of labour is therefore in no way a consequence of the state debt etc., in short, not an invention of the credit system. It has *its roots in the specific mode of realization, mode of turnover, mode of reproduction of fixed capital*" (732).

The potential importance of this observation lies in relation to understanding the vast expansion in financialization and the credit system over the last forty years or so in the history of capitalism. The impacts of this shift have been widely studied and commented on, but no coherent explanation has been proposed, let alone accepted, for how and why this shift occurred. Theorists have been reduced to saying it just happened, that capital changed its spots in favor of financialization, as it has periodically done throughout its history, and that is that. But, if Marx's comment is correct, and if we adhere to the perspective of the totality and the principle that any major transformation must be endogenously accomplished and explained rather than exogenously imposed, then the place to look for an explanation is not within the credit system and finance but within the changing dynamic between fixed and circulating capital. This has been hinted at more than once throughout this section (e.g., the earlier chatter on annuities). The inevitable shift within the spiral form from circulating toward fixed capital exaggerates and exacerbates the need for an adequate credit system and financing. The more capital creates fixed capital of an independent kind, the greater the need to integrate the circulation of credit into the circulation of fixed capital.

The most obvious example I have encountered of this relation in motion was in Second Empire Paris, where the newly empowered imperial regime of Louis Bonaparte set out to save capital from crisis by rebuilding Paris (Haussmannization), and that required the creation of new credit institutions and novel structures of public urban finance. The most recent example is massive urbanization in China, with new housing accounting for as much as 15 percent of growth, backed by the rise of new credit institutions (including a shadow banking system and mortgage finance) that has produced a massive increase in both public and private indebtedness. The question of how the rise of financialization and new credit instruments occurred is redirected to ask how the limitations and possibilities inherent in circulating capital led to a vast expansion in the flow of capital into fixed capital of an independent kind. It is important to note, in addition, that much fixed capital, particularly that of an independent kind, circulates in accord with the circulation of interest-bearing capital without concern for earning profit. The built environment therefore provides a convenient sink for the investment of surplus money capital.

Marx will not let go of what is in effect an obsession with understanding everything he can about the relationship between fixed and circulating capital. The result is a good deal of repetition, reformulations and speculative commentary, punctuated by occasional summary statements. He shows, for example, that "fixed capital itself can be renewed as capital only by becoming a value-component of circulating capital, and *its elements are thus reproduced through the transformation of circulating capital* into fixed capital. *Fixed capital is as much a presupposition for the production of circulating capital as circulating capital is for the production of fixed capital*" (734). The logical structure of this argument appears tautological until the idea of perpetual motion and of movement of capital internal to the totality is introduced. In the summary statement he provides on pages 738–9, he goes on to show how fixed capital "creates value not in so far as it has value—for the latter is simply replaced—but rather only in so far as it increases relative surplus time, or decreases necessary labour time. In the same proportion, then, as that in which its scope grows, the mass of products must increase, and the living labour employed relatively decrease."

This opens the path toward another chapter in the saga of Marx's analysis of fixed capital. "*The less the value of the fixed capital in relation to its effectiveness, the more does it correspond to its purpose. All unnecessary fixed capital appears as faux frais de production*, like all unnecessary circulation costs" (739). This seems a strange statement given the initial importance of fixed capital in raising the productivity of labor. He had earlier pointed out that fixed capital circulation is increasingly captive to the need to find outlets to absorb the "monstrous" quantities of surplus-value and surplus product that capital generates. When "money is immobilized in the hands of bankers" and "when money cries out for a field of employment" (621), then what better place to go than to invest in urbanization or other forms of fixed capital of an independent kind. In this case, it is vital that fixed capital does not contribute to the increasing productivity of labor and that the cycle in which rising productivity becomes self-sustaining be broken. "The value of the fixed capital is therefore never an end in itself in the production of capital." In other words, from the standpoint of production, the value of fixed capital is measured by its contribution to surplus-value production, but from the standpoint of the totality of production and circulation, fixed capital has another vital role to play in absorbing surplus product in unproductive ways. This will, later on, play an important role in counteracting the falling rate of profit (750). The landscape of capital is therefore littered with unproductive fixed-capital investments, the "white elephants" of a capitalist mode of production. Along with military expenditures (which Marx had characterized as tipping value into the ocean), the field of fixed capital formation of an independent kind has a perverse utility as a dumping ground for the investment and perhaps devaluation of surplus capital.

Before proceeding, however, Marx has one more issue to discuss. "The final and last distinction cited by economists is that between movable and immovable." The latter is physically fixed in the land. This covers "improvements sunk in the soil, aqueducts, buildings; and machinery itself in great part, since it must be physically fixed, to act; railways; in short, every form in which the product of industry is welded fast to the surface of the earth" (739–40). While this "adds nothing" to our understanding of fixed capital as an economic category, in this case the "material presence" and the economic usage converge. It can, however, continue to circulate in title form (e.g., as railroad shares) even though its use-value is fixed in space. For this reason it must also be used in situ. Circulating capital must flow in such a way as to facilitate the realization of the value of the fixed capital:

> Originally, the growth of movable property, its increase against immovable, indicates the ascendant movement of capital against landed property. But once the mode of production of capital is presupposed, the level to which it has conquered the conditions of production is indicated in the transformation of capital into immovable property. It thereby establishes its residence on the land itself, and the seeming solid presuppositions given by nature, themselves [appear] in landed property, as merely posited by industry. (740)

The production of what he elsewhere refers to as "second nature" gets under way. Investments in the built environment are often as much oriented toward consumption as production. This is the case with parks, hospitals, schools or, most classically, housing. The house is a form of circulating capital for the person who builds it, but when the house is sold, it goes into the consumption fund, unless somebody decides to use it as a sweatshop, in which case it becomes a form of fixed capital for production. In either case, the lifetime of the house is relatively long-term and the standard period of payment in the United States for its use will be thirty years or so in the form of a mortgage. Most housing lies in the consumption fund. But it is the use, as we have noted, that matters. A house can switch from being in the consumption fund into textile production, which could be turned into condominiums, and thus have switched from the fixed capital category into the consumption funds category.

The fixity of fixed capital has certain implications for how the metabolic relation to nature is understood. Fixed capital that is incorporated in the land will, after it has been amortized, remain behind embedded as a permanent improvement that appears as part of "second nature," the nature modified by human occupancy and productive activity. This poses the immediate problem of the relationship between creation of infrastructures on the land and landed property. The production and use of physical infrastructures, the creation of urbanization and uneven geographical developments, all rest upon (presuppose) the existence of landed property: "The growth of movable property . . . indicates the ascendant movement of capital as against landed property."

Two observations with potentially significant consequences are then taken up. "Capitals are (1) divided into fixed and circulating capital in unequal proportions" and "(2) [have] an interrupted or uninterrupted production phase and return from more distant or nearer markets." As a result, "the surplus value created in a given time, e.g. annually, must be unequal, because the number of reproduction processes in the given period is unequal"

(741). Value creation depends upon how many repetitions of a production process occur during the year as well as upon the continuity in the application of labor in production itself. In agriculture, for example, the application of labor is episodic over the year, and in some regions double-cropping is possible. While Marx does not elaborate, the implication is that processes of unequal and uneven development are internalized within the capitalist mode of production.

It then follows that "the production process, as containing within itself the conditions of its renewal, is a reproduction process whose speed is determined by various relations developed above, which all arise from differences of circulation," such as those arising from the circulation time to distant markets. The result is that "production is on all sides subordinate to exchange. These exchange operations, circulation itself, produce no surplus value, but are conditions for its realization." In other words, to take a tangible example that was never far from Marx's thoughts, the production of surplus-value in the cotton factories of Manchester was constrained by the time taken to get the cotton from the plantations in the Carolinas to Manchester, as well as by the time taken to get the finished product to the primary markets in India. But never forget that "the transformation into money is necessary for the reproduction of capital as such, and its reproduction is necessarily the production of surplus value" (741). Throughout this whole presentation we are invited again and again to recognize the continuity over space and time of the process of production and realization of surplus-value and the various conditionalities that must be reproduced for the process to be successfully renewed.

11

The Falling Rate of Profit and Other Matters
Pages 745–78

Not for the first time, Marx uses the opening of a new notebook to announce a new direction to his investigation. Up until this point, he has considered production and circulation as separable fields of inquiry. In the analysis of production, he was primarily preoccupied with the relation between necessary and surplus labor time. When he turned to questions of circulation, he disaggregated different circuits of capital with particular emphasis on the circulation of fixed capital relative to circulating capital. But henceforth, he now tells us, capital is "posited as the unity of production and circulation" within the totality (745). He now sets out to explore the contradictory unity between them, with particular concern for the impact of fixed capital circulation upon the productivity of labor in production.

Because of its inclusion in circulation as a totality, "surplus value *appears* no longer to be posited by its simple, direct relation to living labour." Marx in effect adjusts his lens to look at the circulation of capital as a whole (Figure 2), and from this perspective surplus-value appears as "merely a moment of its total movement," rather than the culminating end point of a linear process going from money capital to surplus-value realization via production.

From the perspective of the totality, capital "relates to itself as self-increasing value . . . A capital of a certain value produces in a certain period of time a certain surplus value . . . Capital thus posited as self-realizing value—is *profit*, regarded not *sub specie aeternitas*, but *sub specie–capitalis*." It is the search for profit that appears to incentivize and drive capital to do what capital does. "The product of capital is *profit*" (746).

Reinvestment of some of the profit then follows. "In so far as the newly posited value . . . is itself in turn taken up into the production process, itself in turn maintains itself as capital, to that extent the capital itself has grown, and now acts as a capital of greater value." Hence, capital "grown by the amount of the profit, now begins the same process anew in larger dimensions. By describing its circle it expands itself as the subject of the circle and thus describes a self-expanding circle, a spiral" (746). Note the emphasis here upon growth, the growth of capital. Profit is no longer the end point of the circulation process but the vehicle within that circulation process which generates growth of and within the totality.

This transformation from the "virtuous infinity" of a never-ending repetitive cycle (of the sort we experience as day follows night) to the potentially "bad infinity" of the spiral form of endless cumulative exponential growth, is of the utmost theoretical significance. We neglect consideration of it at our peril. The growth syndrome of capital now takes center stage.

From the standpoint of the spiral form in which capital magically accomplishes its endless self-expansion, surplus-value and surplus labor appear as mere moments subject to the hunger of capital for profit as the central vehicle for growth. From this standpoint, capital shows little or no concern for the reproduction of labor power. As long as the worker turns up every day to give of their (alienated) labor, that is all that matters. They will do so because they have to give up alien labor in order to live as well as possible in their world of social reproduction. This is how the circulation of capacity to labor works. Marx is often reasonably criticized for his neglect of social reproduction, but here he is strictly concerned with the perspective of capital's growth, and from that perspective capital does not give a hoot about the conditions of social reproduction. Marx seems to feel justified in ignoring it, too, at least at this point in his inquiry.

The operative word in much of this initial argument is "appears." Whenever Marx uses this word (as he does in the very first sentence of *Capital*) he is referring to something that is real but which conceals its underlying force or meaning. The sun appears to go around the earth, but it is the earth that is spinning. It appears as if capital produces profit, but its origin lies in surplus labor. As Marx notes elsewhere, if everything was as it appears to be on the surface, there would be no need for science. But we have to react to surface appearances and symptoms even when we know that the underlying causes lie elsewhere. Human agents perforce respond as much if not more to surface appearances rather than to underlying causes. A psychologist may try to reassure us that the violence we might witness on the street stems from the insecurity of the participants, but the first practical step is somehow to disarm the agents. The correct analysis of surface appearances is just as important as the identification of underlying causes. Capital is focused on profit-making and appeals to price signals. It cannot recognize the true origin of profit in surplus labor time. In economic analyses, Marx suggests, we need to keep the dynamic tension between appearances and underlying realities constantly in play. This is what he seeks to do in the pages that follow.

From the perspective of the totality, capital appears as if it is self-replicating, searching for profit and building endlessly upon the spiral form of growth. But within that form, it encounters some serious contradictions. "The *rate of profit* depends on the relation between the part of capital exchanged for living labour" (what he will ultimately refer to as variable capital) "and the part existing in the form of raw material and means of production" (which he eventually terms constant capital). "Hence the smaller the portion exchanged for living labour becomes, the smaller becomes the rate of profit." In other words, "the more the relative surplus value grows . . . the more *does the rate of profit fall*" (747). In manufacturing, for example, the more fixed capital is employed, the more raw materials must be used, "while the part exchanged for living labour decreases." Rising productivity means less labor power is needed to produce the same output or more output is produced by the same labor. Note the introduction of the concept of relative surplus-value here, since it is not much appealed to in the *Grundrisse*, as opposed to in *Capital*, where it dominates Volume I. But Marx here notes an important oddity. "*Presupposing . . . [the] equal relation of surplus labour and necessary labour*" (what he will, in *Capital*, refer to as an equal rate of exploitation of labor power) "there can therefore be an unequal profit, and it must be unequal relative to the size of the capitals" (747).

The "gross profit" (what I will refer to as the "mass" of profit) "will grow on the average *not as does the rate of profit, but as does the size of the capital* . . . A capital of 100 with a rate of profit of 10% yields a smaller sum of profit than a capital of 1,000 with a profit of 2%." This is an obvious but all too frequently ignored fact. More generally:

> if the rate of profit declines for the larger capital, but not in relation with its size, then the gross profit rises although the rate of profit declines. If the profit rate declines relative to its size, then the gross profit remains the same . . . and that of the smaller capital remains stationary. If the profit rate declines more than its size increases, then the gross profit of the larger capital decreases relative to the smaller one in proportion as its rate of profit declines. This is in every respect the most important law of modern political economy. (748)

This is a much-cited statement, and it is vital to decipher Marx's meaning. Under the usual conditions of interpretation, the "this" would be presumed to refer to the argument set out in the passage cited above. The context of "this" would then be the relation between the rate and the mass of the profit. But in much of the Marxist literature, the statement is presumed to refer to the falling rate of profit alone. Most economists (including, unfortunately, many Marxists) tend to favor the study of rates of change, and to adjust their interpretations, commentaries and policies accordingly while neglecting problems that derive from an increasing mass of product. For example, a detailed study by the Bank of England in 2019 of the impacts of quantitative easing upon wealth distribution in Britain estimated that "the 10 per cent of least wealthy households" saw "a marginal increase in their measured real wealth of around £3,000 between 2006–8 and 2012–14, compared to £350,000 for the wealthiest 10 per cent." This seemed to confirm the popular view that central bank quantitative easing benefited the wealthy more than it did the least well-off. But the BofE report came to the opposite conclusion. "The UK's Gini coefficient, a commonly used measure of wealth inequality, declined slightly." The £3,000 received by the least well-off was proportionately more given their initial average wealth than the £350,000 received by the wealthiest 10 percent.

But, Marx would ask, in what sense is it better to receive a 10 percent increase on £100 as opposed to a 5 percent increase on £1 million? £3,000 over six years is less than £10 a week, which hardly adds anything to a person's well-being, let alone political and economic power. It is a trivial gain. The wealthiest in Britain got more than £1,000 a week, which is significant. Over six years, the difference would be between a few extra cups of coffee a week for the least well-off, or having enough money to buy a studio apartment in Manhattan for the top 10 percent. If money is a key form of social power, then a low rate of return on a huge mass of wealth (such as that of Jeff Bezos or Bill Gates) confers an enormous increase in social power relative to someone who fashions a high rate of return on a small stash of capital.

Exclusive concentration on rates rather than the mass introduces a systematic bias into economic analysis. If the Bank of England report is anything to go by, this bias all too often benefits the affluent classes. The mass of wealth and power they control is

monstrously increasing relative to everyone else, even with a falling rate of profit. The higher rate of growth for the least well-off is,
it turns out, as much a reflection of their initial poverty as a measure of real benefit. If the bottom 10 percent have close to zero
wealth, then it would not be hard to generate a 100 percent gain for
them by gifting them a small pecuniary benefit. It is the mass that
needs to be addressed and not only the rate. Strangely, the BofE
economists considered that the public failure to read the data right
was the key perceptual problem, rather than outrage at the rapidly
increasing mass of capital controlled by the top 10 percent.

Marx clearly recognizes the significance of this, as evidenced by
his statement which begins: "if the rate of profit declines for the
larger capital, but not in relation to its size, then the gross profit
rises although the rate of profit declines." This is what Marx declares
to be "in every respect the most important law of modern political
economy, and the most essential for understanding the most difficult relations. It is the most important law from the historical
standpoint. It is a law which, despite its simplicity, has never before
been grasped and, even less, consciously articulated" (748).

However, in much of Marxist literature, this statement is
appealed to and cited as a simple assertion of the centrality of the
falling rate of profit in Marx's theorizing of the laws of motion of
capital. This law of falling profits often has pride of place in theories of crisis formation. While it is clear that Marx takes great
pleasure in clarifying and articulating this version of the law (or
tendency) in itself, as we shall shortly see, it is not that simple. To
begin with, Marx is just as concerned in his initial statement with
the gross (or mass of) profit as he is with the falling rate. He sees
the rate and mass as moving contrary to each other. It is only after
asserting details as to how this contrariness works that Marx
ventures his opinion as to the centrality of the law. In the parallel
passages in Volume III of *Capital*, Marx is equally adamant that he
is dealing with a double-edged law: that of the falling rate and
rising mass of profit. The *Grundrisse* text supports this view. It
makes a considerable difference if the law in question is judged to

be that of the falling rate and rising mass of profit, or just the falling rate of profit on its own. From the perspective of the totality, Marx makes clear that it is the absolute growth of capital (the mass of value) that is the essence of what capital is about. If the rate of profit is a primary vehicle for sustaining that growth and if there is a tendency for it to fall, then another mechanism must be found to accomplish the absolute growth that the capitalist mode of production demands. An obvious answer is that the number of productive workers must increase far beyond that needed to compensate for the loss of surplus-value resulting from the rising productivity of labor power. In other words, if the mass of workers employed expands dramatically, this will overwhelm the tendency for the mass of surplus-value to fall because of rising labor productivity. Although the rate of profit falls, the mass of profit can and does increase.

Wealth in capitalist society is measured in terms of command over value (or its representation, monetary values). Amassing sufficient command over values is the aim and object of the pursuit of wealth. The rate of profit is an important means to that end. But the more wealth that is accumulated by some entity (individuals, corporations, institutions, states), the less relevant the rate of profit becomes. During the 1990s into the twentieth century, China registered exceptionally high rates of growth (above double digits). By 2019, the mass was so huge that a 5 percent rate of growth implied unthinkable further accumulation of wealth, with China projected to surpass the United States as largest economy in the world in the not too distant future. This would be the kind of case that Marx would have relished analyzing. But he would also surely have noted that the high rates of growth in the 1990s were predicated on the mass mobilization of low-wage labor recruited from the countryside, shortly followed by the rise of mass consumption (both productive and final) that turned China into a premier market for, among many others, German export industries such as BMW, Siemens and machine-tool products. The dialectics of rate and mass are critical in forging new configurations within the totality.

It is not entirely clear, however, whether Marx is clarifying (and presumably criticizing) a widely held foundational law of classical political economy or stating the law as his own. This is a pervasive problem in studying Marx's writings. From what follows, it seems that Marx did accept Ricardo's law of falling profits as a basis but radically transforms it by way of changing the mechanism and incorporating the rising mass. Ricardo's stand-alone version of falling profit was well-known throughout political economy. What Marx grasps is the particular form taken by the law, the endogenous (internal) rather than exogenous (external) mechanisms that produce and modify it, and its relation to the rising mass. There are also, as we shall later see, other conditions and caveats regarding the operation of the law that in both the *Grundrisse* and *Capital* restrict its operation.

Since my interpretation here runs somewhat counter to a certain line of Marxist economics which fetishizes falling profits without acknowledging (other than in passing) the importance of the rising mass, some justification beyond the textual argument (which I regard as irrefutable) is called for. There are many serious problems confronting global capitalism at the present time and, since the claims for the power of the law are so central in most Marxist theories of crisis formation, the question arises as to which version of the law is most robust in addressing these problems. Consider, for example, the problems of environmental degradation and climate change; the production of the world market (globalization); speedup in turnover times; increasing financialization; rising social inequalities; and the massive increase in the global proletariat since 1980—just to name a few of the most obvious issues. It is extremely difficult to address any of these problems directly and without convoluted reasoning by way of appeal to the stand-alone version of the falling rate of profit. The version that insists upon the contradiction between falling rates and rising masses, on the other hand, makes it relatively easy to address such problems directly. The environmental pressures stemming from a rising mass are clear and present problems that need to be addressed directly. It is significant that, both in the *Grundrisse* and *Capital*, Marx himself attaches to his consideration of the falling rate and rising mass the necessity for capital to forge a world market and to expand consumer markets by any and all means possible, all to accommodate the rising mass. The nature of the contradiction itself would suggest that, the more the profit rate falls (and there is plenty of evidence that it tends to do so), the greater must be the effort to expand the mass (hence the significance of the huge increase in the global wage-labor force since 1980). If profit rates have been falling since 1980, for example, then the consequences that flow from the rapid increase in the mass would readily explain the equally massive expansion in greenhouse gas emissions over the same period as well as the rising inequalities and the frantic creation of new products and markets since 1980 or so. Such a theoretical link is speculative, of course. I merely wish to illustrate here how the problems of the absorption of a rapidly rising mass consequent upon the operation of the double-edged law of the falling rate and rising mass of profits can so easily be brought to bear on such a wide range of pressing problems.

Marx's version of the law draws upon his detailed study of the circulation of fixed capital in relation to increasing labor productivity. The immediate consequences of the operation of the law are multiple. The development of the fixed capital, as we earlier saw, rests on "an enormous development of scientific powers." The relative decline of labor input produces "a great mass of products with low prices." The falling rate produces a rising mass of products even in the absence of any growth. This promotes "intercourse on a magnificent scale, immense sum of exchange operations, large size of the market and all-sidedness of simultaneous labour; means of communication etc., presence of the necessary consumption fund to undertake this gigantic process (workers' food, housing etc.)" (749). What Marx seems to be doing here is implementing the basic insight that production is consumption and that the continuous expansion of productive capacity orchestrated through fixed capital entails, and indeed is, expansion of consumption, even that of the workers. "Hence it is evident that the material productive power already present, already worked out, existing in the form of fixed capital, together with the population etc., in short . . . the greatest conditions for the reproduction of wealth," open the way toward "the abundant development of the social individual" (749). This brings us back to Marx's earlier critique of fixed capital as actually promoting the greater and greater servitude of labor in the service of capital, even as it promises abundant disposable time to emancipated labor. But this time, the consequences of this incipient contradiction are far more catastrophic and dramatic.

"The development of the productive forces brought about by the historical development of capital itself, when it reaches a certain point, suspends the self-realization of capital, instead of positing it." As if this declaration, in itself, were not enough, Marx continues: "Beyond a certain point, the development of the powers of production becomes a barrier for capital; hence the capital relation a barrier for the development of the productive powers of labor." The figure of the emancipated laborer re-emerges from the shadows of history to assume their proper role:

> The last form of servitude assumed by human activity, that of wage labour on one side, capital on the other, is thereby cast off like a skin, and this casting-off itself is the result of the mode of production corresponding to capital; the material and mental conditions of the negation of wage labour and of capital . . . are themselves results of its production process. The growing incompatibility between the productive development of society and its hitherto existing relations of production expresses itself in bitter contradictions, crises, spasms. The violent destruction of capital not by relations external to it, but rather as a condition of its self-preservation, is the most striking form in which advice is given to it to be gone and to give room to a higher state of social production. (749–50)

Humanity has, so far at least, largely seen fit to ignore this advice even though there have been enough "bitter contradictions, crises, spasms" to convince whole populations on occasion that something different might be worth trying out. It is simply not true that all struggles to nurture an alternative have failed. To the degree that we have any residual social protections (such as health care and social insurance in many parts of the world), it has been because of the systematic threat of the communist alternative and active class struggle on the ground. While the foundational class relation of capital and labor remains as solid as ever, the contradictions have become more salient. While some of the outcomes, such as the undeniable and striking "growth in scientific power," which Marx celebrates, have a great deal of positive potential, the aggregate situation is far from reassuring.

As usual with Marx, his detailed thinking leads to an appreciation of the potential countervailing reactions to a falling rate of profit given "the higher state of production" achieved through the application of machinery and fixed capital more generally.

Since this decline of profit signifies the same as the decrease of immediate labour relative to the size of the objective labour which it reproduces and newly posits, capital will attempt every means of checking the smallness of the relation of living labour to the size of the capital generally, hence also of the surplus value, if expressed as profit, relative to the presupposed capital, by reducing the allotment made to necessary labour and by still more expanding the quantity of surplus labour with regard to the whole labour employed. (750)

This is an interesting thesis. Faced with falling rates of profit, capitalists repress wages in order to stabilize their profits, while also employing more laborers to ensure a greater gross (mass of) profit (their true aim) in the face of a falling rate of profit. The capitalists get wealthier no matter what (in much the same way that the economic crash of 2020 produced a new batch of billionaires, while lining the coffers of existing billionaires). This constitutes a very elegant way to connect falling rate and rising mass with increasing class disparities, which will likely in turn give rise to heightened conditions of class struggle. Hence, Marx goes on to argue:

> The highest development of productive power together with the greatest expansion of existing wealth will coincide with depreciation of capital, degradation of the labourer, and a most straitened exhaustion of his vital powers . . . These contradictions, of course, lead to explosions, crises, in which momentary suspension of all labour and annihilation of a great part of the capital violently lead it back to the point where it is enabled [to go on] fully employing its productive powers without committing suicide. Yet, these regularly recurring catastrophes lead to their repetition on a higher scale, and finally to its violent overthrow. (750)

There is a broad-based acceptance that the falling rate of profit is one of the major causes of the periodic crises to which capital is prone. But here we see how the falling rate and the rising mass generate unbearable class disparities along with general economic and social stresses—catastrophes—mediated by way of the uneven impact of the "double-edged" law of falling rates and rising mass.

While in our own times the ability to avoid a collective suicide seems more assured in the short run, Marx did accept even in his own time that capital would likely make every effort to counter the impacts of falling profits. He also recognized that "there are moments in the developed movement of capital which delay this movement other than by crises." He cites "the constant devaluation of a part of the existing capital" (by, for example, technological obsolescence of the mass of fixed capital); "the transformation of a great part of capital into fixed capital which does not serve as agency of direct production; unproductive waste of a great portion of capital etc."

This list is rather striking. What can Marx possibly mean by "fixed capital that does not serve as agency of direct production?"

Does this mean that "a great part of capital" sucks up value in a way that does not contribute to increasing labor productivity even as it performs as a use-value for production? The comment is more readily understandable if it referred to the substantial flow of value into the creation of a consumption fund (of housing, schools, hospitals, roads, etc.). Quite a lot of fixed capital of an independent kind (particularly that embedded in the land) is used by capital as a fixed asset, even as it does not immediately enhance productivity. This is an idea that Marx had earlier advanced with some conviction: "*The less the value of fixed capital in relation to its effectiveness, the more does it correspond to its purpose*" (739). We will later encounter exactly such a phenomenon. Much of this, as we have seen in the case of the road analyzed earlier, rests on joint uses for production and consumption. Wasteful investments in the built environment ("bridges to nowhere") are legendary, and the periodic widespread devaluation of fixed capital is ongoing, even at some points generating crises. The rapidity of technological change and rapid transformations in product markets ensure an elevated rate of devaluation of existing fixed capital. We have to look no further than the recent history of electronics as an example of accelerating (in some instances clearly planned) devaluations through accelerated obsolescence. But the real possibility exists here for investments in fixed capital and the consumption fund to become a speculative dumping ground for surplus money capital that has nowhere else to go. When I look at urbanization in these times, particularly in the Gulf States and China, that possibility looks all too plausible.

Investment in urbanization and physical infrastructure of all kinds is rife with examples of surplus capital being disposed of or devalued in wasteful ways. Unproductive consumption is everywhere in evidence (not least in the field of military expenditures). Surplus circulating capital in the production of, say, cement and steel can be profitably mopped up by long-term investments in the built environment, even if those investments earn nothing in the long run. In that case, the most important thing is maintaining the profitability of production activity in circulating capital (the production of steel and cement), even if the long-term investment in fixed capital does not pay off. The fall in the rate of profit may also be offset by the "omission of existing deductions from profit" such as lowering taxes or reducing ground rents. State-owned enterprises in China may survive by way of state support even in the face of serious losses.

But most important of all, in my view, is the delay attributable to the "creation of new branches of production in which more direct labour in relation to capital is needed, or where the productive power of labour is not yet developed" (751). Marx pays scant attention to these last two items and, in the presentation of the falling rate and rising mass of profit in *Capital*, he omits them entirely. In this, I think he was severely mistaken. Consider some examples. The typical working-class household in Marx's time was very poorly equipped with consumer durables. At the very most, it would entail a kitchen range (wood-, coal- or charcoal-fired) for cooking, a few pots and pans, a table and some chairs, elementary eating and drinking equipment, some bedding and a roof over everyone's head. Lighting would be by oil lamp. These are the kinds of conditions that Dickens described in *Bleak House* as Inspector Bucket finds himself in the brickfields of Hertfordshire. Households of that sort can still of course be found in much of the developing world. But in high-income countries, the range of consumer durables found in all but the poorest households is huge by comparison. Stoves, refrigerators, dish washers, washing machines and driers, cooking equipment, coffee makers, vacuum cleaners, TV and radio, individualized laptops or tablets and mobile phones and for many families two cars per household with, quite possibly, home ownership (mortgage financed), and so on. Electricity and gas, piped water and adequate sewage disposal would be standard. All of this constitutes a huge and ever-growing market for surplus product.

When Marx took up the case of invention becoming a business, he did not foresee or notice how much innovation is oriented to the perpetual creation of new product lines and the creation of new wants, needs and desires, and even whole lifestyles (e.g., the suburban lifestyle in the United States). This has been so successful that final consumer demand appears to be the chief driver of the economy in the high-income economies. The governor of the San Francisco Federal Reserve Bank once commented that the United States typically gets out of crises by building houses and filling them with things. Consumer durables make the consumption fund a vital core of capital's transformation and expansion, responding not so much to the falling rate of profit (though in the early phases of a typical product development cycle, the labor process often tends to be labor-intensive) as to the rising mass of product output (which Marx briefly alluded to above). It is also very much affected by the falling rate of interest. Since 1980 the rates of interest in the most advanced countries have fallen systematically (in the US from 15 percent to less than 1 percent in 2020). But there have also been sectors of capitalist expansion that have evaded the scourge of machine technologies, automation and robotization and will perhaps remain immune to the applications of artificial intelligence. If Marx's definition of value production is anyone who gives over their labor to produce surplus-value for capital, then there is a massive and increasing labor force engaged in, for example, the hospitality, food preparation, care, entertainment, education and recreational industries, all of which are labor-intensive and increasingly organized by capital to be productive of profit (and surplus-value). We often exclude such sectors from consideration since they are usually classified as services as opposed to manufacturing (where value production is presumed to be primarily if not exclusively located). But if we follow Marx's definition, then a teacher employed by a capitalist enterprise is just as productive of surplus-value as a steelworker, and there is no difference in principle between an education or sausage factory (as Marx cogently put it). In this case, the conditions dictating a falling rate of profit are not met, while the problems that attach to an ever-increasing mass of profit become much more salient.

The falling rate of profit theory was a familiar refrain in classical political economy. Adam Smith attributed it to competition, and this leads Marx back into some further reflections on the role of competition more generally. "Competition can permanently depress the rate of profit in all branches of industry"—something Ricardo denied—but only, says Marx, if a fall in the rate of profit "is conceivable *prior to* competition and regardless of competition." This is so because "competition executes the inner laws of capital . . . but it does not invent them" (752). Ricardo, for his part, "flees from economics to seek refuge in organic chemistry" in seeking to explain the inevitable fall in the profit rate (754). As land became scarcer and productivity on the land suffered diminishing returns, his argument went, so land rents would increase and the price of foodstuffs would rise, necessitating an increase in wages such that profits for capital would be squeezed between rising rent on land and rising wages, down to zero. "The falling rate of profit hence corresponds, with him, to the nominal growth of wages and real growth of ground rent" (752). "Modern chemistry," Marx observes, has proven Ricardo's postulate of diminishing returns in agriculture false (754), and the post-Ricardians "have quietly let drop whatever is unpleasant to them in their master's principles, as has the newer economics generally." Not for the first or last time in the field of bourgeois economic theorizing, "to drop the problem is their general method of solving it." "The unpleasant contradictions, antagonisms within which classical economics moves, and which Ricardo emphasizes with scientific ruthlessness, are thus watered down into well-to-do harmonies" (754). Marx was particularly irritated by the work of the French economist Bastiat, who, like far too many Marxist economists of today, "overlooks the trifling circumstance that . . . while the profit rate on capital declines, the capital itself increases" (757). "It is clear, of course, that with large-scale production the total mass of labour employed can increase although the proportion of labour employed relative to capital decreases, and that there is no obstacle, therefore, which prevents an increasing working population from requiring a greater mass of products as capital increases" (757). This last point is significant, since it counters the far too facile thesis that falling wages in response to a falling rate of profit automatically produce a declining effective demand. Against all of this, Marx proudly sustains his version of the theory as internal to the logic of capital rather than exogenously imposed (e.g., in the case of Ricardo, by natural constraints), while using it as a key feature in his inquiry into the more general laws of motion of capital. But he also does respectfully note, in passing, the reservations of Wakefield as to a potential limitation on profit due to problems of realization in the market. The limitations of final consumer demand or of new opportunities for investment (productive consumption) will at some point likely play a role, although Marx does not follow up by showing how or at what point the increasing effective demand deriving from an increasing mass of labor employed, albeit at lower wages, fails to match the rising mass of product.

Ricardo had earlier correctly recognized, contra Bastiat, that "the sum of profit grows as capital grows despite the decline of the rate of profit" (756). Marx on this basis takes the opportunity to reiterate his argument of a rising mass in the face of a falling rate. He works through a variety of Ricardo's numerical examples to show how a total capital starting at 100,000 would continue to grow annually as the rate of profit fell from 20 percent to 17 percent. While there are limits to how long this might go on, the effect is sufficiently powerful for Marx to later insist upon the formulation of a declining rate and rising mass of profit as his version of the key law of motion. He uses this perspective to attack Bastiat, who was deeply exercised by the question of where the market might be to absorb this rising mass when wages and profit were falling.

On page 758 Marx decides to redirect our attention by going "back to our topic," which is that "the product of capital . . . is profit." Marx's objective in the following pages is to probe into the relationship between the realm of appearances and underlying realities, to show how the understandable capitalist concern with profit disguises the origin of that profit in the "free" appropriation of alienated surplus labor by capital. He summarizes this point later on page 767. "The transformation of surplus value into the form of profit, this method by which capital calculates surplus value, is necessary from the standpoint of capital, regardless of how much it rests on an illusion about the nature of surplus value, or rather veils this nature." This names the point where appearance and reality both clash and inform each other.

"By relating to itself as profit, it relates to itself as the *source of the production of value and the rate of profit expresses the proportion to which it has increased its own value*. But the capitalist is not merely capital. He has to live, and since he does not live by working, he must live from profit" (758). For the capitalist this implies that capital is, for him, "a source of wealth," while capital "relates to profit as *revenue*," part of which can be consumed by the capitalist before the rest of it is reconverted into money capital, thus initiating surplus-value production anew. "Thus profit appears as a *form of distribution*, like wages." At the same time profit is "a *form of production for capital*; just exactly as wages are a mere *relation of production* from the standpoint of capital, a relation of distribution from the worker's standpoint." There are echoes here of the formulation of the relations between production, consumption and distribution as laid out in the introduction to the *Grundrisse*. And it leads to a repeat of the criticism of the "fatuous" views of John Stuart Mill, who considers "the bourgeois relations of production as eternal, but their forms of distribution as historical, and thereby shows that he understands neither the one nor the other" (758–9). Sismondi, however, got it right. From the standpoint of exchange, "capital's profit and revenue are impossible." Only alien labor can resolve the contradiction. It is alien labor that "yields an annual fruit which may be *destroyed* each year without the rich man thereby becoming poorer. This fruit is the revenue springing from capital." Marx goes on to comment that "while profit thus appears in one respect as the result of capital, it appears in the other as the *presupposition of capital formation.*" Or, as Sismondi puts it, "thus a part of the revenue became transformed into capital, into a permanent, self-multiplying value, which did not perish; this value tore itself free from the commodity that created it . . . like a metaphysical, insubstantial quality" (759). It is possible for some investors to become passive investors, just drawing upon their revenues. This has the effect of further promoting growth, as investors demand a rate of return on interest-bearing capital.

On the next page, Marx starts to negotiate some of the theoretical quicksands that bedevil his own formulations. "*When capital is posited as profit-creating, as a source of wealth independently of labour, each part of the capital is thereby assumed to be equally productive.*" Each component earns its rate of return. "Since the profit of capital is realized only in the price which is paid for it," then "profit is determined by the *excess of the price obtained over the price which covers outlays.*" Since this is plainly a market transaction, an "individual capital's *profit is not necessarily restricted by its surplus value.*" This raises the thorny question of the fraught relationship between money prices and values. In the marketplace a commodity can trade above or below its value. Money profit can therefore be more or less than surplus value. This does not, in Marx's view, add anything to the total value since one person's gain is another person's loss. "The total surplus-value, as well as the *total profit,* which is only *surplus value itself, computed differently,* can neither grow nor decrease through this operation, ever." The principle of an equivalence between total profit and total surplus-value will be carried over to *Capital* and remain an important feature of Marx's theorizing throughout. He will later formulate this rule in class terms (767). "The *profit of the capitalist class,* concretely expressed, *can never be greater than the sum of the surplus value.*" What is modified, of course, is "*its distribution among the different capitals*" (760–1). But another problem arises "through the separation of interest from profit" in which "a part of the surplus value is posited as production cost even for productive capital itself." The result is "a mass of confusion" that makes it seem as if capital has "some magic power which makes something out of nothing" (761). When we get interest on a bank deposit it seems as if it grew like magic. We certainly did not work for it. While this investigation began with the proposition that "the product of capital is profit," it ends with the proposition that "profit is the source of capital." The inversion is produced thanks to the coercive laws of competition. "So as to impose the inherent laws of capital upon it as external necessity, competition seemingly turns all of them over. *Inverts them*" (761).

"To repeat once more: the profit of capital does not depend on its magnitude; but rather, given an equal magnitude, on the relation between its component parts (the constant and the variable part)." This idea will be taken up by Marx in *Capital* by way of the concept of the organic or value composition of capital and its relation to profit. But here he goes on to invoke "the productivity of labour . . . the turnover time, which is determined by the different proportions of fixed and circulating capital, different durability of fixed capital, etc." He is already aware of how "the inequality of profit in different branches of industry with capitals of equal magnitudes is the condition and presupposition for their equalization through competition." In other words, Marx is already aware of the way in which, under conditions of free-market competition, the equalization of the rate of profit redistributes surplus-value from one production entity (firms, sectors or nations) to another, depending upon the different value compositions (761).

Labor-intensive entities (firms, sectors or nations) in competition transfer value to capital-intensive entities through free-market exchange. Thus, through free-market competition, Bangladesh and China currently subsidize the United States, and Greece subsidizes Germany. The Chinese, possibly recognizing this, are planning a transition to a capital-intensive economy in the coming years—a future which the United States is desperately seeking to forestall. It is a disconcerting historical fact that the pressures to forge an international free market, with its supposed benefits for all, has usually come from the more capital-intensive economies (like Britain in the late nineteenth century and the US in the late twentieth century) and from corporations. The thesis that Marx is exposing here helps understand why that might be so. The Manchester capitalists in Marx's time fostered the Manchester School of economics, which promoted the universal benefits of the free-trade regime that so benefited them.

This also helps us understand a peculiar recent feature of capitalist economic development. In recent years there has been an enormous growth in the hospitality industry, of tourism, restaurant-going and in the marketing of spectacle (everything from large sports and cultural events to the advent of the "Netflix economy"). In all of these areas, final consumption time is close to zero (which parallels Marx's argument that for capital to flourish, circulation time [as dictated by consumption time] should ideally be as close to zero as possible). This sector trades on the monetization and capitalization of ephemeral experiences. Tourism, for example, grew rapidly as an industry after the crisis of 2007–8. The number of international tourist trips increased from something like 800 million in 2009 to 1.4 billion by 2019. Tourism as an industry is typically labor-intensive and therefore offers abundant opportunities for producing and capturing surplus-value. This form of economy facilitates value transfers to the capital-intensive countries, sectors and firms through the equalization of profit rates at the same time that it helps to offset the tendency for the profit rate to decline by fostering labor intensity. The expanding economics of international tourism (e.g., cruise liners) described earlier fits neatly into this requirement.

Marx then returns to restate his main argument. After conceding that under the value theoretic formulation the rate of profit will always be lower than the rate of surplus-value and that "the rate of profit never expresses the real rate at which capital exploits labour" (762). Marx goes on to reassert that the profit rate is "inversely related to the growth of the relative surplus value or of relative surplus labour, to the development of the powers of production, and to the magnitude of capital employed as [constant] capital within production." In other words, it is subject to the *"tendency of the profit rate to decline"* (763). In this, the "action of fixed capital and of raw material and of scientific power" cannot be ignored (764). Marx then feels impelled once more to reiterate the importance of the growing mass. "It is clear, further, that although the part of capital exchanged for living labour declines in relation to the total capital, the total mass of living labour employed can increase or remain the same if capital grows in the same or a larger relation. Hence a constant growth in the population may accompany a relative decline in necessary labour."

This helps understand some of the strange contradictions evident within the global economy. All that we have theorized regarding rising labor productivity and the decline in necessary labor readily helps explain the fact that the share of wages in GDP in almost all of the G20 economies (including China) has fallen steadily since 1980 or so. It has in many countries been cut in half. But over the same period, the global wage labor force has grown from 2 billion (in 1980) to 3 billion (in 2020). This fits neatly with the theoretical proposition of an increasing population and wage labor force subjected to a rising rate of exploitation that can only betoken a huge concentration and centralization of capital in fewer and fewer hands. All of this is going on in the midst of the sharpening tendency for the rate of profit to fall.

Marx reflects briefly on certain "other causes" that might affect the rate of profit. He comes back first to the durability of fixed capital (765). The value incorporated in the fixed capital has nothing to do with its inherent productive force and utility for circulating capital. In fact, certain productive forces can be had for free, such as some kinds of machinery, new divisions of labor, the reorganization of production processes (such as just-in-time systems) and new applications of scientific knowledge. Furthermore, "the growth of population . . . and all the social powers associated with the growth of population and with the historic development of society cost it nothing" (765). Capital happily appropriates all of these "free gifts" of nature and of human nature.

But fixed capital has to be purchased. Its employment "would be a nuisance" if it required more labor for its production and maintenance than it was worth. It follows that "fixed capital is employed only to the extent that its value is smaller than the value it posits" (i.e., the labor it saves) (766). This is a vital limitation to the deployment of fixed capital. The viability of the fixed capital is contingent upon the durability and efficiency of the fixed capital in relation to circulating capital. In *Capital*, Marx notes that much of the new machinery being invented in Britain was not deployed in Britain because labor was so cheap that it was not worthwhile. But in the United States, where labor was scarcer and more expensive, the new machinery was seized upon with alacrity. In China, where labor has been extraordinarily cheap, there was a phase during the 1990s of reengineering the capital-intensive labor processes imported from North America to replace the import of the expensive machinery required with extremely cheap human labor. In recent years, however, this practice of reverse engineering has largely disappeared in China as labor power has become scarcer and more expensive.

There are thus clear limits to the deployment of machine technologies. They only make sense when the cost of the machine is less than the labor saved by using it. When labor power is cheap, mechanization makes little economic sense. When labor becomes scarcer or more militant, machine technologies become more attractive. Furthermore, machine technologies make the most sense in relation to mass production and mass consumption. When invention becomes a business, the cost of machines declines and their field of application can be adapted to niche production and niche markets. It becomes more economically rational to deploy them everywhere. This has an impact on labor productivity and the rate of profit in general.

The issues that Marx is raising here make some sort of sense when projected into the actual history of production in different sectors. Take, for example, the auto industry. This is a very obvious case, in which mass organization (the assembly line) and, later on, robotization and automation of production rested heavily on fixed capital, along with the deployment of science and technology. Rapid periodic shifts in the productivity of labor, the last version of which (post-2000) cut employment dramatically while sustaining output, would make this a classic version of what Marx is talking about. This was all predicated, however, on the organization of society for mass consumption and physical infrastructure to accommodate the use of automobiles. But there are many fields of activity where this does not make much sense. So there is a limitation to the application of fixed capital, backed by science and technology, without the potentiality for mass consumption. Marx does not take up this problem. The automobile industry is a paradigmatic case of industrial mass production predicated on mass consumption. This is an industrial sector in which all of the features that Marx described are in place with respect to increasing labor productivity and a tendency for the profit rates to fall. But this tendency is offset in this sector by the value transfers from labor-intensive sectors achieved through the equalization of the rate of profit under conditions of free-market exchange.

The viability of the fixed capital is also contingently related to the profitability of circulating capital. For example, if someone builds a new airport, then the presumption is that flights will go there and circulating capital will generate enough traffic to redeem the value of the fixed capital investment. Circulating capital is no longer free to circulate wherever it wants. It has a "duty" to validate fixed capital investments. Otherwise, the fixed capital value is lost. During the halcyon days of the property boom in Spain after 2000, a new city—Ciudad Real—was built to the south of Madrid, replete with a huge new airport costing some 2 or 3 billion euros. It was built based on the fantasy that a significant overflow from the congested airport in Madrid would materialize, and that this along with local traffic and a potential transit point for a growing tourist trade would assure enough use. None of this came to pass. And then came the crash of 2007–8, which hit Spain, and its property sector in particular, very hard. The initiating company went bankrupt, and the airport was put up for auction. A Chinese company bid something like 50,000 euros. The bid was refused. The airport was finally bought out by a private investor for an undisclosed but presumably trivial sum, but it has never attracted commercial passenger flights. The airport finally found a use by offering storage space for all the planes that were put out of service during the Covid-19 pandemic.

In this case, the value of the fixed capital was lost because circulating capital was not mobilized to service the debt requirements. But it is also important to recall that fixed capital originates with circulating capital. The construction companies, developers and raw material suppliers in the field of circulating capital made lots of money and surplus-value (profit) out of their contracts to construct the airport, even though it ultimately went bankrupt. The aggregate circulation of the mass of capital was less affected by the bankruptcy of the airport than would otherwise have been the case.

Surprisingly, and rather late in the day, Marx devotes a couple of pages to elaborating the key concepts of absolute and relative surplus-value. The first "appears determined by the absolute lengthening of the working day above and beyond necessary labour time" (768). The second "appears as the development of the workers' productive power, *as the reduction of the necessary labour time relative to the working day, and as the reduction of the necessary labouring population relative to the population*." He quite casually notes the stunning judgment that with the advent of relative surplus-value "there directly appears the industrial and distinguishing historic character of the mode of production founded on capital" (769). Furthermore, he continues, "the tendency of capital is, of course, to link up absolute with relative surplus value; hence [the] *greatest stretching of the working day with greatest number of simultaneous working days, together with reduction of necessary labour time to the minimum, on one side, and of the number of necessary workers to the minimum, on the other*" (770). This contradiction gives rise to different forms of overproduction, overpopulation and other disturbances. A necessary consequence "is the *greatest possible diversification of the use value of labour* . . . so that the production of capital constantly and necessarily creates, on one side, the *development of the intensity of the productive power of labour*, on the other side, the *unlimited diversity of the branches of labour* [and] thus the most universal wealth, in form and content, of production, bringing all sides of nature under its domination." To contemporary sensibilities, the idea of the domination of nature will doubtless be abhorrent in principle, even as it becomes a necessity with the need to eradicate smallpox and other viral infections. What is interesting here, however, is that "capital pays nothing for the increases of the productive force." It can all be organized under the free gifts not so much of nature as improvements that arise out of the reorganization of human labor. Increasing intensity or taking fragmentary work and reorganizing it communally are the sorts of things Marx has in mind (771). On the other hand, growth of population would appear to be a necessary condition but, again, this is something that capital does not have to pay for.

In the pages that follow, Marx examines all sorts of implications and combinations of the contradiction between absolute and relative surplus-value:

> Hence, although *the increase of productive power resting on division and combination of labour rests on absolute increase of the labour power employed, it is necessarily linked with a decrease of the latter, relative to the capital that sets it in motion.* And while, in the first form, the form of *absolute surplus labour, the mass of labour employed must grow in the same relation as the capital employed, in the second case it grows in a lesser relation,* and, more precisely, *in inverse relation to the growth of the force of production.* (774)

It is at this point also that Marx recognizes the importance of the value of capital, what in *Capital* he will define as the organic or value composition of capital. This is closely tied to the production of relative surplus-value, as the "increasing . . . *intensity, speed of labour*" requires "no greater advance in material or instrument of labour" (772). But at some point "the increased productivity of labour requires a greater outlay of capital for raw materials and instrument," while "the growth of the surplus value in all cases presupposes growth of the population" (773).

In exploring these relations, Marx notes a number of peculiarities. For example, given their capacity to increase productivity, it becomes imperative that the application of new technologies work sequentially, beginning with those sectors most closely associated with the supply of raw materials (the extractivist industries), because innovations further down the commodity chain will get blocked if an expansion in raw material production is not already underway. "Thus in spinning before in weaving, in weaving before in printing" (775). An issue of some importance that Marx does not make much of is that the pursuit of relative surplus-value (as opposed to absolute surplus-value) "allows *a larger non-labouring population relative to the labouring one*" (775). This nonlaboring population, as he earlier noted, may be employed as wage laborers against the circulation of revenues. They are simply not engaged in the production of value and surplus-value. The total wage labor force exceeds by far the wage labor force engaged in the production of surplus-value or profit.

For those who have read *Capital*, there is nothing particularly surprising in much of what is said in these few pages. But what is surprising is how casually and matter of factly Marx confidently presents these key concepts a decade before *Capital* was published. But there are some missing pieces in the puzzle of social relations under the contradictory conditions imposed by absolute and relative surplus-value. It is perhaps for this reason that Marx inserts, suddenly and without notice, a brief and controversial comment on the nature of value. This is a rare enough occurrence to be taken very seriously. We take this up in the next chapter.

12

Class and Political Economy
Pages 776–893

The concept of value has a shadowy but problematic presence in the *Grundrisse*. On page 776, Marx, out of the blue, inserts a passage that is remarkably clear, though only up to a point. Value is an immaterial abstraction that arises out of the circulation of money through exchange, but this monetary circulation, and the value form that emerges from it, are consolidated only when money circulates as capital. He will later remind us that capital is based on the class relation between alienated labor and alienated capital. Specific historical materialist conditions and practices "posit" (to use Marx's favorite word) the existence of value as an abstraction. Like gravity, you cannot see it or measure it directly, but its existence is clearly confirmed by its effects. Attention must be paid, therefore, to "the historic foundation" from which categories like value "are abstracted, and on whose basis alone they can appear." Marx's conclusion is unambiguous (again up to a point). "The economic concept of value does not occur in antiquity . . . The concept of value is entirely peculiar to the most modern economy, since it is the most abstract expression of capital itself and of the production resting on it. In the concept of value, its secret betrayed" (776).

Anyone who approaches the text that follows in anticipation that the secret will be revealed will be deeply disappointed. Instead, Marx assembles a mass of materials concerning historical situations along with enough diverse opinion from multiple commentators to fuel a dozen learned dissertations. He notes that "hundreds of volumes have been written in England" on the topic of money and the currency "in the past 150 years" (800). Judging from the excerpts in the text, Marx read many of them. This produces commentary like this:

> The doctrine of the determination of prices by the mass of the circulating medium, first advanced by Locke, repeated in the *Spectator*, 19 October 1711, developed and elegantly formulated by Hume and Montesquieu, its basis raised to a formal peak by Ricardo, and with all its absurdities in practical application to the banking system, by Loyd, Colonel Torrens etc. Steuart polemicizes against it, and his development materially antici-pates more or less everything later advanced by Bosanquet, Tooke, Wilson. (780)

It is hard for the uninitiated to keep pace with authorities cited, let alone pass judgment on the relevance of all of this.

Not having access to modern technologies, Marx spent hours in the British Museum copying out passages in his notebooks on the off-chance that they might provide raw materials for analysis sometime in the future. I sympathize, because that is what I did in the newspaper library of the British Museum for my own doctoral dissertation back in 1960. I threw out my voluminous notes only very recently. Most of them had turned out to be useless. Contemporary scholars have little idea of what that kind of research strategy is like. But from now on in the *Grundrisse*, we are presented with Marx's notes, very often without any commentary.

Marx regales us with all manner of information. Copper was, apparently, cheaper in Rome than in Greece and Asia in the seventh century, and the depreciation of the currency "most cruelly wors-ened the lot of the unfortunate plebeians, who had obtained the

depreciated copper as a loan," but then had to pay it back at a higher
rate, which turned out to be "a five times greater sum than they had
borrowed" (807). There is an eerie resemblance in this to the Third
World debt crisis of the 1980s, when countries that had borrowed
heavily when money was cheap in the mid-1970s found themselves
having to pay it back when money was expensive in the 1980s. When
these countries turned to the IMF for help, they found the Reagan
administration had purged all the sympathetic Keynesians in 1982
and replaced them with hard-nosed supply-siders who insisted on
structural adjustments that used austerity in social expenditures and
labor market "reforms" to favor capital not people. In the *Grundrisse*,
you can also read about the use of iron bars in exchange on the
Barbary Coast along with other "semi-civilized" efforts to "establish
an unchanging value for the unit of money" (797–8). Indebted
Venetian monks melted down their silver chalices to satisfy their
Jewish money lenders. Usurious lending fostered the consumption
and eventual downfall of feudal lords. The long-standing struggle
between Treasury Minister Lowndes versus John Locke in the 1690s
(when the Bank of England was founded) on how to handle the
depreciation of the currency takes up a few pages (802–5). Perhaps
more relevant was a model silk mill erected in Derby in 1719 by one
John Lombe on the basis of an Italian design "which contained
26,586 wheels, all turned by one water wheel." This mill, Marx
opines, "came nearer to the idea of a modern factory than any previous establishment" (784).

I suspect that Marx hoped, by all of this, to get some insight into
the "becoming" of capital and of value, while also making critical
use of the vast trove of analytical documents that practitioners and
economists had produced over the preceding 150 years. Marx
occasionally dialogues with specific authors such as Steuart,
Torrens, Sismondi, Say, and William Blake (the autodidact poet
who wrote tracts on political economy in the post-Ricardian tradition). Some segments are also given over to revisiting questions
earlier addressed—such as the fraught question of money (and, of
course, Proudhon) and of profit as the product of capital. In these

latter cases there is often not much that is substantively new added to what has already been said, though there are some clarifications and occasional nice turns of phrase that can be helpful in presenting Marx's ideas. But there are also some flashes of new insights and possible connections which point in new directions. I propose to concentrate on the new contributions, however sketchy, while skating over much of the rest.

Marx begins, however, with the comment that the expansion of surplus-value from the reduction of necessary labor costs capital nothing, whereas value has to be expended to buy the machinery that raises the productivity of labor. "It is easy to develop the introduction of machinery out of competition and out of the law of the reduction of production costs which is triggered by competition." His ambition, however, is to develop the imperative to raise labor productivity "out of the relation of capital to living labour, without reference to [competition from] other capitals" (776–7). This he manages to do with the help of a convoluted arithmetic argument in which the lengthier turnover time of fixed capital has an important role to play.

He then cites Steuart at some length (779). Marx had a lot of respect for Steuart, in part because Steuart did not have a rosy view of primitive accumulation but recognized its class character, the role of slavery, and its violence. Steuart also struggled to come up with adequate categories at a time when it was not at all clear as to how to respond to the question of where profit comes from. Steuart proposed "profit on alienation" (profit extracted from market exchange), which Marx accepted as an adequate way to think of a world in which the activities of merchant capital and artisanal production prevailed. Marx likewise does not criticize William Blake for highlighting the role of a motley class of otherwise parasitic consumers "whose power of demanding arises from seats, mortgages, annuities, professions and services of various descriptions" with the government taking up "the most prominent station." Considerations of this sort could understandably take pride of place "in countries where simplicity reigns" (780).

All of this drives Marx back to the question of monetary circulation in relation to the overall circulation of capital. The main point seems to be that capital drives beyond the rules of "simple" monetary circulation (of the sort that Steuart was dealing with). "Within circulation itself, the point of return may be different from the point of departure; in so far as it bends back into itself, money circulation appears as the mere appearance of a circulation going on behind it and determining it, e.g. when we look at the money circulation between manufacturer, worker, shopkeeper and banker" (790). Marx elaborates "money as the *measure* of value is not expressed in amounts of bullion, but rather in accounting money" with arbitrary names. "Money is a *measure* only because it is labour time materialized in a specific substance, hence itself *value*" (791). Since the purpose here is to compare values, the "confused notion of an *ideal measure*," which was developed by Steuart, among others, is rejected. Marx spends several pages debunking the idea of an ideal form of money. But he sustains the relation of money to labor time materialized in a specific substance.

Issues also arise around what Marx calls the "double standard" of trade between nations deploying different metallic bases and utilizing different monetary systems, linked together by exchange rates. There is, Marx insists, no "ideal monetary unit" or even "ideal money commodity" capable of representing value everywhere. This does not deny the role of exchange-value as an indicator, component or measure of value. But he shifts the emphasis from money, which is in essence a rather static conception, to currency, which is money perpetually in motion. For the most part, however, Marx simply goes over much of the ground he had covered at the beginning of the *Grundrisse*, dealing with the different monetary forms required to efficiently mirror the different monetary functions.

The circulation of money (the currency) re-emerges as the means to track value in motion, which is, after all, the definition of capital. After pages of citations and commentary, he arrives at the proposition "that prices regulate the quantity of currency and not the quantity of currency prices, or in other words that trade regulates currency (the quantity of the medium of circulation), and currency does not regulate trade." This is a conclusion that may have contemporary relevance. The massive increase in money issue and money circulation has, over the last forty years, had no serious effects on price levels. It has not produced the inflation in the core countries, as many predicted. If "price is only value translated into another language," and if "value . . . [is] determined by labour time," then the price level is set by forces other than the quantity of money in circulation (814). But it is then also important to remember that "the determination of value by pure labour time takes place only on the foundation of the production of capital, hence the separation of the two classes" (817). The question of class analysis and the class relation briefly re-emerges. The production of capital and value cannot be analyzed independently of the relation between alienated labor and alienated capital.

Marx then alerts us to a methodological point of general application. "All of these fixed suppositions themselves become fluid in the further course of development. But only by holding them fast at the beginning is their development possible without confounding everything" (817). This is, in fact, one of the most troubling and potentially misleading barriers to a proper understanding of where Marx is at and, even more importantly, where he might be headed in his writings. For purposes of analysis, he will hold much that is fluid and in motion as fixed.

He immediately offers an opinion as to what he might hold fast. "Since equivalence is determined by the equality of labour time or of the amount of labour, the difference of value is of course determined by the inequality of labour time, or, labour time is the measure of value" (818). But "it is practically sure", he then adds, that "the standard of necessary labour may differ at various epochs and in various countries . . . In consequence of the demand and supply of labour, its amount and ratio may change." For purposes of analysis, he presumes, however, that necessary labor is fixed, even though it plainly is not (817). This is also the tactic he deploys in *Capital*. The theoretical as well as the practical consequences of rendering the value of labor power (or any other key magnitude) as changeable, fluid and uncertain, could be substantial. The assumption that value is singular and universal in its most advanced and competed form is not necessarily warranted. If the different and diverse currencies are all representations of value, why can there not be different value regimes?

This prompts a return to the relationship between machinery and surplus labor and the question of fixed versus circulating capital. Machines will be employed only if they cost less than the labor power saved through their use. "The introduction of machinery can take place only if the rate of surplus labour time does not merely remain the same, i.e. grow relative to the living labour employed, but if it grows at a greater rate than the relation between the value of the machinery and the value of the dismissed workers" (820–1).

But Marx reminds us once more that "the product proper of capital is profit. To that extent, it is now posited as the source of wealth. But in so far as it creates use values, it produces use values, but *use values determined by value*." This is, of course, a critical point because much needed social use-values will not be produced unless they are profitable and value-creating. For Marx, however, the important point is that the permanent demand for certain use-values for consumption provides an important field for profitable activity (822). But the flow of value has to be disaggregated into fixed and circulating capital. The limitation on the deployment of the former affects how "capital will be posited as profit-bearing in a different form" (823). This prompts a reminder that "under the rule of capital, the application of machinery does not shorten labour; but rather prolongs it. What it abbreviates is necessary labour, not the labour necessary for the capitalist. Since fixed capital becomes devalued to the extent that it is not used in production, its growth is linked with the tendency to make labour *perpetual*" (825). The necessary continuity of flow of circulating capital is achieved by the deployment of efficient "just-in-time" production and procurement systems (versions of which could be found even in Marx's time).

The development of industrial capital under such conditions cannot but result in an increasing alienation of labor. "One of the moments of social activity—objective labour—becomes the ever more powerful body of the other moment, of subjective, living labour." But from the standpoint of capital, "the objective conditions of labour assume an ever more colossal independence, represented by its very extent, opposite living labour." Consequently, "social wealth confronts labour in more powerful portions as an alien and dominant power. The emphasis comes to be placed not on the state of being *objectified*, but on the state of being *alienated*, dispossessed, sold." The problem is that "the monstrous objective power which social labour itself erected opposite itself as one of its moments belongs not to the worker, but to . . . capital" (831). Furthermore, this objectification "appears as a process of dispossession from the standpoint of labour or as appropriation of alien labour from the standpoint of capital." This appropriation is real, not merely supposed and imagined in the minds of both capitalists and laborers. This is the condition that cries out to be suspended and to vanish. "The propertylessness" of the worker and "the appropriation of alien labour by capital . . . are fundamental conditions of the bourgeois mode of production, in no way accidents irrelevant to it . . . These modes of distribution are the relations of production themselves," rendering inane John Stuart Mill's insistence that the laws of production are fixed by nature but that distribution is a matter for history. "The 'laws and conditions' of the production of wealth and the laws of the 'distribution of wealth' are the same laws under different forms, and both change, undergo the same historic process" (832).

While capital uses machines in ways not to labor's advantage, "it is just as easy to perceive that machines will not cease to be agencies of social production when they become e.g. property of the associated workers" (833). Such a "changed distribution would start from a *changed* foundation of production, a new foundation first created by the process of history." This does not imply that capitalist technologies can be taken over lock, stock and barrel and used for socialist purposes. But it does suggest that there is no inherent barrier to their adaptation and future use by emancipated labor operating on a changed foundation. The rising productivity of labor is something to be taken advantage of and not decried.

After citing many excerpts from contemporary commentaries on topics such as colonialism, storage costs, credit, and media of exchange, Marx converges upon "the marvellous inventions of Dr Price, which leaves the fantasies of the alchemists far behind." Price had discovered the power of compound interest and growth. He wrote:

> Money bearing compound interest increases at first slowly. But, the rate of interest being continually accelerated, it becomes in some time so rapid, as to mock all the powers of the imagination. One penny, put out at our Saviour's birth to 5% compound interest, would before this time (1772), have increased to a greater sum than would be obtained in a 150 millions of Earths, all solid gold. But if put out to simple interest, it would, at the same time, have amounted to no more than 7 shillings 4½ d. (842)

This "discovery" of the powers of exponential growth had a powerful influence over late-eighteenth-century thought. It was critical, for example, to Malthus's theory of overpopulation, and it led William Pitt to propose a sinking fund that would use the power of compounding to retire the whole of the national debt within a certain number of years. It also led Peter Thelusson, a wealthy Swiss banker living in London, to set up a trust fund of £600,000 to be invested at 7.5 percent compound interest when he died (in 1797), with the stipulation it not be touched for 100 years. His immediate heirs were not amused. Nor was the government, since even at 4 percent the fund would have exceeded the national debt after 100 years. The government responded with a law to limit trusts to thirty years. The immediate heirs sued, but the case was so convoluted that it was not decided until 1859, when it was discovered that all the moneys had been used up in lawyer's fees. This formed the basis for the celebrated case of *Jarndyce v. Jarndyce*, which is the backdrop to the narrative in Dickens's masterpiece *Bleak House*. As Dickens describes it, the day the case was decided—only to find the cupboard was bare—was a moment of great hilarity in the High Court of Chancery. But Price's calculation is important. Capital has grown at the compound rate of between 2 and 3 percent annually since its inception, which was no problem in Marx's time, when it was on the slowly increasing part of the exponential growth curve. But it is now in its accelerating phase, which poses a clear and present danger on all manner of fronts. Marx thought the whole idea of compound growth forever was ridiculous. Price had no idea where the interest might come from (e.g., the surplus-value that is its ultimate source). But Marx does highlight capital's internal necessity for endless growth, which implies compound growth for ever. Getting out of the clutch of the exponentials spells the end of capitalism as we know it. The belief that growth is good, inevitable and desirable at all costs is widely accepted, even at the popular level. The necessity of compounding growth is today one of the most serious yet totally ignored contradictions of contemporary capital.

It is interesting to read through some of the snippets of commentary that Marx assembles, if only to appreciate how far contemporary opinion had come in developing critical perspectives on the capitalist mode of production. Here, for example, is an economist called Fullarton, writing in 1844:

A periodical destruction of capital has become a necessary condition of any market rate of interest at all, and, considered in that point of view, these awful visitations to which we are accustomed to look forward with so much disquiet and apprehension and which we are so anxious to avert, may be nothing more than the natural and necessary corrective to an overgrown and bloated opulence, the *vis medicatrix* by which our social system, as at present constituted, is enabled to relieve itself from time to time of an ever-recurring plethora which menaces its existence. (849–50)

This is immediately followed by a brief discussion of "the division of profit into interest and profit." The question of interest has already cropped up at various points in the *Grundrisse* in relation, for example, to problems of smoothing out the money flows associated with differential turnover times and even more explicitly in relation to the circulation of fixed capital. This division of profit into interest and profit "becomes perceptible, tangible as soon as a class of monied capitalists comes to confront a class of industrial capitalists. *Secondly: Capital* itself becomes a commodity" which has a price determined by supply and demand, which fixes the rate of interest. It is in this form that "capital as such enters into circulation." The circulation of interest-bearing capital thus joins the other forms of circulation within the totality (851).

"Monied capitalists and industrial capitalists can form two particular classes only because profit is capable of separating off into two branches of revenue. The two kinds of capitalists only express this fact; but the split has to be there, the separation of profit into two particular forms of revenue, for two particular classes of capitalist to be able to grow up on it" (851). "The form of interest is older than that of profit," but as is the case with many other political-economic categories that Marx deploys, the positioning changes with the rise to dominance of the capitalist mode of production. Profit "originally appears determined by interest. But in the bourgeois economy interest determined by profit" (852). This presumes that the gross profit "must be large enough to allow of a part of it branching off as interest." The relation between profit and interest depends on competition, but this depends also on class configuration. "The real difference between profit and interest exists as the difference between a moneyed class of capitalists and an industrial class of capitalists. But in order that two such classes may come to confront one another, their double existence presupposes a divergence within the surplus value posited by capital." This division is not a feudal residue. It is, rather, a consequence of the expansion and evolutionary trajectory of capital in itself. It is important to state that "both interest and profit express relations of *capital*" (853). But "interest-bearing capital stands opposite, not labour, but rather opposite profit-bearing capital." This is a statement of the utmost importance. The possibility of active struggle between industrial and banking/finance capitals to the exclusion (and possibly the detriment) of the working class then exists. For many years now, the relations between British manufacturing and the bankers in the City of London have been antagonistic rather than mutually supportive, as political power has typically supported the latter rather than the former with highly negative consequences for industrial employment. In pursuing the matter further, Marx also contemplates lending for purposes of consumption. In Marx's time, this meant either accommodating the needs of merchant capitalists or lending capital to the wealthy for purposes of final consumption (854). In our own day, of course, the ubiquitous use of credit cards would make this a topic of major significance.

After subsequent commentary on the role of merchant capital, Marx likewise suggests that "in the preliminary stages of bourgeois society, trade dominates industry; in modern society the opposite" (858). "Capital arises only where trade has seized possession of production itself, and where the merchant becomes producer, or the producer mere merchant" (859). While the significance and role of merchant wealth is acknowledged, Marx thereafter proceeds mainly to cite a host of economists.

There is more than a hint of a suggestion here of how Marx proposed to approach the question of class formation within a capitalist mode of production. Classes are not invented in heaven or even in the minds of humans out of nothing. They do not descend from the heavens even though in past times it was fashionable if not mandatory to suggest that God's will was involved in designating this or that group as a ruling class. But for Marx, the class structure of capitalism crystallizes out of a flow of socio-economic practices that become widespread and repeated often enough to support a specialty within the overall division of labor in the production and circulation of surplus-value. The handling of money in this instance connects with the uses of money capital, and certain individuals specialize in how to handle, concentrate and manage it. If there are enough individuals of this sort, then at some point this will define a set of interests and practices which will ultimately justify the designation of a class. In the *Grundrisse*, it seems that Marx has decided that money capitalists have evolved to the point where they are worthy of being considered a class. This is in addition, presumably, to his argument elsewhere to the effect that the basic class structure of capitalism is constituted by workers, capitalists and landlords. I am not making a determination here as to whether this designation of the money capitalists as a class is consistent with his other writings, but I think it is interesting to consider how he typically approaches such questions. It is worth noting in this regard that Marx switches his attention to the whole history of money dealing and money management. In the *Grundrisse*, these statements on the class character of the bankers and financiers in relation to industrial capital are followed by brief consideration of the historical and contemporary role of merchant capitalists, but in this instance he does not care to designate the merchants as a class. It was almost as if he felt the need to get the history in his historical materialism right to better understand processes of class formation during the rise to dominance of a capitalist mode of production. In the case of merchants, their historical role is undoubted, but Marx considered their role in a mature capitalist mode of production to be collaborative and not oppositional to industrial capital. There is nothing analogous to the distinction between interest and profit, or, as in the case of landowners, ground rent, to warrant the designation of the merchants as a distinctive class. The "profit upon alienation" that Steuart proposed and Marx accepted as a transitional category, might be revived. In the *Grundrisse*, he contemplates but rejects depicting the merchants as a distinct class, "While the action of commerce concentrates the movements of circulation, hence money as merchant wealth in one respect the first existence of capital . . . this form appears on the other side as directly contradictory to the *concept of value*. To buy cheap and sell dear is the law of trade. *Hence not the exchange of equivalents, with which trade, rather, would be impossible as a particular way of gaining wealth*"

(856). The fact that money exists "as trading wealth" reflects its role as "a mediating movement between two extremes, which it does not dominate, and presuppositions which it does not create" (857). I doubt Marx would take this position today, given the extraordinary contemporary monopsony power of the merchant capitalists (including Apple, Ikea, Walmart, Nike and other brand names, particularly in the clothing industry but also in agriculture) in relation to industrial capital. The case for the identification of a distinctive merchant capitalist class living by means of "profit upon alienation" would be much stronger in our own times. To the degree that class is a fluid category, I doubt Marx would have objected to such a modification. The exercise of monopsony power in relation to the direct producers (with clear downward pressure on wage rates) with the objective of supplying cheap consumer products to a mass market is a clear enough process in our times to warrant specific treatment in class, or at the very least "class faction," terms.

The final pages of our version of the *Grundrisse* are taken up with a brief and clearly very incomplete commentary on value and specific critical engagement with the French economist Frédéric Bastiat (a militant advocate for laissez-faire) and the American Henry Carey (a militant advocate for Hamiltonian infant industry protectionism). All three snippets of commentary were apparently meant to be "brought forward" into a revised introduction. The excerpt on value merely covers the distinction between the use-value and exchange-value of commodities but does not mention value at all. The materials on Bastiat and Carey are of greater interest, in part because Marx clearly sees their differing takes on economic theory as materially grounded in the radically different class and state configurations of the United States and France. Marx begins, however, by noting the antithesis between the Englishman Ricardo (a proponent of Say's law, free trader and influenced by the Manchester industrialists) and the Frenchman Sismondi (a critic of Say's law and proponent—along with Malthus—of a "general glut" theory that rested on the inherent tendency toward overaccumulation). Bastiat, living in a world of all kinds of barriers to trade (tolls on roads, licenses and state regulatory interventions) naturally supported laissez-faire economics, whereas Carey, writing in a situation where US industrial capital was crimped by the overwhelming power of British industry in competition, would naturally seek to protect infant industries from ruinous competition.

This immediately raises, for us, the question of the materialist grounding of Marx's critique. Marx was fully aware that his material base lay with British industrialism, in which the world, he averred, could see the image of its own capitalist future. But it was the Manchester version of British industrialism to which he appealed (helped, of course, by Engels's deep knowledge of it). Had Engels's family factory been in Birmingham, with its Marshallian form of decentralized small-scale industrial organization, contrasting with the dark satanic mills of Manchester, Marx's theory of capital might have read rather differently. A prominent conservative business leader, "Radical Joe" Chamberlain became a reformist mayor of Birmingham and introduced public education and other measures to improve the life of the workers from the 1860s on. He was the leading figure in what became known toward the end of the nineteenth century as "gas and water municipal socialism" (or "sewer socialism" in the US). Marx was either unaware of or uninterested in the characteristics of industrial structure in Birmingham and made short shrift of the impacts of local bourgeois reformism on the part of the manufacturers, even though he clearly supported state regulation of the length of the working day and the provisions in the factory acts oriented to worker education, which presumably inspired Chamberlain.

The geography of the production of Marxist knowledge is in itself a topic worthy of study. I am only too aware that the qualities of my own thinking and working have been profoundly affected by my lived experience in the United States and Britain, lightly modified by some experience in Latin America and Europe and illuminated by flashes of insight (or more properly, startling questions) emanating from visits to East Asia, and China in particular.

13

Concluding Thoughts

In his pioneering book on the *Grundrisse*, called *The Making of Marx's Capital*, Roman Rosdolsky observes that, when he first encountered this virtually unknown text in the 1950s, "it was clear from the outset that this was a work which was of fundamental importance for Marxist theory. However, its unusual form and to some extent its obscure manner of expression, made it far from suitable for reaching a wide circle of readers." I wholeheartedly concur. The *Grundrisse*, from the moment that I first tried to read it in English translation in 1973, confused me at the same time as it changed my whole perspective on Marx's approach to political economy. It continues to do so until this day.

Whenever I have tried to teach the *Grundrisse*, I have invariably found myself coming up with a different angle from which to examine it. This is, for the most part, a testimony to the richness of Marx's theoretical imagination, his dedication to the *historical* in his historical materialism and the intensity and depth of his writing, although my own changing interests and the shifting global context has also had something to do with it.

This time around, I have been mightily impressed with how the concept of capital as an ecosystemic and constantly expanding organic whole or totality, constituted by different circulation processes, all with their distinctive moments, provides a convincing and insightful framework to comprehend what capital is all about. The operative word here is "totality." Reading about and constructing a theory of the political economy of capital from the perspective of capital as an evolving totality is enormously rewarding. But, as I noted in my introduction, this perspective is strangely ignored in the commentaries on this text that I have come across.

Among the various circulation processes at work within the totality, that of the circulation of labor capacity takes, in my view, a certain pride of place (Figure 1). The very idea of the daily life of a working person, embedded in what Marx calls the "small-scale" circulation of labor capacity, is both revealing theoretically and politically instructive. The worker is exposed to radically different material experiences in the course of the circulation process; as seller of labor capacity (in a competitive labor market); as participant in a labor process (designed and commanded by capital); as recipient of a wage (which confers the discretionary freedom that goes with money power); as buyer of commodities in the market (both necessities in order to live and discretionary goods); and, finally, as participant in and product of the multiple forms of social reproduction (including socialized provision) in the daily life of a household (however defined) in a physical neighborhood. Diverse experiences across the different moments of this circulation process tend to generate different political subjectivities. If the identity of working persons as workers is, as Marx puts it, "extinguished" (420) when they are purchasing commodities in the market and they all assume the identity of buyers, how can class consciousness be articulated, let alone sustained, across all the moments within this circulation process? The different political subjectivities that attach to the different moments disguise the overall class character of the capitalist mode of production. It is only from the perspective of capital's totality that this class character becomes clearly visible.

In practice, working persons typically relate differently to the different experiential worlds they encounter. The account earlier set out bears repeating. Some workers might succumb to the temptation of a compensatory consumerism, in which they are offered access to a cornucopia of cheap consumer goods as compensation for horrific alienation at the point of production. Others may reluctantly consent to the alienation of their labor and general exploitation in the hope that they may be able to put sufficient money by to someday open a bodega or a coffee shop. Yet others may consent to everything in this circulation process, provided they have time and money enough to create for themselves a meaningful family or household life. Taking the kids to little league soccer games or music classes or just romping with them in the backyard may afford enough pride and pleasure to mask the miserable alienating experience of working for capital and going to the shopping mall. The creation of a solidary and amicable neighborhood life has been, for many working-class populations, a compensatory though not unproblematic joy that makes class struggles against capital in production seem a remote and even unnecessary engagement. Many of the active struggles we are now witnessing are over such matters as exploitation in the market (protests against monopoly power and price gouging of pharmaceutical products or housing rents, for example); the perversions of the credit and mortgage debt system; the qualities of social provision in the state sector, the qualities of daily life, etc. Workplace struggles against capital are just one form of many social struggles and by no means always the most immediately important, eye-catching or feasible. The deterioration of the qualities of neighborhood life and stresses within families, or household reproduction units, much of which can be traced back to deindustrialization, unemployment and the political turn to neoliberalism, now lies at the root of much of the political malaise experienced by many working people. The production of a vibrant and satisfying daily life is, for many working persons, just as important as holding a satisfying and well-remunerated job. The ideal, of course, is to achieve both, but such a privileged affluent worker is harder to find in these neoliberal times. Some professional positions are, however, sufficiently well-remunerated to allow for such a life.

Like all the other circulation processes at work within the totality, we have to recognize the contextual forces that affect the circulation of labor capacity. While the social reproduction "moment"
has a narrow definition in its direct role in capital accumulation,
all manner of contextual conditions, many of which are produced
by capital, affect everyday life in the household and in the residential neighborhood. Environmental pollution and degradation,
much of it due to capital treating the environment as an externality
for which capitalists are not responsible, have unequal impacts on
health, life expectancy and capacity to labor. Public education is
contingent on the uneven circulation of tax revenues, and
consumer habits are very much driven by the creation of new
wants and needs (like cell phones) at the behest of capital. Workers'
savings are likewise subject to devaluation in the course of a financial crisis, while collapses of energy networks and hurricane and
tornado damage all affect, unevenly and sometimes devastatingly,
this circulation process. It is in the sphere of social reproduction
that older cultural relations of laboring, of patriarchy and gender
dominance are both preserved and enhanced with major consequences for employment structures and economic inequality. It is
here too that discussions over sexual and reproductive mores are
centered, again with consequences elsewhere for the circulation of
labor capacity. To point all of this out in no way invalidates Marx's
simple representation of the circulation of labor capacity. It
remains helpful for thinking through political barriers and options.

I suspect that Marx's purpose in defining the circulation of
labor capacity in this way is to offer a framework in which working
people might reflect upon their situation and come to terms with
all of the forces that condemn them to conditions of living and
working that are, to say the least, so inadequate and oppressive to
them (while being thoroughly "adequate," of course, from the
point of view of capital) as to conjure up the prospect of revolt. It
is almost as if Marx plans to invite workers to join with him in
dissecting the body of their discontents. The historical materialist
and anti-idealist method laid out in Marx's "Introduction" suggests

how workers might look upon and appropriate the totality of their life experience, their culture, as political subjects in the process of becoming class-conscious beings. "The concrete totality is a totality of thoughts . . . a product of thinking and comprehending . . . of the working up of observation and conception into concepts. The totality as it appears in the head, as a totality of thoughts, is a product of a thinking head, which appropriates the world in the only way it can," even as "the real subject" (society) "retains its autonomous existence outside the head just as before" (101). Only in this way can working persons see their lives as "a rich totality of many determinations and relations," while fully recognizing the material condition that "the concrete is concrete because it is the concentration of many determinations, hence unity of the diverse" (100–1). We will return to the question of how this all plays out both theoretically and politically at the end of this concluding chapter.

In the *Grundrisse*, Marx strives to come to terms with the "becoming" of capital as a totality. Recall: "This organic system itself, as a totality, has its presuppositions, and its development to its totality consists precisely in subordinating all elements of society to itself, or in creating out of it the organs which it still lacks. This is historically how it becomes a totality. The process of becoming this totality forms a moment of its process, of its development . . . This society then seizes hold of a new territory, as e.g. the colonies . . ." (278).

Many things can go wrong with this process, and Marx frequently gestures toward the crisis-prone character of the circulation of capital. From the standpoint of the laborer embedded in the circulation of labor capacity, the crisis is more or less chronic (low wages, alienation, impoverishment, unemployment, insecurity, low living standards, etc.). What is adequate for capital is inadequate for labor. One thrives at the expense of the other. Not that there have not been places and times when the lot of the working class has been more acceptable and more stable.

From the standpoint of capital, crises threaten the production of surplus-value and the reproduction of capital in foundational ways. But the disruptions that turn into major crises can come from almost anywhere. This would be expected in any complex organic ecosystem. As in the case of the human body, the collapse of any one of the several circulation systems that comprise capital's totality will lead to the demise of the whole, unless remedial action is taken immediately. This elementary principle unfortunately gets lost in much of the Marxist literature, in which the search for the holy grail of "the" one and only theory of crisis often dominates. But crises also provide capital with opportunities for renewal and transition to a different brand of capitalism. "Never let a good crisis go to waste" is a frequently cited maxim. The adaptability of capital is astounding.

This is the totality that Marx is describing. No one circulatory process or moment within the totality is more important than all of the others. Moments of production, of distribution, of realization, of consumption, of fixed-capital circulation, of the circulation of interest-bearing capital, of labor capacity of state provision are all engaged, and each takes its relevance and meaning through its relation to all the others. The nature, definition and location (geographical or sectoral) of crises varies greatly. But it is then crucial to establish in each crisis whence it comes and, equally important, where it goes to. If someone goes to a hospital with acute pain in the stomach, it does not help to treat it as a heart attack. In the case of capital, it matters whether the primary blockage point lies in production, realization, distribution, or in fixed-capital circulation or wherever. Different kinds of crises have different remedies and effects, depending on where they are located. The falling rate of profit typically results (unless remediated) in massive devaluations of both capital and labor. But experience suggests that capital recovers from such crises to start the cycle again, though often in a different guise, emphasizing a different technological and organizational mix. Crises due to the rising mass are, however, very different. They have become more threatening and dangerous with time because the mass to be absorbed grows exponentially. They are products of the spiral form. They have invariably entailed geographical expansions or what I call "spatial fixes," but the world market is approaching saturation and stalling demographics means intensive rather than extensive responses are required. Such crises can easily turn lethal through environmental degradation, habitat destruction and the accelerations in turnover time that drive beyond human capacities to manage and sustain. I can derive the threat of climate change from the theory of the rising mass of profit, but not from the theory of its falling rate. Nothing appears to have been learned from the Covid-19 pandemic that put a pause on endless growth. The global response is to climb back on board the spiral train of rising mass as quickly as possible.

If one part of the totality fails, then the whole system is threatened. Trouble in one moment in circulation sparks troubles elsewhere. Devaluation, we have seen, is inherent in the capital circulation process. Larger-scale devaluations can occur when, for example, a new wave of cheaper and more efficient technologies is introduced before the lifetimes of the existing fixed-capital assets expire. The penchant of capital for "creative destruction" (to quote the famous phrase from Joseph Schumpeter) is legendary. It includes the radical transformation of the whole landscape of capital with the coming of the railroads and the subsequent victory of the internal combustion engine, which rendered the previous landscape of spatial relations largely redundant. The crisis of deindustrialization from 1980 onward unfolded in the advanced capitalist economies piecemeal (a factory closure here and another there). It was slow-moving and gradual, with occasional spikes, such as the mass closure of all Sheffield or Pittsburgh steel production in just a few years in the 1980s. The deindustrialization of the primary areas of industrial capital in the "rust-belt" regions of North America, Europe and even parts of Asia (e.g., Mumbai) after 1980 entailed major changes with all sorts of political and geopolitical implications. In the Marxist literature, this form of slow-moving crisis is rarely discussed under the rubric of crisis theory. Yet these crisis processes are far more significant than the short, sharp contractions that arise from the financial and merchant capitalist forms of crisis.

Marx makes clear that continuity of flow within the circulation of capital is foundational to its existence, and that any interruption to that flow contains the threat, if sustained, of major crises. In approaching this question Marx appropriates a language of "limits" and "barriers" to be overcome, transcended or evaded (e.g., 409). These constitute "so many mines to explode" the continuous circulation of capital. Some of these mines are planted by forces external to the becoming of the inner structure of capital's totality. Earth-shaking events such as a volcanic eruption in Iceland, a tsunami in Japan and the recent pandemic are treated as "acts of God" (amusingly defined long ago by Blackstone as an act that "no man of reasonable and sound mind would ever commit"). But the impacts of so-called natural disasters depend on prior (and often reckless) human activity (e.g., building in a known earthquake or flood hazard zone). Habitat destruction and climate change almost certainly have had a lot to do with the production of viral diseases and other so-called "natural hazards."

"Production founded on capital," however, requires "the greatest absolute mass" of necessary and surplus labor, and hence "maximum growth of population—of living labour capacities" (608). Current signs indicate a demographic future of diminished global population growth (which is good for protecting the metabolic relation to nature but bad for endless accumulation) and of aging populations. In this regard capital may be shooting itself in its foot. In its thirst to expand labor supply it has happily drawn more and more women into education and labor force participation, which are the two primary triggers accounting for declining demographics in the long run. The immense surge in the global wage labor force (including the increasing participation of women) after 1980 cannot be repeated, although Africa still constitutes the last great labor reserve for capital to feed upon. Capital will have to adapt to this new and less favorable demographic profile. Marx's presumption that population growth would always be there to support capital accumulation is no longer valid. But it will probably take a few major crises to hammer that point home. The need to address acute stresses in the metabolic relation to nature will almost certainly contribute to the same problem in the long run.

But beneath all this another kind of crisis lurks: that of alienation and of loss of meaning. One component of this is the orientation of humanity to a singular but empty definition of wealth.
Capital defines wealth as money and property rights to key assets.
And that is it. Marx postulates wealth as disposable time. Even in
his day, abundant disposable time existed in principle. But it was
and still is appropriated by capital as surplus-value in production.
There is incessant pressure (much of it emanating from capital in
alliance with a bureaucratic state) on social reproduction to create
forms of consumerism and modes of reproduction of labor capacity "adequate to capital." Potentially disposable time is mopped up
in endless and thankless household tasks and labors (both necessary—such as caregiving—and unnecessary). Setting up new
wants, needs and desires to match capital's expansionism is as
endless as the spiral form of production can dictate.

A study of the *Grundrisse* is a return to basics, to the very foundations upon which Marx built his theoretical insights into the
nature of capital. Such a return is invaluable, if only to shore up the
foundations upon which the whole edifice of Marxist thought has
been and continues to be built. There are, of course, features of that
foundation which over time have decayed, been neglected or
become irrelevant. But the theory is robust and universal enough
to hold out new ways to look upon a dominant economic system
that is dynamic, self-transformative and constantly changing.
While all of Marx's texts should be read as historical documents
pertaining to a particular place and time, the potential insights
generated about the essence or inherent nature of capital as an
economic system, along with its potentially fatal contradictions,
can indeed illuminate the anxious present in sometimes startling
ways. The *Grundrisse* is, in short, a prescient text as well as one
relevant to our world today, and it is hard to dispute that this is by
far the most sophisticated and in-depth presentation of Marx's
critical political economy available to this day.

One of the more remarkable features of Marx's text is the fluidity
and adaptability of the conceptual apparatus. What sometimes

appears as sloppiness of usage, for the most part (though not always)
is an acknowledgment that meanings change to reflect the movement of history (and, I would add, the place of geography, since
China, Bolivia and Finland are not easily comparable territories).
Categories such as debt, land, money and even labor transform their
meanings as modes of production change. The internal dynamics
and historical trajectory of capital likewise "posit" conceptual shifts
within the dominant mode of production, which is itself constituted
as a palimpsest of uneven geographical developments. This fluidity
of meaning across both space and time invites us to ask how we
might read these basic categories in the here and the now.

For example, Marx initially interrogates the category of fixed
capital against the background of the temporary devaluation of
capital through its "fixation" for a certain time in various states (as
money, commodities, labor processes) within a circulation process
marked by often radically different turnover times. Fixed capital
(primarily in the form of machinery) becomes, when widespread,
a crucial agent for increasing the productivity of labor power. The
circulation of fixed capital consequently "hardens" into a separate
circulatory process relative to that of circulating capital. Its effect is
to reduce the demand for labor and diminish necessary labor time
(reducing wages and increasing surplus-value). Overall labor
input tends to be reduced, with profound implications for the falling rate of profit and even for any version of value theory based
upon labor input. Machine technology, however, transforms the
category of labor input from the individual to the sociality of the
laboring mass (e.g., within the factory). So-called "productive
labour" (i.e., productive of surplus-value) can no longer be assessed
from what an individual does within an increasingly complex division of labor because it is the organization of collective labor that
now matters. Also, fixed capital comes into its own only under
conditions of mass production, and mass production implies mass
consumption (making the fixed equipment of the household a
vibrant market). The rising mass of ever-cheaper final product
necessitates (posits) an expanding market for use-values (e.g.,

globalization), while rising productivity creates ever-greater surpluses of use-values of both commodities and labor. Such surpluses constitute, however, the preconditions for expanding fixed-capital investment even further. Fixed capital, in short, helps produce the surpluses of circulating capital and labor power that are required to facilitate even more fixed-capital investment. This seemingly closed loop propels a downward spiral in the profit rate. One way to halt this is to invest in forms of fixed capital (as well as in the consumption fund) that do not increase the productivity of labor. This becomes, Marx suggests, a major countervailing influence contra the falling rate of profit. Fixed capital and consumption fund investment is diverted into non-surplus-value-producing projects. Not only does capital specialize in building bridges to nowhere, but it adopts, for example, forms of urbanization that are predominantly capital absorbing rather than capital creating. This creates a field of massive speculative investments often accompanied by spectacular devaluations and bankruptcies.

Marx insists that fixed capital cannot be defined by its physical material qualities but by its usage in relation to accumulation. He is here showing us not only that the category of fixed capital is changing its usage, its role and meaning over time. He is also showing us exactly how and why such changes occur. Fixed capital starts by confronting the problem of differential turnover times. It then becomes a primary means to raise the productivity of labor, before ultimately being used as a sink (analogous to that of military expenditures) in which to dump as much surplus capital and absorb as much surplus labor as possible. Roosevelt's creation of the Works Progress Administration in 1935 is a classic early case of the conscious use of such a strategy. The spectacular urbanization projects of contemporary capitalism are very much of this sort. Something that was marginal in Marx's time has become foundational for ours. The international difficulties of 2007–8 arose, for example, around the finance of housing and other aspects of consumption fund formation in the built environment, primarily in the United States but also in Spain, Ireland and a host of other countries. The crisis was resolved, ironically, in large part by a massive surge of investment into fixed-capital and consumption fund formation in China, the productivity of which is moot. While the image conjured up of fixed capital in Marx's time was that of the machine, it is now that of the Shanghai or Dubai skyline. It surpasses all imagination to think that the thoroughly wasteful investment in Hudson Yards in New York has anything to do with increasing labor productivity. A new tunnel under the Hudson River would be something entirely different. Hudson Yards stands, instead, as a monument to the need to create a countervailing force to the falling rate of profit through the absorption of as much surplus capital and labor as possible in the production of mindless urbanization (Figure 3).

The Hudson Yards monument to mindless and wasteful urbanization rests, however, upon its integration with another circulation process that has come to be of paramount importance to contemporary capitalism: that of the circulation of interest-bearing capital. Interest, debt and credit are all familiar concepts from the antediluvian period of capital's origins. With the rise of industrial capitalism, Marx notes, these categories radically changed their functions and their meanings. The money market became a significant servant of accumulation. There was, for example, no money market in ancient Sumer, and it only started to assume consolidated market forms toward the end of the seventeenth century with, for example, the foundation of the Bank of England (historical antecedents could be found with the banking activities of Jacob Fugger in Augsburg as early as the fifteenth century). In most accounts the major force behind the earlier changes was the need to fund state debt and military expenditures and ventures. The fiscal-military state became particularly active in the transition to industrial capital. Many features of it persist into our own times (including the Bank of England). But Marx disputes this as the primary force behind the growth of money market activities once industrial capital became dominant. He sees the rise in the circulation of interest-bearing capital as reflecting the need to find ways to fund long-term investments in fixed capital and in the consumption fund (e.g., the mortgage market for housing and the bond market for long-term additions to the built environment such as roads and highways, water and sewage, etc.). Contemporary credit, Marx argued, "has *its roots in the specific mode of realization, mode of turnover, mode of reproduction of fixed capital*" (732). With capital periodically crying out for new investment opportunities consequent upon the massive surpluses of both capital and labor that often become both dormant and salient at times of crisis, the financialization of flows into fixed capital and consumption fund formation, lubricated by interest-bearing capital and accompanied by financial innovation, became critical for the survival of global capital. The dramatic case of China over the last two decades illustrates the point. Rapid urbanization (in part mandated by strong currents of accumulation) demanded construction of a financial system adequate to fixed-capital and consumption fund formation there. In China, this new financial system was built by way of financial bricolage and occasional advice from US investment banks, through all manner of opportunistic financial innovations. But that is what had happened earlier during Haussmann's urbanization of Paris, in which new institutions (such as the Crédit Immobilier) had to be constructed to facilitate the rebuilding of the city. It is not as if China longed for or just happened to get a sophisticated financial system and credit market. After all, banks had effectively been abolished during the Cultural Revolution. It simply could not do without financialization as it urbanized during the 1990s in its struggle to absorb the global surpluses of capital to which its own rapid development was so mightily contributing. The result has been an escalating crisis in the financing of the property development sector, with massive companies, like Evergrande, lost in a morass of financial difficulties. Whether or not these investments turn out to be productive and viable remains to be seen. But that is not their point. The immediate need is to absorb surplus capital and labor in the field of circulating capital through spectacular urbanization and massive investment in physical infrastructure (the metabolic relation to nature be damned!). Maintaining the viability and profitability of circulating and extractive capital by way of potentially unprofitable investments and later devaluations in fixed capital and consumption fund formation, is, Marx's theory would suggest, a critical arm of capital's game at a certain point in capital's evolution. It is against that background that we can better grasp the spectacular financial expansions and the imaginative innovations in credit instruments worldwide after 1980 or so, even as we are mesmerized by the skylines of today's great cities. My intuitive guess is that two-thirds of the recent investment in urbanization and physical infrastructure is designed to be "adequate to capital," leaving one-third open for desperate attempts by well-meaning social movements and progressive public servants and politicians to shape an urbanization "adequate to the needs of people."

But there is yet another twist to this story. Much of the money that the financiers lend to invest in long-term fixed capital flows almost instantaneously into the coffers of the circulating capitalists engaging in construction and development. Value and surplus-value are instantaneously produced and recuperated by the activity in these spheres. It is the production of value in the form of factories and houses, schools and hospitals, toll roads and public works of all kinds that we are concerned with here. At some point the question of how the value embodied in such assets can be recuperated has to be answered. Clear property rights to the realization of these values in the built environment have to be established. Some of the value can be recuperated directly by the imposition of user charges (e.g., toll roads). Otherwise, the recuperation is indirect through state taxation to support the use of assets held in common. The flow of values can be capitalized to form market rights to these financial flows. This calls for further elaborations within the financial system in which mortgages, annuities, long-term bonds, and the like, become crucial. One consequence that Marx mentions a number of times is that the circulation of interest-bearing as opposed to profit-seeking capital then prevails. The separation out of profit from interest is critical. Whereas the industrial capitalist is expected in Marx's initial formulation to gain a surplus-value that combines profit with interest, the holder of the fixed-capital or consumption fund asset will demand interest only in the pursuit of their claims to a part of the overall surplus. Marx sees this also as one of the counteracting influences to the falling rate of profit. To the degree that long-term investments of this kind have become far more prominent in capital's overall portfolio, then the circulation of interest-bearing capital "hardens" into a distinctive circulatory system that locks on to the vast trove of monetizable assets that litter the landscape. Marx, alas, does not pursue this in any detail, even as he tentatively registers its potential relevance. The idea that investments in nonproductive long-term fixed capital might help counter the falling rate of profit is mentioned only once, for example. But the historical evidence of its growth in significance is overwhelming.

The startling thing is that no one seems to have advanced a good explanation as to why and how financialization occurred. In most accounts, it just sort of happened "naturally." But, as Marx insists throughout the *Grundrisse*, transitions of this sort need to be theorized as a distinctive product of capital's own nature. Marx anticipates theoretically (though not at all specifically) the need to engineer a sharp diversion of surplus capital and labor flows into long-term fixed-capital formation that ultimately became the spectacular urbanization of today. This was done with the help of a credit system which became the main vehicle for the circulation of interest-bearing capital in asset markets. In this way, modern pension funds can become heavily invested in real estate assets, provided those assets can earn a rate of interest that can then be distributed among the pensioners. The flow of interest can be capitalized to form a market for what Marx will later conceptualize in *Capital* as "fictitious" capital.

Marx designates the bankers and financiers as a distinctive class in the *Grundrisse* (but not elsewhere). This class does not for the most part confront the workers directly (except in modern times by way of credit cards, which, I suspect, would have astonished Marx). The financiers wage their class war, such as it is, against other classes or factions of capital (such as landlords and industrial and merchant capitalists). Marx was, on this point, prescient. The financial system as we know it may have originated as the servant of fixed-capital formation and therefore of industrial capital. But, after a few abortive attempts, it emerged after 1980 as the master of the circulation and accumulation of capital within the totality. Capital has equipped itself with a central nervous system adequate to the needs of the circulation and accumulation of contemporary capital. "In the money market," Marx presciently observed, "capital is posited in its totality; there it *determines prices, gives work, regulates production, in a word, is the source of production.*" But the partitioning of surplus-value between interest and profit has widespread consequences that are largely ignored (even when mentioned in passing) in the *Grundrisse,* though they are taken up in Volume III of *Capital.* The relation between these two claims on surplus-value is too complex to go into here. But it is significant that the falling rate of interest prevailing since 1980 or so has had a vital role to play in steering more and more money capital to invest in fixed-capital and consumption fund formation, particularly of a long-term and independent kind. Much of this investment has no role in promoting the rising productivity of labor. Most commentators indicate that there has been an actual fall in the rate of profit since 1980 or so, and almost certainly there is some relation of this to an equally important (but largely ignored) falling rate of interest over the same period. It is the latter that has permitted if not stimulated the kinds of long-term fixed-capital investments that help check the tendency of the profit rate to fall.

But there is another angle (perhaps better dubbed a contradiction) to all of this that cries out for elaboration. When Marx first introduces the figure of the capitalist, he observes that "it is a law of capital" to "create surplus labour." But it can do this only by "entering into exchange with the worker" and "setting *necessary labour* in motion." There results a tendency "to create as much labour as possible," on the one hand by, for example, soliciting population growth—which in these days is beginning to decline—and producing an industrial reserve army, while at the very same time there exists a "tendency to reduce necessary labour to a minimum" through the application of labor-saving technologies. Capital perpetually seeks, therefore, "to increase the labouring population," at the same time that it constantly seeks to reduce labor's presence in production (399–400). This is a major contradiction. This is similar to what bourgeois economists call a "backward-bending supply curve." When prices fall, the conventional theory says production should decline until supply and demand are in equilibrium. But if producers have fixed costs or objectives, then a fall in prices will lead them to produce more to cover their costs, which probably means further falls in price. The long-run effects can be catastrophic. Conversely, when prices rise producers may supply less. This is a common problem in capitalist countries with a large peasant sector. Far more significantly, it has plagued the oil and other commodity markets. Oil states typically have a certain level of revenue in mind to fund their functions, so when oil prices decline more oil is typically produced, which leads to lower prices (and vice versa when oil prices rise). The instability thus imparted to both oil prices and oil output induced the major producers to found the oil cartel OPEC. But in recent years, OPEC has become less effective, with the Saudis breaking ranks. It is strange, however, that contemporary economics still insists upon supply and demand equilibrium thinking when so much of the world functions on backward-bending supply models. For Marx, of course, a version of the latter is a central contradiction and therefore a powerful shaping force for the evolution of capital in general. The Keynesian version is the liquidity trap, but that also is now anathema for contemporary economics.

If capital is primarily concerned to increase the mass of wealth (usually measured in money form), then any tendency to reduce the rate of profit will automatically stimulate the employment of more workers ("side by side"). Marx then shows how the greater the mass of capital, the lower the rate of profit can go in the quest to amass and centralize more wealth. A 2 percent rate of return on $1 billion adds far more to somebody's total wealth than a 20 percent rate of return on $100. This relationship between rising mass and falling rate of profit explains why capital can and will respond to any fall in the rate of profit by the counterintuitive move of increasing the mass of labor employed, without interfering in any way with the coercive laws of competition that continue to pressure for labor-saving innovations.

All of this helps to explain a central contradiction of contemporary capitalism. On the one hand, the share of wages in national product has systematically declined in almost all of the world's major economies, with the United States and China in the lead, since the 1980s. On the other hand, the global wage labor force has increased from circa 2 billion in 1980 to circa 3 billion now. It is hard to tell what proportion of this increase is engaging in wage labor for capital and how much wage laborers are exchanging their labor capacity against revenues (of the state, of the various factions of capitalist consumers or even from other workers in the case of child-care or care for the aged). But the social (as opposed to individual) labor that is mobilized either directly or indirectly in support of surplus-value production now encompasses more and more millions of workers apparently condemned to ever lower levels of remuneration. This is hardly the description of an economy in a happy state. It works well for the capitalist class (it is "adequate" for capital), but it produces relative penury for everyone else.

Marx's account of the negative impacts of fixed capital on both profit rates and labor capacity, as well as on any value theory based on labor, turns out to have rested on one side of a major contradiction. It comes from the conclusions drawn from theorizing capital from the standpoint of fixed capital alone. When Marx does a deeper exploration of the ineluctable relation between fixed and circulating capital, he encounters powerful forces that negate the earlier propositions in favor of a double-edged theory of the rising mass and shrinking rate of profit. This contradiction is, however, only an elaborated version of the original contradiction in which capital is destined to seek out more and more labor power at the same time as it seeks to reduce necessary labor time to a vanishing minimum. This is the base condition that underpins the current troubling condition of astonishing increases in the mass of capital on the world stage in the midst of a continuous diminution of the share of labor in total value produced.

The perpetuation of this condition rests, however, on a law that Marx hints at but which he seems reluctant to spell out explicitly: the law of the ever-increasing disempowerment of the laborer even when the demand for labor is exceeding its supply (a rare but locally important condition). This law of the declining power of labor—both economically and politically—can only be countered politically. The first step, Marx held, was the regulation of the length of the working day in Britain, followed by a series of factory acts that opened a space for formal education of the labor force. In later years, when social democracy became prominent, the impact of this tendency to disempowerment was mitigated. But the law rules like an unchallenged iron fist over labor relations in the era of neoliberalism, which signaled a frontal assault by the capitalist class against the social democratic attempt, as, for example, in Roosevelt's New Deal and in the experimentation with social democracy in postwar Europe, to empower labor politically (mainly by supporting unionization).

I have, in this *Companion*, taken quite a few liberties to speculate, and even on some occasions to fantasize, about the relevance of Marx's theoretical propositions to an understanding of our contemporary global condition. I justify taking these liberties for two reasons. First, the Marxist tradition of critical theorizing in political economy needs to be something that is kept alive. Marx's texts are not sacred, but are invitations to explore in the here and now the relevance of the universal categories of capital that Marx uncovered and extracted from his studies. I therefore felt it incumbent upon me to illustrate, as much as I could, situations in which Marx's theoretical propositions not only resonated but also illuminated various facets of our contemporary reality. Second, while Marx is deeply concerned with the history of capital's becoming, and even though his thinking is mainly drawn from experience of Manchester industrialism and its accompanying rationalizations in the Manchester School of economics, he constantly searched for

a universal theory of the evolutionary nature of industrial capital
in a pure and unalloyed state. Marx sought to distill abstractions
(universals) that would hold anywhere and everywhere that industrial capital was and is dominant. Today, the rule of industrial capital and its laws of motion are far more dominant throughout the
world than they were in Marx's time, when they were largely
confined to Britain, some parts of Western Europe and the Eastern
seaboard of the United States. But we also know, from Marx's theorizing, that industrial capital is by no means the only or the final
form that capital can take. The rise to importance of fixed capital
circulation necessitated, for example, construction of a credit
system, thus calling forth the circulation of interest-bearing capital
and the rise of a class of all-powerful financiers who ultimately
were in a position to lord it over industrial capital (as they have
done in Britain since the 1920s, from the 1970s in the United
States, and perhaps now are on the verge of doing in contemporary
China). The question is then posed as to whether a new theory of
financial capital is now required, one that supplants the industrial
model on which Marx almost exclusively relied.

While Marx may have begun with a teleological presupposition
regarding capital's evolutionary trajectory, in the *Grundrisse* he
undermines this presupposition. It is the abandonment of teleology
that is one of the outstanding features of this text. By freeing us from
it, Marx confers on us the obligation to identify where we are at now
and where we might go in the context of capital's penchant for
endless accumulation, exponential growth (the dreaded spiral),
uneven geographical development and intense competition between
states or power blocs for economic and political hegemony.

All of these processes take place in space and time. The central
part of the *Grundrisse* is taken up with exploring the spatio-temporal configuration of accumulation and its barriers. This is, by far,
the most neglected (if incomplete) contribution of the *Grundrisse*
to understanding how the totality of capital unfolds. Change of
location creates value (which means it can also be a sphere of
economic activity for the production of surplus-value). As

production systems become more complex and supply chains become more diffuse, so must change of location become a more critical mediating link within production processes, at the same time as transport and communications become ever more important spheres of value and surplus-value production. By the same token, realization in the market is highly dependent on the mediating link between production in one place and consumption in another. If, after all, capital is defined as value in motion, then that motion must go somewhere and it perforce takes up valuable time in so doing. Surplus-value may be realized in a different location from where it is produced, and the cost and time of flows of both inputs and outputs constitute potential barriers to and deductions from value production. As a consequence, technological innovations that further annihilate space through time or accelerate turnover times are internalized within capital's drive to constantly improve the productive forces at the expense of social relations. How this question is answered, both in daily reality and inside the "thinking heads" of the participants, then becomes critical for how the landscape of capital evolves. The fact that this evolution is to a large extent defined by investments (often nonproductive ones to protect the profit rate) in fixed capital—of an independent kind (along with investments in the consumption fund) and embedded in the land—solidifies and, some would say, ossifies the landscape of capital on an ever-increasing scale. The production of second nature requires much closer analysis than Marx gives it.

In his historical explorations, Marx suggests that fealty to the clan is, over time, displaced by fealty to a territory. While questions of state formation and of territorial organization are invariably included in Marx's plans for future work, they have almost no serious place within the text of the *Grundrisse*, except peripherally in the historical sections. This is a pity, since there are propositions within the *Grundrisse* that have important implications for state formation and interstate relations. While the circulation of interest-bearing capital also does on occasion get a mention (particularly with respect to the circulation of fixed capital and the management of capital flows over differential turnover times), a full-fledged analysis of its changing role within the totality of capital is also lacking. There is, however, an interesting moment when Marx considers the argument between John Locke and Secretary to the Treasury William Lowndes on state policy with respect to the depreciation of the currency in the 1690s in Britain (802). This was the decade in which the Bank of England was set up, and we see the formation of what I like to refer to as the "state-finance nexus" that deals with macroeconomic matters such as the currency, central banking and the national debt. This is the institutional arrangement by which the often oppositional alliance between (in today's terms within the United States) the Treasury and the Federal Reserve step in (as they jointly did in 2008–9) to manage the crises of capital.

While international trade and bullion drains the colonization of territories and markets by way of a ruthlessly expansive capital, ultimately producing the world market and all manner of uneven geographical developments (including city formation), all warrant a mention, they are not integrated into the analysis of the totality in any systematic way. But there are some propositions which Marx advances in the *Grundrisse* that are helpful in defining the intricacies of our current reality. We have already noted, for example, the double product of a falling share of labor in national income along with a massive expansion in the world's wage labor force. But this is then cut across by the redistributions of value by way of the equalization of the profit rate. This, as Marx shows, redistributes value from labor-intensive to capital-intensive corporations, sectors, regions and states. These value transfers are contingent, however, on the equalization of the profit rate, and under the Bretton Woods system this was rather weakly enforced. Capital controls meant that corporations and states (and their labor forces) were protected from the full blast of international competition. But the abandonment of the Bretton Woods system in the 1970s opened up corporations, labor forces and states to the force of reasonably open competition. The capital-intensive regions, corporations and states flourished (as did their labor forces to some degree), whereas value was being drained at a critical rate from the labor-intensive economies (Bangladesh, China and the like). The formation of the World Trade Organization (WTO)—an international version of the state-finance nexus—confirmed this system, all in the name of supposed market exchange equality and efficiencies hiding value transfers to capital-intensive (already rich) regions from labor-intensive (already poor) economies. But there was an important sub-agreement within the WTO dealing with intellectual property rights (TRIPS). Contrary to neoliberal theory, this permits corporations to monopolize and monetize knowledge and patents, giving an extra privilege to capital-intensive economies and thereby freezing the disparity in access to technology. The mechanism that makes the rich regions and sectors richer and the poor regions poorer is doubled down on and made relatively permanent by enforcement of the TRIPS agreement. This was not the case under the Bretton Woods system, partly for political reasons. Under Cold War conditions, the US was concerned to foster economic development in Asia (Japan, South Korea, Taiwan and Singapore to contain China) and in Europe (contra the Soviets) and therefore sanctioned technology transfers. By the 1990s this was no longer necessary. Hence the WTO and TRIPS as central global pinions for the state-finance nexus.

The situation of landed capital and the persona of the landlord is somewhat confusing in Marx's account. On the one hand, this is a precapitalist form that Marx would expect to be converted into the distinctively capitalist form of land ownership and ground rent only after the circulation of capital becomes dominant. But land is a foundational means of production, and the separation of the direct producers from this means of production had to precede the rise of wage labor in its capitalist form. Some sort of partial conversion to a proto-capitalist form of land holding and ground rent had therefore to occur before the rise of capital. Henry VIII's dissolution of the monasteries is an example of such a measure, even though it led to the creation of a landed aristocracy rather than a purely capitalist landlord class. The latter would entail the full monetization of land rents and the commoditization of land into a land market in which land would have a price even in the absence of any value creation on the land as occurs in capitalist agriculture. This confirmed the circulation of interest-bearing capital through the channel of land markets and land ownership, a powerful feature to this day.

But from the 1970s onward, the requirements for the circulation of fixed capital (particularly of a nonproductive kind) accelerated and the circulation of interest-bearing capital (the butterfly form of highly mobile capital) became more prominent. Marx's depiction of this form of circulation as independent and autonomous but subsumed within the laws of capital as a totality is here instructive. I earlier likened this in my introduction to raising a teenager in a middle-class household—they perpetually proclaim their right to independence and autonomy, but depend financially on the household and, when they get into trouble, they look to Mum and Dad to bail them out. This, as I earlier noted, is precisely how the banking industry behaved after 1980 or so, though it was usually young and ambitious "quants" (the "swinging dicks," as they were called in London) who raked in the profits by doing outrageous things that senior management could not understand. The New York fiscal crisis of 1975 led the way in defining a general system of moral hazard in the financial sector. The banks and financial institutions could lend without constraint, and if the loans turned sour the state would bail the banks out at the taxpayers' expense. In the United States, the problem was first registered in the savings and loan sector crises of the 1980s, when the state had to bail out a whole raft of institutions that had made bad loans to property development. Internationally the Third World debt crisis of the 1980s had to be resolved through the agency of the International Monetary Fund and the world's central banks. And on Black Monday (October 19, 1987), a sudden global stock market crash that in some cases involved 40 percent declines in share values rocked the world and had to be resolved through coordinated action by the IMF and the world's central banks. In the postmortem on that crash, US economists collectively tried to understand what had happened. Larry Summers, a leading economist then and now, wrote a paper that concluded that the choice was between moral hazard coupled with strong and adventurous economic growth or tightly regulated banking and slow economic growth. He advocated for the former. A later financial study from JPMorgan in the later 1990s concluded that moral hazard had been a major force behind whatever economic growth that had occurred since 1980 or so. The world's financial system had become a casino, a playground for unruly and undisciplined financiers with the mentality of teenagers blessed with too much testosterone and demanding independence and autonomy from all government regulation. When it all crashed in 2007–8, it was the Mum/Dad state that had to bail them out.

This is the economic world we all live in. What is so striking is how some of the propositions in the *Grundrisse*, when set in motion, give such a clear understanding of the central dilemmas that are currently so obvious within global capitalism. They also do it in a way that is simple enough and powerful enough to be readily comprehensible, though Marx's language does a lamentable job of communicating this.

There is, however, one other piece of unfinished business to be engaged with. At one point, Marx comments that capital's penchant to reduce human labor, and the expenditure of energy, to a minimum "will redound to the benefit of . . . labour," and that this constituted "the condition of its emancipation" (701). While Marx only uses the concept once, the voice of this "emancipated labourer" can be heard from time to time, as Marx asks how things would look if the associated workers would take command of machine technologies and artificial intelligence to reduce their material burdens to a minimum and thus liberate their own time for other more joyful and worthwhile things. Marx's appeal to this figure of the emancipated laborer as a kind of in-house commentator on the text is of interest because it indicates where the occasional commentaries on a possible alternative to capital might be coming from. There are passages where it seems that Marx is shaping his argument from this standpoint without specifically invoking it.

What, for example, would the emancipated laborer say or do with the superior productivity conferred by machine technology? How would the emancipated laborer capture the possibility of free time in place of capital's use of it to produce surplus-value? It is through the voice of this emancipated laborer that Marx can pose such questions and perhaps venture some opinion on what might be done with this world that capital has created. The political issue is not what would Marx do, but what would the emancipated laborer, in full cognizance of their situation, do to make this world a better place for the masses of people rendered marginal, impoverished and disposable within the current system? Marx seems to have hoped that the knowledge necessary for transformation would be the product "of the working up of observation and conception into concepts" so that "the totality as it appears in the head, as a totality of thoughts" would function as a guide to political action.

The emancipated laborer presumably has their existence within the circulation of labor capacity, possessed of that "double consciousness" that needs to be transcended and converted into a practical consciousness. The task of the emancipated laborer is therefore not to draw up blueprints for a future socialist society from outside or to explore utopian options and schemas (however interesting). Marx's explorations of the mechanisms of capital's becoming taught him that the building of an alternative mode of production—in the *Grundrisse* the transition from precapitalist to a capitalist social formation—would entail the slow but persistent "dissolution" (and Marx makes much of this word) of older material and social forms, which had somehow or other created situations or contradictions in which the transition to "something else" was made possible. That something had already to be in process so that the emancipated laborer would or should know and be ready to guide, foment and exploit it in the search of relief from daily burdens and oppressions.

But what would those laborers have to be emancipated from? The answer to this question today will be very different from the answer in Marx's time and place. As Marx discovered late in his

own life, the initial conditions in peasant Russia were very different from those in working-class Manchester. It would be just as
different in "Jim Crow" Mississippi and caste-bound Gujarat.
Today, in the United States, we could not go very far with this
question without recognizing the importance of emancipation
from imperialism and neocolonialism, from racism, sexism, religious and ethnic bigotries along with relief from all repressions of
sexual identity. The need to counter state violence and resist draco-
nian forms of regulation would not be far behind. All of these
emancipatory struggles would now be considered as essential
precursors to or co-evolutionary with struggles for emancipation
from the travails of alienated wage slavery, debt peonage, impoverishment, environmental degradation and all the troublesome
consequences of capital's need for increasing centralization of
wealth. Relief from all the other forms of oppression will be meaningless in the long run without relief from the endless exponential
growth path in the mass of both use-values and exchange-values
that the reproduction of capital mandates.

One of the most important corollaries of this spiral form is a drive
for greater and greater centralization of capital. By far the most
important and profitable activity for the investment bankers over
the last few decades has been negotiating mergers and acquisitions
between firms and corporations. The increasing mass of capital in
fewer hands in the major metropolitan regions is now paralleled by
a rising mass of the global workforce. Much of it is dedicated to the
production of surplus-value in low-income countries like Bangladesh
(or, until very recently, China), which produces the mass of the
surplus-value that is appropriated by large corporations and other
economic entities in wealthier and capital-intensive regions
(particularly the metropolitan economies) of world commerce.

When Thomas Paine wrote his famous revolutionary pamphlet
Common Sense in 1776, hundreds of thousands of copies were
almost immediately diffused across the English-speaking world,
largely through independent printers reproducing it at will (intellectual property rights were irrelevant). This work became the

popular manifesto for the American Revolution. His later work *The Rights of Man* (1791) was almost as popular. I mention these works not because they were in any way influential with Marx (his critique of Locke's individualism would apply to them) but to illustrate the kind of potential audience for whom Marx was writing. To be sure, it was a minority within the rapidly increasing mass of the illiterate working class, but a very significant minority nonetheless. The self-taught free-thinking artisan (think William Blake) would be capable of reading and understanding Marx (though, obviously, not the *Grundrisse*, for the reasons Rosdolsky pointed out). They are the ones who can engage with "the working up of observation and conception into concepts" from their grounded positionality in the circulation of labor capacity. While the artisan culture of the manufacturing period was under assault in Marx's time, as factory labor became more the norm, at least in Manchester, the autodidact laborer has never disappeared and to this day forms an important segment if not the core of what the emancipated laborer is all about. The autodidact worker has been a powerful force in capital's history. Today, this is most strongly present within the ranks of cultural producers, along with the self-educated leaders of many social movements. This sensibility can also be found among those public servants who, in spite of a neoliberal ethic that systematically diminishes their status and their standing (e.g., school teachers), put the public first and their own private interest last.

But Marx also had in view another kind of audience that was the product of capital's own development and which he perhaps naively hoped would turn out to be the gravediggers of capital's future. To be sure, industrial capitalism shaped a labor force of machine minders and mindless labor practices tied to lifetime positions within a soulless division of labor. But capitalist development also pointed to the emergence of a new kind of educated, flexible, adaptable and potentially revolutionary labor force. This is what Marx identifies in the *Grundrisse*. The general development of the forces of production, supplemented by "the universality of intercourse, hence the world market as a basis," creates "the possibility of the universal development of the individual." The result is "not an ideal or imagined universality of the individual, but the universality of his real and ideal relations. Hence also the grasping of his own history as a *process*" (542). "The richest development of the individuals" rests on "the highest development of the forces of production" (541). Again, "capital's ceaseless striving towards the general form of wealth drives labour beyond the limits of its natural paltriness, and thus creates the material elements for the development of the rich individuality, which is as all-sided in its production as in its consumption, and whose labour also therefore appears no longer as labour, but as the full development of activity itself." These were the people who would surely be in the frontline of recognizing how the development of the "productive forces themselves encounters its barrier in capital itself" (325). Once this barrier is clearly recognized for what it is, Marx holds, so the consciousness of the need for an alternative cannot be far behind.

In this, ideas can become a material force for change, but ideas that are grounded and directed. In a well-known passage in *Capital*, Marx asserts that "what distinguishes the worst architect from the best of bees is this, that the architect raises his structure in imagination before he erects it in reality. At the end of every labour-process, we get a result that already existed in the imagination of the labourer at its commencement." Ideas can be, Marx concedes, a material force for historical transformation, but only if they are realized through social and material practices. We can daydream about a socialist revolution all we want, but these daydreams go for naught if they can find no meaningful material or social expression. Conversely, transformations in material and social practices are unlikely to hold without the support of ideas "adequate to" their new anticapitalist reality. It is the practicality of "the emancipated labourer," searching out those cracks in the armor of capital through which, as Leonard Cohen has it, "the light gets in."

The problem, of course, is that mass education (of the sort Marx approved of in the educational clauses of the British Factory Acts) is not necessarily harnessed to this end. As Mr. Dombey in Charles

Dickens's *Dombey and Son* remarks, he is all in favor of public education, provided it teaches the public its proper place. Feminists and critical race theorists as well as Marxists can all too easily appreciate the point.

The self-reproduction of capital is enabled, of course, by all manner of active agents, chief of which is the admittedly fragmented but still all-powerful capitalist class, along with its comprador factions (insanely wealthy merchants, industrialists, landlords and financiers) and a largely self-satisfied bourgeoisie backed by military and police power. It is in this context that Marx called upon the figure of "the emancipated labourer" to evaluate the socialist potential within capitalist technologies and organizational forms. At a time when there is a pressing need for creative and extensive intervention in the foundations of economic life, and at a time when there is a clear need for collective action to address problems of environmental degradation and the devaluation of human life to almost nothing, the voice of the emancipated laborer needs to be heard and to be magnified by all possible means. Our world is a world that capital has made in the image of its own self-reproduction. We have to confront the various symptomatic and egregiously noxious effects of this process in the here and now. But this must be done with the long-term aim of going to the root of the problem, which is the process of capital's self-reproduction as a totality. Going beyond the fragments to understand the totality is a message that saturates the pages of the *Grundrisse*, concluding that it is time for capital to be gone, to make way for a more civilized, egalitarian and environmentally acceptable mode of production.

To read the *Grundrisse* and absorb its messages is to awaken a sleeping giant that can animate mass movements calling for transformation to an alternative. The voice of the emancipated laborer has yet to be heard loud and clear. The magnification of that voice is our immediate collective task. Acting upon it immediately follows.

APPENDIX
Marx's Plans for Future Work

Quite frequently in the *Grundrisse*, Marx mentions topics which "do not belong here yet" or will be dealt with later. This suggests that he had some general strategy in mind (or more likely in formation) as to the order of presentation and whether or not this or that topic or category could or should not be deployed where. It is difficult to discern much of what he had in mind. But there are certain topics—such as the circulation of interest-bearing capital and the role of the credit system and the financial class—which appear at various points, only to be actively suppressed on the grounds that they do not belong here yet. On some occasions, however, Marx lays out a whole plan of work for the coming years. I think it useful to bring them together to get some sense of the huge project that Marx at that moment had in mind. Clearly, he did not complete these work programs, leaving it for future generations to fill in the gaps. But the plans are illustrative of the state of Marx's thinking in the run-up to writing *Capital* and in some ways may help define the initial context in which he wrote this later work.

PLAN ONE (PAGE 108)

The order obviously has to be (1) the general, abstract determinants which obtain in more or less all society, but in the above-explained sense. (2) The categories which make up the inner structure of bourgeois society and on which the fundamental classes rest. Capital, wage labour, landed property. Their interrelation. Town and country. The three great social classes. Exchange between them. Circulation. Credit system (private). (3) Concentration of bourgeois society in the form of the state. Viewed in relation to itself. The "unproductive" classes. Taxes. State debt. Public credit. The population. The colonies. Emigration. (4) The international relation of production. International division of labour. International exchange. Export and import. Rate of exchange. (5) The world market and crises.

PLAN TWO (PAGE 227)

In this first section, where exchange values, money, prices are looked at, commodities always appear as already present. The determination of forms is simple. We know that they express aspects of social production, but the latter itself is the precondition. However, they are not *posited* in this character [of being aspects of social production]. And thus, in fact, the first exchange appears as exchange of the superfluous only, and it does not seize hold of and determine the whole of production. It is the *available* overflow of an overall production which lies outside the world of exchange values. This still presents itself even on the surface of developed society as the directly available world of commodities. But by itself, it points beyond itself towards the economic relations which are posited *as relations of production*. The internal structure of production therefore forms the second section; the concentration of the whole in the state the third; the international relation the fourth; the world market the conclusion, in which production is posited as a totality together with all its moments, but within which, at the same time, all contradictions come into play. The world market then, again, forms the presupposition as well as its substratum. Crises are then the general intimation which points beyond the presupposition, and the urge which drives towards the adoption of a new historic form.

PLAN THREE (PAGE 264)

I. (1) General concept of capital. – (2) Particularity of capital: circulating capital, fixed capital. (Capital as the necessaries of life, as raw material, as instrument of labour.) (3) Capital as money. II. (1) *Quantity of capital. Accumulation.* (2) *Capital measured by itself. Profit. Interest. Value of capital*: i.e. capital as distinct from itself as interest and profit. (3) *The circulation of capitals.* (α) Exchange of capital and capital. Exchange of capital with revenue. Capital and prices. (β) *Competition of capitals.* (γ) *Concentration of capitals.* III. Capital as credit. IV. Capital as share capital. V. *Capital as money market.* VI. Capital as source of wealth. The capitalist. After capital, landed property would be dealt with. After that, wage labour. All three presupposed, the *movement of prices*, as circulation now defined in its inner totality. On the other side, the three classes, as production posited in its three basic forms and presuppositions of circulation. Then the *state.* (State and bourgeois society. – Taxes, or the existence of the unproductive classes. – The state debt. – Population. – The state externally: colonies. External trade. Rate of exchange. Money as international coin. – Finally the world market. Encroachment of bourgeois society over the state. Crises. Dissolution of the mode of production and form of society based on exchange value. Real positing of individual labour as social and vice versa).

PLAN FOUR (PAGE 275)

I. *Generality:* (1) (a) Emergence of capital out of money. (b) Capital and labour (mediating itself through *alien* labour). (c) The elements of capital, dissected according to their relation to labour (Product. Raw material. Instrument of labour.) (2) *Particularization of capital:* (a) Capital circulant, capital fixe. Turnover of capital. (3) *The singularity of capital:* Capital and profit. Capital and interest. Capital as *value,* distinct from itself as interest and profit. II. *Particularity:* (1) Accumulation of capitals. (2) Competition of capitals. (3) Concentration of capitals (quantitative distinction of capital as at same time qualitative, as *measure* of its size and influence). III. *Singularity:* (I) Capital as credit. (2) Capital as stock-capital. (3) Capital as money market. In the money market, capital is posited in its totality; there it *determines prices, gives work, regulates production,* in a word, is the *source of production*; but capital, not only as something which produces itself (positing prices materially in industry etc., developing forces of production), but at the same time as a creator of values, has to posit a value or form of wealth specifically distinct from capital. This is *ground rent.* This is the only value created by capital which is distinct from itself, from its own production.

Index